Feminism as Life's Work

Feminism as Life's Work

Four Modern American Women
through Two World Wars

MARY K. TRIGG

RUTGERS UNIVERSITY PRESS
NEW BRUNSWICK, NEW JERSEY, AND LONDON

Library of Congress Cataloging-in-Publication Data
Trigg, Mary K., 1955–

    Feminism as life's work : four modern American women through two world wars /
Mary K. Trigg.

        pages cm

    Includes bibliographical references and index.

    ISBN 978–0–8135–6523–1 (hardcover : alk. paper) — ISBN 978–0–8135–6522–4 (pbk. :
alk. paper) — ISBN 978–0–8135–6538–5 (e-book)

    1. Feminists—United States—Biography. 2. Feminism—United States—History—
20th century. I. Title.

    HQ1412.T75 2014

    305.420973—dc23

    2013033863

A British Cataloging-in-Publication record for this book is available from the British
Library.

Portions of chapter 6 first appeared in *Journal of Women's History* 7, no. 2 (Summer
1995): 52–85. Copyright © 1995 The Johns Hopkins University Press.

Visit our website: http://rutgerspress.rutgers.edu

Manufactured in the United States of America

*For my daughters, Laurel Trigg Rapp and
Sarah Kathleen Trigg Rapp, and in memory of my mother,
Margaret Katherine McLaughlin Trigg*

Contents

Acknowledgments

This book and the four women in it have traveled with me for many years, and I have had the unique opportunity to consider the topics raised here—love, sex, marriage, motherhood, work, feminism—from my own evolving vantage points over time. Since the very beginning of the idea for this book my husband, friend, and life partner Ronald Rapp has been a source of inspiration and fierce support. I could not have finished this without his kindness and loving encouragement. I am greatly in his debt.

I have also been richly blessed with intellectual mentors and cheerleaders who have played an invaluable role in shaping *Feminism as Life's Work* and spurring me on to complete the book. Mari Jo Buhle introduced me to the field of women's history and advised me through early versions of this book with intelligence, friendship, and faith in its potential. Mary S. Hartman read the book early on and employed her sharp eye, large historical mind, and wide-ranging knowledge about marriage to offer wise suggestions. Nancy Hewitt has taught me a great deal about the history of US feminism, and about generosity. Her gracious willingness to read and comment upon numerous drafts and to steadfastly insist on the project's merit is humbling. I can only try to emulate these unstinting intellectual mentors and pioneer scholars; I am touched beyond words by their generosity.

Many have read this book in various stages, and I am grateful for the support and help of each one of them. I want to acknowledge Richard Meckel, Barton St. Armand, and the late William McLoughlin for their incisive comments and early confidence in the project. I thank Cynthia Gorman for her astute, close reading of the manuscript and her invaluable ideas for revision. I thank the anonymous readers for the time and care they took with the manuscript, and for their liberal sharing of their scholarly expertise. I thank Heather O'Neill for her important reading and suggestions, and Adam Wilson for leading me to Heather at a critical moment. I am grateful to Rutgers University, especially the Institute for Women's Leadership and the Department of Women's and Gender Studies, for giving me an academic home and a source of inspiration. I thank the School of Arts and Sciences for the research leave that allowed me to work on this book.

I am grateful to the staff at the Schlesinger Library of Harvard University for their help in accessing the papers of the four women in this study, and the Woodrow Wilson Foundation for its endorsement. I extend my gratitude to Rutgers University Press and its fine staff, especially director Marlie Wasserman and my editor Katie Keeran. I appreciate more than I can say your patience and diligence in helping me to make this book as strong as it could be.

This has been a labor of love, and I have been buoyed up on this journey by the love of those most important to me, both living and dead. I thank my incredible daughters Laurel and Sarah, to whom this book is dedicated; my beloved mother Margaret Katherine McLaughlin Trigg, my father Warren Magruder Trigg Jr., my four sisters, my niece Kelly Kaems, and my loving husband. You are my force field and I have invoked you more than you know in the process of completing this book. I am eternally grateful.

Abbreviations

AWA	American Woman's Association
CESL	College Equal Suffrage League
CU	Congressional Union
DS Tapes	Doris Stevens Tapes, in DSP
DSP	Doris Stevens Papers, 1884–1983; MC 546. Schlesinger Library, Radcliffe Institute, Harvard University, Cambridge, MA
ERA	Equal Rights Amendment
IACW	Inter American Commission of Women
IHGP	Inez Haynes Gillmore Papers, 1872–1945; A25. Schlesinger Library, Radcliffe Institute, Harvard University, Cambridge, MA
II Correspondence	Inez Irwin Correspondence (in NAWSA Papers)
IWW	Industrial Workers of the World
LPC	Lorine Pruette Clippings, in LPP
LPP	Lorine Pruette Papers, 1915–1974; MC 306. Schlesinger Library, Radcliffe Institute, Harvard University, Cambridge, MA
LWV Papers	League of Women Voters Papers, Library of Congress, Washington, DC
MB Papers	Eli F. Ritter and Mary Beard Papers, DePauw University Archives, Greencastle, IN
MBPSL	Mary Ritter Beard Papers, 1935–1958, A-9. Schlesinger Library, Radcliffe Institute, Harvard University, Cambridge, MA
NAWSA Papers	National American Woman Suffrage Association Papers, Library of Congress, Washington, DC
NCNW	National Council of Negro Women

NWP Papers	National Woman's Party Papers
SL	Schlesinger Library, Radcliffe Institute, Harvard University, Cambridge, MA
SSC	Sophia Smith Collection, Smith College, Northampton, MA
WCWA Papers	World Center for Women's Archives papers, Schwimmer/Lloyd Collection, Ms. Division, New York Public Library Archives
WJCC Papers	Women's Joint Congressional Committee Papers, Library of Congress, Washington, DC
Wood Papers	C.E.S. Wood Papers, Huntington Library, San Marino, CA
WTUL	Women's Trade Union League
WRC	Women's Rights Collection, Schlesinger Library, Radcliffe College, Cambridge, MA
WTUL	Women's Trade Union League

Feminism as Life's Work

Introduction

Middle-class, highly educated, and white, the quartet of women profiled in this book are an elite group, but they offer insights into the transformations taking place in the lives of middle-class American women in the 1910s, 1920s, and 1930s. The post–World War I disillusionment, revolution in manners and morals, and changing understanding of love, sex, and commitment are all evidence of the profoundly altered world in which these four American feminists found themselves.[1] Still, they experienced and interpreted the vicissitudes wrought by modern culture in different ways. A writer, a historian, an activist, and a psychologist, they devoted their careers to women's causes while struggling to compose their own lives in a rapidly changing society.

This book takes up one central question: how did a small, self-appointed vanguard of "modern" women carry feminism forward in life and work at a point when the organizational center of the movement had shrunk? Through the lives and thought of Inez Haynes Irwin[2] (1873–1970), Mary Ritter Beard (1876–1958), Doris Stevens (1888–1963), and Lorine Pruette (1896–1977), *Feminism as Life's Work* explores what we can learn from their struggles. In the years after the 1920 suffrage victory, feminists such as these established new sites of experimentation that I will examine in this book. These sites included the National Woman's Party, sexuality and relations with men, marriage, and work and financial independence.

Being a modern feminist was not easy. Combining marriage and career was difficult, as was conceiving of oneself as a heterosocial feminist, one who devoted her life to the cause of women, while living in the midst of men. Even resolutely modern women like Stevens worried at times that their "detention by the male" would endanger their feminist commitment and that the emancipated man was more myth than reality. Stevens's, Pruette's, and Irwin's unhappy unions showed how difficult "willed equality" could be to realize. Pruette eventually recognized the danger an overemphasis on marriage held for women's self-realization and for feminism itself. In their utopian efforts to reshape work, sexual relations, and marriage, modern feminists ran headlong into the harsh realities of male power, the double sexual standard, the demands of motherhood, and gendered social structures. As Pruette noted in 1940, "Here in the frosty afternoon," modern feminists sometimes forget "the bright gay dream of equality, of freedom, of a relation between men and women that should be a little finer than anything the world had known before."[3]

The women in this study not only devoted their lives to women's causes but they also used their lives as laboratories for feminist experimentation. Their feminism was not just political but also intensely personal. Their private experiences fueled their ideas and activism, as the historian Ellen DuBois has noted of other feminists in history. "Feminist theory reaches out to movements for political change, and reaches within, to the inner reality of women's lives," DuBois wrote. "Women's lives, when women strive to understand and change them, have always been the source of feminism's most profound insights."[4] In mapping the routes these women took as they practiced in their lives, the ideas emerging from a collective women's movement in a changing society, this book examines the pain, conflicts, and confusion that sometimes resulted from crafting "modern" lives.

In addition to exploring these feminists' lives as wives, lovers, potential or actual mothers, *Feminism as Life's Work* also analyzes the changing nature of the women's movement across three turbulent decades rent by a world war, a revolution in Russia, a global depression, the rise of fascism in Europe, and an impending second world war. It chronicles the shared and conflicting ideas in the long struggle for women's rights in the United States, a struggle that continues in our own time. Although separated by twenty-three years, Irwin, Beard, Stevens, and Pruette belonged to the same generation, born in the last thirty years of the nineteenth century—a group considered by some historians to constitute the second distinctive generation of American women reformers and activists.[5] Three of the four were energetic, leading suffragists who, when the Nineteenth Amendment was ratified, were still young enough to have decades of productive work ahead of them. The book charts the ways these activists moved from the suffrage victory to new goals, as well as the impact their experiences in the suffrage movement had on their lives.

None of this was without controversy. Feminism, sexuality, marriage, work, motherhood, and gender equality were all contested, provocative topics in the United States between 1910 and 1940. A period of transformation from Victorian to modern America, these decades ushered in a new age. The old philosophy of separate gender spheres, which had linked white women to domesticity and the home, and men to the broader public sphere of the marketplace and politics, was fading away.[6] Whereas nineteenth-century cultural arbiters had equated white, middle-class women with the piety, purity, domesticity, and submissiveness of "true womanhood," the twentieth century witnessed the dawn of a new woman.[7] She was sexually liberated, comfortable with men, worked for wages, supported egalitarian marriage, and desired autonomy and self-understanding. The rise of women's higher education, the entry of middle-class women into the labor force, an explosion of consumer culture, and feminism all propelled this new woman into being.[8] Journalist Dorothy Dunbar Bromley pronounced in her 1927 *Harper's* article "Feminist—New Style": "She is acutely conscious that she is being carried along in the current of these sweeping forces, that she and her sex are in the vanguard of change." A new emphasis on individualism was rising, as Bromley stated: "Feminist—New Style professes no loyalty to women *en masse*, although she staunchly believes in individual women."[9]

Being modern meant not only living in the city and engaging with new movements in the arts, but also earning a wage, having political rights, and experiencing a new psychological consciousness and (hetero)sexual expressiveness, as well.[10] The self-consciously female community and separatist ideology of nineteenth-century middle-class womanhood began to dissolve in the 1920s as New Women attempted to assimilate into male institutions and forge close relationships with men.[11] Some historians have asserted that this fundamental change from the separate-spheres ideology of the nineteenth century to the heterosocial world of the twentieth was complete by 1930.[12] The companionship that modern feminists envisioned with men was in part erotic. By the first decade of the twentieth century, a new morality had swept much of urban America, replacing earlier ideals of white, middle-class female "passionlessness" with candid recognition of women's sexual drive.[13] Women's visible new roles seemed at odds with Victorian ideas that sharply distinguished male and female feelings. Modern feminists claimed the heterosexual experience as an experiential site in which to explore physical pleasure and human interaction. They also seized upon marriage as a laboratory of sorts, advocating a new companionate union, which, with its emphasis on sexual intimacy and egalitarianism, made marriage the ideal. The idea of paid work as a way to avoid the overburdens of domesticity and define the self was alluring. College-educated, ambitious, eager to break barriers, these were the first American feminists who believed they could aspire to both marriage and career.

Yet despite the excitement of the new, there were challenges. The poignant, anonymous autobiographical essays by seventeen "modern women" for the progressive magazine *The Nation* in 1926 and 1927 capture many of the trials modern feminists faced in the post-suffrage years. The contributors explored the personal sources of their feminism and demonstrated how these ideals had survived (or not) in the realities and stresses of the female life cycle. "Our object," the editors explained at the launch of the series "These Modern Women," "is to discover the origin of their modern point of view toward men, marriage, children, and jobs. Do spirited ancestors explain their rebellion? Or is it due to thwarted ambition or distaste for domestic drudgery?" Modernity was not linked to youth, politics, or style—the median age of the participants was forty; they included equal-rights feminists as well as social feminists. What distinguished this group of white, middle-class, successful professional women from other self-identified feminists in the 1920s—and what made them, according to *Nation* editor Freda Kirchwey, "modern"—was their desire for heterosexual love as well as paid work. Scholar Elaine Showalter described them as an avant-garde: "In their 'modernity,' their mobility, their choice of careers, and their control of their bodies, the *Nation* women were an avant-garde, different from the housewife of Middletown, who still lived in a sexually segregated world, and also different from the urban and rural women who worked hard all their lives because they needed the money."[14]

Irwin and Pruette were included in *The Nation*'s series, and like their fellow essayists they represent a privileged vanguard of American women. The majority of women at this time did not have the leisure, access to education, or opportunities to choose unconventional marriages, their own forms of sexual expression, or fulfilling vocations. The *Nation* women offer striking parallels between their changing life patterns, professed role conflicts, and occasional disillusionment, and the views of some white, professional, middle-class, highly educated American women of the late twentieth and early twenty-first centuries.[15] Pruette, who often had her finger on the cultural pulse, noted in the early 1930s that modern, middle-class women were still unsure of themselves as they tried to realize their own ambitions as professional women and wives: "Nothing is settled in the woman's mind. She is having to work out new ways of living, about which there are still many disputes. She has not the ready-made justification of the men."[16] Working out ways to negotiate discrimination at work and domestic burdens at home shaped this generation of college-educated women. It is surely no coincidence that the four women examined here eventually settled on independent careers outside of academia or other institutions. They were self-employed professionals, and three of the four divorced and lived as single women for significant periods of time. Only one became a mother. Their lives also demonstrate how women who identified with such an unpopular cause as feminism in these years had an extraordinarily strong commitment to it. Their legacies remind us that social change can be a lengthy process, one that can take several generations to fully measure. Many of the goals these four early twentieth-century American feminists organized for, thought, wrote, and cared deeply about have been accomplished. Others are still contested today.

All four achieved fame during their lifetimes but today are mostly forgotten. Only Beard has been studied and written about in any depth. They left remarkable and rich documents that include personal diaries, letters, dream analyses, menus, novels, poetry, unpublished manuscripts, photographs, resumes, and other artifacts accumulated over long and full lives.[17] Beard's life, however, had to be pieced together from other writings, since she destroyed her personal papers.

I draw on these sources to place these four characters at the center stage of early twentieth-century American feminism, where I believe they belong. This book is an effort to reintroduce their ideas and their lives, so relevant to our own in the early twenty-first century. These women were concerned with questions that resonate today: the meaning of happiness and success; our responsibility to society versus the self; how women and men can achieve egalitarian, autonomous relationships in the home and the workplace; the role that family responsibilities should play in the lives of women (and men). Their lives and ideas also illustrate the challenges of advancing equality. What does equality mean? How is it best achieved? Who should work toward this end and through what avenues? My goal is to deepen our understanding of feminism during "the doldrums," the post-suffrage period that is now generating significant interest among historians of women and feminism.[18]

These four feminists lived long and productive lives. Inez Haynes Irwin was a prolific author who, in her ninety-seven years, published forty-two books, including thirteen novels, five short story collections, seventeen children's books, five murder mysteries, three women's history volumes, and innumerable articles. In 1931 she became the first woman elected to the presidency of the Authors' League of America. Although not always critically acclaimed, Irwin was an immensely popular writer who, in some of her best books provocatively addressed the issues of work, marriage, divorce, and motherhood through a feminist lens. She was the first fiction editor of *The Masses,* a socialist magazine founded in 1911, which, under Max Eastman's editorship, became a lively vehicle for publishing the work of progressive writers, thinkers, and artists. A labor activist and suffragist, Irwin was also a lifelong National Woman's Party member, an equal rights supporter, and a recognized feminist appointed to leadership roles because of her fame and influence.

Mary Beard was a writer and "nonestablishment historian" who has been credited with launching the field of women's history.[19] Married to the eminent historian Charles Beard, she rejected what she saw as the elitism of the academy to create an independent career centered on connecting historical research to social reform. Beginning with her first book, *Woman's Work in Municipalities* (1915), through her most important book, *Woman as Force in History* (1946), Beard argued that women had played a major role in all of history. She believed investigating those contributions required a broad interdisciplinary perspective. She wrote or edited eight books independently and co-authored seven more with Charles, most notably the widely read, multivolume *Rise of American Civilization* (1927) and *The Making of American Civilization* (1937). Throughout her lifetime Beard railed against socioeconomic inequalities and "unbridled capitalism," and supported the cause of working women. She was a suffragist who sought the vote to equip working-class women with a political voice and in the post-suffrage decades firmly opposed the Equal Rights Amendment (ERA). Through her leadership of the World Center for Women's Archives (1935–1940), which was to be a gathering place and clearing house of women's historical documents, Beard spread her vision of historical and cultural relativism and her view of women as civilizing agents in an increasingly uncivil world.

Hailed as "An Apostle of Action," Doris Stevens was a leader in the National Woman's Party (NWP) from the 1910s through the mid-1940s, when she parted ways with her former confidant Alice Paul. She was among the activists imprisoned in Virginia's Occoquan Workhouse and memorialized the striking suffragists in her now-classic 1920 book *Jailed for Freedom.* A riveting speaker, superb organizer, and successful fundraiser, Stevens was a leader or participant in virtually all the radical tactics initiated by the NWP in the final years of the suffrage movement. Her zealous commitment to public activism illustrates some of the most effective, inspiring characteristics of American feminism in the early twentieth century. Her elitism and class bias also demonstrate its less admirable side. Stevens's vision extended to women's sexual emancipation, birth control, and marriage reform. She headed the organization's Inter American Commission of Women from 1928 to 1939, and during those years was a recognized leader of international feminism. At the same time, she developed a long and complicated relationship with her mentor, millionaire feminist Alva Belmont.

The fourth woman, Lorine Pruette, was a psychologist and social critic who studied with original Freud disciples G. Stanley Hall and Alfred Adler in the 1920s and 1930s. Her 1924 Columbia Ph.D. dissertation, "Women and Leisure: A Study of Social Waste," became a popular book that catapulted Pruette into the public eye as a feminist spokesperson. An insightful theorist committed to women's "self-characterization," her own painful, ultimately doomed efforts to achieve a happy marriage and fulfilling career fueled her ideas. She initially embraced the sexual revolution of the early twentieth century but eventually changed her mind, concluding that sexual freedom was dangerous to the women's movement and to female self-realization. For nearly half a century she advocated women's right to both family and career and proposed innovative solutions to make both possible, such as part-time work and job sharing for married women. Like Beard, she believed women were different from men and opposed the ERA.

The lives of the four women crossed at multiple points. Stevens joined Irwin's College Equal Suffrage League as an Oberlin student. This was her introduction to stumping on street corners for the suffrage cause. The two combined forces through their leadership in the National Woman's Party and later work for Beard's World Center for Women's Archives. Beard was drawn to Stevens's exuberance, and expressed sincere fondness for her, sustained through decades (although Stevens was at times wary of Beard, calling her a communist in 1939 and privately expressing doubts about her broader vision). Yet Stevens may have turned to Beard for advice in the lonely years after she lost the chairmanship of the Inter American Commission of Women and left the National Woman's Party.

Pruette and Irwin were friends: Pruette attended Irwin's twenty-fifth wedding anniversary celebration in 1941 and supported the archives project that Irwin chaired on Beard's behalf in the 1930s. Still, Pruette bowed to no one in her admiration for Beard. When Franklin D. Roosevelt won the presidency, Pruette suggested he nominate Beard for secretary of state (as part of an all-female cabinet, an audacious proposal featured on the front page of several American newspapers). When Pruette wrote a book manuscript on husband-wife teams, Mary and Charles were among them. She admired Charles Beard and recalled a stormy evening she spent in a log cabin with him and Mary. Pruette was fascinated by his description of his grandmother's courage and pluck in shooting a mountain lion while on horseback, which inspired his own feminist belief in women's strength. Pruette was such a Beard enthusiast that sustaining Mary's legacy became personally important to her. She wrote the sociologist Alice Rossi decades after Beard's death to complain about Rossi's exclusion of Beard from her anthology of seminal American feminist thinkers.

Three of the four women were connected to Columbia University, and all four spent much of their lives in that creative center of feminist modernity, New York City. Mary Beard was a Columbia graduate student in the 1900s (and Charles earned his Ph.D. and was a professor there from 1904 to 1917). Pruette earned her Ph.D. from Columbia in 1924, and Stevens was a doctoral student there from 1929 to 1931. Their activist and social circles overlapped. Although they pursued feminist ends through a variety of means, all four came together through their organizing and intellectual contributions to the cause. They read and reviewed each other's books, joined each other in both public organizations and personal celebrations, and supported each other's efforts.

As the traditional historical narrative has often concluded, American feminism did not die after 1920, the year that woman suffrage was won, but feminism faced new challenges. After a democratic, diverse, inspired, and impatient suffrage coalition finally won the Nineteenth Amendment, the organizational base constricted significantly. The National Woman's Party, led indefatigably by Alice Paul—who had helped revive the US movement by borrowing the militant tactics of British suffragettes—was in part responsible. After the suffrage victory, the NWP appointed itself feminist flag bearer, narrowing its program to achieving another amendment to the Constitution that would abolish all legal distinctions based on sex. Some feminists like Beard disagreed with this approach. Irwin and Stevens stayed closely tied to the NWP for decades beyond its 1923 introduction of the Equal Rights Amendment to the US Constitution, which extended the idea of egalitarian relations between women and men into the law. Beard eventually split with the party over the proposed ERA, which she believed would endanger the protective legislation that benefited working women and mothers in the labor force, and Stevens ultimately left the party as well. But they did not leave feminism.

American feminism faced another challenge after women won the vote: the question of need and relevance. Was feminism still necessary? What were its purpose and its goals?[20] Feminist anxiety and drift were reflected in a lack of consensus and declining interest in social reform and single-sex initiatives among younger women. Overt debate about feminist ideas contracted. Concerns with women's emancipation gravitated from political causes to popular culture. Some commentators sounded a note of alarm that modern culture, especially the dynamics of consumption, could alienate women from their self-development and ensnare them in economic dependence on men.[21] The newest New Women of the 1920s were cigarette-smoking, rouged and lipsticked, jazz-listening, pleasure-seeking "modern girls," then known as flappers.[22] Feminism became passé to young women of the 1920s, without the tinges of glamor and adventure that had spurred on those who had poured into the suffrage movement a decade earlier.[23]

Ex-suffragists scattered across the gamut of women's causes, some, like Irwin's friend Maud Wood Park into the League of Women Voters, others into the political parties. Those drawn to labor threw their energies into trade unions, local and state public welfare agencies, and the Women's Bureau of the Department of Labor, created during World War I. Retrospectively called social feminists, these women viewed suffrage as a tool for reform, were involved in public policy issues dedicated to the needs of working women, and advocated a feminist welfare state. Social feminists came to play an important role in the 1930s New Deal, closely allied with First Lady Eleanor Roosevelt and trade unions. Frances Perkins, for instance, the secretary of labor, was a social feminist.[24]

Racial tensions were another challenge facing American feminism in the post-suffrage years. Jim Crow laws and racial segregation, lynching of Black Americans, and character attacks on Black women had reached an all-time high in the decade before the vote was won.[25] African American women's organizations were often founded in part because of Black women's exclusion from white women's groups. At least twenty Black women's groups endorsed woman suffrage during the 1910s, yet some white suffragists held to a double racial standard and allowed their prejudices to dictate their actions.[26] Alice Paul, for instance, overlooked the needs of African American women in her single-minded focus on winning the vote and later on equal rights.[27] Some white suffragists—Beard is one example—walked a fine line in trying to satisfy both white and Black women in the movement. Other white suffragists such as Stevens professed a belief in racial equality that served as a veneer for her own prejudices.

African American women's disillusionment with the white-dominated women's movement extended through the next two decades and led them to participate in few organized feminist activities. Nor were they interested in the Equal Rights Amendment that preoccupied white feminists in the 1920s. Instead they focused on issues that affected both men and women of their race, including lynching.[28] In these decades, Black feminists tended to identify with the struggles of third world peoples more than with white American feminists, joining organizations like the International Council of Women of the Darker Races and the Women's International League for Peace and Freedom.[29]

The four women here illuminate how race and class informed feminist ideas and movements of the early twentieth century. There is little indication that Irwin, Beard, or Pruette viewed themselves as racial superiors. Instead of connecting feminism to white women's rights or Black women's inferiority, they strove to recast it as inclusive and anti-racist. In her eloquent "Open Letter to Feminists," which Beard wrote in 1937 and published in the NWP newspaper *Equal Rights*, she argued that feminism was only one important goal of social change. She equated women's enemies with democracy's enemies: "war, fascism, ignorance, poverty, scarcity, unemployment, sadistic criminality, racial persecution, man's lust for power and woman's miserable trailing in the shadow of his frightful ways."[30] She challenged both factions within the post-suffrage movement to demand "decency of life and labor all round" and encouraged women to take leadership in creating a better world. Beard insisted that collectors gather histories of racially and ethnically diverse women for the World Center for Women's Archives, demonstrating her commitment to inclusivity. Irwin and Pruette articulated ideas on race relations that were progressive, even radical, for the times, though they occasionally reflected the racial views of their era, working behind the scenes to address racism in women's organizations rather than directly confronting it.

A dueling set of ideas shifted uncomfortably beneath the feminist movements of the 1920s and 1930s, contributing to post-suffrage challenges. These were the idea of difference, which inspired social feminism, and the idea of sameness, which informed equal rights feminism, symbolized by NWP feminists in these years.[31] The idea of sexual difference holds that women's biology and cultural roles, particularly as mothers, makes them more different from men than like them. This approach argues that women have special needs that deserve recognition and response (in schools, the workplace, and the courts, for example). Maternalism, an influential idea between 1910 and 1940 and one of the intellectual strands I trace in this book, draws on the difference ideology. Maternalism glorified women's capacity to mother and applied to society the values of nurturance attached to that role.[32] In contrast, the idea of sexual sameness maintains that, as fellow human beings, women are more like men than they are different, and thus deserve equal treatment with no favors.[33]

Historians have debated the depth this impasse created among early twentieth-century women's advocates. Estelle Freedman contends that after 1910 a younger generation rejected the "difference" argument in favor of women's identification with men as human beings, which set the stage for claims to equal rights but alienated more moderate Americans. She argues that these diversions split the US women's movement for nearly half a century.[34] Nancy Cott claims that what historians had previously interpreted as the demise of feminism in the 1920s was more accurately the early struggle of modern feminism. That struggle centered on a very large task: finding language, organization, and goals that would speak to and for modern women in all their diversity.[35] Yet there was intense disagreement on how best to do this. American feminists' stubborn unwillingness to move beyond antagonisms forged in the fire of the suffrage movement weakened their abilities to present a united front during these decades. Yet, the four women examined here also demonstrate how some feminists in the 1920s and 1930s who split over fundamental issues like protective labor legislation could still come together on shared goals, from the movement to save women's historical documents to the call for women's economic equality within marriage.

A number of scholars have noted the paradox that the equality versus difference argument presents to feminism and its history. Feminists have had to refuse the ideas of sexual difference that established their inferiority, at the same time that they have had to focus on women as a collectivity on whose behalf they advocate.[36] Or as Cott captures the conundrum, feminism "aims for individual freedoms by mobilizing sex solidarity. It posits that women recognize their unity while it stands for diversity among women. It requires gender consciousness for its basis yet calls for the limitation of prescribed gender roles."[37] Burnita Shelton Matthew, a lawyer who joined Stevens in international work, summed up the contradiction neatly when she described a good feminist as one who "knows a discrimination when she sees one, and is loyal to women as women."[38]

Most historians of US feminism have valued the idea of equal rights more than that of difference.[39] The 1920s debate over the ERA was a defining moment in the history of women's politics as well as in the development of legislative and legal frameworks of equal rights, workplace protections, and the welfare state. It is often written about as pitting working-class women who highlight difference versus middle-class women who demand equality. In her study of labor feminists in the mid-twentieth century, Dorothy Sue Cobble argues for the need to reexamine the historical narrative in which equal rights feminism is favored over difference feminism. She advocates the necessity of acknowledging multiple forms of American feminism and the possibility for a productive, simultaneous engagement with ideas of "difference" and "equality" among feminists.[40]

The affiliations and ideas of Irwin, Beard, Stevens, and Pruette suggest that some American feminists—on both sides of the fence—argued for a simultaneous belief in equality and difference, or equality with difference, as early as the 1920s and 1930s. All four of the women held complex, synthetic views that were contextualized and evolving.[41] Their comprehensive visions suggest a post-suffrage feminist theoretical process striving to reconceive gender equality in the modern world. None of their ideas fits into neat boxes, which demonstrates the complexity and possibility of a more nuanced approach to feminist ideas in these years.

In addition, these four illustrate the ways feminist thought resists limitations. Historians have systematically documented the shared and conflicting ideas in feminist theory, but as many scholars have noted, feminist thought is multifaceted and has been so since its inception. It reflects a multiplicity of perspectives that challenge any clear boundaries and has included liberal, radical, Marxist/socialistic, psychoanalytic, care-focused, multicultural, global, colonial, ecofeminist, and postmodern perspectives.[42] Although some of these theories had not yet been dreamt up or named in the early twentieth century, the thought of Irwin, Beard, Stevens, and Pruette pulled from a number of them, illustrating the unruly messiness of intellectual categories as well as the capacious, wide-ranging nature of their ideas. Their multipronged approach to feminism on a variety of fronts over decades demonstrates the persistence, and variety, of feminism(s) during these years. Moreover, traces of their thought are alive in forms of feminist theory today, making their lives and ideas instructive to contemporary audiences.

As a term, "feminism" is a relatively modern word. It was first coined in France in the 1880s and spread through Europe in the 1890s and to North and South America by 1910.[43] What was referred to in the nineteenth-century United States as woman's rights, woman suffrage, or the woman movement—with emphasis on the singular woman symbolizing the presumed unity of the female sex—gave way in the 1910s, the height of the American suffrage movement, to the modern term "feminism."[44] Feminism in the 1910s included not only collective goals like occupational advancement and political rights but also a changing consciousness, which represented an individual transformation. Marie Jenney Howe, founder of Heterodoxy, the renowned New York City feminist club that drew together women professionals, artists, and intellectuals, took a stab at defining feminism in a 1914 socialist publication: "No one movement is feminism. No one organization is feminism. All women movements and organizations taken together form a part of feminism. But feminism means more than this. . . . Feminism is not limited to any one cause or reform. It strives for equal rights, equal laws, equal opportunity, equal wages, equal standards, and a whole new world of human equality. But feminism means more than a changed world. It means a changed psychology, the creation of a new consciousness in women." Although single-sex, Heterodoxy aimed to expand women beyond gender norms and was one of the earliest American organizations to use the term "feminism." Irwin, a member for nearly forty years, described Heterodoxy as "the easiest of clubs . . . no duties or obligations. There was no press. Everything that was said was off the record." Stevens honed her feminist ideas in Heterodoxy as well.[45]

"Feminism" began and has persisted as a contentious term, due to both its connection to radicalism and disagreements about its meaning. Considering feminism globally, Estelle Freedman has argued that from its origin in the 1910s through the social upheavals of the 1960s, "feminist" "remained a pejorative term among most progressive reformers, suffragists, and socialists around the world." Even as universal suffrage for both sexes spread around the globe—to England in 1928, Japan, Mexico, France, and China by the late 1940s—feminism was still associated with extremism and with race and class elitism.[46] In some parts of the world, feminism has been used to reinforce imperialism; in others, feminists have linked their movements to the anticolonial uprisings of which they were a part. During the national revolution from 1919 to 1922, when Egypt gained nominal independence from Great Britain, for example, feminists joined nationalist leaders to organize mass demonstrations against colonial rule. Similarly, feminist organizations in India joined the movement for Indian independence during the 1930s and 1940s.[47] The subject of feminism has been highly contested in more recent times as well, as exemplified by critiques from women of color and lesbians in the United States in the 1970s, 1980s and 1990s, as well as from the political right. Feminism in the early twenty-first century has also been co-opted in the national interests of both liberal modernist states and religious fundamentalism.[48]

The multiple strands of feminist thought represent varying ideas about the reasons for women's oppression and the best ways for eliminating it. Noting the major traditions highlights some of the important differences in feminists' theories and practice that shaped these four women's lives and ideas. Liberal feminism, often identified with Mary Wollstonecraft's *A Vindication of the Rights of Women*, John Stuart Mill's "The Subjection of Women," and the nineteenth-century woman suffrage movement, argues that women's subordination is rooted in customary and legal constraints that block women's access to enter and succeed in the public sphere. It was this philosophy that most ignited Beard's wrath. Linked in the mid-twentieth century with the National Organization for Women (NOW) and Betty Friedan, one of its founders and its first president, liberal feminism claims the importance of individual rights and believes the single most important goal of the women's rights movement is sexual equality.[49] Hoping to free women from oppressive gender roles, liberal feminists argue that biological sex should not determine an individual's psychological and social gender. Critics have challenged this perspective for advocating a male ontology of self, individualism, and considering only the interests of white, middle-class, heterosexual women.[50] Of the four women investigated here, Stevens most fully represents the liberal feminist position.

In contrast, radical feminists advocated displacing the social and cultural institutions of patriarchy, especially the family and organized religion, rather than simply retooling legal and political structures. Some radical feminists argue for androgyny—both women and men exhibiting masculine and feminine qualities—while others want to affirm women's essential "femaleness." Marxist and socialist feminists integrate class and sex in their effort to understand women's subordination to men. Their analysis often focuses on women's work within the home and family as well as in the labor market, and they advocate the destruction of capitalist economic structures. Irwin, Beard, and Pruette all included radical analyses in their thought, and Irwin and Beard were both anti-capitalists, if not explicitly socialists.

While liberal, radical, and Marxist-socialist feminist thought considers the macrocosm (patriarchy or capitalism) in its varying explanations of women's oppression, psychoanalytic feminists consider the microcosm of the individual, looking for the roots of women's oppression within the female psyche. One version of this approach considers care-focused feminists, who are associated with interdependence, community, and connection (in contrast to men as a group being linked to independence, autonomy, and selfhood). This strand of thought privileges a feminist ethic of care at the same time that it seeks to reduce women's burden of nurturance so that, like men, women can develop themselves as full persons. Pruette was a psychoanalytic feminist who addressed the issue of care, but so, too, did the other three women.

Other diverse and complex categories of contemporary feminist thought include multicultural feminism, global feminism, and postcolonial feminism, which, broadly described, are committed to understanding the multiple differences that exist among women both nationally and transnationally, and the meanings of those differences for coalition work and shared social justice struggles. Finally, ecofeminists take up women's (and men's) relationship to the nonhuman world of nature, while postmodern feminists analyze language and discourse to understand the systems of meaning that construct and define sex and gender.[51] Denise Riley has argued that the category of "women," and therefore feminism, is always contingent.[52]

Some contemporary scholars have criticized the standard division of feminist activism in the United States into a series of historical waves: the first wave woman suffrage movement (1848–1920), the second wave women's liberation and equal rights movements (1960s and early 1970s), and the recent third wave.[53] The women's rights movement in which Irwin, Beard, Stevens, and Pruette participated and that they led during the 1920s, 1930s, and beyond is not represented in this model of US feminism. They could be viewed as contributors to the final years of the "first wave," but they had decades of activist and intellectual work still ahead of them in 1920. Ignoring that work reinforces the myth that feminism in the United States "died" in the post-suffrage years.[54] Beard, Irwin, Stevens, and Pruette doggedly spoke, wrote, organized, demonstrated, and advocated for the rights of women for decades after the Nineteenth Amendment was ratified.

While these four women were part of the crest that pushed the seventy-two-year-long suffrage movement to victory, they continued to propel the US movement forward from the 1920s to the 1960s.

Three of them lived long enough to witness the resurgence of feminism in the late 1960s. Pruette, who died in 1977, read and publicly critiqued advocates of the emergent movement, including Kate Millett and Shulamith Firestone. In her habitually feisty way she challenged historian William O'Neill, who described his influential 1969 *Everyone Was Brave: A History of Feminism in America* as "first of all an inquiry into the failure of feminism." Pruette wrote O'Neill to object to his argument and shared her reservations with other scholars who would listen. She wrote historian Sherna Gluck: "No doubt you've seen Bill O'Neal's [*sic*] book on the woman's movement. He claims this was a failure. I think he's nuts." Pruette believed O'Neill personally "damned" her because he faulted early twentieth-century feminists for limiting their visions to the vote instead of reshaping marriage and the family, which Pruette did try to do. She was one feminist intellectual who lived to read the historical assessment of her movement's failures.[55]

Even before Pruette's recognition of the ways that history could be rewritten, or reevaluated, all four women advocated the significance of historical memory among American feminists. This included Beard's belief that women's minds would be set on fire by understanding their own historical importance and Irwin's insistence that college women link their suffrage activism to the memory of the pioneers who opened doors for them. They placed themselves generationally, wrote from this perspective, and extended their hands both forward and backward through time—forward to pull up a new generation of feminists, as Irwin did in co-founding the College Equal Suffrage League, and as they all did when they joined the youthful National Woman's Party—and backward to clasp the hands of the older generation that was passing.

The visionary feminists I write about in *Feminism as Life's Work* recognized the danger of forgetting what came before and to whom debts were owed. They paid homage by writing books, creating and supporting archives to hold women's documents, and chronicling a history they were still very much in the midst of. They recognized the challenge of reenergizing a movement after an exhausting collective victory like the Nineteenth Amendment, and they all felt, often personally, the factionalism that marked the women's movement in the early twentieth century. They were increasingly disappointed in a younger generation that seemed uninterested in women's issues. They tried valiantly to achieve in their own lives the egalitarian marriages, accomplished careers, and full lives that the modern interpretation of feminism suggested was possible. Their life stories offer fresh insights into the history of a pivotal social movement over several critical decades. They link the suffrage movement to the rise of women's liberation, and their lives suggest that no matter the roadblocks ahead, feminism's forward movement is clear.

Together these four women offer a unique perspective into the transitional years in early twentieth-century feminism, as it moved from a separatist to a gender-integrated world.[56] They stood at the crossroads as American feminism redefined its goals and strategies, joining and leading what was at times a raucous, contentious, painful debate. Feminists like these began with high hopes of achieving egalitarian lives with men in love and sex, marriage and family, as well as work. This proved more difficult than their ideas and capacious visions suggested. Yet their courageous defiance of early twentieth-century gendered stereotypes contributed to social change that has rippled down to our own time. Their struggles prefigured the conflicts of a later generation.

CHAPTER 1

Planting the Seeds

The years 1880 to 1920 saw dramatic changes in America. The nation was transformed from a rural economy and landscape to an urban, industrialized one. By 1900 almost two-thirds of working Americans no longer labored on farms but in offices, factories, stores, or banks; on railroads or in the trades; and the nation's population was increasingly concentrated in the cities.[1] These changes set the stage for the development of various types of feminist thought, embodied by the four women examined in this book. The early family lives and childhood experiences of Inez Irwin, Mary Beard, Doris Stevens, and Lorine Pruette shaped their feminism, as did their educations, mentors, and the vibrant women's movement of the last quarter of the nineteenth century. The spirit of activism and public involvement that characterized this energetic, innovative period in US women's history spilled over into their lives and stirred their developing minds and imaginations. The ideas of none of these women were exactly alike, as is true of feminism today; however, they all shared a commitment to woman suffrage. Their points of intellectual convergence and dissonance will be one of the central themes of this book, as it illustrates the variety of parallel feminisms that existed in the early twentieth century.

The four families this chapter profiles demonstrate in microcosm the larger forces of change sweeping the United States in these years. The transformation from an agricultural to an industrial economy is seen in each family: while each woman had at least one grandfather who was a farmer (and one parent who grew up on a farm), their fathers labored in urban professions. Irwin's father was a prison warden and politician, Beard's a lawyer and reformer, and Stevens's and Pruette's both worked in small businesses. Three of the women were born and grew up in cities: Boston (Irwin); Indianapolis (Beard); and Omaha (Stevens). Only Pruette was born on a farm, in Tennessee, but her family moved to a town when she came of school age. Of the four, only Beard's family belonged to the booming middle class of the late nineteenth century. The other three knew bouts of poverty and genteelly aspired to the solid middle class.

Nineteenth-century debates precipitated by the women's rights movement—about property rights, education, and privileges within marriage—fed into the two emerging lines of reasoning that influenced both the developing and mature ideas of the women. Evolving as early as the 1830s, the "difference" approach argued that women's power in society came from their abilities to influence the men in their families through education, example, and persuasion. This approach justified women's public activities, like education and participation in reform societies, as part of women's separate sphere and distinct calling. The nineteenth-century middle class broadly accepted this view, championed by women like Sara Josepha Hale and Catharine Beecher. Those who supported the second line of reasoning—egalitarianism or "sameness"—stressed rights over influence, arguing that women should exercise power as men did, through political and economic rights. Led by Susan B. Anthony, Lucy Stone, and Elizabeth Cady Stanton, this more controversial approach held that women should receive the same rights as men in society and government, including the right to vote.[2]

Ideas about gender hierarchy in the home were in flux during the later nineteenth century. Changing beliefs about husbands' and wives' roles were influenced as much by new notions of the marital relationship as by a growing women's rights movement in North America and much of Western Europe, which considered reform of marriage laws an important part of its agenda.[3] In addition, the sharp distinction between separate spheres was eroding, even in the most conservative circles.[4] Although middle-class women still needed to marry in order to survive financially, some women—like the mothers of the two younger women in this study—imagined broader horizons in college, which made them chafe in their subsequent lives as wives and mothers. Traditional Victorian values associated with marriage—male dominance, female economic dependence—challenged feminist ideas and the possibilities that higher education held out to women. While "good morals" of Victorian women and gendered marital roles maintained the stability of most marriages, they took a toll on women's and men's personal lives and created a great deal of discontent.[5] This discontent was palpable in the childhood homes of Stevens and Pruette, and it influenced their adult feminist agendas.

The middle class of the early twentieth century feared the American family was in crisis.[6] Statistics validated this concern. In 1870, there were 1.5 divorces for every 1,000 marriages. By 1920, the figure had ballooned to 7.7 divorces per every 1,000 marriages.[7] A declining birth rate freed women from a lifetime of pregnancy, childbirth, and childrearing. The total fertility rate in the United States fell 50 percent between 1800 and 1900. While the average number of children per family in 1800 was 7.4, by 1900 it had plummeted to 3.5. Together, the mothers of Irwin, Beard, Stevens, and Pruette gave birth to twenty-five children in all; collectively their daughters, the four feminists in this study, gave birth to only two.[8] Combined with falling birthrates among "native-born" Americans, the divorce rate stoked fears about the survival of the family and the "American race." Politicians, reformers, and social analysts who referred to "the American race" in the late nineteenth century meant whites who lived in the United States and were usually of northern European or Anglo-Saxon descent.[9] Three of the four women's families profiled here were "native-born" (only Stevens's mother was an immigrant, from Holland). Irwin, Beard, Stevens, and Pruette fit the profile of the white, childless, educated woman upon whom xenophobic fears about "race suicide" came to rest (although Beard did ultimately have two children). Historians have asserted that early twentieth-century anxieties about the family were connected to the changing roles of women.[10]

Increasing immigration and urbanization compounded this nervousness. New immigrants from southern Europe and Asia fanned the flames of fear among American elites—including reformers—that "American values" and way of life were being lost as immigrants brought customs from their native countries to the United States. This anxiety and suspicion led to pronatalism, the selective promotion of reproduction by the state. In the early twentieth century, coercive means of reproductive regulation as social control were linked to cultural constructions about the family. Nostalgic idealizations of motherhood, family, and home were invoked to create and legitimate social policies concerning reproduction.[11]

These idealizations hearkened back to earlier, agrarian representations of home. In the mid-nineteenth century United States, the idealized home was a moral space that reflected and/or shaped the character of those who lived there, and counteracted the unsettling influences of industrialization. By the end of the nineteenth century, a new ideal of home took root among middle-class Americans, one that celebrated consumption, good taste, and self-expression rather than self-restraint and morality.[12] At the same time, Progressive reform movements stimulated Americans to seek solutions to problems caused by the surge in immigrant and urban populations. Progressive reformers advocated government legislation to address child labor, dirty and overpopulated neighborhoods, impure food and water, government corruption, and unsafe working conditions.[13]

Nostalgic idealizations of home and motherhood led to ideas of maternalism, which played a central role in dividing American feminists in these years. Maternalist ideas emphasized women's differences from men and celebrated their unique abilities to mother and care for children. They reinforced notions of immutable sexual difference; blurred distinctions among women based on class, race, and ethnicity; and promoted white, middle-class definitions of the family and the family wage system. Maternalist thought included two interpretive strands: the first emphasized the reconceptualization of women's roles in public

policy in terms of the wider application of maternal values of care and nurture, the approach Beard took. A second strand emphasized the reformulation
of women's roles in public policy in terms of the biology of motherhood and a
eugenic ideal of bettering the family and the race.[14] Both strands—which cannot
be completely separated—invoked an essentializing image of women as repro-
ducers, which would lead many equal rights feminists to oppose the maternalism
advocated by social feminists. Yet some, like Beard and Irwin, applied maternalist ideas toward feminist ends, as they tried to bridge earlier feminist ideas with
modern ones. To better understand these four women as adults, it is necessary
to first come to know them in the beginnings of their feminism, beginnings that
planted the seeds for fruitful lives of feminist dedication.

My Mind Seethed in Those Days: Inez Haynes Irwin

Irwin was a militant and freethinking girl, born in Brazil in 1873 and raised in a
large, struggling, middle-class Boston family. The eighth of ten children born to
Gideon Haynes and Emma Jane Hopkins, Irwin spent her first two years in Rio
de Janeiro, where her entrepreneurial father, previously a Massachusetts politician and prison reformer, was attempting to market a device for shelling coffee
beans. While the Hayneses were in Rio, a yellow fever epidemic swept the city;
one of Irwin's older sisters contracted the fever and died. The Hayneses immediately returned to Boston, their South American venture a failure, their family
in mourning.[15]

Her dramatic first years and unconventional family were well suited to the
liberal, independent woman Irwin became. Her father, Gideon Haynes, was born
in 1815 into an old American family of Scottish-English roots, and was raised in
a female world: the only male in a household consisting of his widowed mother
and eight sisters, he grew up believing in women's rights and social reform. By
the time he married Irwin's mother, he was a forty-two-year-old widower and
single father of seven. Irwin's mother Emma Jane Hopkins Haynes, born in 1841
and boasting English descendants who came over on the *Mayflower* and signed
the Declaration of Independence, was a Lowell mill girl who married at nineteen.
Emma shocked their close, conservative Boston community when she ice-skated
or rode horseback up to the day each of her ten children was born. One Haynes
ancestor married a Native American (in which Irwin took great pride), a fact her
future husband would facetiously refer to when he stated, "One of Inez's ancestors came over on the *Mayflower*, and another was on the reception committee."[16]

Irwin warmly identified with her father's idealism, liberal political instincts,
and love of drama and adventure, all attributes that characterized her own long
life. Gideon Haynes began his eclectic career as a Shakespearean actor, served
two terms in the Massachusetts House of Representatives, and in 1857 was
appointed warden of the state prison in Charlestown, after the previous warden

and deputy warden were killed in a bloody riot. In his fourteen years as warden (which spanned the Civil War years), Haynes began a prison lecture series. He invited such luminaries as abolitionist Wendell Phillips and William Lloyd Garrison, editor of the radical antislavery newspaper *The Liberator*, to speak. Haynes became a noted prison reformer and wrote a book about his experiences, *Pictures from Prison Life.*[17] "My father was a handsome person," Irwin admiringly recalled in her fifties, "the black-haired, oliveskinned, gray-eyed type, with a figure like a blade of Damascus steel, romantic, chivalrous, gallant, gay—*dashing* was the word they used to describe him."[18]

Her mother's spirited energy and independence also influenced Irwin, although she rebelled from the domesticity that circumscribed her mother's life. Emma Jane Hopkins's mother had died in childbirth when she was ten. Although her father, left alone with eight daughters, immediately remarried—"the makeshift matrimony of a man left alone with an unsolvable problem," Irwin wryly commented—she virtually brought herself up and went to work at an early age. Irwin recalled her mother as "beautiful in a delicately robust way," and vain, extravagant, temperamentally capricious, illogical, with "a natural instinct for beauty," "a strong streak of common sense," and "the sparkle of . . . mother-wit." "Physically and nervously she radiated life," Irwin wrote. "She was the quickest creature I have ever seen." In 1926 Irwin described the characteristics she believed she inherited from both parents. "It is, I believe, my father's blood—a long line of farmers—which has most influenced my thinking and is responsible for a kind of militant idealism which marks many of my family. It is, I believe, my mother's blood—a long line of mill-workers and mill-owners—which has most influenced me aesthetically. That strain has given me an intense love of beauty; a feeling, more poignant perhaps, when beauty is expressed in color rather than form."[19]

Her parents' marriage was passionate and exciting—providing the positive model of marital love and friendship Irwin achieved in her own second marriage—but it was also traditional in its assumption that Emma's place was in the home and prolific motherhood was her vocation. Emma was a box-maker in her uncle's factory when she first saw Gideon, then the Massachusetts State Prison warden, at an 1858 political rally. "When she was seventeen my mother heard my father make a speech," Irwin wrote. "She came home, waked up all her sisters, and kept them laughing half the night in spirited girlish imitations of him. The next year she met him. A few months later they were married." Twenty-four years younger than her new husband, Emma not only assumed responsibility for the big warden's house, she also became stepmother to seven children from his first marriage (his wife had died two years earlier), the eldest of whom was only four years younger than she was. To add to this heavy domestic burden, she and Gideon had ten children of their own; twelve children of the combined family survived to adulthood.[20]

Irwin's father lost the wardenship when a new political administration took office, and he was unemployed when Irwin was born. The family's strained finances and her father's advancing age (he was fifty-eight at her birth) marred her childhood. After his ill-fated Brazilian business venture Haynes retired to his home, and for the remainder of his life earned a meager income running small hotels and publishing occasional magazine articles. Irwin's dramatic description of her father in the diary she kept as a teenager illustrates the idealized, mythic vision she carried of him: "Injustice fired him as the red rag the bull. . . . He had flung himself into a leading reform of the day with the whole souled devotion of his manhood's prime. . . . He succeeded in finally working changes in the penal code which put the prisons and the prison discipline of his native state foremost in the world. But at the cost of his health and the ultimate chilling of his heart."[21]

Many years later, when Irwin was sixty-five, she considered the challenges her mother had faced due to her aging husband's growing reclusiveness. While in his youth and years as warden he had enjoyed entertaining on a lavish scale—holding masquerades, for example—in his later years he withdrew more and more into his home. If relatives and friends wanted to see Gideon Haynes they had to call on him. "It made life, I now realize," Irwin commented, "rather difficult for my mother. She was twenty-four years younger than he and still full of life, activity and vivacity when he retired from the fleshpots." The family's refined poverty, which placed the rising consumerism of the late nineteenth century out of the Haynes's reach, strongly influenced Irwin in her early years. "We were poor . . . not poor enough to live in the slums . . . but poor enough to float along at a dead level of a lamb-stew existence." "As I look back upon my youth," she wrote in 1912, "it is like gazing upon a long, gray, dusty, arid stretch of desert. My girlhood was buried in a period of family history which trailed prosperous, stirring, and romantic days. Of all social atmospheres this is the most deadly."[22]

A starry-eyed, idealistic child, Irwin escaped from the "strangling gray fog of poverty" that shrouded her family through the cultural institutions and education to which her parents introduced her, as well as the fertile world of her own imagination. "The family life was informed with that idea of plain living and high thinking which was the New England ideal fifty years ago," Irwin wrote in 1925. "As I look back on my life, it seems to be bound by the Boston *Transcript*, the Boston Public Library, the Boston Symphony, and the *Atlantic Monthly*." Her early years were also influenced by her attraction to "that scarlet-and-gold-country of the footloose male," to which she longingly watched her brothers escape. Even as a girl Irwin began to feel a growing impatience with the woman's lot. "From the moment I was able to think for myself," she wrote in mid-life, "I regretted bitterly that I had not been born a man." She recalled living "a negative life of the flesh, a positive life of the spirit." In the "world of faery" that she spun in her mind she was happy, ambitious, and mentally eager. In her actual world she remembered being quite a different person, one who was bored, lonely, and unmotivated. She equated her romantic longing for adventure with travel, work, the outdoors, and the masculine public sphere. "I wanted to run away to sea, to take tramping trips across the country, to go on voyages of discovery and exploration, to try my hands at a dozen different occupations. I wanted to be a sailor, a soldier. I wanted to go to prize-fights; to frequent bar-rooms; even barber-shops and smoking-rooms seemed to offer a brisk, salty taste of life." Irwin was drawn to this masculine culture her entire life, the culture she envisioned her quixotic, adventurous father inhabiting in the glory days before her birth.[23]

Since she rebelled from the domesticity her mother represented, Irwin sought out unmarried career women and suffragists for role models in her youth. Her unorthodox eighth grade teacher, "a perfect type of the women who were fighting in those days for what was called Women's Rights," introduced her to the ideas of nineteenth-century giants Susan B. Anthony, Elizabeth Cady Stanton, Lucy Stone, the Grimké sisters, Lydia Maria Child, and Lucretia Mott, which marked a turning-point in her life. "Once she suggested that the subject of the next composition be, *Should Women Vote*," Irwin wrote. "That was the first time I had ever heard that question. It was a great moment in my life, for a star burst in rainbow vastness in my mind and then settled into perpetual glowing existence there." The adolescent Irwin respected this influential teacher so much that one day she slipped an anonymous love poem on her desk. Over sixty years later she could still recite the first verse: "Lovely woman, full of grace / I can read it in your face / That you have done much good on earth / Ever since your day of birth."[24]

Like this much-admired teacher, her two unconventional, progressive aunts also helped sculpt Irwin's emerging feminism and intellectual liberalism. Her father's youngest sister Lora was ordained a minister in 1875 and quickly gained a reputation as "the wittiest" of all the "women clergymen." When Irwin came home from school "agog" with the revolutionary idea of votes for women, her Aunt Lora (a household familiar) calmly responded, "I have believed in woman's rights all my life, and so has your father." As an old woman, Irwin was still "breathless with admiration" of her Aunt Lora, who in the nineteenth century challenged gender barriers and was in the professional vanguard. Although women made up the majority of church members at the time, most mainstream denominations did not allow women into the ministry.[25]

Women found more leadership opportunities in the "new" religions of the late nineteenth century, which also influenced young Irwin and her developing ideas. Spiritualism, a movement whose participants believed they could communicate with the dead, peaked in the second half of the century, and women were considered superior mediums. A second aunt of Irwin's was a devoted spiritualist who introduced her to social change movements and radical ideas, which both grew out of and contributed to this popular movement.[26] As a teenager, Irwin spent six weeks during the summers of 1889, 1890, and 1891 at a Massachusetts spiritualist community with her aunt. The ideas disseminated there stretched her mind in ways that reverberated far into her future: "I heard discussed there every possible system of ethics, every possible theory of humanitarianism." She explained: "I listened to teetotalists, spiritualists, atheists, agnostics, theosophists, socialists, anarchists and to a dozen other ists. All these ideas flowed like lava over the white tablet of my sixteen- and seventeen- and eighteen-year-old-mind leaving a fiery impress behind. . . . My mind seethed in those days."[27]

Irwin arrived at young womanhood rebellious, ambitious, and independent, determined to break out of "the woman's life" and already articulating feminist principles. She graduated valedictorian from Bowdoin Grammar School in 1887 and from Girls' High School in 1890. At her high school graduation she read an original composition on Romantic poets Byron, Shelley, and Keats; the *Boston Transcript* reported, "Rather an ambitious attempt it was, but as a product of girlhood, a wonderful thing." When Irwin read this she determined, "If this is true, I can learn to write. I am going to be an author." She resolved to go to nearby Radcliffe College to prepare for a brilliant career.[28]

Her parents' deaths in 1892 and 1893, however, interrupted her dreams and transformed living as she knew it. The loss of both parents within close proximity overwhelmed Irwin with grief, yet the diary she kept in these years suggests that, enigmatically, it also freed her to launch her own passionate, creative life. Irwin was only nineteen when her father died of natural causes. Her mother, distraught, in mourning, and possibly financially overwhelmed, hanged herself a year later, at fifty-four. Irwin and her younger sister Daisy discovered their mother's body.[29] Suicide in the late nineteenth century—particularly by women—was unusual, and like suicide today left feelings of abandonment, anger, guilt, and social censure in its wake.[30] Irwin never alluded to this personal trauma in any of her many published writings. Yet its impact was clear; she later proposed suicide as a civil disobedience tactic in the suffrage movement, and wove suicide into several of her novels. Newly motherless, one month after her mother's death Irwin sadly wrote in her diary, "I would be of that class of persons who have not 'pet' subjects or mamas. All mamas should be mine." As a twenty-year-old, on July 28, 1893, two months after her mother's suicide, Irwin scrawled "Freedom!" in bold, black letters across the top of her diary page, and underneath it dizzily wrote: "The second climacteric has arrived. I begin to live formerly I have existed. I approach life, trailing clouds of glory. My coming is heralded by the trumpet, lots of grand emotions, sickened love, great despair, all-conquering ambition. . . . Intensity, passion lies all before *me*. How shall I end? My dual life, my life of dreams, must merge with the practical events of day. . . . Life came to me at my father's death. . . . To have two great sorrows at once is after all a blessing. Each in some part over-powers the other." Reeling from shock and sorrow and faced with the prospect of having to support herself, Irwin took a teaching position to save money to attend Radcliffe. She taught for three and a half years at an elementary school in Charlestown, which she found both difficult and a professional mismatch. "Looking back on my pedagogical career," she later wrote lightly, "I have come to the conclusion that, although I was not the worst teacher the Boston Schools ever knew, I was close to it."[31]

When Irwin finally achieved her long-held goal of attending Radcliffe, her two years there marked a watershed in her life. It was at Radcliffe where she first consciously identified as a feminist and began a close, lifelong friendship with classmate Maud Wood Park, who became the noted leader of the National League of Women Voters and an influential social feminist.[32] The two young women had much in common when they met in a Chaucer class in 1896. Like Irwin, Park was born in Boston, had been a bright high school student, and taught school before attending college. Out of a class of seventy-two, they were the only students to believe in woman suffrage.

Displaying the lively spirit of rebellion that characterized her, Irwin organized her first suffrage meeting at Radcliffe. Park later remembered Irwin in her college years "as small and dark, with so-called Spanish coloring, which appeared to point to the environment of her Brazilian birthplace as having more influence than the New England heredity of her parents. Her liking for bright colors, particularly for neck ribbons of brilliant red, always seemed to me symbolic of her amazing zest for life."[33] When a Radcliffe donor invited the class of 1897 to a tea at her home and circulated an anti-suffrage petition, Irwin and Park were irate. Consulting neither the administration nor faculty, they invited Alice Stone Blackwell, daughter of women's rights advocates Lucy Stone and Henry Blackwell, to address the students on the woman suffrage cause. "The day of the meeting," Irwin later recalled, "Maud and I cut every college class. We stood in the main hall of Fay House, stopped every girl who entered, described the situation and asked her to come that afternoon to hear Alice Blackwell. When Maud introduced Miss Blackwell, she faced a hall, so filled with girls that the steps, windowsills and aisles were packed." Despite the fact that she and Park were "plunged into hot water" as a result of the incident, Irwin graduated from Radcliffe in 1898 with Honors in English and prepared to become a writer.[34]

Irwin's friendship with Park blossomed around their shared passion for feminism. Irwin and Park first heard the term in the 1890s from a fellow student recently returned from France, who pronounced it "in the French way: feminisme," as Irwin later recalled. Throughout her life Irwin credited Park with stimulating and shaping her incipient feminism. She wrote her in 1938: "your ideas on feminism, so perfectly formulated, guided and brought to precision the unformulated ones, adrift in my head. These were in the old Radcliffe days, when after we had finished comparing notes on the Kittredge Chaucer course, we talked over women and women's affairs. You exercised an enormous influence in these ways in those days. I am grateful for it, so grateful that I won't attempt to put it in words." As Irwin wrote of her half century of friendship with "dear dear Maud": "We discovered . . . [a] tie, so strong, so fiery, so compelling, that it turned our studies pallid. Deathless, unique, it has kept our friendship a solid thing all these fifty-odd years. We were both feminists."[35] Their friendship survived their leadership of opposing sides of women's factions in the 1910s, 1920s, and beyond.

The seeds for Irwin's feminist modernity were planted in her early years. In admiring and romanticizing masculine culture (and her father), she dismissed female culture as trivial and dull. She rebelled against the feminine conformity expected of nineteenth-century middle-class women, scribbling defiantly in her 1893 diary: "I wonder if there is anythings [*sic*] forbidden women to say, that I have not already said. If I thought so, I should look them up and say them."[36] She turned her considerable energies and gutsy rebellion to challenging the separation of male and female spheres and improving the status of women.

Irwin recognized this tension, this pull between the male and female spheres, in her own experiences. As a girl, she wrote of her "dual life," her life of dreams—a "masculine" life—and her real life—a "feminine" life. Later, when her need for companionship overcame her reluctance to marry, Irwin alternately entitled the diary she kept as a young wife, "The Two Lives of a Woman," "A Two-Lived Woman," and "The Double Life."[37] Her embrace of modern feminism exacted a toll—a failed first marriage, struggles to sustain a creative life as a writer in a period that dismissed women professionals, years of unhappiness. But like the other three women in this book, her commitments were unwavering, and she self-consciously and courageously used her own life as a testing-ground for her feminist beliefs and work.

The Freedom to Dare: Mary Ritter Beard

Beard's childhood and youth are much more difficult to bring to life than Irwin's, because she intentionally destroyed her personal papers. Why she, a pioneer in women's history and one of the first champions of an archive for women's personal and public documents, should choose to destroy her own is enigmatic. Several historians have speculated on her motives: one suggested Beard lacked the self-confidence to be examined critically; another remarked, "her desire to remain elusive is itself a statement about her personality." Beard's daughter suggested that her Quaker background made her overly modest. With good humor, she held "a strict outlook on life," and wanted to help people "personally and impersonally," without claiming public credit. In her last book, a brief memorial volume to her husband Charles A. Beard, Mary may have supplied the answer when she quoted a journalist who wrote of both Beards: "'By our works shall ye know us' is their notion." Charles also destroyed his personal papers. The paucity of sources makes an investigation of Beard's formative years sketchy, speculative, and episodic, particularly in comparison with the other three women in this comparative study.[38]

Born three years after Irwin on August 5, 1876, Beard grew up in a stable, conservative, upper-middle-class Indianapolis family. The fourth of seven children, she was the eldest daughter of Narcissa Lockwood and Eli Foster Ritter. Her mother was the cultured daughter of a southern planter; her father was a Quaker, lawyer, and temperance activist. Mary had three older brothers, two younger brothers, and one sister born when she was seven. Her secure childhood and youth knew none of the tragedy, scarcity, or familial loss of status that Irwin's did. The Ritters owned an impressive home, spacious and beautiful, with a top floor large enough to serve as a ballroom for adults and a roller skating rink for the children and their friends.[39]

Eli Foster Ritter was a stern, zealous man who, like Irwin's father, sparked his daughter's life-long commitment to reform. He was born in Indianapolis to southern Quaker parents who had moved from North Carolina in 1822. He left his parents' farm in 1859 to attend Indianapolis's Northwestern Christian College and then Asbury University (later renamed DePauw), a prestigious Methodist university in Greencastle, Indiana, in 1861. When the Civil War erupted, Ritter left Asbury and his Quaker principles to join the Union army. In 1863 he married Narcissa Lockwood and then returned to active combat duty for the duration of the war. A reformer and an advocate of the temperance movement, he was approached to run as a presidential candidate for the Prohibition Party, but refused. A Republican, in the 1870s Ritter and his family joined the Central Avenue Methodist Church, a bulwark of midwestern conservatism. Ritter served on the church's board of trustees and in 1877 was in charge of the Sunday school. His daughter Mary echoed his reformist sympathies but never shared his attraction to organized religion. When she was young, her father encouraged her to read the *Western Christian Advocate* on Sundays: "I was more than lukewarm about this matter," she later exclaimed. "I was frigid."[40]

One historian has suggested that Narcissa Lockwood was the model for Beard's later belief that women play powerful roles in the family and in civilization. The second of three daughters, Beard's mother came from an old American Protestant family that left Kentucky for Greencastle, Indiana, before the Civil War. Prominent in the local Methodist church, the Lockwoods developed strong ties with DePauw, the university that all the Beard children eventually attended. Beard's mother was remembered by her grandchildren as "the musically gifted daughter of a Southern planter," an elegant lady who "liked nice things," and was "quite formidable." Unlike Irwin's mother, who had worked in a factory, Beard's upper-middle-class mother attended the Brookville Academy in Thockton, Kentucky, and taught briefly before her marriage. Beard's description of her mother suggests her influence in Beard's later critique of twentieth-century women's embrace of the male career model, which puzzled her feminist contemporaries. "Narcissa Lockwood . . . [never] thought of herself as a 'careerist.' . . . I don't know whether my mother was paid a cent but I doubt it. My mother . . . read law to my father when his eyes were too weak from exposure in the Civil War to read for himself. Through her aid to him, he passed the examination for the bar and with the rest his eyes had he became a distinguished lawyer."[41]

The idea of "the lady" was powerful in Victorian society. Cultured, patient, polite, well mannered, "the lady" was collectively endowed with a public role as the civilizer of men and implicitly coded as white and middle-class. Emily Putnam, the first dean of Barnard College, noted in her 1910 history *The Lady* that "the lady has established herself as the criterion of a community's civilization."[42] This idea of woman as a civilizing influence in a turbulent, materialistic world served as a metaphoric life raft to Beard. This idea, to which she returned again and again in her books and thought about women, men, and feminism, was a powerful concept she had developed as a girl observing her mother both in and outside the home.

The belief that women were more nurturing and moral than men had great influence in Victorian America and was tied to the later politics of maternalism. Used to justify female confinement to domesticity and the home, some women turned the tables by using this idea of innate gender difference to demand access to political rights and to transform traditionally private issues (motherhood, child care) into public discourse.[43] By the late nineteenth and early twentieth centuries, women reformers like Jane Addams and Mary Beard argued that women should apply their housekeeping skills to society and sweep away the corruption and dirt of a masculinized culture. Nineteenth-century constructions of masculinity, in contrast, were rigid and often harsh. The middle-class ideal of the male provider was paramount: Americans questioned the manhood of husbands who lost their jobs (as Iwin's father had) or saw their businesses fail.[44]

Influences outside her home and family also shaped Beard's developing thought. She was an outstanding student, noted for her academic skills and leadership abilities. She attended Indianapolis public schools and, like Irwin, graduated valedictorian of her high school class. Her parents sent Beard to DePauw University, where she arrived in 1892 at the age of sixteen. DePauw was coeducational, having admitted women in 1867, but the curriculum was gendered—girls were to study "belles lettres" and boys, politics. Beard majored in Roman law, was senior class president, and chosen a Phi Beta Kappa member. Like Irwin, she was fortunate to have a gifted teacher and mentor who expanded her to new ideas and ways of thinking. "It is not too much to say that the greatest stretching of my mind during my undergraduate days at DePauw occurred in your classroom and in your home," she wrote this male German professor in 1931.[45] When Beard graduated in 1897, the editors of the DePauw yearbook aptly described her as "Both the practical and good, well fitted to command."[46]

Although her college was coeducational, Beard joined a DePauw sorority, Kappa Alpha Theta, which may have inspired her later to join women's organizations that challenged gender norms and advocated women's access to traditionally male opportunities. She met two sorority sisters who questioned the sharply gendered worlds at DePauw. Over forty years later she remembered them and the stimulus they provided to her developing thoughts on women challenging convention. Writing in 1936, Beard recalled one sister who "took as a matter of course her right to enroll in classes for the study of political science even though this was 'not done' by members of the sorority that long ago." The way she conducted herself, Beard remarked, caused her to be "accepted by the men in her class at her own value." Her second "rebellious" sorority sister led Beard to believe that "even a young woman could really break the social conventions which called for pseudopatrician or genuinely bourgeois manners and be guided in her human relations by a more creative sense of values. She too did things that were 'not done' by her clan sisters." As for herself at DePauw, Beard remarked: "I too was a 'sport' in that I responded to such innovators beyond the conventions of a clan. . . . The thing that lingers with me in this connection is not the thought of clannishness itself and its tendency to standardize and defeat creative intelligence, for after all, the . . . class involved . . . protected their errant sisters. It may be that the freedom to dare sprang from that very protection."[47]

Mary Ritter met Charles Beard at DePauw. Charles had arrived in the spring of 1895, near the end of Mary's sophomore year. They met shortly after the university repealed its no-dance law; Mary was one of a group of students who got together to practice dancing, and Charles came to watch. Years later, she reminisced about their first meeting: "Charles Beard came. But he just sat in a big dormer window and talked. He talked and talked, and I didn't understand much of what he said. But that was the beginning." It was the beginning of an eventual loving, successful marriage that spanned nearly half a century and a fruitful intellectual collaboration that produced classic historical works.[48]

Mary and Charles's courtship revolved around shared studiousness, an enthusiasm for bicycling, and a deepening interest in social issues. One classmate remarked: "they read and studied together a great deal . . . and appeared at that time to be inclined socialistic [sic] in thought and expression." Another's observation suggests Mary was the outgoing one in their college years: "Charles was quite shy socially and probably didn't care much for social life." Two photographs of the young couple at DePauw depict a serious, matronly-looking woman and a tall, handsome, gangly young man.[49]

Even as undergraduates, the Beards were at the forefront of Progressive-era social movements. On an 1896 freshman field trip, Charles visited Hull House, the settlement house Jane Addams co-founded in a working-class immigrant neighborhood on Chicago's New West Side. When he graduated in 1898, Charles Beard moved to England to study British and European history at Oxford, where he played a leading role in the founding of Ruskin Hall, a "free university" offering correspondence and evening classes to working-class men. At the same time, he was working on an institutional history of England's office of the justice of the peace, which became his Ph.D. dissertation. Mary, who had graduated from DePauw a year earlier and taken a job teaching German in the Greencastle, Indiana, public school system, married Charles Beard in March of 1900, and moved with him to Manchester, England, one month later.[50] A new world was about to open up for her.

Mary Beard's early feminism was grounded in a conservative, Quaker, middle-class background that left her with a respect for the traditions of female culture, separatism, and gender difference. She neither rebelled from domesticity nor, so far as we know, felt distanced from her mother. It has even been suggested that her mother, cultural provider and nurturer to the Ritter household, first sparked her daughter's enduring belief in women as civilizing agents and potential world saviors. Yet her "errant" sorority sisters—who broke DePauw convention by taking political science courses and rebelling from "bourgeois manners" expected of young college women—also stirred her feminism. What Beard took from their examples was a "sportish" support for women's rule-breaking and a respect for the female community (in this case, a sorority) that provided the protection to offer women "the freedom to dare."

SAME RULES FOR GIRLS AND BOYS: DORIS STEVENS

Stevens was born into a world in which the Victorian ideal of separate gender spheres was rapidly disappearing. Twelve years younger than Beard and fifteen years Irwin's junior, she was born in Omaha, Nebraska, on October 26, 1888, into a middle-class, Presbyterian family. Her mother, Caroline Koopman Stevens, was born in Holland in 1863 and immigrated with her family to the United States when she was three. Her mother's father was a pastor in the Dutch Reformed Church for forty years. His rise from rural Dutch poverty to clerical leadership made him exemplify the American dream to his family.

Stevens's father, Henry Stevens, was born in 1859, shortly after his British family immigrated to the United States. His father died when Henry was six, and—unable to support her four sons—his widowed mother placed Henry and one brother in an orphanage. Henry's childhood was spent bouncing among state institutions, his mother's small New York City apartment, a Long Island farm where he worked as a laborer, and culminated in his mother's death when he was thirteen.[51] To his wife's disappointment and his children's chagrin, he was never able to achieve the masculine material success that late nineteenth-century Americans celebrated.

Stevens was raised in a modest household bounded by a forty-year membership in the Lowe Avenue Presbyterian Church and staunch Republicanism. She was the second of four children. When Democrat William Jennings Bryan challenged President William McKinley in 1896, in the historic election that symbolized the death of Populism—the agrarian revolt against corporate expansion—the Stevens family taped McKinley's picture to their windows. The Stevens children wore pins of tiny buckets on their clothes, signifying the full dinner pail McKinley promised his constituents if reelected. When President McKinley was assassinated in 1901, Stevens's weeping mother took thirteen-year-old Doris by the hand to the piano and softly played "Lead Kindly Light," explaining, "This was his favorite hymn. He was a good man." A conservative Republican in her later years, Stevens liked to recall a childhood incident in which a friend took her doll's blanket and refused to return it. When she told her mother, Caroline Stevens testily responded, "You can not trust a Democrat; you must never [trust one] again." In her mature years Stevens considered this wise advice.[52]

Stevens had a happy childhood, tarnished only by her parents' mismatched marriage. She and her older sister Alice presided over the affairs of their two younger brothers, Harry and Ralph. A self-described good child, the only punishment Stevens recalled receiving was one box on the ears from her indomitable grandmother. She described her mother as a "regular Elijah [sic] Root on arbitration," who settled most of the children's feuds peacefully.[53] Stevens depicted herself as a dreamy child whose long, thin legs, abundant brown hair, and prominent teeth led her siblings to dub her "Dukie," because of her alleged resemblance to Duke, the family horse.[54] As an adult and a well-known feminist, she was renowned for her lanky beauty and stylish grace.

Stevens's parents Carrie Koopman and Henry Stevens differed in temperament and ambition. They met in Paterson, New Jersey, married in 1883, and moved to the heart of the Midwest in Omaha, where they remained all their lives. Her mother, described in her obituary as a woman "nurtured in the old time religion [who] lived the simple and faithful life of a sincere follower of our Lord and Master" was unfulfilled, ambitious, and restless in marriage. While Carrie was practical and exacting, Henry was idealistic, ascetic, and spiritual. Carrie never forgave her husband what she considered his "countless incompetencies": she scorned his "clean, upright" Christianity, his "almost ridiculous" honesty, his innocence and financial naiveté. "Had he not got done in by a man who sold him bad land in the Dakotas, trusting to the godliness in mankind instead of examining the title to the acreage? Had the family not been threatened with eviction repeatedly because [Henry] had inconveniently gone out on strike—solitary strike—and lost?"[55]

Intellectually curious, as an adolescent Carrie Koopman read medical journals "when she should have been playing the organ and making woolwork mats." She dreamt of becoming a doctor. Stevens's mother insisted on limiting the size of the family: "But for me," she dryly remarked, "[Henry Stevens] would have fathered fourteen instead of four children, with his 'God will provide' doctrine." When her own waylaid career ambitions could not be vicariously fulfilled in a successful career for her husband, she grew bitter. She described her happy, thriving youth to her children; "and then your father came along," she pointedly remarked. After her mother's death, Stevens remembered her as courageous, kind, valiant, and unfulfilled. "[I] hope," Stevens wrote, "that in a later epoch to come, a woman of her abilities may have a fuller life and less frustration. She was born ahead of her time but I am deeply grateful to her for everything I got from her." "I always felt," Stevens wrote of her close, positive relationship with her mother, "that I had her loving approval and her complete confidence and that is about all the security a parent can give a child. Our relations were . . . those of two persons at ease with each other."[56]

While her mother's dissatisfaction pushed Stevens toward feminism, her father's underdog status earned her sympathy. In childhood, Stevens and her siblings shared their mother's contempt for their emotional, gentle father, as she later elucidated in a thinly veiled fictionalized account. As she grew older, Stevens came to appreciate her father's morality and unworldliness, although these traits cut against the grain of an increasingly materialistic culture. Like her mother, her father supported her ambition and activist career. Because he encouraged his children to pray aloud at the dinner table, she asserted, Henry Stevens prepared them to take part in family, and later public, life. "That I was nervous then, and still am, does not, you see, prevent me from going on praying in public," she once told a feminist audience. Stevens believed her father's humble example and consistent encouragement motivated her to seek equality in human relations. After her first public speaking experience stumping for woman suffrage at an Omaha theater after her freshman year in college, her father emerged shyly from a corner and stated, "Well, daughter, if you feel so strongly about this matter, this is what you have to do."[57]

Like the other three women, Stevens continued to mull over her parents' relationship for much of her life, and it influenced one of her key contributions as a modern feminist: her effort to remake relations between women and men. On Father's Day 1946, more than fifteen years after her father's death, she stated before a National Woman's Party audience: "when we first meet up with our fathers, we are usually very small and helpless. Some women I've known have become feminists because their fathers were tyrannical. I was more fortunate. . . . This is not the time to try to decide whether feminists are born or made, but if they are made, fathers have had something to do with it!"[58] When Henry Stevens died, Stevens issued a public statement on the family's behalf: "Man of impeccable character, integrity and honesty—all the homely Christian virtues—an idealist to the end. . . . We children are all very proud of the deeply spiritual gifts our father possessed. An intense and generous person, by nature a gentle ascetic, he always exacted the highest devotion to principle in others, which he himself tried to give." Privately, however, Stevens wrote, "Fantastic father he was but as a person who lived so utterly alone one could not but find him pathetic. Somehow it fits father to finish while mowing the lawn. It was as if [he] gave final testimony that he had tried or *meant* to try. Even over the humble chores. You know she [Stevens's mother] always believed he never *did* try." Sixteen years after her mother's death, when she herself was sixty, Stevens expressed her feelings about her mother's high expectations in "A Letter to Mother": "Often, we as children thought you exigent with father. There was many a hurdle you set for father that he couldn't take. . . . Then you felt frustration when your dreams did not come true. . . . I think you kept on dreaming to the last breath. Such perfectionism and idealism breeds fine people. But they pay a hard price when reality does not keep pace with their dreams."[59]

Despite her parents' incompatible marriage, Stevens was an outgoing, popular teenager. In high school she was already noted for the charisma that character-ized her as a feminist leader. Vice president of her Omaha High School sopho-more class, she was also vice president of the Athletic Association and athletic editor of the yearbook. The verse accompanying her picture in the 1905 year-book suggests Stevens was already noted for heterosociality, which distinguished modern feminism from the nineteenth-century interpretation: "She vows that her heart is a wide open book—/ I fancy therein I should much like to look,/ and read there the secrets of short tete-a-tetes,/ Of church Sunday evenings, and some other dates."[60]

Stevens's four years at Ohio's Oberlin College, the first in the nation to admit women and African Americans, served as an important catalyst for her developing feminism. According to a colorful account, she arrived at Ober-lin with a generous scholarship, a rifle for shooting jackrabbits, an aversion to fudge parties and feminine gossip, and twenty-two dollars borrowed from her younger brother. She took German, Shakespeare, psychology, French, and English composition her freshman year, played sports, joined the French Club, the Oberlin Chorus, and enrolled in voice and cello lessons. Like Irwin, Stevens discovered the woman suffrage movement in college and immediately joined the College Equal Suffrage League, which Irwin had co-founded with Maud Wood Park in 1900.[61]

At Oberlin, Stevens pursued the two key goals of the equal rights feminism to which she devoted her life: legal equality and companionship between the sexes. "I had only one plank on my reform platform on equality at college," she later wrote. "Same rules for girls and boys (Legal side), permit dancing between boys and girls (Social side)." Her reminiscences included few of the warm recollec-tions of female friendships and organizations that moored the college experi-ences of Irwin and Beard in the 1890s, and demonstrate in microcosm how the feminist tide was beginning to turn. Beautiful, spirited, and always sought after by men, she was as known in her college years for her multiple romances as for her suffrage activism. One contemporary later described Stevens as boy-crazy and a flirt: "She enjoyed playing with her male colleagues and they liked her."[62] She was reprimanded repeatedly for staying out after hours and once for riding in a surrey with a young man.

When she applied for a loan after her sophomore year, the dean of women turned her down as a bad risk and suggested she transfer to a women's college. According to Stevens, this dean nursed a "secret and guilty passion" for the president of Oberlin, which led her to report that Stevens "played with too many men and then jilted them." Originally a music major, Stevens graduated in 1911 with a bachelor's degree in sociology. In her yearbook, Stevens playfully declared, "The day has passed when we form an ideal of a man and then hunt for one like it to fall in love with." A professor's response, "Well, Miss Stevens, how do you fall in love?" suggests that Stevens had earned a reputation at Oberlin for being "a firebrand" who liked men, fell in love easily, and was distinctly modern in her approach to heterosexual relationships.[63] This reputation followed her into the US and international feminist movements, where Stevens sometimes met harsh criticism for it.[64]

Like Irwin in her early years, Stevens rejected domesticity and female culture. She liked men and identified with them as companions and potential allies. Her spirited, unruly image at Oberlin, one she may have intentionally cultivated, was later described as identification with male pursuits: "Doris Stevens was already a feminist. She had refused to submit to the gently feminine variant of the college yell at football matches, and she preferred felling trees and practicing with a Colt revolver, to fudge parties and fuss."[65] Her later feminism embraced a vision of men and women as partners and comrades, and identified gender as the primary culprit in women's unequal access to rights and resources. She, too, would pay a price for her resolute dedication to creating singularly new relations with men and insisting on women's right to fulfilling work in the public sphere. Her identification with her mother, the heterosociality of her youth, her lack of interest in female culture and domesticity, and her discovery of the woman suffrage movement all awakened Stevens to feminism and sculpted her later ideology and activism.

A Career as Much Like a Man's as Possible: Lorine Pruette

Lorine Pruette was born on November 3, 1896, in Millersburg, Tennessee, and later credited the circumstances of her difficult birth for her original impetus toward feminism. Her mother, a "frightened hysterical twenty-one year old girl with the dull gold hair, the gray-blue eyes and the 'strong' nose," was delivered of her first child by her new husband's brother-in-law, a country doctor. He refused to administer anesthesia during the labor and birth; chewing on his cigar he declared, "Women should suffer; that's what makes them love their babies." Pruette later sardonically remarked that he was the first male chauvinist she encountered in life. "Apparently it never occurred to him," she wrote, "to wonder how men learned to love their offspring." Had her mother had a different obstetrician, she believed, her own life would have been different. Although her mother eventually bore three more children (one died in infancy), the pain and humilia-tion of that first childbirth stunned and embittered her. "My mother . . . maintained throughout her life that nothing was so terrible as pregnancy, and that the only meaning in life was your children," Pruette wrote.[66]

In contrast to Stevens's midwestern roots, Pruette was raised a daughter of the South. Her Scotch-Irish maternal great-grandfather, whom she described as a feminist and the ancestor she would most have liked to know, was a country doctor who firmly believed in women's education. He sent his daughter, Lorine's maternal grandmother, to college. A strong, resourceful woman, she later nursed the Civil War wounded. Widowed while pregnant with her fifth child, she sold the family's debt-ridden farm and opened a store to make ends meet, but still managed to send Lorine's mother, Eulalia Miller Pruette (born in 1875) to Tennessee's Soule College, the same college she had attended.[67] Although so poor she attended classes with a hole in her shoe, Eulalia was an outstanding stu-dent who later used her college papers—most of them marked "Excellent"—to teach Lorine to read. After graduating in 1895, she taught at a small rural school for one year before marrying. Pruette remembered her maternal grandmother, elderly when Pruette knew her, as dictatorial. She enrolled Pruette in the United Daughters of the Confederacy, a women's association dedicated to honoring the memory of those who died in service to the Confederate States of America. In addition, her grandmother insisted Pruette accompany her to deliver stipends to the old Confederate soldiers.[68]

Pruette's father, Oscar Davis Pruette, also born in 1875, came from a relatively wealthy, old land-owning Tennessee family. He too was college-educated, and described as "the best-looking man in seven counties, who drove the fastest horses." The Pruette plantation on which he was born had boasted five thou-sand acres before the Revolution. Although whittled down to a few hundred by the mid-nineteenth century, it escaped the Civil War untouched, apparently because his father, a horse trader, was wealthy enough to bribe Yankee officers. Pruette remembered her paternal grandfather, of French Huguenot and Ameri-can Indian ancestry, as enormous (at 250 pounds he was exempted from fight-ing in the Civil War), lusty, and kind. Her paternal grandmother was a difficult, demanding Welshwoman.[69]

Eulalia and Davis Pruette's marriage was, according to their daughter, des-tined to unhappiness from the start. "After my old-gold mother accepted the squire's son, who told her she would live wherever she wanted to," Pruette wrote, he "promptly took her home to his aged Pa and Ma." The new bride was immedi-ately insulted by her father-in-law who, noting how much prettier her sister was, remarked to his son in her hearing, "Why, Davis, I believe you married the wrong girl." The morning after their wedding night Eulalia's mother-in-law stormed into the bedroom and scolded her son's new wife for waking him. "This was long before Freud, but certainly a Freudian situation, the old mother competing with the young wife," Pruette, who became a psychologist, later wrote of the incident. "I shall never forgive your invasion of my parents' nuptial chamber," she exclaimed to her dead grandmother. When Pruette's mother finally demanded a home of her own, Davis's parents gave them a small cottage and one hundred acres on their land where they raised pigs, hens, cattle, and horses. This rural, isolated home was the place Pruette spent her first five years.[70]

The New South that arose after the Civil War slowly moved from the single-crop agricultural system—cotton, tobacco, sugar, or rice—to new manufacturing sectors such as textiles, furniture, cigarettes, and cigars. While white women and men found opportunities in these industries, African Americans, 90 percent of whom lived in the South, led lives that were redolent of slavery. Sharecroppers lived for generations in one-or two-room cabins, farming and giving white landowners their share of crops, unable to stay ahead of expenses and debt. In 1900, over 90 percent of all southern African American working women were domestic servants—housemaids, cooks, or laundresses. Laundry workers were paid such low wages that some white working-class and most middle-class white families—like Pruette's—had at least one laundress.[71]

Racial inequities in work opportunities and income joined segregation and racial violence to create a dismal landscape for African Americans, especially in the South. The Jim Crow era solidified in 1896, two years before Pruette's birth, with the Supreme Court's *Plessy v. Ferguson* decision, which upheld segregation by approving "separate but equal" facilities for African Americans and whites, providing new legal justification for racism. Between 1889 and 1898 over eleven hundred African Americans, mainly in the South, were brutally killed by lynch mobs, who justified the murders by often-false accusations of Black men raping white women. When Pruette was a child in Millersburg, Tennessee, a vigilante mob seized a young African American from prison, dragged him to a nearby bridge, and shot him to death. This incident profoundly influenced Pruette, who described it in an essay she wrote decades later. "When I was a child we had a lynching in our town. They took this black boy out of the jail, the sheriff helping them; they took the black boy down to the bridge across the river, riddled him with bullets, and no doubt went home feeling virtuous. The sheriff was briefly confined, then came home to a hero's welcome. This had marked me, so in college I made a talk against lynching. The college boys told me that this was so impressive, coming from a southern woman. Apparently, I was supposed to urge on the lynchers, who were out to protect my 'purity.'"[72] Race riots fanned across the South in the 1890s, from Phoenix, South Carolina, to Wilmington, North Carolina, to New Orleans. Public responses to lynching, including race riots, and Ida B. Wells's widely circulated pamphlet "Southern Horrors: Lynch Law in All Its Phases" (1892), led to an international antilynching campaign.[73]

In addition to being influenced by southern culture and race relations, the dynamics in her own home also shaped Pruette. Her parents were temperamentally mismatched: her mother was ambitious, pragmatic, and practical, while her father was dreamy, romantic, and unmaterialistic. "She had a very stubborn jaw," Pruette wrote, "while Davis had a dimple and a rose-bud mouth." Her mother never lost the scars of her childhood poverty, a poverty her father ("of Latin blood . . . the true l'homme moyen sensual") never knew. "My mother was a child of her times," Pruette wrote. "Gone were the wide horizons of before the war. Here were the penny-pinching days of the Reconstruction, and somehow a relic of Calvinism and more than a relic of Victorianism moved into the south." Her father, the only son of his parents' old age, was a pampered child brought up to ride a good horse, instruct the family help, and be kind to the descendants of slaves who still lived on the family plantation. "In business my father has always been the kind of man who comes out of a trade poorer than he went in," Pruette remarked. "He has the need to be generous and lordly and superior to money; he wants to give things away in order to assure himself that he is of some importance in the world." As an old woman she wrote of her father: "[He was] able to accommodate himself to anything, to make friends of anybody, and to get whatever joy was to be got."[74]

The only child for the first seven years of her parents' contentious marriage, Pruette was often caught in the middle of their marital strife. "My father loved everything that lived. . . . My mother hated and feared everything that moved. . . . I am standing between them, the apex of the triangle." Pruette later remembered her parents' bitter arguments over money, the family's residence, and how to raise their daughter, and she described her painful childhood position as pawn in their marital matches.[75]

Pruette's mother, whom she described as "the true daughter of the hierarchy of a small southern town," forbade her to play with the children of neighboring white tenant farmers, whom she considered "white trash," as well as the children of the Black sharecroppers who still lived in the slave cabins that dotted the Pruette land. The only childhood companions Pruette had were the two daughters of the family's Black laundress, and her mother. "So we lived with the bluegrass hills and the rattlesnakes," she wrote of the early years of her childhood, "the mocking birds and the darkies, my mother in a terror of childbirth and I in a loneliness not greatly mitigated by the contempt in which I was taught to hold all other children in the vicinity. . . . Those lonely, bitter years were a crime against childhood; I shall not ever lose their scar."[76]

Her parents' unhappy marriage became for young Pruette a metaphor of the female-male relationship and fueled her incipient feminism. Given this, it is not surprising that much of her adult writing focused on the institution of marriage, a key site of feminist experimentation in the 1920s. She later recalled two pivotal childhood incidents that shaped her emerging thoughts on men, women, and marriage. "I learned that everything, everything, was Davis' [her father's] fault. When

I was perhaps four my mother was complaining and carrying on, while I suffered from her sorrows. We had a large square oak dining table. I can still recall clinging to this table, my hands behind me, and speaking my mind to this brute, this torturer of fair women, the despoiler. 'I hate you,' I declared." "I was not allowed to love my father . . . I thought I idolized my mother. Perhaps I did," Pruette later recalled. A bitter argument between her parents inspired Pruette to begin writing her first book, on sexism and gender inequities in marriage. "By age nine," she wrote, "I was convinced that all the evils of the world came from these intolerable males. So I sat on the front porch, with my lined school tablet, and began to write my first novel. Its name was 'Husks: A Story of Modern Marriage.' It began, 'Women are the packhorses of civilization.'" Near the end of her life Pruette commented, "Looking back over the years it seems to me now a sad thing that a child should find such a name for life. HUSKS. No doubt my mother had been screaming out her injustices, her complaints against life. Probably she had been smashing a few dishes too. So I took refuge on the porch and turned to a word for help."[77]

Pruette grew up with a sense of being different from other children, of being "the odd ball." She later related her feelings of nonconformity to her family position as first-born ("the wounded one, most loved, most hated"), the sickness (asthma, whooping cough, croup, depression, allergies) that plagued her childhood, and her exceptional brightness. She was an outstanding and precocious student. "Later my brother's wife told me he had told her that it was 'awful, having to grow up in the shadow of *that*,'" she wrote. "I was the *that*. For I was the *bright* one." Like Stevens's mother, Pruette's mother was college-educated and impatient in her domestic role. Frustrated by her own stagnating intelligence and discontented in her marriage, she poured her energy and aspirations into her only daughter. Before Lorine was old enough to attend school, Eulalia had taught her to read, to recite the Greek alphabet, and to sing Scottish mountain songs. "Down on that lonely farm I began to learn to think," Pruette wrote. When, at four, she was the only Sunday school child to know the shortest Bible verse— "Jesus wept"—she was declared a genius on the spot, and her mother redoubled her efforts to ensure her daughter's brilliance. "My mother was pink cheeked and laughing, while the other mothers clustered round. My father had tears of pride in his eyes. People touched me, petted me, admired me. . . . I think that I must have shivered as I looked into my mother's shining eyes. For I was looking at my fate. I was going to have to be the Bright One. If it killed me." When she was five, the Pruettes left the farm behind for the small town of Christiana, Tennessee. Two years later they relocated to Chattanooga, where her mother's family (more prosperous now) got her father a job, which he took "on sufferance, always with the threat that he would soon be going back to the country." Her brother Miller's birth relieved Pruette of some of the "injurious strain" of her mother's single-minded devotion.[78]

Both as a child and an adult, Pruette was stridently honest, unorthodox, and defiant. She once aptly described herself as "a rebel. An 'agin' person. A non-conformist. A dissenter, a French Huguenot, doubly stubborn. A person whose habitual response is like to be 'It ain't necessarily so.'" When she was six years old and attending Christiana's Southern Methodist Church one Sunday morning in 1902, the revivalist minister shouted, "Everybody who is *saved*—set down." Pruette, fiery, stubborn, and sincere, was the lone standing recipient of the preacher's wrath. She later described the memorable incident: "Now I had long been a faithful attendant at the Sunday School. I grieved over the Crucifixion [*sic*] just as I grieved over Robert E. Lee. . . . From the words of Jesus I had learned that the truth would make us free. . . . So now I had come to a moment of truth, in that little middle Tennessee village. The song ended. Everybody sat down. I remained standing. Nobody had told me whether I was saved or not. SO I felt that the only honorable thing was to remain standing. . . . The pastor preached a real Hell fire and damnation attack. . . . I remained standing all through the blast."[79]

Her youthful courage, unorthodoxy, and painful participation in her parents' tumultuous marriage led teen-aged Lorine to reject home life and marriage, and like Inez Irwin embrace the masculine model of a career and life in the public sphere. "By the time I reached my teens," she wrote in 1925, "I had a well-developed dogma on the world's injustice toward women because they have to bear the children, and a lack of interest in God because he was a man." "I was . . . determined to have a career as much like a man's as possible," she wrote. "And no babies. And no matrimony."[80] Inspired by Portia in Shakespeare's *The Merchant of Venice*, she considered becoming a lawyer, and later a journalist, but was discouraged by others in both endeavors. She eventually decided to earn a Ph.D. and become a psychologist.

While Pruette's adolescence appeared to be that of a typical white southern middle-class girl of the 1910s, there are indications it was troubled. She characterized herself as a "dreamy, moody, romantic" teen who read voraciously: John Keats, Edgar Allan Poe, French avant garde writer François Rabelais, and François-Marie Arouet (better known by his pen name Voltaire), sophisticated fare for a teen. She studied rabidly, admired or adored her teachers, and grieved in the summer when school was out. Like her childhood, her adolescence was solitary: "I wandered lonely as a cloud." She did not date in high school, supposedly because of her dislike for men, but more likely due to her sharp-tongued mother's tendency to "tear down any tentative swain who presented himself." "When . . . boys made advances to me I turned them down with incredible ease," Pruette remembered. She never mentioned female friendships in her recollections of her teenaged years. At sixteen, Pruette took a leave of absence from high school for "some mysterious malady called a nervous breakdown." Taken from doctor to doctor, she had no strength or energy, walked "like a feeble old person," and thought she was going to die. Her condition, which she later believed to be a thyroid disorder (one of her multiple adult illnesses) was never diagnosed. Although she recovered she was, in her mid-to-late teens, "always low on energy, and often depressed."[81] Depression plagued her adult life as well.

Although not the turning point it appeared to be for the three other women, Pruette's college life was successful, social, and happier than her childhood and adolescence had been. She graduated from Chattanooga High School in 1914, missing salutatorian by two/tenths of a point (valedictorian was reserved for a male), and entered her local public university, the University of Chattanooga. Here she shook off her youthful isolation by joining a sorority, acting in plays, editing the college newspaper, and playing a violin in the orchestra. Pruette's college years overlapped with the outbreak of World War I in Europe in 1914, which the United States joined in 1917.

She became a noted public speaker in college, already lecturing on controversial topics, as she did throughout her career. Her 1918 antiwar speech garnered Pruette first prize in the university's speaking competition and second in a statewide contest. Even in college, Pruette could not escape from her ever-dominant mother. Although Lorine directed her not to attend her speeches, Eulalia sat in the audience anyway. "I can see her now," Pruette wrote late in life, "when I told her not to come, sitting on the second row, tossing her strong chin and her old-gold hair, smiling at me, knowing I could not throw her out." Pruette graduated from the University of Chattanooga in 1918 with a bachelor's of science degree in chemistry and then moved to Washington, DC, where she worked for the Division of Venereal Diseases, part of the Bureau of the Public Health Service.[82]

As Pruette stated on numerous occasions, her feminism was born out of her mother's discontent. "I learned my feminism, in a manner of speaking, at my mother's breast," she concluded. The marital oppression her mother complained of became Pruette's oppression and shaped her first feminist convictions, which had a decidedly anti-male cast. At thirty, Pruette wrote anonymously, "there have been many nights when I have stayed awake planning desperately how to make a great deal of money and take my mother away from my father."[83]

Throughout her life and career Pruette tried to vindicate her mother, to realize her mother's aspirations. "I was the bright one . . . Looking back over a . . . life . . . I can see how that fact shaped my life. That, plus my mother's dreams." Pruette's mother raised her daughter to have the profession she never realized herself. "Probably she had marked me down in her heart as the writer she meant to be," Pruette commented. As she grew older she criticized her mother as unloving, sharp-tongued, even brutal, "and yet, a great woman." "It was many and many a year," she concluded, "before I accepted the fact that my mother was a good bit of a devil and that she had marred me, marked me, made me."[84]

Although other influences gave Lorine Pruette's awakening feminism a nudge, including the woman suffrage movement, her own rebellious unorthodoxy, and the "male chauvinists" she encountered early in life, her all-consuming relationship with her frustrated, idealistic mother was what really made her a feminist. She too used her life as a testing ground for her theories about sexuality, marriage, and women's financial independence, and ultimately determined that modern feminists' wide-eyed, utopian visions were much more difficult to realize in practice than in theory.

CHAPTER 2

Setting the Stage

Mary Beard, Inez Irwin, and Doris Stevens joined the American woman suffrage movement during its final two decades, and the experience was one of the richest of their lives. The movement exposed them to strong, inspiring women and gave them the opportunity to become activists and to develop their voices as public speakers, organizers, and authors. It moved Beard to canvass door to door, to involve working-class women, and to join a myriad of organizations, including the fledgling Congressional Union/National Woman's Party. It inspired the dramatic Irwin to propose a suicide pact between women as a form of suffrage activism and civil disobedience and to brainstorm the idea of picketing the president of the United States. It sent Stevens to prison for picketing the White House and provided fodder for her first book, *Jailed for Freedom*. The movement also provided a forum for the application and refinement of their feminist ideas. Their suffrage engagement between 1900 and 1920 not only sheds light on the lives and philosophies of Beard, Irwin, and Stevens, but also provides insight into the movement during its final climactic, combative years, a movement that set the stage for the objectives and challenges of post-suffrage feminism.

The American woman suffrage movement was born in the abolitionist, reform spirit of the 1830s, matured amid the surging women's rights movements of the late nineteenth century, and was realized in 1920, marking a watershed in US women's history.[1] For seventy-two years US suffragists fought against an opposition that ridiculed them, trivialized their intent, and used legal and constitutional maneuvers to block them. By 1900, the movement had already charted a contentious history. Black males were made citizens after Reconstruction and enfranchised by the Fifteenth Amendment in 1870, which split the woman suffrage movement into two factions. Boston's Lucy Stone led the American Woman Suffrage Association, agreeing that in "the Negro's hour" it was right that Black men be given the vote before women. The rival National

Woman Suffrage Association, led by New York–based Elizabeth Cady Stanton and Susan B. Anthony, rejected the Fifteenth Amendment for its exclusion of women. In 1890, these two predominately white, middle-class organizations merged to form the National American Woman Suffrage Association (NAWSA), and the movement gained momentum. Wyoming joined the union as a suffrage state in 1890, and three more extended the vote to women during that decade: Colorado in 1893, followed by Idaho and Utah in 1896. But then no new suffrage states were added until November 1910, when Washington raised the number to five. Throughout these years, African American, working-class, and immigrant women participated in increasing numbers. They joined a diverse assortment of women politicized by their civic engagement in women's clubs, trade unions, churches, and settlement houses.[2] By the 1910s, according to Christine Stansell, "women's suffrage commanded a far-flung mass movement, one of the most socially heterogeneous in American history."[3]

In 1913 the association's tiny Congressional Committee broke away from the NAWSA and evolved into the radical, independent National Woman's Party, an organization that played a critical role in the final years of the movement as well as in the lives of Irwin, Beard, and Stevens.[4] The party became a controversial site of feminist experimentation in the post-suffrage years. The transformation that occurred within the ranks of the movement, including changes in leadership, was startling. Alice Paul, described by at least one historian as "perhaps the single truly charismatic figure in the twentieth-century suffrage movement," took the reins of NAWSA's Congressional Committee in 1913, and by 1916 founded the NWP. Launched with her Irish coworker Lucy Burns, the NWP became renowned for militant action and intransigent feminism, and during the 1910s attracted both elite and working-class women to its ranks. By the end of 1915, the movement's focus shifted from the state to the national level, marking a distinct turning point.[5] Partly a byproduct of the times, which witnessed the peaking of progressive reform and the outbreak of a world war, it was also a logical outcome of extending the model of British militancy to the United States.

Irwin, Beard, and Stevens were members of the Congressional Union/NWP in the 1910s, and Alice Paul loomed large in each of their lives. Highly educated and never married, she eventually earned two law degrees and a Ph.D., but what set Paul apart as a leader was her ability to inspire and motivate others to disregard public opinion. She was able to mobilize both impatient younger women like Stevens and discontented older women like Irwin and Beard, who by 1910 had both worked in the suffrage movement for over a decade. According to historian Christine Lunardini, "Paul represented the force that made them willing to take uncommon risks, including imprisonment and possible estrangement from families, friends, and peers."[6] Stevens first met Paul in 1913 when, en route to an Adirondacks respite, she stopped in Washington to join a CU demonstration on the Senate. When asked to stay on in lieu of her vacation, "I was lost," Stevens later wrote. "I knew I would stay. . . . And it was years before I ever mentioned a holiday again."[7] Although Stevens later broke bitterly with her former mentor, through the 1910s and 1920s, she was consummately loyal.

As some earlier women's rights advocates had done, twentieth-century feminists courted male allies and reached across class and age to build powerful coalitions. The NWP attracted younger women like Stevens, who strove to dissolve the political, social, and physical boundaries that separated them from men. "Oh, do have done with this eternal talk about women!" was the characteristic response of younger suffragists, according to an activist of an older generation. "Sex-consciousness," declared a young woman, was "one of the first things which has to be left behind" by those who are "serious-minded."[8] They saw themselves as rebellious youth replacing dowdy Victorian matrons who had ground the movement to a halt.[9] Both Beard and Irwin were warmly attracted to this vibrant spirit of youth.

INSTRUMENTS FOR CIVILIZING FORCE: MARY BEARD AS SUFFRAGIST

Beard's two decades of leadership in the woman suffrage movement reflected her social feminism and her progressive commitment to improving the lives of women, men, and children across class and race. As a young newlywed in 1900, she spent three years in England with her husband Charles and acquired a transformative political and social education. Here she first resolved to dedicate her life to women. After a wedding "with all the trimmings," the married couple settled in Manchester, the heart of industrial England and a center of feminist and labor activism. On an evening stroll they bumped into a group of rowdy, working-class girls celebrating one of the first British military feats in the Boer War. Beard was never quite the same. She described the pivotal incident in a 1936 interview: "Mrs. Charles Beard—remember she is a young bride on her honeymoon—is suddenly confronted with a crowd of girls, about sixteen years old, from the mills. The girls are drunk, in the gutter, singing something about 'We're the stuff that's made Old England great.' I was shocked. At that moment I knew I must try to do something for women. If the incident hadn't occurred, I suppose I would have gone on giggling my way through life." Her distress at meeting the inebriated girls no doubt reflected her midwestern Quaker and temperance background (her father was reluctant to let her marry a man who drank beer). Her daughter later tried to explain why this incident so influenced her mother. "To a sheltered woman who had never been in *any* crowd in any city, and had led the quietest, most Quakerish life, this was pandemonium. It astonished even much tougher persons."[10] Beard consistently connected the causes of women with that of the working class with a resolve that at times left her standing alone among feminists.

Beard was one of several American feminists in Europe during the early twentieth century who witnessed the actions of the suffragettes, in some cases worked directly with them, and brought the revolutionary educations they gained back to the United States. She developed a close friendship with the Pankhursts, both Emmeline, who in 1903 founded the Women's Social and Political Union, and her daughter Christabel. The Beards's involvement with the British Socialist and labor movements also changed Mary's consciousness in these years. As cofounder of Ruskin Hall, Charles Beard was hailed as "a coming leader" by the New Labour Party. Years later, Mary reflected on how those acquaintances in England "changed the whole course of my life." She wrote in glowing terms: "They were nearly all cooperators in ideology and they mostly belonged to that wonderful cooperative movement in England. . . . It was all based on the idea of *civil*-ization and loyal to that great creative formula for living."[11]

Mary Beard returned to the United States in 1902 transformed. Two years later Charles completed his doctorate in political science and was appointed lecturer in history at Columbia University. The Beards lived on New York's Upper West Side, and in 1909 bought an old farmhouse in New Milford, Connecticut, where they spent summers. Charles Beard joined the Department of Public Law and three years later was appointed to a newly created chair in Politics and Government.[12] Mary Beard immersed herself in reform organizations, the suffrage movement, and motherhood.

The suffrage organizations Beard joined reflected her loyalty to working women as well as her identification with the women's organizations that grew out of progressive reform. Her affiliations foreshadowed the bridge-building role she would play in the contentious 1920s and 1930s. In 1907 she joined the Equality League of Self-Supporting Women, a group begun by her friend Harriot Stanton Blatch (Elizabeth Cady Stanton's daughter), with the dual purpose of making the American movement more dramatic and creating a militant suffrage organization based on a coalition of working-class and middle-class working women.[13] Renamed the Women's Political Union in 1910, it spearheaded a campaign to force the New York legislature to authorize a referendum to amend the state constitution to grant women suffrage. Beard also joined the Women's Trade Union League (WTUL), a cross-class organization formed in 1903 that encouraged working-class women to join suffrage campaigns but also provided support for laboring women's initiatives.[14] Beard served as secretary to the WTUL legislative committee in 1908, participated in the league's support of the New York Shirtwaist Makers' Strike in 1909, and joined the organization's investigation of the notorious 1911 Triangle Fire, which killed 146 young women factory workers in New York City. In 1910 Beard joined the New York City Woman Suffrage Party, an organization that described itself as "a new movement in politics—a political party which is the expression of a moral cause."[15] Beard eventually became vice chair of the New York State Woman Suffrage

Party, whose membership of twenty thousand grew to a half million by the time the suffrage amendment passed.

African American women were among the groups that contributed to the broad coalition in the final, successful decade of the suffrage movement. In their struggle for the vote, Black women fought racism and sexism simultaneously.[16] They considered the vote a way to address their sexual exploitation, affect the prohibitions against interracial marriage, widen their influence with legislators and school boards, and sway labor issues. The "expediency" strategy that the NAWSA took in the late nineteenth century drew on white fears of Black and immigrant domination. This strategy aimed to prove that the enfranchisement of white women would strengthen, rather than weaken, the power of a white ruling class.[17] African American women responded by forming their own suffrage organizations. By the 1900s, Black suffrage clubs had sprung up around the United States, and state suffrage societies were created from coast to coast. In 1913, for example, Ida Wells-Barnett formed one in Chicago. In 1914 Nannie Burroughs, head of the Baptist Women's Convention, convinced the central body of the Negro Baptist Convention (boasting 2.5 million members), to endorse woman suffrage.[18] Until 1916, African American women primarily led their own suffrage campaigns, but after World War I increasingly joined mainstream, white suffrage campaigns.

In New York State, African American women mobilized for suffrage early in the century and as early as 1910, white suffragists in New York City approached Black clubwomen, inviting them to form "colored" chapters of various organizations. Wealthy suffragist Alva Belmont was one of the first to include African American women in the world of white suffragists. She met with the Negro Women's Business League in 1910 and offered to fund a meeting room for African American suffragists, to be affiliated with her organization, the Political Equality Association.[19]

It is possible that Beard was present at the subsequent meeting that Belmont, Ella Hawley Crossett (president of the New York State Woman Suffrage Association), and other white suffragists held with over two hundred African American women at a Black Baptist church in midtown Manhattan. This was probably the moment when interracial woman suffrage cooperation in New York City was initiated. At the meeting Crossett invited African American women to affiliate with the New York State Woman Suffrage Association. Within six months, over one hundred African American women had joined the "Negro" branch of Belmont's organization, and Belmont opened a headquarters for the group in Harlem. Later, however, Belmont secretly donated $10,000 to the Southern Woman Suffrage Conference, an organization that opposed a federal suffrage amendment on the grounds that it would give southern Black women the vote, a tactic African American women had feared in their initial association with Belmont. Nonetheless, by 1915 a suffrage headquarters for Black women opened on West

Sixty-third Street, which may have been funded by the New York State Woman Suffrage Association.[20]

Like the newcomers to the suffrage fight, including urban reformers who streamed into the movement in the 1910s, Beard cared as much about issues of labor, poverty, and class as she did about women.[21] She considered the ballot a tool for reshaping society along egalitarian lines, a means by which women could exert their civilizing influence. As she wrote many years later: "votes for women are but instruments for civilizing force." Despite her own comfortable upbringing, like her husband Charles, Mary was committed to addressing socio-economic inequalities, which both Beards believed were caused by capitalist greed and laissez-faire economics.[22] Once women won the vote, Beard believed, they would work together to eradicate the harsh social conditions engendered by rapid industrialization and urbanization. She wrote, "When women in the home come to see how the forces of the outside world are breaking in upon them at every point; when the women in the workshops and factories come to learn how real protective legislation is to be secured through politics, then the cause of woman suffrage is won."[23] "*Working women need to vote*," she declared in 1912, "because their brothers regard them as inferiors and the vote will win more respect from them. They need to vote because the vote will give them more independence and self-respect. . . . They must make political issues as their brothers are doing." Beard urged working women to "make themselves felt as human beings with minds and hearts." She wrote trade unionist Leonora O'Reilly "a very long and very earnest letter pointing out what seemed to me the blind folly of ignoring political action." Apparently she convinced her, for Beard noted that O'Reilly is "circularizing the trade union girls very hard for the [suffrage] parade."[24] Like the many groups that united under the suffrage banner in the 1910s, Beard believed that feminism could not be detached from other goals and considered it part of a collective, grand democratic push.[25]

Beard had a daughter Miriam in 1901 and a son William in 1907, and her years of young motherhood coincided with, and shaped, her suffrage activism. She was concerned about the social and economic vulnerability of mothers, especially working-class mothers, as well as the pronatalist policies and state-sanctioned notions of what constituted "fit" mothers. She cast her suffrage activism in this light. Beard wrote in 1912: "as suffragists and mothers (most of us), we . . . quarrel with many of the premises laid down at the opening ceremony of the New York School of Mothercraft. One speaker . . . laid all the blame for juvenile delinquency, crime, vice and immorality in general on mothers—individual mothers." She described another speaker who struck "a social note" at the inauguration of this adult school designed to teach women how to be "better mothers." This was an officer from the Board of Health who discussed the city's efforts to obtain money for milk stations and "baby-saving." Beard challenged: "He did not, however, come out for Votes for Women as a possible helper in that struggle. Perhaps he thought it untimely. To some of us it seemed vital." She connected woman suffrage with policy issues that affected the lives of working-class and poor women, such as labor conditions, urban poverty, and the economic vulnerability of single mothers. Beard declared: *"Everything that counts in the common life is political. If dilettanti reformers really understood this, they would understand the scope and power of the suffrage movement. It is because of the persistent pressure of these real facts of every-day experience (such as 'wages, unemployment, industrial accidents, wife desertions, tenement work, hours, congestion, drink') for the majority of women that equal suffrage is inevitable."*[26]

During the early 1910s, Beard applauded the militant tactics of the CU/NWP, including the controversial strategy of punishing the party in power, in this case Democrats, for not passing suffrage. She was one of the first three initiates to the fledgling organization, along with lawyer and cultural radical Crystal Eastman and wealthy socialite Dora Lewis. Alice Paul notified Beard in 1913, "The Congressional Union has been formed to . . . secure the passage of an amendment to the United States Constitution. . . . [It] is composed of women in all parts of the country who are interested in furthering the federal amendment." Beard immediately joined, largely because her broadmindedness extended beyond the more conservative, mainstream NAWSA. Thirty-seven at the time, Beard exclaimed to Paul, "I am so much more radical than either of the old political parties that, when I get off and think, I lose my whole absorption in the one fight for enfranchisement."[27] She shared the enthusiasm for a collaborative effort with men that her younger peers in the CU/NWP eagerly feted. When a writer for a political science journal asked Beard her opinion of the new gender-integrated politics, she responded that for her and her female colleagues, working with men was a central feature of their efforts—even if most of the work landed on the women, she jested.[28]

Representing her racial justice convictions and signifying the racial tensions that challenged feminist organizations over the next decades, Beard led a contingent of African Americans who marched in the 1913 suffrage parade. Organized by the Congressional Union in Washington, DC, two months after its creation, a divisive issue arose when a group of African American women from Howard University, including Oberlin graduate, educator, and political activist Mary Church Terrell, volunteered to march in the parade with the college women's delegation. When, in response, several white women threatened to withdraw, Paul initially suggested a segregated march. Several white suffragists, including Beard, were determined that the parade be racially integrated. Beard attended a meeting called by African American women to strategize their response and wrote Paul: "Here is a faithful report of the colored meeting," which she described as "small" but "exciting." Beard described three factions represented: those who hesitated to make demands which would hurt the suffrage cause; those who accepted New York's invitation to march with the integrated group; and "those who were determined to put up a fight for marching where they belonged . . . and not just where some women were willing they should march." This group was "indignant over the situation," certain that a southern minority was "terrorizing" the organization's northern majority, and declared they would take the story to the anti-suffragists and the press if forced to be segregated. "After a very heated discussion," Beard wrote Paul, "I proposed that each woman sign her name on a paper saying where she wanted to march and that a committee representing all three factions take this paper to you today. You may not approve my action but I do want, if possible, to prevent trouble on parade day. . . . We ought to be intelligent enough to avoid a race war," Beard concluded. "That is a perfect nightmare to me."[29]

When the parade took place on March 3, the day before Woodrow Wilson's first inauguration, the grand procession of eight thousand marchers and the unruly spectators nearly upstaged Wilson's arrival in the capital. Beard wrote her son decades later:

> I was marshal for that event of a section of the parade in which Negro women marched. I had insisted that they be permitted to participate and, since I was one of the first women to support Alice Paul and Lucy Burns, . . . my insistence that Negro women join the parade was effective. But the fear that the hordes of people from Maryland, etc., who would come to Washington to see the parade, would be so furious to see Negro women in it, that they would resort to violence was so strong that I would get some men to assist me in marshaling that section. . . . I headed that division dressed in a Green Cape and some sort of cap. The men took positions at the sides of the Negro marchers—tall, impressive fellows. AND THERE WAS NOT A SIGN OF TROUBLE ANYWHERE ALONG THE LINE.[30]

The entire Beard family marched in the parade: Charles walked with the men while Miriam, then twelve, and William, six, rode on horse-drawn floats.[31]

Despite the time Beard devoted to complicated suffrage initiatives, she also published a monograph, *Woman's Work in Municipalities*, in 1915. It applied her equation of motherhood and female moral values to social problems, at the same time that it argued powerfully for women's right to work in the public sphere. This volume, like Edith Abbott's *Women in Industry* (1910), drew on social science research to argue for reform. Both books were "labors of scholarship but also outpourings of moral and social responsibility."[32] Echoing earlier US feminists such as Frances Willard and Charlotte Perkins Gilman, Beard advocated a translation of women's nurturing and domestic skills from the private to the public sphere. A policewoman could be "the city's mother to the motherless"; a housing or business inspector was really a "magnified housewife . . . on a huge scale," she asserted. Surveying education, public health, prostitution, recreation, housing, social services, crime control, corrections, and civic improvement, Beard offered a "new evaluation of woman's work in civilization . . . feeling, seeing, judging, directing, equally with men, all the great social forces," and argued for collective solutions to "individual" problems, cross-class sisterhood, female solidarity, and the centrality of the feminine role in society. In response to middle-class criticism of working mothers who did not breastfeed their babies, for example, Beard wrote: "No kind of philanthropy will solve the requirements of infant welfare when poverty or labor conditions are the root of the problems. Babies' milk thus becomes essentially a social-economic problem." She also chastised those who argued that prostitution should be allowed because it protects "our own daughters." Beard proclaimed: "All women are [our] daughters."[33]

Like most working mothers then and now, Beard struggled to balance her responsibilities to her children with her own work. Although historians have portrayed her alternatively as severely hampered by her domestic obligations or blissfully freed by an extensive household staff, the truth likely lies somewhere between.[34] As an adult, Beard's daughter portrayed her mother's lifestyle as one of comfort and relative freedom. "Young people . . . just cannot imagine the ease with which Mary . . . and her other suffragette friends coped with family life. When you always have a cook in the kitchen and a handyman in the garden and a chauffeur-butler type to buy everything and hand round the dishes, besides a nurse for the children, what is there to cope with? . . . Not that the Beards lived in the style of *Upstairs, Downstairs*; . . . [still] Mary never did housework. Charles never ate in a kitchen or carried a dish." Miriam also suggested that her parents were not interested in child-raising or in childhood itself. "I think both Beards, like most Victorians, thought that childhood was something you got over as fast as possible. And William and I did not make problems that would have shocked them; we were never ill or flunked anything; and we did not 'get into trouble,' perhaps because we never found any to get into."[35]

Beard's correspondence during these years is marked by an apologetic tone for her care giving and guilt for letting the suffrage cause down. In the summer of 1913, when her dying mother was living with her, Beard contritely wrote Paul, "You are bricks to stay in the South and work in this weather. I would be by your side at all costs if it were not for the children and a very ill mother who will probably not survive the summer." She wrote NAWSA president Carrie Chapman Catt in June 1915: "I should be throwing my energies now into the state campaign if I could throw them anywhere outside the home. I can't afford to pay the right person to take care of my children in the country and they mustn't be in town this summer. I shall give with whole hearted devotion however the last two months to the state provided you all are not terrified at my co-operation." A year earlier, Beard reminded Alice Paul (who was unmarried) of her family obligations: "I must consider my young children at times."[36]

Yet Beard's relations with NWP work were shaped by more than family obligations. When she became convinced that the NWP no longer shared her commitment to working women and reform, she severed her connection. As early as 1914, Beard made it clear to Paul that she could not separate labor issues from suffrage. She refused to attend the annual conference that year because it was held at Marble House, millionaire Alva Belmont's palatial Newport summer home. "I can't do the Newport stunt," Beard wrote Paul. "I shall probably be the only one who, for labor attachments, feels that participation in the Newport plans, is inadvisable." Remarking that "Newport and money stand in the popular mind for one and the same thing," she concluded: "I ought to be interested in suffrage first and labor second but I am frankly not. They are inseparable in my interest and I do realize to the full that the Union doubtless does have to have Newport."[37]

As the NWP moved closer to the equal rights stance it consolidated in the 1920s, Beard moved further away from the group. She withdrew from the Executive Committee in 1916, the Advisory Council in 1917, and by 1919 had cut all official ties with the organization. "I am well aware that the National Woman's Party calls one merely doctrinaire who cares about means to an end and that I am anethema [sic] because I do," she wrote a party member that year. "I do object to this use of my name as if I sanctioned all the means used by the organization of which I am no longer a member." Her daughter later stated that Beard "broke with Alice Paul and the rest so decidedly" when, after getting the vote, they wanted equal rights: "Mother said they were all bourgeoises who had never done a lick of work in their lives and did not know conditions of working women. . . . Mary worked for protective legislation for women and was not going to see that cast overboard."[38]

WOMEN EVERYWHERE, WORKING AT EVERYTHING:
INEZ IRWIN AND THE SUFFRAGE MOVEMENT

In the same year that young Mary Beard set off for England to immerse herself in suffrage and working-class politics, Inez Irwin and Maud Wood Park co-founded a suffrage organization for college women, which helped funnel fresh energy and new recruits into the stagnant American movement. The College Equal Suffrage League (CESL), organized in Irwin's native Boston in 1900, began with a handful of students at Radcliffe, Boston University, Tufts, and MIT.[39] Those who joined were among the first and second generations of women to enjoy access to higher education, one of the great demands and victories of the nineteenth-century women's movement. Twentieth-century women could add higher education to new rights that few in the generation born before the Civil War could imagine.[40] Park underscored this in her 1908 comments to NAWSA members: "Those of us who have lived and studied in the midst of the opportunities of this generation can hardly realize the tremendous change in public opinion about the education of women wrought by the equal rights movement more than by any other cause."[41]

Through her leadership of the CESL, Irwin demonstrated her gratitude to the forerunners who had paved the way for women to attend college. She and Park launched the organization two years after graduating from Radcliffe. Park conceived the idea after she heard eighty-year-old Susan B. Anthony speak at the 1900 NAWSA Convention of "the struggle, the trials, the sacrifices . . . the long, persistent efforts" to get college education for women. Lucy Stone had died seven years earlier, in 1893 at seventy-five; Elizabeth Cady Stanton would die two years later, in 1902, at eighty-seven, and Susan B. Anthony in 1906 at eighty-six, marking the passing of the pioneer generation. The CESL symbolized a younger generation's thankfulness and willingness to take up the torch.

Irwin revered the women she considered the nineteenth-century heroines of the women's movement, and demonstrated this throughout her lifetime in her fiction, her nonfiction, and her actions. She spoke appreciatively of Anthony, Stanton, Stone, Mary Livermore, John Whittier, and William Lloyd Garrison. She especially admired Anthony: "She was a true devoted creature, giving up everything, even her chance of happiness, to the cause. I wish she could come back now and see how the little seed she dropped has sprouted and grown into a big tree."[42] In the frontispiece to *The Story of the Woman's Party*, Irwin quoted the last public words Anthony spoke on her final birthday: "But with such women consecrating their lives failure is impossible." Irwin also prefaced this book with Anthony's call to the next generation: "Most of those who worked with me in the early years have gone. I am here for a little time only and my place will be filled as theirs was filled. The fight must not cease; you must see that it does not stop."[43] Irwin took up this challenge by organizing college women to push the suffrage fight forward.

The CESL contributed to the blossoming of the women's movement in the new century by bringing younger women into the fold and relating the cause to women's higher education. The organization's two goals were to interest college women, both graduates and current students, in suffrage and to advance the movement among working-class and middle-class, educated women. They launched their new organization by writing letters to fourteen Radcliffe alumnae and began with twenty-five charter members, Park as president and Irwin as secretary. In an initial meeting Irwin compared women's moral obligations to repay college "loans" with their commitments to their feminist forerunners. Every college woman is working on "borrowed capital," she told her small audience, "borrowed energy, borrowed courage, borrowed enthusiasm." The honorable way to repay the pioneers was to take up the suffrage baton. The founders of CESL offered a $100 prize for the best essay on "the equal suffrage theory" and rotated their meetings that first year among the different Boston campuses where women were enrolled. The first flyer Park and Irwin created read, "YOU, AS A COLLEGE GRADUATE, are under obligation to woman suffrage. The college education was won for *you* by the earlier suffragists. Will you liquidate your debt?"[44]

The CESL quickly grew from a small, local organization into a national force that included education leaders M. Carey Thomas, president of Bryn Mawr; Alice Freeman Palmer, former president of Wellesley; Mary Wooley, president of Mount Holyoke; and Columbia anthropologist Elsie Clews Parson. By 1908, the organization had branches in Rhode Island, Pennsylvania, Maryland, the District of Columbia, Illinois, Michigan, Minnesota, Nebraska, Iowa, Wisconsin, California, and Washington. That year the state leagues merged to form the National College Equal Suffrage League and affiliated with the NAWSA. The CESL's growth contributed to the spirit of rebirth surging through the suffrage movement by 1910. "Altogether dear Maud Park," Irwin wrote her friend that year, "this movement which when we got into it had about as much energy as a dying kitten, is now a big, virile, threatening, wonderful thing."[45] League representatives constituted one of a number of delegations Alice Paul sent to call on President Wilson in 1913, to convince him to support a federal suffrage amendment.[46] The CESL represented the voices of college-educated women until it disbanded in 1917 to devote its energies to the national movement.

Through the CESL, Irwin aimed to bring the voices and spirit of youth into a movement that had increasingly become associated with older women. Although some undergraduates hesitated to become suffragists for fear of antagonizing men or losing invitations to parties, Irwin urged them to support the cause and to bring men into the movement along with them. She believed they needed an organization to draw them together—much as she and Park had been attracted to each other at Radcliffe—not only in their common belief in votes for women, but in their shared, privileged identity as college-educated women. Her strategy succeeded: the league served as an entry point for college students who later became important movement leaders. Doris Stevens was one of them. She joined the CESL while an Oberlin student and reminisced decades later: "Maud Wood Park [was] one of my *first* early inspirations, & got me to speak to crowds of men for woman suffrage on the street who hollered at me, when I was still in college. I didn't like it much & had many a quiet vomit before I went on to do my act."[47]

Irwin's life reflected in microcosm the spirit of change and innovation sweeping America in the prewar years, which both fed into and mirrored the women's rights movement. She captured this socially conscious mood when she described the most thrilling years of her life, the years between 1900 and 1914. "Life was full of hope and freedom," she wrote. "Great movements were starting everywhere. In the United States, the loudest voice in the land was that of the liberal. Everyone was fighting for something. Everyone was sure of victory." Irwin recalled that any speaker with a megaphone could proceed to the corner of New York

City's Forty-second Street and Sixth Avenue and announce, "'I am here to gather recruits for a movement to free . . .' And before he could state the object of his crusade, he would be in the center of a milling crowd of volunteers."[48]

At the same time Irwin plunged into suffrage activism, she also married and began her writing career. She wed aspiring author Rufus Gillmore in 1897 when she was a Radcliffe student. In 1908, the young couple moved from Boston to Greenwich Village to join the bohemian, artistic community there. Like Beard, Irwin was radicalized by a visit to prewar Europe, although her education was both in the arts and in politics. There, in 1909, she and Gillmore met American avant-garde writers Leo and Gertrude Stein; visited the studios of the "revolutionists in art" Henri Matisse, Pablo Picasso, and Georges Braque; encountered refugee Russian revolutionaries English Walling and Anna Strunsky; and witnessed the militant British woman suffrage movement.[49]

Like Beard, Irwin insisted on linking woman suffrage with other social reforms and in the 1910s became deeply involved in the labor movement. In 1913, the year she divorced Gillmore, she moved to San Francisco and met Maud Younger, who became a close friend, fellow labor organizer, and NWP member. The historian Christine Stansell has described Younger as an epitome of "the feminist temperament at its most ebullient and least conflicted."[50] She came from a wealthy San Francisco family and was privately schooled and sent on the European tour before moving to New York City's College Settlement in 1901. She emerged five years later a determined trade unionist and suffragist. A WTUL member, Younger organized the Wage Earners' Equal Suffrage League in California, and belonged to the Waitresses Union. Irwin described the day she met Younger as "a turning-point of great importance in my life." "Outside my two sisters I have never loved any woman as I loved Maud Younger," she wrote. "Our friendship, deep, glowing, and exciting, continued until her death in 1936."[51] Her most dramatic suffrage feat—single-handedly driving a team of six white horses in a San Francisco parade—surely impressed Irwin, who was inspired by women taking on men's tasks, especially those that required strength and daring, as well as technical expertise.[52] In 1913 Irwin wrote Maud Wood Park from San Francisco: "I suppose you know who Maud Younger is—the 'millionaire waitress'— first society girl in San Francisco then does settlement work in N.Y.—becomes waitress—joins union—writes experiences for McClure's becomes great labor sympathizer—worked like a trojan for suffrage in California got the eight-hour law for women through in California—has worked for suffrage in many states . . . inspiring speaker." Lest she be jealous, Irwin assured Park that she still held the first place in her heart: "[Her] place is second only to yours in my affection— *Mauds* seem to be my ruin."[53]

The association with labor was central to this generation's belief in women's need for productive work, a belief all four women in this collective biography steadfastly embraced.[54] Younger introduced Irwin, already a labor advocate in her own right, to the California movement, which employed tactics like the picket and embraced the radical "one big union" idea of the Industrial Workers of the World (IWW). Irwin wrote Park: "Did you know I was a fierce labor fan? Yep—second only to feminism with me."[55] She accompanied Younger to the hearings of the Industrial Commission, weekly meetings of the Central Trades and Labor Council, and joined her in a three-month effort to finance a retrial for the Ford-Suhr case, a legal battle involving two IWW members who had organized a 1913 strike among California hop-pickers and were framed for murder. Together that year, Irwin and Younger addressed ninety-one American Federation of Labor unions—sometimes as many as three in a night—in their appeals for funds.[56]

Irwin's efforts on behalf of the convicted men earned her both the loyalty of IWW members and the censure of the press and conservative community. Newspaper editorials referred to her as "the Gillmore woman" (which she described as the time-honored journalistic shorthand for a prostitute). One magazine editor dubbed her "the reddest woman in America!" When Irwin returned to New York in 1914, Secret Service agents tailed her for six months; when the red-baiting backlash of the post–World War I era began, her name was on every one of the blacklists. The IWW did not forget Irwin's efforts on its behalf, inviting her to address nearly every New York City IWW organization about the Ford-Suhr case, which was eventually resolved through a pardon from California's governor.[57] Irwin's activist efforts illustrate her commitment to the kinds of cross-gender partnerships that early twentieth-century feminists embraced.

At the same time that Irwin was involved in labor activism she joined the NWP, the organizational equivalent of her vivid, militant spirit. The independence and audacity of the Pankhursts inspired many American suffragists who had grown discouraged, including Irwin. "Nobody in the world welcomed the militant movement in England as I did," she exclaimed. "I have always said that when they threw the first brick, my heart was tied to it." "At last the tradition of female patience, of feminine taste in deportment, had gone by the board," she declared. "Women were using the tactics that, through all the ages, men had used; the only tactics that were sure to bring results; rebellion and violence."[58] Forty years old in 1913, she had become conscious of "a growing discouragement that began to freeze into doubt." The doldrums of the suffrage movement, that abyss between 1896 and 1910 when no new states enfranchised women, made the state-by-state method of winning the vote appear hopeless. Irwin believed suffragists might have to form a band who vowed to commit suicide for the cause. Given that she had discovered her mother's body after her suicide, this was a powerful statement. Irwin had a model for this in British suffragette Emily Davison, who threw herself in front of the king's galloping horse at the 1913 Epsom Derby and was killed. She explained: "It would be like this. A young woman, able, successful, happy, kills herself in Boston, leaving a note 'I die because women are not free.' . . . Next week, another young woman commits suicide in New York leaving a similar note. The third week it is perhaps Chicago . . . Washington . . . Seattle . . . San Francisco . . . New Orleans . . . You can imagine what a terror, what a horror would spread across the nation, as parents would ask themselves and each other, 'Will our daughter be next?'"[59]

Death did reenergize the movement, but in the form of war rather than suicide. World War I riveted the nation's attention from 1914 to 1918, and suffragists seized on the bloody conflict as another rationale for granting votes to women. The war began in Europe in August 1914, after a Serbian nationalist assassinated the heir to the throne of the Austro-Hungarian Empire. The United States initially pursued a policy of isolationism, avoiding conflict while trying to broker peace. While most US suffragists thus observed the war from afar, Irwin traveled to the battlefront. She married journalist and war correspondent Will Irwin on February 1, 1916, and spent nine months with him in war-torn Europe.[60] Inez kept a detailed, 512-page typed chronicle that she intended for publication, "1916 War Diary."[61] During her months in Europe, the United States had not yet joined the war. Despite an earlier pledge of neutrality, in April 1917 President Wilson signed a declaration of war after German U-boats sank seven US merchant ships. The United States had a small army but drafted four million men, and by the summer of 1918 was sending ten thousand fresh soldiers to France every day. Over fifteen million people were killed in World War I, making it one of the deadliest conflicts in history, though the United States lost only 116,500.[62]

While Will Irwin was at the front, from her hotel rooms Inez worked on her novel *The Lady of Kingdoms* and traveled through France, England, and Italy. While in Europe she dined with Maud Younger's parents, who lived in Paris; met with Christabel Pankhurst; had an audience with Pope Benedict XV in Rome (although she was Episcopalian); and in London met Herbert Hoover. Hoover, who would be president of the United States from 1929 to 1933, was a Stanford classmate of Will Irwin's and in 1916 was in London directing relief efforts for war victims. Irwin also witnessed firsthand the devastation and loss of families, communities, and cities as a result of the war, as well as a new gender flexibility that transported women into previously male-dominated occupations.[63]

Irwin's vivid war diary alternates between narrative and travelogue— descriptions of churches, art, famous sites, people—and provides a glimpse into the rising human cost of what came to be known as the Great War. From Paris in February 1916: "Paris in war! Such a dark, silent, night city! . . . Inside the café . . . a world reversed, where all the color is contributed by the men because three fourths of the women are in mourning." In April 1916 she sadly exclaimed: "War seems to be devouring France like some mighty metal monster, tearing the hearts of the people with blood-red claws; grinding out the very life of the country with its horrible weight. One gets restless away from it." Irwin visited hospitals where she saw the wounded and dying, including a five-year-old Belgian boy whose ten fingers had been amputated. "The German who did it said," she wrote grimly,

"'You'll never fire a shot against Germany.'" His hands had gone six days without medical attention, and the child eventually died.[64]

While men flocked to the US army, women, both in Europe and the United States, took advantage of new work opportunities. Nearly one million American women entered the labor force for the first time during World War I. African American women, segregated in low-wage occupations like domestic service, were able to trade up for better-paying jobs in industry. Women slipped into sectors previously off limits to them—as mail carriers, assembly-line workers in munitions plants, train conductors, and streetcar drivers.[65] Irwin noted this turning point in women's employment with pride: "The women are really working at men's jobs. You see them on trams everywhere, efficient, competent, and very resourceful. . . . I am not surprised when women act or sing or paint, or sculpt, or write well, or make good speeches, or perform extraordinary feats in organization. I already know that they can do all those things and I still can not help thinking they are easy. But successfully to invade the professions, the crafts and the trades, to grapple with machinery, to take positions in which they must make a thousand instant decisions a day—it delights me when I see them doing *that*. I wanted to applaud all those tram women." In April 1916, the *Daily Mail* reported that "now fifty percent of the workers in the [French] munition factories are women, as against thirty percent last December, and that it is expected the number will go on increasing." Irwin wrote exuberantly from London: "And then the women! That's the big touch, the modern touch! Women everywhere, working at everything. This morning as we turned into the Strand the first sight I saw gave me such a thrill that I still quiver with it. There came toward me, in the midst of that incredible tangle of traffic, a motor-camion, as big as a house and, at the wheel, a slip of a blonde girl in a long, white smock and a big, wide, pink picture hat. I have always wanted to see women with their hands literally on the machinery of the world. And here I get it."[66]

Middle-class modern feminists like Irwin viewed working women as their spiritual compatriots, with shared aspirations for economic independence.[67] Like wage-earning women in the United States, European working women were buoyed by their new spending power, which delighted Irwin. She attended union meetings, including women's associations, and described an evening she spent with a certain "Consul T." who, as Irwin noted sarcastically, "was extraordinarily interesting on the effect of the war on the 'lower' classes—I use in quotes, the English term." This patrician woman remarked that the workers, who now had steady jobs with increasing wages, were spending their newfound money on possessions they had never been able to afford. "The sale of cheap jewelry in Birmingham for instance had increased enormously," Irwin related. "Also women were buying the fur coats and pianos that they had always wanted and never had. She seemed to think it was a deplorable state of mind, but my sympathy was entirely with the spenders."[68]

Irwin's *The Story of the Woman's Party* (1921), a history of the National Woman's Party from its founding to the 1920 suffrage victory, offers another vantage point from which to consider her suffrage affiliations, feminist views, and post-suffrage loyalties. In blow-by-blow, journalistic fashion, *The Story of the Woman's Party* offers a detailed narrative of the campaigns—parades and marches, speeches, mass meetings, deputations to the president, lobbying, arrests, and prison experiences—of NWP members as they worked to sway the opinions of President Wilson, members of Congress, and the American public. Irwin drew on the NWP paper *The Suffragist*, newspapers like the *Washington Times* and the *New York Times*, popular magazines such as *McCall's* and *McClure's*, and fresh chronicles of the victorious suffrage campaign, including Stevens's *Jailed for Freedom* and Younger's "Revelations of a Woman Lobbyist" to piece together this flattering history.[69] *The Story of the Woman's Party* demonstrates Irwin's esteem for Alice Paul, her appreciation of the cross-generational nature of the NWP in its early years, and colorfully depicts the electric jolt of youthful energy the group's bold tactics injected into the moribund suffrage movement.

Irwin portrayed Paul as a brilliant, inspiring leader whose goal was to win the suffrage for women, not precipitate feminist infighting. "Before an organizer left Headquarters for parts unknown," Irwin wrote, "Alice Paul talked with her for several hours, going over her route, indicating the problems which would arise and—in her characteristic and indescribable Alice Paul way—suggesting how they were to be met; holding always above these details the shining object of the journey; managing somehow to fill her with the feeling that in spite of many obstacles, she would conquer all these new worlds. 'No matter,' she always concluded, 'what other Suffragists may say about us, pay no attention to it; go on with your work. Our fight is not against women.'"[70] Following Paul's example Irwin virtually never mentioned the rival group, the NAWSA, in her book, although her private correspondence reveals her anger and disillusionment at their treatment of the NWP. *The Story of the Woman's Party* is a careful book that hewed closely to the NWP party line. In doing so, it prefigures Irwin's lifelong loyalty to the party and to Paul. Irwin's involvement in the woman suffrage movement was the highlight of her life. Thirty years after the vote was won, she exclaimed, "This struggle, which engaged all my youth and much of my maturity, is a part of my life on which I look back with a sense of satisfaction, so soul-warming that I find no adjective to describe it. What women I met! What fights I joined! How many speeches I made! How many words I wrote! But best of all—what women I met! How I pity any generation of women who cannot know that satisfaction!"[71]

A MILITANT TYPE: DORIS STEVENS IN THE SUFFRAGE MOVEMENT

While Inez Irwin combined activism with marriage and her writing profession, and Mary Beard intertwined hers with motherhood and crafting history, in the 1910s Doris Stevens made the woman suffrage movement her full-time career. After graduating from Oberlin in 1911, Stevens worked briefly in a Cleveland settlement house. Concluding that settlement work only scratched poverty's surface, she left to teach high school and eventually turned to suffrage organizing. Stevens first joined the NAWSA ranks; by 1913 she dropped her day job and became field secretary of the Dayton, Ohio, branch and organizer of Dayton County.[72] When the Congressional Union was formed, she joined immediately.

Stevens represented the "new" and singular type of woman the National Woman's Party came to symbolize. As journalist Sara Bard Field wrote of the Woman's Party in 1916: "A new sort of woman it took . . . a militant type, unemotional and logical and yet fired by a desire for justice," "a woman with vision, mentality, and political sagacity."[73] Nurse Lavinia Dock, who picketed the White House and served a jail sentence in her sixties, wrote of party activists in 1917: "If anyone says to me: 'Why the picketing for Suffrage?' I should say in reply, 'Why the fearless spirit of youth?' . . . The old stiff minds must give way. . . . The young are at the gates!"[74]

In many ways Stevens personified the paradoxes inherent in NWP-style feminism during the suffrage years. Allied with militancy, attractive to an elite element, tiny in size yet impressive in the vigor and devotion of its members—modern, youthful, nonconformist, in the vanguard—the party was remarkably well-suited to Stevens's animation, her militant flair, her radical, unorthodox feminism, her meritocratic views. Although a dedicated suffragist, Stevens's feminist vision already extended to women's sexual emancipation, birth control, and marriage reform, which took up much of her attention during the 1920s and 1930s.

Stevens's exuberance radiated youth and modernity, which helped make her an effective activist. It did not hurt the suffrage movement that she was young and beautiful and a magnet for the media, which were drawn to her charismatic presence. A *Washington Times* reporter described her in 1914, the year she left the NAWSA to join the CU, as a "wholesome, pink-cheeked college girl" whose fresh ideals and enthusiasm "just stampeded all the time-honored notions the Senator persons have about lobbying for suffrage."[75] Another journalist described her as "very young, very enthusiastic, [and] very logical." In a letter Beard wrote Stevens decades later, she recalled her first impression of her: "Your radiance and quick wit stirred my very soul when I got to Washington in 1915. I was clumsier than any donkey then, as I still am. You were all glow and charm. Keep all of it you can."[76] Her lover Frank Walsh, a suffrage supporter and chairman of the Industrial Railways Commission, informed Stevens that she was so pretty that everyone, men and women alike, stared when she entered a room. He remarked that many considered her "the most beautiful woman in the suffrage movement." In another letter he described a conversation he had with an acquaintance about "that suffrage gal." The unidentified friend, who did not know Walsh was involved with Stevens, heard her give a speech and exclaimed to Walsh: "by God kid, I never saw as good looking a woman, or heard as good a speech in *my* life, so I followed around to two or three other places, thinking I might strike up a chat, but Nothing doing!"[77] Even at forty, Stevens was described in the British women's rights newspaper *Time and Tide* as "a lovely creature, tall, graceful, animated, wearing her beautiful clothes easily, and carrying gallantly her air of triumphant youth. . . . This is Doris Stevens . . . one of the most vivid and significant personalities ever connected with the Woman's movement."[78]

A riveting speaker, superb organizer, and highly successful fundraiser, Stevens quickly emerged as one of the stars in the NWP firmament. Appointed executive secretary in 1914, she organized the national conference that year, conducted the Women for Congress campaigns in Colorado, and opened the Denver headquarters. The next year Stevens planned the first convention of women voters and in 1916 was appointed chairman of the Organization Department; in that year she alone opened NWP branches in eighteen states. When she headed the party's California campaign against President Wilson's reelection during the fall of 1916, a San Francisco political reporter praised her as "one of the most efficient organizers I have ever known, be it man or woman." She co-chaired the organization's Colorado campaign to defeat the Democratic congressional candidates there and make woman suffrage an "ever-present political issue" in the states where women already had the vote. One of the incumbents she opposed was Edward Keating, a Democratic US representative from Pueblo, Colorado, who did win reelection that year but was defeated in 1918. Stevens wrote Paul, "Tomorrow I start for the principal points in Keating's district. I am told it is as much as one's life is worth to go into his district and ask the miners to vote against him,—so if you get a telegram, saying, that Doris has been strung up on a nearby pole, you will understand why." Not only did Stevens raise more money for the CU in the campaign than any other organizer and achieve a Democratic defeat for which the organization could claim credit, she also converted individual women voters to the political tactic of gender solidarity. Recounting her Colorado organizing experiences, she wrote: "One Democratic lady came up to me after the meeting and said, 'I had no idea you women had been so rebuffed by my Party. I am convinced that my duty is to the women first, and my Party second.'"[79]

Stevens's enigmatic relationship with wealthy suffragist Alva Belmont was partially responsible for her quick ascent up the organization's hierarchy. Mrs. Belmont, born in 1853, was an overbearing personality and a key player in the US women's rights movement. She was a southern-born New York socialite who married and divorced William Vanderbilt before marrying rich financier Oliver Belmont. Newly widowed, Alva Belmont came to the suffrage cause in

1909 in England, and soon after joined the NAWSA.[80] According to her biographer, Belmont was obsessed with power and control and had an almost phobic fear of losing her grip on it. "Her combative nature rejoiced in conquests," her daughter Consuelo wrote. "A born dictator, she dominated events about her as thoroughly as she eventually dominated her husband and her children. If she admitted another point of view she never conceded it." Belmont's forceful personality helps explain the odd relationship Stevens had with her for nearly twenty years, in which Stevens was supplicant, companion, speechwriter, fundraiser, and willing messenger for the older feminist. Although lavishly wealthy, Belmont could be unfathomable and had a puritanical, thrifty streak. "She was always in conflict between living sumptuously and selfishly and being amused by a court jester and her marked identification with Joan d'Arc," Stevens remarked.[81] The prospect of being rewarded in Belmont's will also motivated Stevens's desire to please her.

Doris Stevens first met Belmont in Washington, DC, in the winter of 1913 at the NAWSA annual convention. Their close association did not begin until the following year, when Stevens was sent to Newport, Rhode Island, to open headquarters for the CU. Paul was chair, Belmont an executive committee member, and Stevens was put on the payroll at $100 a month and placed in charge of the Bellevue Avenue headquarters. She was also expected to organize a national conference, fundraise, write Belmont's speeches and press statements, and speak publicly at locations as varied as the beach, dance halls, and street corners. Stevens later recalled, she was "at Mrs. Belmont's beck and call at any time of the day or night. She wished me to lunch, dine, ride or stay the night with her at Marble House."[82] Reflecting back on their curious relationship, Stevens stated, "from 1914 on, in the early days, I could not say why I did so many private services for Mrs. Belmont in addition to my work for the organization; except that I was young and obedient, and anyone who knew Mrs. Belmont well knew that when she asked you to do anything you did it or you were no longer needed around the place . . . the more I gave the more she asked and in turn the more I gave."[83]

Stevens's private services for Belmont ranged from fellowship to acting as her personal emissary. Belmont expected her to visit regularly, and Stevens often spent the night with Belmont at her home on New York City's Fifty-first Street, especially when she complained of loneliness. Belmont often called upon Stevens after her regular day's work to accompany her to the theater, to dinner, and other events. Belmont was apparently afraid of being robbed of her jewels, and was reluctant to go out alone with her chauffeur at the wheel.[84] Although Paul was chair of the NWP, Stevens believed it was Belmont who held the organization's reins in her hands.

While Beard's and Irwin's commitment to suffrage was tempered by their family obligations and career demands, Stevens's dedication was so zealous and unabating that her friends and colleagues worried she would lose sight of her own life. This indicates the all-consuming nature of the woman suffrage movement in the lives of some of its leaders and rank-and-file members. Frank Walsh admonished her in a 1915 letter: "I do so thoroughly agree with Crystal Eastman, darling, about you giving up your beautiful young life to this thing you are in, great as it is." A fellow NWP member chided Stevens the following year: "I fear you will give out before this big thing is pulled off.—Don't kill yourself.—It isn't worth it.—You know Susan B.—lived to an age of maturity herself, and Anna Shaw is still fit." When Beard and another party member met Stevens in 1915 to discuss the first Woman Voters Convention, they put her on a train for a few days' vacation instead. At the bottom of Stevens's weekly progress report to Lucy Burns, Elizabeth Colt scrawled: "Mrs. Beard and I both felt it important to get Miss Stevens away for a few days vacation *at once*. She has been really ill." When NWP activists began a civil disobedience campaign and suffragists were jailed, three weeks after her release from prison Stevens reluctantly wrote Paul that her doctor told her it would be "utter folly" to undertake the national speaking tour she had planned to publicize the plight of the incarcerated suffragists. "As soon as I leave the hospital I am going to the mountains—I don't know which ones yet—to read-sleep-eat and tramp. I shall *surely* be made over by Nov. 1st at which time I shall finish the tour." Her notes on the year 1917 reveal, however, that instead of resting that autumn, Stevens visited twelve states and spoke publicly for woman suffrage every day between October and December.[85]

As the rebellious tactics of the NWP drew increasing public attention to the suffrage cause, NAWSA members amplified their criticism. President Carrie Chapman Catt's "winning plan," formally adopted in 1916, introduced key state woman suffrage referenda and simultaneously supported an amendment to the Constitution. As the pressure of the movement increased in its final years, the tension between the two groups escalated. Neither Beard nor Irwin welcomed the split among suffragists, and were aware that such a rift had occurred in the nineteenth century. Believers in female solidarity and women's peacemaking skills, they both warned of the danger of women working against each other. Beard cautiously advised the movement's leaders not to criticize other women, but to throw all their energies into gaining the vote. She counseled Lucy Burns in 1915: "If we can just go on refraining from talking about the National and do our job, the country is ours." In another letter she remarked, "What a pity that all the National suffragists can see is attacking other suffragists."[86]

While Beard encouraged suffragists to support one another despite their differences, Irwin strove valiantly to protect her friendship with Maud Wood Park, now a NAWSA leader. She tried numerous times to explain to Park her decision to side with the NWP. When Park initially discovered Irwin had joined, stung, she remarked, "I suppose a person of my temperament cannot exactly estimate what—to a person of dramatic temperament—is the fascination of a militant movement." Although hurt, Irwin did not respond until 1921, when the suffrage battle was over. She told Park then that it was not her attraction to drama that drew her to the NWP, it was her belief that it would be the swiftest way to enfranchise women. "I think perhaps you—more than any woman alive," she wrote, "could understand how impatient I had grown with the state-by-state method; how my blood boiled at the sodden immovability of Massachusetts."[87]

Irwin believed that Maud Wood Park and Alice Paul, leaders of the opposing sects, had much in common: a quiet temperament, humility, and a sage simplicity. She hoped to end the escalating contention between women by bringing their two leaders together in friendship. She wrote Park in 1921: "I have never—in all my life—met a woman who is so much your own blood-sister as Alice Paul. . . . She is a woman with whom *you*—you personally—could travel around the world and to the two Poles in perfect amity, understanding and *rapport*. I say this, after long study of her which meant living for long periods in the house with her and after my long friendship with you. She doesn't, one half as much as you do, belong, by congeniality of temperament, to me. She belongs, thereby, a great deal more to *you*." Hoping she had not overstepped she concluded: "If it offends you—after I have said that you ought—of all the women in the world—you two ought to know each other—consider it all unwritten."[88] In 1938, when both women were in their mid-sixties, Irwin again tried to express to Park her reasons for joining the movement's radical arm. She credited "a kind of violence—the Indian strain, perhaps—that seems inherent in me." She also described experiencing a "kind of sinister despair," a hopelessness that made her imagine the need for violent, even self-destructive acts to direct the nation's attention to the urgent need to pass the woman suffrage amendment. But she assured Park, "Of course that only floated through my mind. Nobody could ever voice such a plan if she were not prepared, herself, to be the first to commit suicide. The National Woman's Party took care of that feeling. I have always been glad I joined. I have never regretted one word of it."[89]

Both Irwin and Beard belonged to the minority of women who tried to bridge the bitter, widening gap between feminists in the final years of the suffrage movement, which seriously challenged feminist unity in the post-suffrage years. Despite their efforts, hostilities on both sides hardened and rippled forward several decades. Of minister and NAWSA president (from 1904 to 1915) Anna Howard Shaw, Beard wrote Lucy Burns: "Isn't it sad to see her end her life of struggle with hatred gleaming out of her aged eyes? She doesn't know how to hold together the things she has spent forty years in building up . . . To Die hating! God save me from that." When in 1915 Catt denounced the anti-Democratic policy of the NWP as "a serious tactical blunder" and a "stupendous stupidity," Beard wrote her a conciliatory letter. "I wish we might agree on the value of political work as well as educational work, on the power of the

President, and on the advisability of always attacking the enemy rather than on laying defeat to women. . . . I have always considered you so big, because you have not considered those who differed with you, as necessarily beneath contempt. . . . I have long wanted to argue these matters with those of you whom I respect so much."[90]

Despite the fractious climate among suffragists, a 1917 victory in New York State signaled the long-awaited penetration of the previously immovable eastern states and marked a new stage in the movement. After multiple fruitless visits to President Wilson, who continued to refuse to endorse suffrage, the NWP struck upon the dramatic tactic of picketing the White House. NWP activists were the first group of citizens in US history to pioneer this form of political protest, and Irwin probably introduced the idea, drawing from the model of striking labor unions.[91] The first suffrage pickets, described by the press as "Silent Sentinels," appeared at the White House gates in January 1917, holding banners that denounced the president and demanded the right to vote. According to Stevens, the picketers caused a profound stir and made the front page of all the newspapers in the country. When the persistent women went back and back again, the press began to denounce them as undesirable, unwomanly, unsexed, and pathological. At the same time, the US Congress was debating the prospect of the country joining the European war. With the country's entry into war and Wilson thrust into the world's spotlight, the picketing women came to symbolize to some the inconsistency in his support of democracy abroad but not at home.[92] Consequently a large, enthusiastic group of women from the political left joined the NWP in 1917, finding its tactics and antiwar stance attractive.[93]

Beginning in June 1917, the police arrested hundreds of suffragists for obstructing traffic. They were sent to the District jail, the abandoned workhouse connected to the jail, or to Virginia's Occoquan Prison, for terms ranging from three days to seven months.[94] Described in *The Suffragist* as "a Woman's Party leader and speaker of national reputation," Stevens was one of sixteen women arrested on Bastille Day, July 14—the annual commemoration of the 1790 French storming of the Bastille fortress-prison—for picketing the White House. Serving as defense attorney for the arrested suffragists (because they were denied legal counsel), Stevens declared dramatically: "What is our real crime? . . . [We] peacefully petitioned the President of the United States for Liberty. . . . We say to you, this outrageous policy of stupid and brutal punishment will not dampen the ardor of the women. Where sixteen of us face your judgment today there will be sixty tomorrow."[95] Alice Paul led a delegation of women to the White House on October 29, knowing she would be arrested, and was sentenced to seven months. The NWP leader had learned in England how to "politicize the body" to build public awareness and outrage against forced feeding of imprisoned women. When she entered the US prison in 1917, Paul weighed a mere ninety pounds and still suffered from health problems as a result of forced feedings in England. After refusing food for seventy-eight hours, she was moved to the Asylum Hospital and fed by force.[96]

Although Stevens and NWP feminists like her were willing to go to jail and risk their health and even their lives for woman suffrage, many of the arrested suffragists were middle- and upper-class white women whose prison stays were their first encounters with African American and poor women. They did not envision their activism representing women across race and class. Stevens, who was sentenced to sixty days (but commuted to three) when she and her fellow picketers refused to pay a $25 fine, was among one of the first groups to serve prison terms in the aging, poorly kept Occoquan Workhouse. In *Jailed for Freedom* she recalled sleeping "side by side with Negro prostitutes" and said ingenuously of her "dusky comrades": "not that we shrank from these women on account of their color, but how terrible to know that the institution had gone out of its way to bring the prisoners from their own wing to the white wing in an attempt to humiliate us. There was plenty of room in the Negro wing. But prison must be made so unbearable that no more women would face it." When the jailed suffragists were forced to dress in the Black prisoners' garments, Stevens wrote that the "unpleasantness" of wearing the clothes of "these unfortunates . . . made us all wince."[97]

The classist and racist biases Stevens exhibited foreshadowed the conservative turn her thought would take later in life. Though a gifted fundraiser, when the collections were slim she could turn disparaging and nasty. She wrote Paul from Charlotte, North Carolina, in 1917: "I have never seen such illiberality *anywhere.* They say no Jews come to Charlotte because the Scotch Presbyterians [her own background] are more Semitic than the Jews themselves."[98]

At times she complained to Paul about the class of people to whom she was asked to direct her suffrage propaganda. Recalling how she spoke on street corners before clusters of Newport seamen in 1914, Stevens wrote: "I used to stand on a chair and talk to drunken sailors and after speaking I would get off the chair and collect their dirty nickels."[99]

While suffragists disagreed among themselves, and many voiced unsisterly attitudes toward women of color and working-class women, the cause gained new momentum. On January 10, 1918, the suffrage amendment passed the House of Representatives by a vote of 274 to 136—a two-thirds majority with one vote to spare—exactly forty years to the day from the time the amendment was first introduced into Congress and exactly one year after the first picket banner appeared at the White House gates.[100] Appointed chair of the NWP Political Department in 1918, Stevens was one of several women evicted from the Republican Convention that year for flinging from the gallery a banner that rebuked New York Republican Senator James Wolcott Wadsworth for his determined opposition to woman suffrage. It read in part: "We demand his support for the National Suffrage Amendment, or his resignation from the Senate."[101] Impatient with the president's dragging his heels, the NWP escalated its headline-grabbing tactics. Members staged an August demonstration at Washington, DC's Lafayette Monument. Forty-eight women were arrested for holding a meeting on public grounds and for climbing on a statue. Twenty-six were sentenced to ten to fifteen days in the district jail, and immediately went on hunger strike. Paul and Burns were part of the imprisoned group. Disguised in a man's raincoat, Stevens intrepidly smuggled a letter to them before being thrown out by a prison guard.[102]

By the fall of 1918, the woman suffrage issue was so politically charged that President Wilson declared in a Senate address that the suffrage amendment was "vital to the winning of the war. . . . It is vital to the right solutions which we must settle and settle immediately."[103] His change of heart reflected the fact that NAWSA's membership had expanded to two million, seventeen states had passed suffrage referenda, and he hoped to both recognize and deepen women's contribution to the war effort.[104] In December 1918, when Wilson sailed to France to attend the peace conference at the end of World War I, the four hundred NWP officers determined that a new strategy was required. Marching single file from headquarters past the White House and again to Lafayette Park, they applied a torch to a pile of pine logs in the Grecian urn placed at the base of the statue. Eighty-four-year-old Reverend Olympia Brown, one of the first ordained woman ministers in the country and a friend of Susan B. Anthony, threw into the flames the speech the president made on his arrival in France. "Massed about that statue," Stevens, who was part of the procession, wrote, "we felt a strange strength and solidarity, we felt again that we were a part of the universal struggle for liberty." On New Year's Day, 1919, NWP activists began the first of the "watchfires of freedom" in an urn on the sidewalk directly in line with the president's front door, burning Wilson's speeches on democracy as fast as he made them in Europe. Throughout January and the start of February, women of all ages kept the watchfires burning and were arrested, imprisoned, went on hunger strike, and were released. Writing from the West, where she was organizing the Prison Special (a carload of former suffrage prisoners who undertook a national speaking tour and addressed overflowing crowds), Stevens exclaimed to Paul: "It was a beautiful thing to do. I should like to have helped in the deed."[105]

Still one vote short in the Senate, the Democrats set February 10, 1919, as the date on which that body would again consider the amendment. But the Susan B. Anthony Amendment was defeated, sixty-three in favor, thirty-three opposed. In March 1919 Stevens and twenty-four others were arrested for picketing the New York Metropolitan Opera House while President Wilson was inside leading a meeting on his proposed League of Nations. An officer marched the NWP members to the police station, denouncing them as cannibals and Bolsheviks.[106]

The Sixty-fifth Congress with its Democratic majority ended on March 3, 1919, without the US Senate passing the amendment.

On June 4, 1919, the US Senate of the Sixty-Sixth Congress finally endorsed the amendment by a fifty-six to twenty-five vote and sent it to the states for ratification. Suffragists continued their campaigning, and after thirty-five of the required thirty-six states had ratified the amendment, the nation's attention turned to Lorine Pruette's home state of Tennessee where the governor, pressured by President Wilson, had called a special session of the state legislature. On August 18, 1920, a young Tennessee legislator who had previously stood with the anti-suffragists cast the decisive vote in its favor, citing his mother's desire for him to vote for ratification. The Nineteenth Amendment became law on August 26, 1920, marking the culmination of the largest and most momentous phase of the women's movement in American history.[107]

CHAPTER 3

Detention by the Male

Early twentieth-century American feminists were not only interested in gaining their citizenship, they were also concerned about remaking their private relations with men. Sexuality was a central component in that remaking. The vibrant 1910s, which witnessed the triumphant climax of the woman suffrage movement, also fostered a sexual revolution that led to a more open society during the 1920s. By 1920, a consumer society that valued fashion and play had replaced the earlier sober, work ethic–driven culture.[1] As one unhappy reformer stated in 1913, "the commercialization of practically every human interest in the past thirty years has completely transformed daily life. . . . Prior to 1880 the . . . main business of life was living . . . the main business of life now is pleasure."[2] New ideas about women's sexuality emerged from this rapidly changing culture and its post–World War I "live for the day" attitude.[3] The lives of Doris Stevens and Lorine Pruette offer a glimpse into the sexual revolution during the period that F. Scott Fitzgerald dubbed "the Jazz Age," the years between World War I and the Great Depression of the 1930s.[4] They also dramatically illustrate the conundrum modern feminists found themselves facing as they envisioned a dazzling future with eager men at their sides.[5]

The rise of the sexologists and the popularity of Sigmund Freud fed into this changing cultural landscape. Feminists like Mabel Dodge Luhan and Emma Goldman, who considered sexuality self-defining and a critical part of human experience, claimed Freud as a leading authority on the topic. They were charmed by Freud's definition of sexuality as a driving instinct in both genders, one linked to pleasure rather than solely to procreation. Feminists appreciated Freud's uniquely modern assumption that one's sense of self is linked to sexuality, and were anxious to learn more about female sexuality and to explore their own. As the historian Mari Jo Buhle noted, "feminists, like Freud, were coming to understand sexuality as the leading indicator of selfhood or, as later generations would put it, subjectivity."[6] Stevens's almost clinical analysis of her sexual experiences reflects this rising emphasis on the self. As her patient lover and later husband Jonathan Mitchell stated in 1961, "Doris had a feeling that she was pioneering in life, a feeling which overlapped this childish, childlike preoccupation with her own affairs as if no one had ever before existed."[7]

This exploration of self was central in the minds of modern early twentieth-century feminists like Stevens and Pruette, who used their own lives as sites of feminist experimentation. What one historian has described as "the politics of selfhood" was informed by European theories as well as the introspection of psychoanalysis.[8] American feminists read widely in the 1910s and 1920s from recently translated essays by European writers on sexuality, including Iwan Block, Emil Lucka, Auguste Rowel, Richard von Krafft-Ebing, Havelock Ellis, and Edward Carpenter.[9] Some of these theorists affirmed women's desire but also revered their potential motherhood, which they considered the marker of women's difference from men, one that made them uniquely suited to advance civilization. The Swedish educator Ellen Key took this one step further by sexualizing maternity, arguing that the impulse to become pregnant triggered female sexual desire.[10]

SEX RADICALS CHALLENGE ORTHODOXY

The women and men who espoused sex radical ideas believed they were remaking the world, throwing aside their parents' inhibitions to create new relationships that were reciprocal, egalitarian, and superior.[11] Advocates of "modern" sexuality endorsed free love, multiple partners, and interracial sex and marriage.[12] In urban areas like Greenwich Village and Harlem, radical thinkers viewed erotic experimentation as a key component of revolutionary struggle. Although small in number, their influence was far-reaching. Stevens was friend and neighbor to the Greenwich Village bohemian crowd, many of whom became well-known artists, journalists, suffragists, and cultural critics—Georgia O'Keeffe, Margaret Sanger, Emma Goldman, Max Eastman, Ida Rauh, Genevieve Taggard, Ruth Hale, and Sara Bard Field, among others. The Village's famous monthly *The Masses* became, under Max Eastman's editorship, a venue for a new kind of bold writing about topics like birth control, divorce, and prostitution.[13]

Although reproduction had constrained white middle-class women's sexuality and defined their social roles in the nineteenth century, twentieth-century sex radicals championed sex without fear of pregnancy. The nineteenth-century concept of female "passionlessness," which grew out of the separate spheres construct as well as a Protestant culture of moral control, was dissolving.[14] Upright Victorian wives had promoted both husband and wife's abstinence as a way for women to achieve "voluntary motherhood."[15] In contrast, sex radicals endorsed birth control, illustrating their belief that women's sex drive went beyond motherhood.

Emma Goldman was one sex radical who proclaimed women's right to develop their "love nature separate from and independent of [their] maternal nature."[16]

The birth control campaign advocated not only smaller family size but also women's right to nonprocreative sexual pleasure. Linked to feminism and championed by sympathetic men, the campaign arose in radical New York circles in 1912 and spread through the nation via Socialist Party proponents and IWW members.[17] A cross-class movement that drew in modern women, male advocates, and young working women, it was led by public health nurse Margaret Sanger in the 1910s. Her column "What Every Girl Should Know," published in the socialist newspaper *The Call*, led to the founding of her journal *The Woman Rebel* in 1914.

To advocate and use birth control was a symbol of feminism and modernity. The practice challenged postal inspector and moralist Anthony Comstock's efforts to keep the dissemination of birth control information illegal.[18] A Columbia University anthropologist, Elsie Clews Parsons, for example, devised a plan to have women who used birth control stand up in court and make a public declaration at Sanger's 1915 trial on obscenity charges, a parallel to the twentieth-century "We Have Had Abortions" campaign.[19] Pruette's and Stevens's lovers and husbands were adamant that they use birth control, which both women strongly believed in. Stevens's 1925 speech before the Sixth International Neo-Malthusian and Birth Control Conference, entitled "False Social Barriers to Women's Psychic Release," pointed to the close ties between the feminist and birth control movements.[20] Her intentional joining of women's "psychic release" with their physical release through sex without the concern of pregnancy points to the connections radicals made between a healthy psyche and a healthy sex life. Sanger was in the audience and later wrote Stevens that her paper "was the finest paper I have ever had the pleasure of listening to from any woman."[21] The birth control campaign of the 1910s represented the emergence of "a faint, quavering, and sublimated line of thought"—women's right to control their own bodies—that became a critical demand for modern women. What came to be called the reproductive rights movement took shape in these years.[22]

Black women were also interested in controlling their fertility and at the local level established clinics and advocated the importance of contraception to the survival of the family and the Black community. Both white and Black women had used contraception and abortifacients for decades, and abortion was available though dangerous.[23] When the poet Edna St. Vincent Millay—a friend of Stevens—came to visit in London in 1922 she told her about her recent miscarriage, which Millay's mother, a nurse, helped induce through an herbal abortive followed by vigorous outdoor exercise in rural Dorset County, England. Mitchell remembered decades later: "It was an incredible story . . . of her mother, of rolling in the fields! Well, they produced a miscarriage, and it made Edna frightfully sick. There were doctors in London to whom she might have turned . . . and Miss

Stevens would have helped her. But instead the two of them went off like two animals—off together in the hedges of Dorset!"[24]

Despite the risk of unwanted pregnancy, sex radicals affirmed the legitimacy and healthfulness of sexual activity. Stevens spoke openly about female sexual desire. In a 1925 speech she criticized the double standard that downplayed women's "sexual and amatory needs," while exalting men's.[25] Sex radicals hailed from middle- and working-class backgrounds and varied ethnicities, and included Harlem Renaissance poets and novelists as well as blues singers. Ida Cox, Bessie Smith, Ethel Waters, and Ma Rainey all sang evocatively about Black female sexuality.[26]

Still, ideas about sexuality were based on a moral order that was not only gendered but raced. As Christina Simmons has noted, male and class/race privilege created a double sexual standard. White middle- and upper-class women were often desexualized in Victorian America, but gained social status as wives and mothers bearing and nurturing white children. Lower-class women, including domestic servants, prostitutes, and working-class women, were often the targets of an aggressive masculine "sporting culture" that defined them as promiscuous by nature. Most whites reflexively placed African American women in this category, despite the efforts of Black clubwomen and suffragists.[27] White womanhood was articulated at times in relation to Black women and their supposed (hyper) sexuality, which made African American women reluctant to embrace the sexual revolution of the early twentieth century.

This moral order extended to lower-status and racialized men as well. In the South in particular, white female purity was exalted, while white men at times gained their first sexual experiences, and expended their lusts, on Black women.[28] While some higher-status men believed African American and lower-status women should provide them sexual service, lower-class men and men of color were historically denied sexual access to higher-status women. Lynching was one mechanism intended to prevent this access.[29]

FEMINIST GENERATIONS AND SEX

Once women were recognized as sexual beings, romantic female friendships became threatening, and the heterosexual relationship was exalted as the norm and ideal. While many nineteenth-century women had couched feminism in terms of female friendship and difference from men, twentieth-century feminists strove to redefine it in the context of male/female relationships and similarity between the sexes. The nineteenth-century culture of "smashing," when students in all-female colleges and boarding schools exchanged affectionate notes and became infatuated with one another and with female teachers, was passing. Some nineteenth-century professionals pursued lifelong relationships with other women; these "Boston marriages" were visible and accepted. By 1930, all such relationships were suspect.[30]

In their celebration of heterosexual love, sex radicals heaped fuel on the fire that was beginning to smolder against homosexuals. The post-Freudian insistence on the inescapable, uncontrollable nature of the sex drive—in men and women—made intense female relationships appear deviant. With the rise of the social sciences, new labels of normality and abnormality were attached to sexual behavior. Women who chose not to marry were stigmatized as neurotic or lesbian. "The driving force in many agitators and militant women who are always after their rights," one commentator noted, "is often an unsatisfied sex impulse, with a homosexual aim."[31] Even bohemian groups, who earlier had opened space for same-sex relationships, became less accepting of them by the late 1920s.[32] Free lover Floyd Dell borrowed the language of the new social sciences when he wrote: "the intensity of friendships between people of the same sex . . . we now regard as an artificial product, the result of the segregation of the sexes and the low social position of women. As women become free and equal with men such romantic intensity of emotion finds a more biologically appropriate expression."[33] Some historians have contended that middle-class women like Stevens and Pruette, who formed their ties in an age when society still accepted same-sex bonds but lived as adults in an era when such relationships were condemned, represent a cultural and historic turning point. Such an abrupt social shift could prove disquieting and confusing.[34]

Women increasingly internalized the homophobic perspective of the changing times, as frank sex studies revealed. Katharine Bement Davis's ambitious *Factors in the Sex Lives of Twenty-Two Hundred Women* (1929), which she began shortly after World War I, investigated lesbian relationships, birth control practices, and happiness in marriage, including timing and frequency of intercourse. One of her survey respondents suggested a witch-hunt atmosphere rising in the 1920s: "the ethics of homosexual relationships is the most serious problem the business or professional woman has to face today. . . . In my city some business women are hesitating to take apartments together for fear of the interpretation that may be put upon it."[35]

Most feminists raised in the nineteenth century reflected the Victorianism of the era in which they came of age. Even Inez Irwin and Mary Beard, modern feminists in many respects, were uncomfortable with the topic of sex. Not sexually liberal women themselves (and safely settled in monogamous marriages before sexual liberalism was mainstreamed), sexuality was simply not as central to their feminist identity as it was to Doris Stevens and Lorine Pruette. Irwin and Beard were in their mid-to-late thirties in 1910 and entered their forties during the decade. While they might discuss a topic like prostitution because of its social context, the personal celebration and exploration of sexual experience was missing.

Although from early adolescence Irwin had been devoted to eradicating the barriers between male and female spheres, she rarely included sexual relations in her critique. When she came across the novel *And Satan Laughs* in 1891, eighteen-year-old Irwin used Victorian language to describe it in her diary as "a vile novel relating the life of a fallen woman." She stopped reading after twenty minutes, "happy to say such books never attract me long. I am disgusted soon and put them aside."[36] In 1929, after reading *The Terrible Siren*, a biography of nineteenth-century sexual radical Victoria Woodhull, Irwin wrote Maud Wood Park: "I would have liked to be with you every moment while you were reading *The Terrible Siren*. Never, *literally* was I so torn between triumph & disgust as when I read that book."[37]

In her autobiography, Irwin reminisced that, while she and her friends at Boston's Girls' High School in the late 1880s and early 1890s had talked about teachers, books, the Boston Symphony, art exhibits, and "a ragtail and a bobtail of the interests of late girlhood," "we never discussed men—never!" she exclaimed. "I cannot remember that during all our long friendship the word 'sex' was ever used . . . except perhaps with reference to botany or zoology. Any younger generation will say, 'Think what you missed!' And it will be right. But I shall reply, 'It is extraordinary how much there is in the world to talk about besides sex.' And I shall be right too."[38]

The entire topic of sexuality is strikingly absent from Beard's rich analysis of women in history. In the one article she wrote on sexuality, "The Economic Background of the Sex Life of the Unmarried Adult" (1934), she examined the unmarried as a social group and portrayed them as a threat to social stability. Characterizing the new fascist movements in Germany, Italy, and Japan as "a dynamic of unmarried males," Beard argued that the restraining influence of "education, jobs, families and public obligations" and above all the "civil-izing influence" of women were necessary to keep "idle bachelors" from leaping "with the rage of tigers . . . over the barriers which civilized nations had erected for human behavior." Considering celibacy in the Catholic Church, Nazi homosexuality (which she labeled "perversion"), the exploitation of single women workers in the textile industry, and the roving bands of unmarried youth set in flight by the American Depression, Beard concluded that "husbands and maternity are essential to women's mental health" just as "paternity and wives are . . . vital to that of the males."[39]

Only through the topic of prostitution, a hotly contested issue during the Progressive era, did Beard and Irwin ever directly discuss sexuality. In 1909 Irwin wrote Park, describing a letter she wrote to *Collier's* magazine. "I said some exceedingly iconoclastic things . . . for one thing I demanded an investigation of the whole subject of prostitutedom." By the end of the century, prostitution flourished in a highly organized system of urban red-light districts. The world of commercialized prostitution fed a perception of an epidemic of venereal disease and also reminded Americans of men's potential for unbridled lust, which stood in contrast to the refined, spiritualized passion still admired by the traditional middle class. Reformers described commercialized sex as a problem created by men, for the profit and pleasure of men, and linked it to a growing nativist sentiment against European immigrants.[40]

Beard's discussion of "The Social Evil" in *Woman's Work in Municipalities* (1915) was Progressive in its social focus, yet muted in its analysis of sexuality. Declaring that prostitution swallowed up "the unskilled daughters of the unskilled classes," Beard argued that the way to eliminate it was to improve the lives of working-class women: to replace moral precept with industrial training, provide cleaner, safer housing, regulate hours and conditions of labor, control recreational facilities, increase the minimum wage, and provide mothers with pensions. Although she argued for breaking "the conspiracy of silence" on "matters of sex" and an elimination of the double standard which extended "false standards of morals" to young men, Beard concluded that "the same virtue is needed in both sexes for the happy development of that family life on which the security of the race and the progress of civilization depend."[41]

Nineteenth-century feminists found themselves alternately puzzled, distressed, and even repulsed by modern feminism's new emphasis on sexuality. Of Havelock Ellis—who wrote the first medical textbook on homosexuality as well as other sources on sexuality—Alice Stone Blackwell wrote her cousin in 1912, "I have never read any of Havelock Ellis' books. I am sorry if his books are disgusting; but they deal with a disgusting subject & perhaps under the circumstances they can't help being so." When Sanger appealed to suffrage leader Carrie Chapman Catt for support for the birth control cause, Catt responded tartly, "Your reform is too narrow to appeal to me . . . and too sordid." Considering that "a million years of male control over the sustenance of women has made them sex slaves," Catt stated she could offer Sanger no support until "the advocacy of contraceptives is combined with as strong a propaganda for continence." Charlotte Perkins Gilman characterized the "wild excitement over sex" which she perceived in 1924 as detrimental to "race progress" and female self-development, and argued that monogamy was a natural form of sex union and the one most beneficial to civilization. Similarly, Jane Addams commented in 1930 that "the breaking down of sex taboos" seemed odd to the two generations of professionally trained women who lived "completely celibate lives" without thinking themselves "Freudianly abnormal."[42]

The generations Addams spoke for found their sustenance in female friendship and community as well as in lesbian relationships. (Addams herself had a forty-year partnership with Mary Rozet Smith.) Irwin's long friendship with Park demonstrates her own appreciation of same-sex relationships. In nearly every letter she wrote Park between 1904 and 1955, Irwin professed love and comradeship, as well as her deep need for female friendship. Irwin, who as a teenager dismissed boys as "lesser girls," as a woman sometimes suspected that "men ain't exactly people." "Men can't fill in all the chinks," she wrote Park in 1908, and confided, "I often suffer from a kind of sex-loneliness."[43]

In a manner that became foreign to a culture increasingly obsessed with heterosexuality, Irwin naturally described her physical and emotional attraction to her friend. She routinely addressed her as "my angel," "my dear," "my beautiful and beloved Maud," and described their friendship as "ardent." She was drawn to Park's physical beauty, especially her "truly exquisite" nose, which she fondly described "as chiseled as though cut by a fairy sculptor with the most minniken of tools." In 1912 Irwin wrote a tribute to Park, the science fiction novel *Angel Island*, in which she cast her friend as the beautiful, spirited feminist heroine. "'Angel Island' begins in The AMERICAN MAGAZINE in July," she wrote Park. "Remember that you're Julia in it. You may complain of characterization—she differs from you here and there—but by Jove you won't kick at the looks I've handed to her. . . . Yours to command till death, Inez." Several years later Irwin wrote Park, "It was a great delight to me to hear you speak at the Convention of the Woman's Party, to listen to your exquisite voice again and to gaze at your lovely face. . . . I could go on at a greater length, but I know you will laugh at it." After her friend's death, Irwin described herself as a devout worshiper of Park and said wistfully, "She was the most beautiful creature I have ever seen."[44] Such outspoken admiration and open love for another woman became increasingly rare among twentieth-century feminists.

EPISODES WHICH CAUSE TROUBLE: DORIS STEVENS

Stevens's tumultuous love life captures the challenges early twentieth-century feminists faced as they tried to translate their new sexual ideals into real lives with men. Modern feminists were often disappointed in their quest for self-fulfillment and gender equality.[45] In her twenties during the resonant 1910s, Stevens threw herself with abandon into the sexual revolution. She was determined to capture, in the poet Genevieve Taggard's words, "the unity of life, the dance of it." "Life should be lived magnificently," Stevens exclaimed to Beard in 1935, and that is exactly what she tried to do. She celebrated contemporaries like dancer Isadora Duncan, who stated that her body had caused her so much pain from headaches, backaches, and toothaches that it owed her all payment possible in sexual rapture.[46] Like other modern feminists, Stevens believed heterosexual fulfillment would join with independence and a meaningful profession as new ideals for women.[47] Jonathan Mitchell, her lover for twelve years before they married, characterized Stevens's early interest in female sexuality as "almost professional." "[Doris] meant that the sex relationship in her own life was to be not only better than it had ever been in anyone else's life, but to be conceivably of a new and superior character."[48] Like her adventurous peers, Stevens read Ellis and

Carpenter and touted the "new knowledge" and "new light" of modern psychology. "This may be a lone rebel voice in the wilderness," she wrote optimistically in the early 1920s. "But the lone voice is comforted by the hope that modern psychological research, before it becomes crystallized and formalized, may do such irreparable damage to the orthodox conception of women's inferiority that no retreat to it will be possible."[49]

In the early 1920s Stevens bought a summerhouse at Croton-on-Hudson, New York. A group of pleasant, old frame cottages on Mount Airy Road housed close friends from New York City, including Max Eastman and Eugen Boissevain, Crystal Eastman and her husband Walter Fuller, John Reed for a time, Floyd Dell, and other bohemians and cultural radicals in Stevens's circle. "It was as though Greenwich Village in summer array had been dumped down with almost deliberate pageantry upon the grass," one of them wrote.[50] Rural, lovely, and informal, this home served as a retreat for Stevens through decades of intensive work for women's causes and as a gathering place for cultural radicals who shared her modern ideas about sex.

Stevens's friend, the auburn-haired poet Edna St. Vincent Millay, a symbol of sexual emancipation for this new generation, was one of Stevens's frequent visitors in Croton. Millay's 1918 poem "My candle burns at both ends;/ It will not last the night;/ But ah, my foes, and oh, my friends—/ It gives a lovely light!" became the rallying cry of sexually liberated women.[51] In April 1923 Stevens invited Millay to visit her summer home. Millay—who had just won the Pulitzer Prize in poetry—flouted convention and took many lovers (men and women, single and married). She met Eugen Boissevain, who became her devoted husband of many years, at Stevens's home, where they were paired in charades.[52] Stevens's friendship with Millay is one more indication of her changing ideas about female sexuality.

Like nineteenth-century free lovers, 1910s sex radicals believed marriage bound women to men in a property relationship, and they endorsed "free" unions based on sexual attraction and emotional closeness. Yet they departed from their predecessors in their experimentation, with multiple partners outside the bounds of their marriages. Havelock Ellis suggested that variety in partners could fuel the passions and that emotional faithfulness was more important than sexual fidelity.[53]

Although one historian characterized sex outside of marriage in the early twentieth century as "a personal form of direct action as risky, as thrilling, as full of a paradoxical sense of play and deadly responsibility as throwing a bomb," Stevens engaged in a number of premarital sexual unions, at least two of them with married men. She carried on a fervent, secretive correspondence from the suffrage trail with a married radical labor lawyer and the chairman of the Federal Industrial Relations Commission, Frank P. Walsh, himself a suffrage supporter, from 1914 to 1916. He wrote her in 1915: "I wanted to make love to you right there while I was making that speech. I knew all the time the desperate nature of the game a man plays with the Suffragists, but ... 'I don't Care'—I would join the d___d movement on your account. . . . I just love Beautiful Doris, & her eyes, & lovely hair & flashing teeth & 'pinkness' & warm divine little girl-woman body & her sweet understanding mind & all her girly-womany tricks." In 1916 he wrote: "You know Doris darling, My Beautiful One, we Just came together. As a Man and Woman, or boy & girl, & thus it has been & always will be. I hate that awful mixture of beliefs . . . Causes and Sex. . . . You're my girl; my little sweetheart; my Beautiful Doris & would be if you were Queen of the World and I the Ashman, or if you were Mother Jones and I was Secretary to the Most odious Plutarch." In another letter Walsh implored Stevens to "come to me soon again in the flesh" and signed it "Your faithful, faithful Lover." When Stevens deprecatingly called herself "a primitive woman," Walsh responded ardently: "You will always be girlish womanly & fine. The primitive woman indeed! So you are—So you will ever be—That and everything else, though! The Belmonts et al. couldn't remove that unless they cut off your breasts, broke your legs so you would lose your beautiful carriage, took the light from the wonderful eyes, made the soft fingers so they could not twine, dulled your mind & tore out your soul! You primitive ones, free & beautiful will save all, even the faded rheumatics & other."[54]

Although Alva Belmont disapproved of sexual experimentation, New Women like Stevens continued their adventuring. Unlike their feminist forerunners, their lives were lived in the midst of men. In one letter Walsh complained to Stevens, "Your letters contain a running account of your many New Men." In another he queried, "I am wondering how you spent last night. . . . Did you dance? With whom did you dance? Where did you dine? Who was the lucky guy?"[55]

When Walsh refused to divorce his wife or engage in a more open relationship with her, Stevens fell in love with another married man and radical lawyer, Dudley Field Malone, whom she eventually married. In 1919 Malone endearingly dubbed Stevens "my Dutch English love-child economist"; the next year he prompted her, "Don't you think you ought to get me a tiny apartment or small suite at some small family hotel . . . so that whenever possible we can have some privacy." In another letter Malone declared, "All night long, my darling beast I slept with your little old rose colored kimono wrapped in my arms . . . my body is torturing me to bring it to be near you & feel your nearness in glorious contacts." In another frankly erotic letter he wrote Stevens in 1921, eight months before their marriage, "Beautiful love with the white throat & arms & those full glorious pink nippleless breasts. I am mad to lie close by your satin limbs & feel the throb and thrill of your beating body. Plan to come to me soon."[56]

The historian Leila Rupp has speculated that Stevens was not entirely comfortable with her role as "free woman in the sexual revolution," which may have been true.[57] She made all her lovers burn her letters ("it's the hardest sting in the world for me to destroy your letters," Walsh protested), and went to lengths to hide her liaisons from Alva Belmont and Alice Paul who, though near in age to Stevens, was apparently celibate. Stevens cautioned one of her lovers not to write her at NWP headquarters. "Better not send personal cables as they will surely be opened by AP." When she and Paul sailed from Paris together in 1931, her lover Mitchell wrote Stevens: "If you should come back on the same ship as Paul, maybe you wouldn't want me to meet the ship at all. Just cable me, & we'll meet in Croton. . . . (If Paul comes to Croton I could maybe secrete myself in the neighborhood . . .). Or couldn't I masquerade as a suitor of Fanny's, & bring the car in, & take your bags etc."[58]

Despite their expansive rhetoric, female partners in these new relationships were often disappointed in men and privately expressed their conflict, ambiguity, and pain to one another.

Although Walsh refused to divorce (and seemed to ask to be caught in his adultery), when he sensed Stevens drifting away he wrote her with longing: "I know what's the matter. It is another man. You d____d enlightened and independent women have that way about you. I love you more than anyone else I have ever seen. . . . I would give the whole world if I could inhale your presence today. I mean have you right here near me where I could touch you and feel you and smell you. I would love you to death." A close friend wrote her several months later: "I had puzzled almost as much as you over that sudden stoppage of heart-overflow on the part of F.P.W. . . . He is a Roman Catholic at heart. . . . Perhaps, as you say, he is secretly hoping the lady will die. Then . . . he would marry you. . . . But to divorce the wife; much less to come out in a fine, undeceitful free relation with you—that he would never do."[59]

Stevens's closest woman friend, the poet and reformer Sara Bard Field, whom she had met in the suffrage movement, suffered her own heartaches with her philandering lover, the writer and attorney Charles Erskine Scott Wood. He too was married, although they eventually married after a decades-long affair.[60] Poignantly, many of the letters between Stevens and Field brimmed with their doubts about the possibility of achieving equal relationships with men. For her part, Field dealt with Wood's serial extramarital relationships by commiserating with friends like Stevens and befriending her husband's lovers.[61]

Christina Simmons has argued that sex radical practices ultimately fulfilled men's needs more than women's. Part of this dynamic rested on still-prevalent views about male and female sexuality and gendered roles. White women faced more surveillance and social judgment than white men because of their identity as potential wives and mothers. The easy access to sexual knowledge and autonomy that men enjoyed was more difficult for women to achieve.[62] Women of other races were held to different standards as well. Middle-class African-American women were held to a stricter level of respectability and sexual propriety than were men because the racist suspicion of immorality made them potential targets of male assault. Despite their own naïve sense of possibility, modern feminists underestimated the tenacity of social expectations about women's sexual, maternal, and domestic roles.

Feminist social scientists were well aware of the different consequences sexual emancipation posed for women and for men. In *Greenwich Village, 1920–1930: A Comment on American Civilization in the Post-War Years* (1935), the sociologist Carolyn Ware noted that in those circles where the women tried to achieve a genuinely emancipated status trouble often arose because men only paid lip service to the principle of equality and took advantage of the women's seriousness to exploit them. "The changed attitudes toward sex," she wrote, "were much more of a wrench for the girls than for the men, for the latter could fit the facts of freedom and experimentation in sex relations into the tradition of the double standard which they might have officially abandoned, but which remained an essential part of their attitude." In contrast, she concluded, young women had the "whole weight of their tradition against them." When sexually emancipated women talked about and practiced sex equality they really meant it, while the men often did not.[63]

Rather than leading to independence and self-realization, multiple sexual partners placed women at risk of unwanted pregnancy in a time when the success of birth control was uncertain, their financial abilities to support children singlehandedly was quite limited, and social censure against unwed mothers was strong. While sexually "modern" women understood the limitations of marriage, they also recognized that it offered wives protection from social exclusion and economic want. Women needed the protective institution of marriage more than men did, and many women in the sex radical camp, including Stevens and Pruette, still sought to marry.[64] They optimistically believed they could reshape marriage and use it as a laboratory for new ways of thinking about working women and male-female relations. But remaking marriage proved exceedingly difficult for modern feminists.

While non-monogamy ostensibly gave women the extramarital freedom long available to men, many sex radical men were reluctant to share traditionally masculine prerogatives. Some historians have interpreted early twentieth-century men's impulses for multiple sexual encounters as a longing for experience, a desire to "consume" women, tied to male privilege and the new era of consumption. Some men wanted a secure claim on one woman while also having sexual access to others, but were jealous when women took the same liberties.[65] This was true with Stevens and her first husband Dudley Field Malone.

Some progressive men recognized their inability to make sustained commitments. Philandering bohemian Floyd Dell later recalled that lustful men routinely quoted Carpenter and Ellis to convince women "that love without marriage was infinitely superior to the other kind, and that its immediate indulgence brought the world, night by night, a little nearer to freedom and Utopia."[66] Max Eastman, Stevens's next-door neighbor at her summer home, described in his memoir *Enjoyment of Living* how Stevens wryly teased him about his "trunk complex." Whenever a lover moved in with Eastman, if she brought only a small bag or suitcase, the relationship generally went well. But if she came carrying a trunk, Stevens noted, the affair was ill fated.[67]

It is also possible that non-monogamy was simply not as attractive to women although some, like Stevens, valiantly tested it.[68] When, in her first marriage, Malone criticized Stevens's talents and responsiveness as a lover and turned to other women, she retaliated by having a one-night stand with an Italian cavalry officer, "to try herself out as men have always done to confirm their belief in or their distrust of themselves." She described the incident in her personal papers, under the heading "Episodes which cause trouble":

> D [Dudley] accuses X [Doris] of inadequacy—frigidity—repeatedly X solemnly determines that the next time a man not too unattractive pursues her she will try herself out. . . . X does so—ascertains—& dismisses Desmond. . . . She had to be practically lassoed to the rendez-vous and against eloquent pleadings, left promptly after the encounter & did not stay the night.
>
> She got just this from the experience.
>
> If that can be achieved with some one about whom you do not care, it can be thrice achieved with the one you love. And X was pleased & happy in the knowledge that now all would be well.

Stevens described the pivotal encounter in an unpublished fictional piece. "She had a delightful time and found out what she wanted to know, that there was nothing terrible nor frightening about making love and also that she was not a frigid woman. . . . She would have had qualms at so having used him as an experiment except for the fact that her new knowledge and her new estimate of herself were the most important results of this encounter. She felt grateful to him and liked all the world." When Stevens told her unfaithful husband about her own adulterous adventure, however, he was infuriated, dashing her hopes to bring the experience as "a gift" to their faltering relationship.[69]

With her marriage to Malone deteriorating, Stevens began a long-term extramarital affair with journalist Jonathan Mitchell. They initiated a correspondence two years after she married Malone, during the summer of 1923, using pseudonyms. She signed her letters as Julia, Peter, or Dreka, and he called himself Hans; they both referred to Stevens's husband as Mr. Tebrick. That year Stevens wrote Mitchell from Paris, and remarked that she had bought the ancient Indian text on human sexual behavior, *The Kama Sutra*, in a tiny French book shop: "It purports to be an amply appendiced source book on the art of Brahmin lovemaking," she informed him. "Casually I survey the sub-titles and find one which reads, 'Obstacles aux rapports avec une femme mariée.' . . . Aha, thinks Doris, I'll see what they are and circumvent them. I give you the opening sentence as is: 'One is allowed to seduce the wife of another, if one is willing to court the danger of dying of love for her.' There you are. I thought I'd better hasten and tell you what will be expected of you according to the wise ones."[70]

In their twelve-year affair, Stevens and Mitchell believed they were breaking new ground, inaugurating new and finer associations between men and women that would lead to a gender-egalitarian world. They were not alone in their idealism. By the 1920s, Americans associated sex with leisure and self-expression, and popular culture made love and sex increasingly visible as men and women mixed and mingled in public spaces.[71] Feminism would pave the way to the prevalence of the "human sex," only incidentally divided into male and female.[72] When Malone reacted with violent jealousy to his wife's admission of infidelity, Stevens turned to Mitchell and, as he later recalled, "she tried to impart . . . to give . . . her treasures to me." Unlike the possessive Malone, Mitchell was open-minded about sharing Stevens's past experiences. Stevens was adamant he accompany her to Fiesole, Italy, the place hallowed by the cavalry officer, whom Mitchell philosophically viewed without competition or anger, but rather "as a part of Doris, as much as her father and her brothers." In a 1927 debate in London, Mitchell publicized his and Stevens's sexual philosophy, advising the audience on how to improve their sex lives and reshape the world at the same time. He suggested that "the highest grade of love affair" could only be achieved by a mutual, wholly free giving and taking between partners. He maintained that leisure and play were essential to successful love affairs, and were the key to "enabl[ing] these love affairs to blossom to their fullest extent, to imprint the love pattern upon the whole of life, and to make a world of loving men and women."[73] Mitchell's emphasis on leisure and play suggests how far the pendulum had swung for white middle-class men, who in an earlier period viewed self-control and delayed gratification as key to successful lives or greater perfection. His vision also underscores supportive men's embracing the modern feminist ideal of a world where the sexes mingled, as "fellows in a world-building enterprise."[74]

Homosexuality never entered Stevens's analysis of sexual liberation, despite the fact that she discussed it with friends, some of whom were lesbian or bisexual, and she recorded dreams of sexual experiences with women. Since (hetero) sexuality became a symbol and testing-ground for the beauty and equality possible between modern women and men, homosexual relations seemed backward looking, life without a mate of the opposite sex, unfulfilled and intellectually barren.

Both Mitchell and Stevens at times invoked the anti-lesbian ideologies and language increasingly circulating in the 1920s. Mitchell contended that both Alice Paul and British women's leader Lady Rhondda had "serious defects," due to "their retreat from the most important relationship of living." The next year, as Stevens's relationship with Paul grew increasingly strained, Mitchell was less charitable. "I don't see anything to be done about Paul," he wrote Stevens in 1932, "except to say she has partial paralysis of her social impulses & make allowances for her. You can't reason with or about sick ones."[75]

It is possible that Stevens's ambivalent attitudes toward love, sexuality, and marriage led to her homophobia. Leila Rupp suggests that Stevens's love for Sara Bard Field, if not placed in the context of their mutual heterosexuality, would have been too threatening.[76] Some of the correspondence between Stevens and Field does point to an extremely close attachment. Shortly after she began her affair with Malone, Stevens wrote Field that, although Dudley was devotion personified, still Sara was "the only human in my life whom I love without reservation." "I love you more than any human being—yes my love for Dudley doesn't touch yours." Field responded by relating her need for Stevens and warmly recalled "that night when I held you close for a time and kissed your dear eyes and brow and felt I was laying my love at your heart's door." In the same letter Field returned to the topic of men and their tendency to disappoint: "He really loves me, Doris, as much as men *can* love which, except when they are about ready to die . . . is not very much."[77]

Both Stevens and Mitchell ultimately believed Stevens's most important contribution as a feminist leader was her embodiment of the symbolic potential of heterosexual love. "Auxiliaries are dreadful bores," she declared in 1927 to an audience in her hometown of Omaha, Nebraska. "The only fun in life is where men and women play together, and men and women work together."[78] In 1928 Mitchell proclaimed Stevens "an artist in human relationships." "Because of that" he declared, "there is no person alive who compares with you as a leader of women." "There is no one who sees life with as high & lovely an [*sic*] conception of it as you do," her lover rhapsodized. "I've read Ellis, & seen or read everyone I can find who is excited about living beautiful lives, & I know no one who has put themselves into the thing, & come out with such satisfying conclusions as you have." When Stevens was named chairman of the Inter American Commission of Women in 1928, Mitchell wrote her excitedly:

> It's magnificent, sweet, sweet, heart, my heart. . . . It means new broad avenues down which men & women can go hand in hand.
> Hand in hand is a swell phrase. Not one helping the other, taking his or her arm, not one guiding the other, nor carrying them, nor leading them— none of that. Two people walking free & erect, & touching each other for no other reason except they love each other. . . . I think, & professionally believe, that if the right people & enough people could know you, that is all that need be done to make feminism all established as a policy of society. . . . Firsts are what Dinsche [his pet name for Doris] accomplishes. Her life can be told with each part beginning "the first time a woman ever . . ." You are the lovely shoot which our tree of society sends out into the sun & wind.[79]

This statement captures the buoyancy and faith with which modern feminists and their male allies viewed the newly gender-integrated world. Their ultimate inability to realize gender equality and dismantle in one generation deeply rooted attitudes did not dampen their public enthusiasm for sexual emancipation and modern marriage. Their private conclusions, however, were different.

Even a dedicated sexual modern like Stevens wondered if love with men was really so much more magnificent than female friendship. In a letter to Frank Walsh, she described love as "Old stuff" and "dangerous for a feminist." When Field agreed, admitting that her lover C.E.S. Wood "covers me as a man *can* love," Stevens responded that this made her "quite sad for I know it's true. Even dear unselfish Dudley hems me in so that it is he or no one." She was torn over whether separatism in institutions, organizations, and possibly even love relations could be the more effective route to feminist strength and self-determination. Despite her commitment to the NWP, a woman-only organization, her strategy emphasized cooperation and collaboration with men.[80] She defined feminism in 1946 as "nothing more than the attitude of women toward the relations between them and their menfolk."[81] Occasionally Stevens doubted her own ability to live with and sexually love men while devoting her life to the causes of women. In 1924 she described to Mitchell a telling dream:

> Had a wild dream the other night—several other girls and I were more or less in bed with a strange, unidentified, unattractive male. All the others got out—I stayed against my inclination mostly because he maneuvered to keep me there. Finally I too got away but not in time to be on the dot for a memorial meeting at somebody's tomb. I had carefully prepared a small white silken banner on which I had written in ink in very round clear letters the names of all the 250 women who went to jail. My contribution to the ceremony was to cast this banner into the tomb before it was closed. I got there and the ceremony was over. Reproachful looks were thrown at me until I explained how disappointed I was, and what my memorial plan consisted of. Then the other women became sweet and tender and said "never mind. We'll have a bigger and better ceremony soon and then you can deposit your banner." Which I took to mean that my work would survive in spite of any detention by the male.[82]

Perhaps a feminism that believed in the possibility of a life lived on equal terms with men and that discounted patriarchy and men's dominance of power was misguided. Twentieth-century feminists had to reckon with this uncertainty.

The Evolution of Disenchantment: Lorine Pruette

Pruette offers a second example of a modern feminist's encounter with the early twentieth-century sexual revolution and represents another cautionary tale. As a psychologist, Pruette interpreted changing sexual behavior and attitudes; as a New Woman, she plunged into the maelstrom. This dual positioning—one foot resting on theory, the other on personal experience and practice—makes her vantage point unique. Pruette recognized the double-edged sword sex could be for women, because of men's and women's different resources and power and the persistence of social attitudes about gender-specialized roles. Ultimately she concluded that sexual "freedom" was repressive for women and dangerous to feminism.

Eight years younger than Stevens, Pruette's twenties spanned World War I and the postwar era (1916–1926). Like Stevens, Pruette married twice but she also divorced twice: she married in 1920, divorced in 1930, remarried in 1932, and divorced two years later. She then remained single for the rest of her life, more than forty years. She experimented with non-monogamy and hoped men would join women in "new unions" which would allow women to remain independent, continue their careers, and reject domesticity.[83] In their idealized efforts to forge new, egalitarian relations in a world in which women joined men in the public sphere, both Stevens and Pruette prefigured the conflicts of a later generation.

On the one hand, Pruette epitomized modernity and the feminist embrace of sex radical ideas and practices. When she embarked on a national speaking tour in the early 1930s, she was introduced as "one of the most alert and capable analysts of American psychology today," and as "a distinct product of the twentieth century" (though she was born at the tail end of the nineteenth). In her frankness about sexuality, her Freudian insistence on its centrality in infancy and childhood, her ranking of birth control as more important than suffrage, and her advocacy of sex education in school and home, Pruette's ideas were removed from nineteenth-century views. She too hailed Edna St. Vincent Millay as "the prophet of my generation" and believed a "magnificent new freedom" would emerge from the loosening of Victorian sexual restraints.[84] When she donned her social scientist's hat, her views became more sober.

The pros and cons of women's careers, the link between masculinity and breadwinning, and gender roles within the family were all topics taken up by social scientists in the 1920s, who believed their expertise was critical to the modern social order. The disciplines of sociology, psychology, anthropology, economics, and political science were carved out and rapidly growing. A new emphasis on sex differences in mental functioning held sway as psychologists reexamined femininity and opposed the goals of feminism, including women's desires for self-definition. Influential psychologists John B. Watson and Floyd Allport applied an instrumental approach in the decade to argue that individuals should adjust to social norms.[85] Pruette, whose master's thesis was titled "A Study of the Mores and the Totemic Concept," believed the opposite. She argued that the development of reason and scientific inquiry gave individuals the tools to free themselves "from the necessity of giving blind, unreasoning obedience to the demands of the group and to the force of old traditions and mores." "More and more as this process of rationalization goes on," she wrote, "will each of the great institutions, the church, the family, the state, become secularized and open for experiment."[86] As a young psychologist lecturing and writing about the problems of reconciling women's desires for love, work, and individuality, Pruette raised her voice against this reactionary tide.

She launched her early career in a period of unprecedented debate and scholarly contention in the field of psychology. In the final year of the suffrage movement, 1919 to 1920, Pruette earned a master's degree in sociology from Clark University in Worcester, Massachusetts. It was there that she met G. Stanley Hall, who was recognized for launching the new psychology at Johns Hopkins University in the 1880s. The founder and president of Clark University for thirty-one years, Hall was one of Freud's earliest American supporters. Of Hall, Freud wrote in his 1914 history of the psychoanalytic movement: "Who could have known that over there in America, only an hour away from Boston, there was a respectable old gentleman waiting impatiently for the next number of the *Jahrbuch*, reading and understanding it all, and who would then, as he expressed it himself, 'ring the bells for us'?"[87] Organizer of the famed 1909 Clark Lectures, the first and only forum in which Freud presented his theory of psychoanalysis to an American audience, Hall and his students anticipated many of Freud's ideas in their own work on sexuality, genetic psychology, and child psychology.[88] Never totally devoid of his Puritan worldview or his idealization of women, Hall initially believed the sublimation of sexual urges led to human creativity and that "the woman soul" would elevate humanity. In Pruette's words, Hall "dreamed of a feminism in which women should be free to follow the dictates of their hearts, but in which those dictates would make them increasingly feminine. For the older rebel type of feminism, aping man's roughness and man's attire, he had little use; but for the aspirations upward and outward of the woman he showed an eager interest."[89]

Although Pruette knew Hall for only the last four years of his life, she met him at an impressionable time. Twenty-two years old and casting about for a profession, trying to break free from her mother's dominant influence, Pruette found Hall (seventy-six in 1920) the mentor and father figure she needed. She was Hall's graduate student for one year, attending all his lectures and auditing his famous Monday night seminars. When troubled at Clark, she visited his office and left "revivified, new-made, able to face again the problems of living." For four years Hall read and critiqued everything Pruette wrote, including her Ph.D. dissertation *Women and Leisure*, which like his major work *Adolescence* (1904) focused on teenagers.[90]

Pruette considered Hall's 1924 death a catastrophic event in her life. Three years later she published *G. Stanley Hall: A Biography of a Mind*, her tribute to the man who brought her "stimulation and joy," inspired her career, helped her better understand her own psyche, and eased her occasional gloom. After graduating from Clark, Pruette moved to New York City and entered a Ph.D. program in psychology at Columbia. Much later she recalled the youth culture, intellectual elitism, and narcissism of the times. She described "the childish cynicism of the twenties in America" for youth as a period when "obviously anything was possible and the world was our oyster." In her first year of graduate study, Pruette announced carelessly "to a small enraptured group—some of whom were older and should have known better" that she planned to die before forty. There was no reason to live beyond that age, she declared, as in fact there was no reason to live in the present, except it was rather fun. Later she described this pleasure-seeking, youth-centric philosophy as "the modern version of hedonism."[91]

Despite her immersion in this existentialist academic circle, her first real mentor had powerfully imprinted Pruette's thought. Because Pruette's enigmatic ideas on masculinity and femininity reflected Hall's influence, his theories are worthy of a brief description. Like many of his contemporaries, Hall feared that "overcivilization" endangered men and argued that American boys should receive a "virile" education. He considered modern civilization effeminizing; middle-class men could remake manhood by getting in touch with the "primitive" and "savage." In his youth Hall suffered from a tortured sexuality, absorbing the common cultural belief of the time that sexuality was sinful and must be restrained or it would drain "nerve energy." Ambivalent about manly self-control, he believed in the masculine power that stemmed from an iron will and strong character.[92] After *Women and Leisure* was published, Pruette went on a national tour delivering two popular lectures, "The Modern Woman" and "The Decline of the Male." The ideas she disseminated strongly bore Hall's imprint and publicized men's insecurities about women's entry into the workplace and other public arenas.[93] In these talks Pruette sympathized with men, whom she described as being manipulated and outmaneuvered by the sexual, newly mobile, public Modern Girl.[94]

After Hall died, Pruette began reading the work of Alfred Adler, whose ideas on the inferiority complex and men's "striving for power" predicted some of the challenges modern feminists encountered as they tried to forge egalitarian lives with men. She first met Adler in 1926, when he visited the United States. In 1930 she traveled to Vienna to study with him, attending his lectures, meeting regularly in a coffeehouse with him and his graduate students, visiting his country home, and for a time helping edit *The International Journal of Individual Psychology*. A Swiss general physician, Adler succeeded Freud as president of the Vienna Psychoanalytic Society in 1910, but broke with him a year later over Freud's emphasis on sexuality as the basis for neurosis.[95] With a small group Adler established the Society for Free Psychoanalytic Research, through which he developed and spread his theory of Individual Psychology. A socialist who wrote the first paper on Marx and psychoanalysis, Adler emphasized the sociological—rather than the repressed—consciousness. Inferiority and its compensation, a desire to rule or be above—which, significantly, he termed the "masculine protest"—formed the cornerstone of his theory.[96]

Hall and Adler influenced other psychologists in the early decades of the twentieth century who, like Pruette, found masculinity and femininity deeply interesting areas for exploration. Their fascination hinged on the very real stakes at play—as women entered the public sphere, who would tend to the private sphere of home and family? Would men lose authority and power as women joined them in workplaces and as newly enfranchised citizens and political actors? Three American psychologists were included in feminist journalist and editor Freda Kirchwey's series of seventeen self-reflective autobiographical sketches by feminists published in the *Nation* in 1926–1927.[97]

The psychologists Beatrice M. Hinkle, John B. Watson, and Joseph Collins contributed to the "modern women" series. The tone of their essays, published under the heading "Explaining Women," ranged from optimistic approval to misogynist rants, and demonstrated the aggressive role social science played in prescribing sexual and marital roles in the 1920s. Beatrice Hinkle, a feminist, Heterodoxy member, and Jungian psychoanalyst, was reluctant to make sweeping generalizations. "What is the real inner cause of the revolt in the souls of these women?" she asked. Adler, she stated, would call them "victims of the masculine protest" and would interpret their revolt as an expression of an inferiority complex that led them to refuse to accept the traditional submissive role. Freud would diagnose them as "suffering from a castration complex" and explain their rebellion as an inner protest against the fact that they were not born men. She believed their attitude was "a normal protest against external collective restrictions." Although she did note that this group of women was "weak on the side of their women's nature," she concluded that "their attitude is part of a great rolling tide which is bringing to birth a new woman," one who could stand beside man as his equal.[98]

The male psychologists' sexist, stereotyped interpretations illuminate the very real threat feminism and women's new public roles posed to the masculine establishment. Titling his essay "The Weakness of Women," Watson, arguably the most influential American psychologist of the decade, declared: "These women were too modern to seek happiness; they sought what? Freedom. So many hundreds of women I have talked to have sought freedom. I have tried to find out diplomatically but behavioristically what they mean. Is it to wear trousers? Is it to vote—to hold office—to work at men's trades—to take men's jobs away from them—to get men's salaries? Does their demand for this mystical thing called freedom imply a resentment against child bearing?" Continuing in this dismissive tone he queried, "When a woman is a militant suffragist the chances are, shall we say, a hundred to one that her sex life is not well adjusted?" Neurologist Joseph Collins focused on the feminists' reluctance to become mothers: "There are many good reasons why the majority of women should not have ten to twenty children, but there are many more and better reasons why they should have from five to ten." Sounding the pronatalist

tone then endemic in the United States he declared, "the 'best' stock is showing the smallest reproduction," and determined, "I have a hunch that the sex-
coefficient of many of these writers is low." He ended his essay by stooping to
the level of speculation and asked, "which of these women should I have liked
to companion?" He selected two, the first Pruette, of whom he wrote: "[She]
had strong, lusty desires and she wished more than anything else to have
'swift feet that she might run after them.'" At thirty-one one of the youngest feminists included, Pruette poignantly titled her essay "The Evolution of
Disenchantment."[99]

Pruette changed her mind about the "magnificence" that would flow from
heterosexual freedom because she believed the younger generation misunderstood it and men misused it. She was troubled by flappers' disinterest in
feminism and their apolitical focus on men, sex, beauty, and self-fashioning
the body. She argued that they translated her generation's independence
in responding to "primal urges" into "the old game of follow the leader."[100]
Whereas her generation linked sexual emancipation with revolutionary ideas
(gender equality, emotional liberation, freedom), 1920s youth knew nothing
of this historical context in their conformist compulsion to be sexually active
at all costs.

The available statistics on early twentieth-century sexual practices among
American youth point to a dramatic behavior shift in the 1920s. A 1938 survey
of 777 middle-class women revealed that although 74 percent born between 1890
and 1900 retained their virginity until marriage, only 31.7 percent born after 1910
did.[101] In Alfred Kinsey's landmark *Sexual Behavior in the Human Female* (1953),
based on 5,940 white women, he found that young women of the 1920s differed
more from their generational predecessors than any subsequent generation differed from them. The largest increase in "petting" and premarital sexual intercourse, extramarital intercourse, and orgasm in marital intercourse occurred
between the group born before 1900 and those born in the first decade of the
twentieth century.[102] By 1934, Ira S. Wile, M.D., could state in *The Sex Life of
the Unmarried Adult* (Margaret Mead, Mary Beard, and Lorine Pruette were
the three female contributors to the collection): "the old pleas for freedom and
individualism have found expression in freer sex behaviors and more open sex
relations between unmarried men and women."[103]

In addition to her trepidations about oversexed youth, Pruette voiced concerns about homophobia. Women who grew to maturity in the late nineteenth
and early twentieth centuries, she argued, often experienced overt homosexuality and emotionally powerful relations with women that were safer and more
satisfying than modern women's trysts with men. Citing Davis's study, Pruette
noted that one-third of the one thousand married women interviewed had
experienced homosexual encounters after puberty. Half of the 1,200 unmarried women had participated in relations with other women. When she was

a fourteen-year-old schoolgirl in 1910, Pruette recalled, "we were not so well informed about the proper names for things; there was a little edge of disapproval about the girl who paraded her 'masculinity,' and the girl who went 'too far' was, of course, frowned upon, but within limits there still remained a genuine and important outlet for eroticism, without any guilt attachment." That outlet was "the schoolgirl crush," when one girl "thrilled to the young loveliness of another girl," and acted on that attraction by "innocent" caresses and exclamations of love. Pruette recalled at twelve being "jointly in love with the minister and the minister's daughter." She believed attitudes toward close female relationships shifted from acceptance to distrust in her lifetime. "The closing of other channels," she warned, "may conceivably send the girl at an increasingly early age into the frankness of a heterosexual relation."[104]

Although she rebelled against the sexual hypocrisy and repression rampant in her native South, such a culture, Pruette concluded, at least "allowed the individual some chance of living according to his own tempo." Modern sexual mores forced young people to "busy themselves with flaming bright red when all they want is to be a mild and more salubrious pink." When, in her early thirties, Pruette attended a college gathering that turned into a drunken orgy, she returned home feeling old, sick, and disillusioned. "Sex may be for those boys and girls a tragedy and a glory, a diversion and a nuisance, but that night, for most of them, it was merely a trivial extra stimulant." "Certainly if this was being modern," she fumed, "no one would ever again have the right to hurl that epithet reprovingly at me."[105]

When young people felt compelled to be sexually active, Pruette asserted, they gave up choice and lost sight of the emotional and spiritual meaning that informs sex. She urged the flapper generation to revive romanticism, "based not on the Victorian gulf between the sexes but on a very binding acquaintance." "Love is an art to be learned like any other," she argued, and sex is "exactly what we make it." Sex without context or commitment became a physical reflex rather than an ideal of conduct which "involve[s] the pursuit of the good and the significant in human relations in preference to the commonplace and the trivial."[106]

While Pruette believed flappers misinterpreted (or knew nothing of) her generation's idealistic rationale, she was most angry about men's misuse of women's commitment to sexual freedom. Her resentment stemmed from her own disappointing relationships with men. Yet her thought and writings on men and masculinity are conflicted and contradictory, both feminist and anti-feminist, which may reflect the fraught nature of these discussions in the 1920s as well as her own internal demons. Although she moved through her teens "secure in the shadow of the virgin's blue veil," Pruette lost her virginity as a Columbia graduate student in 1920, with a fellow student to whom she was engaged. She recalled this as the first of many unremarkable sexual encounters. "Since this was the Flaming

Twenties, and we were intellectuals," Pruette wrote, "we felt morally obligated to anticipate the ceremony. Scared half to death, we checked into a small hotel. We tried, we really tried. And in the morning, the small pin prick of blood, attesting virginity on both sides."[107]

Pruette believed her life was burdened by men's insatiable sexual demands, which undoubtedly influenced her thoughts on male and female sexuality, as well as the potential that new relations with men had for reshaping modern feminism. Like Stevens, she was attractive, with thick red hair, small features, and what she described as "a husky voice and sensual mouth" which "made the men conclude hopefully that I was much more passionate than I really was." "All my life," Pruette candidly noted, "I have felt sorrowful, even guilty because I could not participate in all of the tangoes [sic] that were proposed to me. It was not that I was easily tempted to love; I was easily impelled to compassion when the pallor and the damp brow, the short breath and the trembling indicated a state of heat." Such intense pressure for heterosexual relations was, Pruette concluded, the final outcome of sexual emancipation, one dangerously repressive to women.[108]

There were deeper personal reasons for Pruette's guilt and obligation to sexually satisfy men: they reflected her ambivalence about her parents' marriage, and her intellectual admiration of G. Stanley Hall's ideas about masculinity. In his early writings Hall argued that puberty predisposed men to an inappropriate sexual expression, which exhausted their social "capital" and weakened their development into masculine men. By the time Pruette met him he had changed his ideas, arguing in the two-volume *Adolescence*, which Pruette surely read, that rather than being dirty, sex was holy. If boys' sexual energies were properly channeled, their sexual awakening was like a spiritual awakening in the Protestant tradition of religious conversion. Herself conflicted, partly because of her childhood role as the apex of the triangle made up of her demanding mother, her gentle father, and herself, Pruette found herself torn between Adler's theory on the masculine need to rule and Hall's beliefs about men's needs to be manly. She also was responding to an apparent crisis in masculinity. According to the historian Michael Kimmel, American men in the 1920s anticipated a return to normalcy after World War I, but instead many grew increasingly restive as work seemed dull and routine, women invaded previously all-male sanctuaries, and the machine age led them to question their own meaning and potency. The financial crash of 1929 and the ensuing Great Depression exacerbated these concerns. Such a climate may help explain men's reluctance and inability to meet the high expectations modern feminists like Stevens and Pruette brought to their "new" relationships.[109]

Despite her own hesitation about sex radicalism, in the early 1930s Pruette had an intense extramarital affair with the man who became her second husband. Even though she fell in love—"the earth-shaking, intolerable, obsessive, devastating thing"—with an educational theorist and painter, John Woodbridge Herring, her attitude toward sexuality differed from his. A pair of poems Pruette and Herring wrote for each other offer some suggestive glimpses.[110] While Herring's "Lines for a Lady," published in *Poetry Quarterly* in 1931, focuses on his sensual attraction to Pruette, her responding "Courage," printed in the *New York Herald Tribune* in 1933, depicts male sexuality as burdensome and divorced from love.

LINES FOR A LADY

I
Elinor of the strange and lovely eyes
Of the brave and tender eyes that have grown used
To inward gazing on images of poignant beauty
Upon a world that has too little time
Or thought, or skill, or grace for dreams and beauty.
Sometimes I think I see within these depths
A deeper conflict moving, where eager wings
Are tugging at the weights that hamper them,
In protest that outlives their wearying,—
Until my lips do tremble as I smile at you.

II
The night is lighter than the day,
      Or so it seems to me,
When banished stars come back to beck
      The heart's rich errancy.
The clumsy thrusts of median sun
      I banish joyously.
Exultant that the soul defies
      The wilting of the noon.
You are to me an Indian night
      Suffused with intimate stars
Where earth and heaven are gently met
      In one another's arms.

III
You have lived luxuriantly from the brown earth into the upper air.
You have sunk your roots deeply and without fear.
You have drunk up only the clear liquor of the soil.

You lift with graceful strength your spirit in the air,
I cannot share with you in the upper air
Until I have twined my roots with yours

Until I have drunk from the nurture of the soil.
My roots are pulsing through the earth to yours . . .
I feel the thunder of primeval song.

Courage
Now that I no longer know you as pressing need, inescapable urgency;
Now that the light beat of your hands holds no threat of anguish, and
    no promise;
Now that you have ceased to be the encompassing night
Wherein I formerly hung suspended, impaled and crucified;
Now that desire is fled and we sit quietly in remembrance and kindness
I can say what then I dared not say—I love you.[111]

The contrast between the two poems exemplified Pruette's evolving thought on the differences between male and female sexuality and the broader implications this held for early twentieth-century feminism. Herring's poem was erotic; although he recognized Pruette's romanticism and daring (her "strange and lovely eyes" searched for the world's "dreams and beauty"), he could not join her "spirit in the air" (he compared her to an Indian night and a graceful, strong tree) until he "twined" his roots with hers and drank with her from the nurture of the soil. He concluded the poem with a thinly veiled statement of sexual intent: "My roots are pulsing through the earth to yours . . . / I feel the thunder of primeval song." In contrast, Pruette's sexual experience in the poem is set in the context of *his* need, which is described as "pressing" and "inescapable." Only after desire ebbed and they ceased to be lovers and became friends did she tell him what then she "dared not say," that she loved him. The courage that she lacked was the bravery to insist on the connection between love and sex, an association early twentieth-century male sex radicals scorned. All Pruette's sexual metaphors in "Courage" are violent and intrusive. She believed sex radicalism was detrimental to women's self-development. At the same time she thought women had a responsibility to sexually satisfy men, a conundrum that contributed to a life that was often unhappy.

Pruette took up the topic of sex in a controversial novel she published in the later years of the Depression. In *School for Love* (1936) she proposed that commitment and love be returned to sexual intimacy. Heralded in the *New York Times* as a book that "goes as far as any of the young English writers have gone on the road to frankness concerning what used to be forbidden subjects," *School for Love* treated premarital sex directly, disdained promiscuity, featured male impotence, and ultimately celebrated sex as a communion between two people in love and about to marry. The story of a twenty-one-year-old woman from Chattanooga, Tennessee, who visits post–World War I Paris to buy her trousseau and has her first sexual encounter with an older married man, the novel is frank in its treatment of sexuality, yet describes a philosophy of sex in which the emotive, spiritual components are foremost, the purely physical a distant second. Of their hometown daughter's "French novel with localized characters," the *Chattanooga News* admonished, "We shudder to think of the arguments that will be forthcoming when local pride focuses attention on this book.... Certainly Miss Pruette could not have written this book in Chattanooga.... She could not have been mentally in Chattanooga and written it."[112] Forty years old and living in New York City as a twice-divorced writer and consulting psychologist, Pruette had traveled a long distance, both physically and mentally, from Chattanooga, Tennessee.

Pruette offered two solutions to the problems she believed the new sexual code inflicted on women: restore commitment and meaning to heterosexual intimacy or return to the homosocial world. Although both were conservative in their avocation of a return to earlier sexual mores, her message was often misunderstood as radical. Pruette argued that the new morality met neither woman's physical nor emotional needs and that the consequences of promiscuity affected women much more negatively than men.

In a 1934 article on the sex lives of single men and women, Pruette maintained that due to the automobile, sexually stimulating movies, the disappearance of the chaperone, the increased freedom of working girls and women, the dissemination of birth control information, the greater ease of association between the sexes in smoking, drinking, and athletics, "we no longer protect the virginity of our girls." She did not welcome this as a positive trend for women or society. Pruette defended abstinence as a legitimate choice for both sexes. In 1927 she had published *Saint in Ivory*, a novel commemorating the fifth-century Parisian patron saint and virgin, Genevieve. Three decades later, when she witnessed the 1960s sexual revolution, Pruette expressed her disapproval to historian William O'Neill, stating, "Promiscuity is not the road to freedom."[113]

During the 1920s. Pruette recognized the younger generation's amnesia about modern feminists' venturesome efforts to remake the human sex.[114] She linked women's increasing interest in men to their diminishing commitment to each other and to the loss of the single-minded dedication that a profession had represented to an earlier generation. She understood how difficult it would be for women to fulfill both public and private roles. She wrote in 1924: "When I was fourteen, back in the dim ages, wild horses could not have dragged from me the admission that I wanted a boy. Probably I did, although I cannot now resurrect any memory of such a yearning, but when I had much later come into an awareness of some of the delightful possibilities of the defective sex, I know that I was a little ashamed to admit this to myself because it seemed that I was deserting from that stern band of young maidens who were growing up with contempt for such silliness and with a masculine protest that made them whisper 'careers' in the rapt tone of the god-inspired. But, another day!"[115]

Although they adopted the new sexual mores as their own, the younger generation increasingly considered feminism old-fashioned and irrelevant. In 1924, when she published *Women and Leisure*, feminism was "still a fighting cause, with some remnants of glamour." Three years later, Pruette described American women under fifty as falling into three groups: first were "those who struggled for independence of action, who have against legal and social disqualifications fought their way into positions of importance, who bore the brunt of the fight begun in their day and who never quite lost their bitterness toward men." Second was "a younger group which knows less bitterness because it has known less of the struggle." The third was "a still younger group that is frankly amazed at all the feminist pother and likely to be bored when the subject comes up." She wrote: "The flapper knows nothing of that tedious world against which the old-line feminists rebelled. She knows nothing of the fight and cares less. 'Feminism?' She asks nonchalantly. 'Oh, you mean antiman stuff? No, I'm not a feminist.' Nothing is so dead as the won causes of yesterday; there is no reason why she should think of herself as a feminist; she has inherited feminism."[116] The historian Nancy Cott's analysis of 1920s youth concurred. "The younger generation looked across the generational divide and saw Victorian sensibilities," she wrote, "as though the venturesome Feminists of the 1910s had never existed."[117]

Stevens and Pruette ultimately believed that sexually liberal relationships primarily benefited men and acknowledged that women continued to be splashed with the paint of the old double standard. As Stevens told her first husband Malone, "I was the poor apostle of freedom; you were the communicant who profited from my doctrine."[118] She may have expressed her true feelings in an unpublished play she wrote about a sexually emancipated woman who, ultimately disappointed, concludes that "the world is full of lies. . . . The man, if he is celibate, is called a holy man. The celibate woman, a spinster." The play highlights sex radical men's duplicity in saying one thing to women and believing and practicing another. "We've been fools to believe you so long," Stevens's fictional protagonist concluded. "If virginity is good for us it's good for you. If it's not, it's bad for both."[119] Pruette concurred, remarking in 1934 that despite the fact that the term "double standard" was no longer fashionable, as a social control it continued to flourish. She wrote, "The double standard is simply a protective device used by both men and women to proclaim that what is sauce for the goose is not sauce for the gander, or vice versa."[120]

Still most women of this new generation believed male-female relations and marriage were the sine qua non of savoring life's pith. Yet combining marriage and career was difficult, as was conceiving of oneself as a heterosocial feminist, one who devoted her life to the cause of women while living in the midst of men. Even such a determinedly modern woman as Stevens wondered pensively at times if her "detention by the male" would lead to the destruction of her work for women. In what must have been one of her darker moments, Stevens wrote her equally pioneering friend Sara Bard Field, "I am sure the emancipated man is a myth sprung from our hope and eternal aspiration."[121] Such were the bogeys that confronted modern American feminists as they danced on the edge of a new and heterosocial world.

CHAPTER 4

Old Ideas versus New

MATERNALISM AND EQUAL RIGHTS

Where most sex radicals sought to separate women's sexuality from marriage and reproduction, maternalists elevated motherhood. In social policy, they focused on maternal and child welfare and drew on maternalist language and strategies to transform motherhood from women's main private responsibility into public policy. The meanings of the term were ambiguous, but historians have defined maternalism as "ideologies and discourses that exalted women's capacity to mother and applied to society as a whole the values they attached to that role: care, nurturance, and morality."[1] Maternalism was the powerful idea that Mary Beard had summoned in *Women's Work in Municipalities* when she argued that women's care work in the home should extend to cities and societies.[2] Motherwork—women's unpaid work of reproduction and caregiving—was at the heart of maternalist philosophy.[3]

The roots of maternalist thought lay in republican ideas about gendered citizenship (mothers' roles in raising citizens), the Victorian separate spheres ideology, and mothers' politics of the late nineteenth and early twentieth centuries that emphasized women's political significance to the state.[4] Maternalists generated searching critiques of government and society. Their visions included a caring state in which women played roles as voters, policy makers, administrators, and workers, both within and outside the home. That the majority of maternalist thinkers and movements could not muster the political capital to reshape social policy does not diminish the historical importance of their vision or legacy.[5]

Maternalist discourses were often competing and taken up by diverse interest groups, including legislators and government personnel, social workers, philanthropists, employers, and wage earners of both sexes, who disagreed on the "proper" social roles of women, children, and the family.[6] Maternalist narratives existed in relation to other discourses—about citizenship, class, gender, and national identity, among others.[7] Maternalist thinking ultimately reinforced

95

gender roles, as it emphasized women's responsibilities within the family. Its prescriptions modernized gender inequality by politicizing and codifying social roles and relations. Maternalist ideas impaired women's ability to operate in the labor market as equal workers with men and challenged the modern feminist idea that women could have meaningful work in the world and egalitarian relationships with emancipated men. In connecting women's citizenship to the maternal ideal, such prescriptions ultimately denigrated the role of women's paid labor, and legitimated a gender-segregated work force.[8] The National Woman's Party (NWP) challenged these old ideas as it unswervingly stood for women's right to equal opportunities in the labor force.

THE BEST WAY FORWARD

Feminists jockeyed for new positions and goals in the post-suffrage years. The press and jittery male politicians were uncertain what impact the "women's vote" might have on the nation.[9] Former suffragists were concerned that women with whom they had worked closely might join different political parties with contrasting points of view. Friendships forged during suffrage might be endangered. The *Woman Citizen*, the publication of the National League of Women Voters (LWV), cautioned in September 1920: "Now that the vote is won . . . women who have worked hand in hand for years find themselves split up into members of all the different political camps. They are sometimes aligned in opposition to those who have been their closest friends. This opposition is inevitable; but let us resolutely make up our minds that it shall not interfere with the friendship."[10]

Despite this advice, feminists sustained the divisions of the suffrage movement as they sought to influence legislation and public policy. Maud Wood Park presided over the creation of the Women's Joint Congressional Committee (WJCC) in 1921, an umbrella group intended to coordinate the legislative agendas of women's organizations that shared the social reform emphasis of the LWV. The NWP was not one of its ten member organizations, which included the General Federation of Women's Clubs, National Consumers League, National Federation of Business and Professional Women's Clubs, National League of Women Voters, National Women's Trade Union League, and the Women's Christian Temperance Union, all organizations that supported maternalist thinking.[11] The WJCC's adoption of a maternalistic program and rhetoric explains the legislative success and public approval the committee enjoyed in the early years of a politically conservative decade.

The 1921 campaign for the Sheppard-Towner Maternity and Infancy Bill, led by the WJCC, exemplifies the ways social feminists invoked maternalist ideas. Addressing infant and maternal mortality and expanding Progressive era concerns with children's health and welfare, if passed by Congress the bill would place the administration of babies' and mother's programs under child welfare divisions within state boards of health. On April 25, 1921, the Senate Committee on Education and Labor opened hearings on the bill. Park testified that nearly every national women's organization supported it (the NWP was glaringly absent), and the millions of women represented made the pending bill their first legislative priority. The Senate approved it by a wide margin and sent it to the House. After a twelve-hour debate, the House passed the bill in November 1921, also with a large margin. The successful women's lobby had drawn powerfully on the language of sex difference and maternalism, appealed to politicians' and the public's reverence for motherhood, and cast themselves as mothers with "mothers' hearts." The passage of the bill represented the government's acknowledgment of the importance of healthy mothers and children to the public good.[12]

In sharp contrast, the Equal Rights Amendment (ERA), proposed two years later, called for the recognition of women's rights as individuals and citizens, rather than as wives and mothers. Authored by Alice Paul, the succinct amendment read: "Men and women shall have equal rights throughout the United States and every place subject to its jurisdiction." The ERA conflict strained friendships and divided women's organizations. The ERA struggle came to center on protective labor legislation, but the ideas of maternalism were deeply embedded in the controversy. Social feminists had worked long and hard to win minimum wage and maximum-hour work laws for women (keeping in mind women's needs as child-bearers); they were concerned that the proposed amendment would eliminate such laws. Early on Paul was willing to be flexible on this point, suggesting in 1921 that the problem be addressed "by raising the standard of protective labor laws for men until they are equal to those now in existence . . . for women." At this critical juncture, organizational jealousy, personal hostility, and ideological conflict won out, and the differences hardened on both sides.[13] Some feminists, like Inez Irwin and Mary Beard, sought a middle ground and a conceptual umbrella large enough for both sides. However, singular efforts went nowhere.

Women's economic independence was also at stake in the struggle over protective labor legislation and the ERA. Tied to liberal theory rooted in individual rights, equal rights feminism equated economic independence and political participation to full citizenship. Independent wage earning—trumpeted on the *Equal Rights* masthead as "a man's chance, industrially"—meant discarding the legal protections social feminists had spent two decades working to win. New state labor laws adopted at the end of the nineteenth and early twentieth centuries had included restrictions that recognized women's vulnerability to exploitative or arduous working conditions and the value of their dual roles as mothers and wives as well as workers. At the same time, these laws denied women the liberty enjoyed by other workers, as they wrote into legal precedent a conception of citizenship that was rooted in motherhood and family life.[14]

Like earlier suffrage organizations' disagreement over tactics, women's rights groups in the 1920s squabbled over the most effective way to address gender discrimination. A blanket amendment, NWP leaders believed, would make all discriminatory legislation illegal, and they advocated equality for women across the board. In opposition, the LWV endorsed gradualism to attack inequality. Park reflected in 1933: "The LWV from the beginning has stood for step-by-step progress. It has been willing to go ahead slowly in order to go ahead steadily. It has not sought to lead a few women a long way quickly, but rather to lead many women a little way at a time."[15] NWP members were unwilling to wait for the myriad discriminatory state laws to be individually overturned.

Party members objected to the ways that gender-specific labor legislation set women apart as a separate group of seemingly second-class citizens who were unable to care for themselves and required protection. Attorney Alice Paul alleged that legal equality was incompatible with acknowledging gender difference. While not all equal rights feminists agreed, most did concur that women should be granted the same legal status as men. In contrast, maternalists emphasized women's gender and their roles in the family as rationale for their opposition to the ERA. They contended that the NWP's naïve, reckless approach overlooked the complexity of women's lives.

The ERA symbolized divisions over class and social philosophy that went to the root of the meaning of women's emancipation. It captured differences in ideas and strategy between social feminists and equal rights feminists, still smarting from their disagreements in the suffrage years.[16] In addition, the 1920s NWP was tiny and provoked hostility among women who led other organizations. Whereas the WJCC boasted twelve million members and twenty-one affiliated organizations at its 1924 peak, the NWP at its height in 1920 had only fifty thousand members.[17]

Although small, the NWP continued to exert an outsize influence. In a 1922 *Ladies' Home Journal* article titled "Women as Dictators," Alva Belmont— elected to the titular role of NWP president in 1922—argued that women must remake the political structure by creating a third, all-female political party.[18] Even more radical was her suggestion that until the NWP could remake the maculinized political system, American women should abstain from voting. While the *New York Times* conceded that "Much might be said for the view that men have made a mess of the world, and that government by women or even by children couldn't be worse and might be more intelligent," it concluded that Belmont's vision was both unrealizable and flawed. Paul privately agreed, concerned that the NWP did not have the resources to become a third force in American politics, and quietly downplayed the idea, redirecting energy and attention to equal rights. She was able diplomatically to convince Belmont that this was the best way forward.[19]

An Internationalist Bolshevist-Feminist Plot

In addition to intrafeminist disagreements, a conservative shift in national affairs made politicians wary of all women's organizations, which made a collective feminist project difficult to realize. The speculation that women would vote as a unified "bloc" had been disproved, which caused women to lose their political standing and potential clout. Between 1924 and 1930 conservatives, patriotic groups, former antisuffrage organizations, and employer associations joined forces to "red-smear" any one they believed was trying to increase the role of the federal government in industry and human welfare. The 1917 Russian Revolution, which had destroyed the tsarist autocracy and led to the creation of the Soviet Union under the Communist Party, fueled this fear. American women's organizations, especially the WJCC and its far-reaching legislative agenda, were caught up in the witch hunt.

Right-wing attacks greatly diluted organized women's ability to advocate for social reform during the 1920s. Successful attempts to link the WJCC's membership and agenda to communism weakened the committee and its public support. Rebuttals from groups like the Boston-based Woman Patriots (formerly the National Association Opposed to Woman Suffrage) followed the victorious passage of the 1921 Sheppard-Towner Maternity and Infancy Bill. In congressional testimony, Woman Patriots dubbed the bill "an internationalist Bolshevist-Feminist plot . . . to put over Russo-German 'welfare' measures and systems leading to a Soviet form of government." The WJCC's subsequent crusade for a child labor amendment to give Congress the power to "limit, regulate and prohibit" the labor of those under eighteen passed both houses of Congress in 1924. Despite valiant efforts by social reformers, it ultimately went down to defeat. Due to resistance from manufacturers, farmers, and laborers (who often depended on their children's incomes), in the end only six states voted to ratify the amendment.[20]

Conservative assaults led to the publication of the notorious "Spider Web Chart" showing connecting threads among US women's groups, Russian communist groups, and international pacifist organizations. On March 15, 1924, the *Dearborn Independent*, a newspaper founded by Henry Ford, published an article, "Are Women's Clubs 'Used' by Bolsheviks?" The anonymous author described US women's organizations controlled by an "interlocking directorate" of communists, socialists, pacifists, and other subversives who were following orders from Moscow. It specifically targeted the WJCC consortium. One week later, the newspaper published a chart depicting fourteen national women's organizations linked in a web of communist conspiracy. Although conservative attacks on organized feminism had a history in the United States dating back to the early nineteenth century, the fact that a number of 1920s women's rights organizations did have ties to international and peace-oriented groups and that several of the leaders were socialists gave sticking power to these assertions.[21]

Despite its militant suffrage activism and radical call for an equal rights amendment to the Constitution, Paul's NWP was not included in the Spider Web Chart. The party's stance against sex-based industrial legislation placed it in agreement with the National Association of Manufacturers, which waged a vigorous fight against the child labor amendment, considering it an entering wedge for protective laws for all workers and a greater federal role in industrial affairs. WJCC members duly noted the similarity between the NWP's views on protective legislation and those of manufacturers.

This was the broader context in which Irwin, Beard, Pruette, and Stevens pursued their feminist goals in the 1920s. Beard, who had split with the NWP over what she considered its increasingly elite focus, tried to stay aloof from disagreements that divided friends and colleagues, though her ideas in the 1920s and 1930s demonstrate her sympathy with maternalist philosophies. For her part, Irwin chose to stick with the NWP after suffrage and endorsed their equal rights goal, but like Beard she too engaged with the ideas of maternalism. A reading of their ideas in these decades deepens our understanding of the diverse, creative ways that a small, self-appointed vanguard of modern women carried feminism forward in life and work in the post-suffrage years.

Mary Beard Deploys Maternalism

Beard's ideas in the post-suffrage decades reflected her confidence in maternalism. She rejected the individualism she believed women's professional ambitions represented and was drawn to the reform agenda and collective philosophy of social feminists. In books she published in these years, especially *On Understanding Women* (1931) and *America through Women's Eyes* (1933) Beard articulated the importance of women's concerns with "the care of life" and the magnitude of their roles in the home.

Beard's stance reflected her conviction that the single-issue goal of legal sexual equality was too narrow an approach to gender questions. She anticipated some of the dangers and limitations of the modern feminist ideal. Advocating sexual equality, in her view, embraced meritocracy and overlooked the needs and interests of women of different races, ethnic backgrounds, and classes.[22] Her sustained attention to mothers' long working hours, sweatshop abuses, and wage-earning women's need for legal protection led her to disagree with the ERA. Beard shied away from confrontation, however, and instead moved deeper into studying and writing women's history as a way to seek unity for all women. She privately expressed her objections to the proposed amendment and on occasion shared lengthy explanations with close colleagues and friends. In July 1921, she wrote Elsie M. Hill, then NWP national chair: "As for the federal amendment, it seems to me it would overthrow all protective industrial legislation for women and I can't see why it wouldn't also do things like conscript women for war. If 'equal opportunists to the bitter end' want that result, the amendment seems to hit the mark. I am not one of the party especially since my return from this last trip abroad where there is so much industrial equality that women sweep the streets and till the land while the men drink in the cafes."[23]

She described feeling more comfortable with state bills to address women's rights, because they left room for protective legislation. She contended that, because of potential maternity, women required special protections under the law. "I am perfectly aware," Beard remarked, "of the factions that rally around that [federal] policy. I am not an ultra feminist on that point because in my mind children do add a complexity to women that they cannot add to men and I see no way of removing it entirely for the best interests of both sexes as well as the children." Beard told Hill that she was continuing to pursue feminist goals, but in her own manner. "Best wishes to my erstwhile pals," she wrote, "and please tell them that I am working as hard as they in the way that seems to open best for me."[24]

The method that seemed best to Beard for furthering feminism in the quarrelsome 1920s was through intellectual collaboration and co-authorship with her husband. Mary's forty-eight-year marriage to Charles Austin Beard—warm, exciting, and compatible from all accounts—offered her a positive experience of marriage and motherhood that informed her writings and thoughts. The two historians spent much of their married life in a rambling, sixteen-room Connecticut farmhouse, which they shared with their two children and a myriad of visiting friends, fellow activists, and political comrades. A former boys' school, it was, their daughter later noted, "too big for an ordinary household," but "not for *their* household, *their* weekend guests, their house was like Grand Central Station, filled with people coming and going, and father letting out his enormous voice from dawn to dusk."[25] A visiting journalist described the Beard home, which boasted seven thousand books but had no telephone, radio, or television, as a paradise for bookish people and artists.[26]

If it became a problem to harmonize so many different types of people ("father's lawyers and sewage engineers might not mesh with his historians; none of them went very well with the . . . suffragettes or fiery personalities like Rosika Schwimmer," their daughter recalled), her parents avoided giving parties and instead invited certain groups at a time to their home. When Mary or Charles were less than enthralled with each other's colleagues or friends—"Father's municipal experts bored mother; her wild women got on father's nerves," their daughter explained—they both simply saw their "difficult chums" in town.[27]

Not only was the Beard marriage rooted in a network of kin, neighbors, friends, intellectuals, and activists that extended the boundaries of their family, it was moored in a shared commitment to work. Their careers overlapped: while his drew Mary into the worlds of academics and international relations, hers drew Charles into the universe of suffrage and feminist politics. Charles Beard taught at Columbia for thirteen years until he resigned in 1917 in protest over the "arbitrary dismissal" of several antiwar faculty members. In 1940 he accepted a one-year position as professor of history at Johns Hopkins University in Baltimore. Yet despite a prolific career as scholar and public intellectual, after he left Columbia he never again had a permanent affiliation with an established institution of higher education, nor did Mary Beard.[28]

Her marriage to, and collaboration with, Charles deepened Mary's commitment to labor issues and strengthened her belief in the need for gender-specific legislation. In 1920 she published *A Short History of the American Labor Movement*, intended as "a brief and simple story of the labor movement in the United States," directed at an audience of busy citizens.[29] With other activists and educators, the Beards created the Workers Education Bureau in 1921, described as a national clearinghouse for workers' education enterprises. The bureau, independent of any union or labor federation, sponsored conferences for workers, created correspondence courses, and sent a traveling library to unions across the United States.[30] It represented both Beards' belief, which stemmed from their experiences with Ruskin Hall at the dawn of the century, that education should be connected to social change. "Mere learning in the form of collection of facts will never free the world," Charles remarked in a 1900 speech. Mary echoed this belief in a 1933 talk before the International Congress of Women: "action without thought is perilous," but "without action, whatever our thought, we are futile. It is not enough to know; action is as essential as knowledge."[31]

Mary and Charles were professional collaborators who coauthored nine important, widely read books. Their co-authorship began with *American Citizenship*, a 1914 high school civics textbook, included the highly praised 1927 *The Rise of American Civilization*—which historian Richard Hofstatder said "did more than any other such book of the twentieth century to define American history for the reading public"—and followed with *America in Midpassage* (1939), *The American Spirit* (1944), and *A Brief History of the United States* (1944).[32] Because no letters between the two are known to exist, their collaborative method is something of a mystery, which seems fitting since their shared philosophy was to shun publicity and let the writing stand on its own.[33]

Although Charles Beard's career was more publicly recognized than Mary's, their attitudes suggest a marital camaraderie. When editors, critics, and readers overlooked Mary in their collaborative ventures, Charles protested. Mary Beard privately wrote Florence Kitchelt, "Reviewers often imply that the whole product is C.A.B.'s in spite of the fact that he had never written on cultural themes before so I appreciate your willingness to count me in, in view of the way I drudged on the work for three years and especially since the cultural side was my hunch—not just women."[34]

Mary Beard publicly made light of her lack of recognition in her shared work with her husband, although it must have been disheartening and frustrating. She good-humoredly recounted to Rosika Schwimmer an incident that occurred at the conclusion of a meeting about the World Center for Women's Archives, a national archives project Beard led during the 1930s. "I was so amused by the remark of one of the Southern women present yesterday," Beard wrote in 1935. "'I know your husband's work very well,' she said. 'Why don't you do anything yourself?' I was so proud of myself for smiling only. I think I am moving ahead in my personality." When her magnum opus *Woman as Force in History* was published, Beard wrote a friend: "I am deeply moved by Mr. Stonier's commendation of my book, even though he does not realize that I have published several books independently of my good husband."[35]

Yet if the public slighted Mary's part in their collaborative writings, Charles contributed in important ways to the work that was considered hers alone. Both she and the Congressional Union had depended on his reputation to support their suffrage activism. When she testified before the U.S. House of Representative's Committee on Rules in 1913, Beard prefaced her remarks with "Gentlemen of the committee, I always represent my husband when I speak on suffrage."[36] Not only did he contribute his constitutional knowledge to the struggle for a federal suffrage amendment but Charles also aided Mary in the research and writing of *Woman as Force in History.*[37]

During the 1920s, Beard deepened her maternalist ideas as she moved forward on what would be an enduring legacy of her life's work: to generate historical research for the purpose of social reform.[38] Her views on women's history evolved dramatically over her lifetime. As a newlywed in England she had read Charlotte Perkins Gilman's *Women and Economics*, which led her to criticize women as overly domestic, excessively feminized house slaves. Her very first article, published at twenty-four in two parts in the journal of Ruskin Hall, "The Twentieth-Century Woman Looking Around and Backward" (December 1900) and "The Nineteenth-Century Woman Looking Forward" (January 1901), foreshadowed a theme she carried forward doggedly the rest of her life: the incompleteness of history without "the deeds and the words" of women. Yet early in her analysis she saw women contributing nothing to civilization but children, and women and wives as beasts of burden or male property. Although she did not cite Gilman in this early article, her words channeled her ideas. Beard affirmed, "Woman has never been human. The desire to be feminine and to please men has made for a most unnatural, oversexed individual." Like Gilman, Beard exhibited "a principled disdain for domesticity" and proposed collective solutions to women's domestic servitude, including communal cooking and shared laundry services. Only through education and paid involvement in the production and distributions of wealth outside the household could women take their proper place beside men in the world outside the home.[39]

Beard wrote *On Understanding Women* (1931) later in the 1920s, when she first called for a more complex view of the feminine past. In doing so, she intentionally complicated the discourses about maternalism. Beard was fifty-five when this book was published. Ranging over prehistory, ancient, and modern history, she wove women into the tapestry. She argued that women had always been active historical agents, whether as upper-class housewives in ancient Greece (who, "from that center of seclusion exerted an influence reaching beyond the boundaries of cities and states"); as soldiers in the Roman Empire; or as settlers in the New England wilderness. She praised women's essential and historical role as caregivers and preservers of life.[40] In a 1932 book review in *Equal Rights*, Sue Shelton White described Beard as "a feminist sounding a challenge to modern men and women, to reinstate the woman-principle in the study of history and in social thinking." *Cherchez la femme*, she noted, is the guide Beard suggested for those who seek historical truth. "This would mean," White realized, "a complete re-writing and a new approach almost revolutionary." She described Beard's concern with the woman-principle as different from mawkish sentiment praising the "mother instinct," but as something more profound. "The individual 'mother instinct' may be translated into social philosophy and action."[41]

Beard's 1933 anthology *America through Women's Eyes* brought together women's documents in a reader she hoped would demonstrate that women had been an integral part of the development of the United States. Again she argued for women's centrality in history: "woman has always been acting and thinking, intuitively and rationally, for weal or for woe, at the center of life." Taking a swipe at the nineteenth-century US women's rights movement, she criticized the rapid industrialization that brought it into being, and forced women out of their homes and into factories and workplaces, where like men they embraced "competition for place, income, and power." "Women were no longer women," she wrote, "they were competing units in a society of competing units called 'human beings.'" Trumpeting her maternalist views, she exulted: "If there is in all history any primordial force, that force is woman—continuer, protector, preserver of life, instinctive, active, thoughtful, ever bringing thought back from sterile speculation to the center of life and work."[42] Recognizing a volley at the NWP's equal rights agenda, an anonymous reviewer in *Equal Rights* sniffed, "We would not have chosen from such material as Mrs. Beard did," and faulted her for barely mentioning the women's rights movement and its pioneers Susan B. Anthony and Elizabeth Cady Stanton, ignoring Emma Willard and her fight for women's higher education, and overlooking Margaret Sanger and the birth control crusade.[43]

Beard expressed a sense of loss over the historical narrowing of the social functions of the family, the shrinking of its role as the site of production, the institution responsible for educating children, caring for the elderly and ill, and transferring craft skills. Because she believed modern career women and men had replaced the mutuality of this older system with individualistic values, she denounced "careerists" as "capitalistic entrepreneurs or retainers of the bourgeoisie." In a revealing 1939 article, Beard praised American pioneer women who, in contrast to "the 'career girl' morbidity of a machine age," worried little about recognition or women's place, but "simply went about their businesses perfect and imperfect doing what they could and liked to do." She lauded her own dead mother, who first worked as a schoolteacher for no pay and after marriage devoted herself to furthering her husband's career. Modern feminists, "so rabidly competitive and so capitalistically confident . . . divorced from the good earth, dweller[s] in cities . . . bourgeois to [their] toes," would do well to explore women's history, Beard believed, and understand the economy and culture of an older America which underlay their own activities and desires.[44]

Because Beard admired women and men who were motivated by collective rather than what she considered individualistic goals, she denied throughout her lifetime that she had a career. "I'm not a 'woman of achievement' or a 'career woman' or a Ph.D.," she stated unequivocally in 1946. "I'm a woman who works. Works at what? Works at self-education, and I've been brash enough to write my feelings." In 1955, on the publication of her fifteenth and final book, *The Making of Charles A. Beard*, a reporter for the *Indianapolis Star* interviewed Beard. When the female journalist asked Beard, then seventy-nine, how she felt about having provided such a great educational heritage for the American public, she responded that she viewed it all as simply "no career." "I just did what I thought I might be able to do," she stated quietly. "But in your books on women," the reporter persisted, "*America through Women's Eyes, On Understanding Women. . .* wasn't that a career?" "Why no," Beard replied, "I just got interested in them— being one myself."[45] Her sympathies led Beard to devalue or ignore the very real dilemma some middle-class women faced, of how to achieve satisfying lives in both public and private spheres. Her stubborn thought on this issue was closely linked to her conception of women as creative actors in history who brought a uniquely feminine, life-preserving, and civilizing force to masculine enterprise and action.

While Beard celebrated the positive aspects of women's traditional familial roles, she never admitted the oppression women could experience as wives and mothers. Nor did she empathize with women who succumbed to patriarchal authority. "Women who are willing to cringe before nasty husbands are weak creatures by choice," she tartly wrote in a personal letter to a friend. In response to a woman who wrote her proposing a research project on women's role conflicts between marriage and career, Beard curtly responded, "I have told you face to face and by letter that I do not regard the state of mind respecting domesticity and a career or women's problems of domesticity itself as a proper phase of collegiate education."[46]

Although Mary was Charles Beard's closest collaborator, it was he who was recognized, publicly lauded, given awards, and offered academic appointments at prestigious universities. She worked on her own, from her home, as an independent scholar. She made light of this and did receive a certain amount of recognition for her scholarship and activism, but in many ways Mary worked in the shadow of Charles's gigantic reputation. "Not only as an historian but also as a political scientist and educator, Charles A. Beard was one of the most influential social thinkers in the United States from about 1912 to 1941," the *International Encyclopedia of the Social Sciences* appraised two decades after his death.[47] Male historians of the 1950s and 1960s who kept the memory of Charles Beard alive— whether through praise or condemnation—paid no attention to Mary's role as coauthor of nine volumes. Such normative thinking resounded in Howard K. Beale's literal erasure of Mary Beard's labor and name from their coauthored texts: "No one knows the nature of their collaboration. . . . Hence, I have always spoken of the joint works as Charles Beard's."[48]

Mary's own generous, loving help to Charles is testament to her belief that women should be supportive of their husbands, as her own mother had sustained her father. When, for example, Charles grew hard of hearing, Mary was faithfully by his side. She wrote Lena Madesin Phillips in 1935, when Charles was to testify before a congressional committee, "I just have to stick pretty close to CAB and his enterprises because he is so helpless without me, being so deaf and generally so dependent on my cooperation. Even so, we generally have the same urges and points of view, if not in every instance." After four decades of marriage, Mary openly told a friend that, because "we are still in love," she would accompany Charles in his year of teaching in Baltimore.[49] More than one outside observer believed the Beards represented an ideal. When Lorine Pruette began a book on husband-and-wife teams (which is itself interesting, given her eventual disillusionment with marriage), Mary and Charles were among them. A 1944 book on "Love in America" included a section on the Beards. When Elizabeth Schlesinger wrote Beard to inform her that she and Charles were included, Beard responded, "We know a lot about love to be sure. Have we advertised that fact?"[50]

Two weeks before Charles died, Mary wrote a friend: "My *beloved* seems much better today—at long last," and added, "You must not think that I deserved any part of CAB's Gold Medal Award. It was given for his *total* work—and justly. (Don't carry sheer feminism too far.) . . . I have been at the hospital after midnight every night but this one."[51] She wrote to their son William about her and Charles's comradeship in work, politics, and life itself: "Outsiders and even you and Miriam because of your comparative youth could not fully comprehend our mutual happiness in working, jabbering, and getting such exercise as we took in our simple ways. THIS IS THE ABSOLUTE TRUTH."[52] As she moved into her late seventies, Beard insisted, over her children's objections, on remaining in the sprawling New Milford house in the summers, because it was the home she and Charles had shared for forty-five years. She lined the walls of her office with his pictures, and kept Charles's study just as he had left it. In 1951 she confided to a friend, "Come April, I plan to be back in my home. . . . I shall have my precious workshop and the open door to Charles' workshop with the memories of our togetherness as my treasure for abiding here while I keep able to work and remember." When, after three years of widowhood, a friend inquired if she were lonely, Beard responded, "Lonely? Yes—at times for my departed perfect Charles with whom I could chatter, as he could talk to me, for nearly fifty years. But I must refuse to let loneliness make me obviously miserable or wretched of soul. Work is my salvation."[53] Realizing that "work on my part is courage," she carried on as a widow "for the mastery of grief and the enrichment of the invisible continuing companionship."[54]

Inez Haynes Irwin Challenges Maternalism

At the same time that Beard was crafting nonfiction to influence feminist and historical thought, Irwin was writing novels that plunged into the debate over maternalism and equal rights. In *Angel Island* (1913), *The Lady of Kingdoms* (1917), and *Gertrude Haviland's Divorce* (1925), she reconceptualized motherhood as a route to women's liberation and self-actualization and a stimulus for change in a violent, masculinized world. Like Beard, Irwin was influenced by Charlotte Perkins Gilman, who offered a forceful vision of motherhood along with a call for a radical reconstruction of family life. On the eve of World War I, Gilman had optimistically declared the dawn of "motherhood as social service instead of man-service." Men, she maintained, "have wasted women's lives like water, and the children of the world have been sacrificed to [their] sins. Now we will have a new world, new-born, new-built, a mother-world as well as a father-world in which we shall not be ashamed or afraid to plant our children."[55] Although a bloody war eclipsed the new world she envisioned, Gilman's interpretation of maternalism attracted Irwin, who built upon it in her novels.

Although she enjoyed a long and happy second marriage, Irwin's thoughts on marriage and motherhood were influenced by an unhappy first marriage and the punishing domesticity she observed female relatives shouldering in her youth. After her first, seventeen-year marriage ended in divorce, Inez married her longtime friend William Henry Irwin three years later and shared her life with him until his 1948 death. Like the Beards, Inez and Will Irwin shared the same profession and seem to have mutually supported each other's work. An 1899 Stanford graduate, Will Irwin was managing editor of *McClure's Magazine* and *Collier's Weekly* before becoming a free-lance journalist and war correspondent. His *New York Times* obituary described him as one of the most valued and distinguished of the popular journalists of his era.[56]

From most reports, the Irwins were sympathetic colleagues who helped and abetted each other's careers. Inez described authorship in the house with Will Irwin as a double delight; both morning writers, "we two fortunates could play together all the afternoon and evening." "We read each other's manuscripts, accepted each other's suggestions amicably, or indulged in battles royal.... I never interfered with his work. And I was not one of those wives who went snooping through his waste-basket looking for scorned and rejected masterpieces."[57] The early years of their marriage, however, may have been different. Bohemian poet Louise Bryant suggested that the two were professionally competitive. She wrote her lover John Reed in 1917 (the year after Inez married Will) that the Irwins were "so *jealous* of each other's work." In Will Irwin's 1942 memoir *The Making of a Reporter* he described his travels with Inez during World War I, but she is featured as an unnamed wife lacking any profession.[58] A 1923 *Time* magazine article on Will Irwin and his younger brother Wallace, a novelist, was titled "Their Wives Are Literary, Too," which suggests that despite her prolific publications, Inez Irwin, like Mary Beard, was often overshadowed by her husband. The article describes Inez as an author of children's books and short stories.[59] Despite these hints of competition, Irwin portrayed their shared vocation as a positive. "He developed in me a mental curiosity, a passion for logic of thought and clearness in the expression of it," she wrote. Like Charles Beard, Will assisted Inez with the research and writing of her women's history book *Angels and Amazons*.[60]

The Irwins lived in a century-old brownstone on West Eleventh Street in Greenwich Village for thirty years and summered in Inez's large house overlooking the ocean on Boston's North Shore. Although Irwin shared much of her life with Will Irwin, she also shared it with her sister Daisy, who lived in Inez's home for decades. Their brother Harry Haynes built a summer house next door, demonstrating her deeply rooted family ties. Although she had no children of her own, Irwin borrowed other people's babies and toddlers by inviting them to live with her, and she enjoyed a warm relationship with her stepson from her second marriage. She wrote Charlotte Perkins Gilman in 1921, urging her to come and visit at their Scituate, Massachusetts, home, which she painted as a communal, multigenerational, summertime paradise.

> Our household, when *you* come, will consist of (1) the angel-husband, Will Irwin, (2) My sister Maud Duganne (mother of Phyllis who is, as you probably know, at twenty-one the author of a book and a baby) (3) Mrs. Thompson, one of Heterodoxy and (4) her lovely baby (nearly two and a half) Inez-Elizabeth, known as Duck and (5) myself. . . . Our house is a lively one; people appearing often in the course of the day. . . . We are not fashionable. . . . No company in the morning because everybody writes; . . . There is clematis and honeysuckle under your window. . . . Lobster right out of the water; sword-fish, fish chowder; fresh berries; . . . Everybody laughs all the time; Come or I'll MURDER you.[61]

The only way Irwin could accept being married was as a financially independent woman, tied down neither by domesticity nor a husband's competition or demands, a theme she powerfully echoed in some of her finest novels. The imperative for financial independence was stronger for Irwin than for Beard.

Beard's childhood home had been comfortably upper middle-class, while Irwin's parents had struggled with money problems, many children, and constant efforts to stretch the family budget. Irwin vowed she would never find herself in her parents' predicament, and she never did. She also considered women's economic self-sufficiency a feminist imperative.

Irwin was able to find the "angel-husband" willing to meet her requirements, an important achievement that provided her an emotionally sustaining marriage with autonomy to pursue her own creative work. Like Beard, Irwin described her married social life as "constant and surging," and wrote Park: "Will Irwin is the most gregarious of mortals, and in addition, is more full of talk—comment on the news, on books, on things; reminiscence, episodes; anecdote, experience. In this respect, he is the most brilliant creature I have ever known. He loves people. Because he loves them so much, I entertain as many for him as I can manage." The Irwin marriage was brightened by laughter and mutual respect. Husband and wife good-naturedly teased each other over their leadership in competing writer's organizations and their differing college allegiances. When he questioned her grammar, asking, "Didn't they teach you better spelling than that at Harvard?" she retaliated, "Stanford, a western man's idea of a university." They not only laughed together, they cried together as well. Irwin wrote Park that she must go see the film version of *A Midsummer Night's Dream*: "Will Irwin and I wept together over it."[62]

However compatible they were, Inez and Will Irwin's marriage also allowed room for individual opinions and, like the Beard marriage, decades of intellectually companionable talk. When deported anarchist Emma Goldman was allowed to briefly visit the United States, Inez presided at the dinner in her honor; the same evening Will chaired at a very different dinner, one for Herbert Hoover. When word spread at the Hoover dinner that "Will Irwin is chairing here and Mrs. Irwin is chairing for Emma Goldman," one man tersely commented, "the Irwins would!" Irwin explained the success of their marriage by describing their relationship as not only that of husband and wife, but of very good friends.[63]

The fact that Will Irwin was himself a feminist who was proud of his wife's life-long commitment to women also enhanced their marriage. One of several male speakers at the First Feminist Mass Meeting held in New York's Cooper Union in 1914, in 1944 he proudly described Inez as "the devil who invented the idea of picketing the White House to get publicity for the Woman Suffrage Cause." When an interviewer asked Irwin if she was afraid to picket herself, Will briskly interrupted: "You don't know Inez or you wouldn't say that."[64]

Will Irwin died the same year Charles Beard died, and he left his comrade and wife Inez as bereft, as Mary found herself after the loss of her "departed perfect Charles." "And then, in 1948," Irwin wrote, "death struck me its direst blow. Will Irwin died." "Ah," she recalled, "everyone tried to fill the vast stark, black void of Bill's absence." Nightly after his death, Irwin, who believed in the occult, searched the dark and in the daytime looked out into the bushes and through the trees in their yard, hoping to catch a glimpse of her deceased husband bending over a stone wall, or cutting dead underbrush away.[65]

Four years after his death, a friend sent Inez a picture of the Irwins at work, side by side. "Thank you from the bottom of my heart for sending me that article with so pleasant a picture of my husband and myself working over a manuscript together," she responded. "It brought the inevitable sense of agony, but I am quite willing to pay that price to possess this lovely souvenir of our wonderful life together."[66]

The issue of success, fame, of leaving one's mark on the world as scholar or artist was not one that Irwin or Beard commented on at any length, but it is there nonetheless, in the margins of their own self-assessments and occasional self-denigration. They were both women who found disciplined, creative, intellectual work to be at the center of life and self-identity. At the same time, they were wives who suspected that their husbands—whom they loved deeply—were smarter and more gifted than they. Beard's private letters reveal a lifelong ambivalence about her own capabilities. Sprinkled throughout her letters and speeches—and Irwin's as well—are disclaimers and apologies. Beard had no advanced degree, never held an academic appointment or full-time, paid position, yet she was an intellectual of major stature. She was confident enough about her feminist reading of history that her persistent vision fueled decades of research, writing, and publication, yet she was also quick to call herself "insane" and "a low-brow."[67] Irwin was similarly hasty to denounce her own writings as not important enough to have been written.

In fact, she believed she would have been more successful had she remained single. "I think I might have been a better writer if I had not known Will Irwin," she wrote. "He was so good, so noble, at the same time so electric, so fascinating, the nearest approach to a word I want to use is lovely, that I was more interested in him than in my work." Like Beard, Irwin derided her own work, calling it trivial and unimportant. Much of Irwin's writing has been forgotten. She did, in her own lifetime, however, reap the rewards of public recognition and financial success. She also enjoyed the companionship and love of Will Irwin. She described their marriage as "a forty-four-years old friendship . . . which . . . crystallized into a marriage." "It seems to me," she wrote of their years together, "that it was one long adventure, overlaid with conversation."[68]

In her early feminist years however, Inez believed marriage trapped women in lives of monotony and "soullessness," and vowed she would never marry. In her 1894 diary she wrote grimly of "woman," who "drudges out her meager, pale life . . . giving her roses of cheek and lip, the fire of her eyes to her babies, toils for them unceasingly and dies." "A marriage," she confided to her diary later that year, "would scatter forth all thought of high achievement. I must . . . forget such dreams." In a 1926 essay, "The Making of a Militant," Irwin recalled that in the early stirrings of her young-girl thinking the woman's life had filled her with a profound horror.

> All about me I saw lovely young things marrying, producing an annual baby, taking care of too many children in the intervals of running their houses. It seemed to me that early they degenerated into one of two types: the fretful, thin, frail, ugly scold or the good-natured, fat, slatternly slut. . . . Nothing terrified me so much as the thought of marriage and child-bearing. Marriages seemed to me, at least so far as women were concerned, the cruelest of traps. . . . I made all kinds of resolutions against matrimony. All the time, though, I was helplessly asking myself, how was I going to fight it— when I so loved companionship?
>
> One way, I decided, was not to let myself get caught in any of those pretty meshes which threaten young womanhood. I made a vow that I would never sew, embroider, crochet, knit—especially would I never learn to cook. I made a vow that if those things had to be done, I would earn the money to pay for them. I married, but I kept my vow. I have always paid for them.[69]

Irwin's youthful thought on the hopelessness of combining profession and family was reinforced by her first failed marriage to fellow writer Rufus Gillmore. She married Gillmore in 1897, when she was twenty-four and a Radcliffe student, and he was nineteen. In 1904 she wrote in her diary that Rufus was disgusted with her financial independence; four years later she scribbled, "Arguments with . . . Rufus about the itinerary . . . interrupting all my stories by reading from a magazine and then 'go on with your stories about your girls.'"[70] In 1912, the year before she filed for divorce, Irwin published two searching articles in *Harper's Bazaar*. In "The Life of an Average Woman" she described marriage as "a world which holds out . . . no hope of real independence, personal freedom, or spiritual privacy" and depicted the average woman as "a slim, weak, pale, bowed, weary figure— meek, humorless, inarticulate, standing timidly on the threshold of life, peering through the open door, but not daring to enter." In "Confessions of an Alien," she described herself as "alien to this world." "It seems to me that sociologically," Irwin wrote, "I hang in a void midway between two spheres." While her avocation, which took enormous time and energy, put her beyond the reach of the average woman's duties and pleasures, the conventional limitations of the female lot made the male sphere inaccessible to her. "Life has favored me above most women," she wrote, "in that it has permitted me to do the man's work and has paid me the man's pay." But "the double standard clutches me in an iron grip," she continued, because "it has never allowed me to play the man's game." "And perhaps," she concluded, "I have paid high for my independence—in that feeling of alienage to which I have confessed."[71]

Irwin's 1913 feminist fantasy novel *Angel Island*, first serialized in *American Magazine*, represents her strongest indictment of marriage and brutal masculinity. It also reveals her thoughts on male domination of the female body, as well as the redeeming possibilities of motherhood. It is likely that *Angel Island* was the inspiration for Charlotte Perkins Gilman's utopian novel *Herland* (which has become a feminist classic), which Gilman began writing the year Irwin's book was published. There are striking similarities between the two.[72] Both authors drew on mythic archetypes of communities of women to interrogate gender relations, but Irwin's book is the harsher condemnation of marriage. Dedicated to Maud Wood Park, *Angel Island* is the story of five men who are shipwrecked on a remote, semitropical island and find it inhabited by five beautiful winged women. Physically strong and free, united in their female world and speaking their own language, the winged women are initially curious about the men, who lay claim to them: "I'd like nothing better than the job of taming her," one declares. Playing with the Angel of the House metaphor, another of Irwin's shipwrecked males inquires: "what happens to a man if he marries an angel? Does he become angel-consort or one of those seraphim arrangements?" Increasingly frustrated by the women's elusive, hovering visits, the men begin to consider marriage by capture. "I'm not for it," one says. "A man doesn't get a run for his money. It's too much like shooting trapped game." A second responds: "Oh, well, if the little darlings are not accustomed to chivalry from men . . . that explains why they stand us off."[73] In their desire for the women, the men violently capture them, cut off their wings, and marry them.

To Irwin, who wrote this short fantasy novel during her divorce proceedings, marriage represented women's loss of freedom, the ability to soar, create, enjoy community with women, and control one's own body. Irwin was a life-long lover of the ocean and in the warmer months swam daily up until her seventies. It is significant that the women of *Angel Island* are, until they meet the men, free creatures of the sea and air.

The same physical alterations Irwin had noted with revulsion in her married female relatives she ascribed to her diminished flying women characters. After three years of marriage there were "devastating changes": wingless, fat, domestic ("even though she chattered, she sewed; her little fingers fluttered like the wings of an imprisoned bird"), petulant, restless, melancholy and longing for something more, the five women of *Angel Island* powerfully depict Irwin's worst fears of marriage.[74]

Motherhood, however, infuses new meaning into their circumscribed lives and inspires the women to launch a feminist revolt, which means that the island may see a new type of men and women—equals—who can both fly and walk, as companions.

Three years after the publication of *Angel Island* and at age forty-three, Inez married Will Irwin and the happy, loving, feminist union they achieved must have in part mitigated her earlier despairing assessments of marriage. When Park wrote to congratulate her, Irwin responded, "Thank you dear Maud. I have been terribly unhappy for years. But now I think it's going to be better." Like Beard, Irwin relied on outsourcing, including paid domestic help, to free her from the clutches of housework. Still, she realized the burden domestic chores posed for most women. She exclaimed to Park, "What a problem housework is! I have thought a great deal about it over the years, for I hate it, myself, as I find most women do. My only solution is that everybody in the family must do it—men, women, and children."[75]

Although on her second try Irwin successfully combined marriage and career, she believed motherhood would not be conducive to her work, and like many of her college-educated contemporaries chose not to have children. The fact that her own mother bore ten children and was stepmother to six more undoubtedly influenced her, as did the dictates of maternalism, which held that mothers belonged at home with their children.[76] Irwin's thoughts on wage-earning mothers changed over time. In her "1916 War Diary," Irwin described her sorrow at observing young children in a French child-care center. "They take us through playrooms which have been provided for children and a *crèche* where working women can leave their babies. There are about a dozen of these babies, most of them in the toddling age. As we enter, one of them—very tiny and with great plaintive eyes—comes forward calling 'Maman! maman!' in a voice so wistful that it has haunted me ever since.... I wonder if governments will ever learn that, in the end, it is economy to keep the mother with her baby."[77]

Irwin's reflections reveal her support at the time for mothers' pensions, government payments to mothers who lacked other means of support. The Progressive era campaign for mothers' pensions was led by a loose coalition of child welfare officials, clubwomen, social feminists in organizations like the National Consumers League and the US Children's Bureau, and local mothers' clubs.[78] Mothers' pensions were meant to allow mothers without a male breadwinner to forgo paid employment so they could stay at home with their children. Between 1911 and 1928, forty-four states passed mothers' pension statutes.[79] The historian Gwendolyn Mink has argued that, like other early twentieth-century maternalist policies, mothers' pensions offered financial support to needy women in exchange for public regulation and supervision.[80]

Mothers' pension programs distinguished between deserving and underserving mothers, limiting benefits to those who were morally worthy and culturally assimilable. While widows and deserted women were eligible, most states excluded divorced women, African Americans, and single mothers (considered morally suspect).[81] Most had rules barring mothers who received pensions from wage work, although the meager allowance was not a survivable income for most female-headed households.

Ironically, the middle-class women who had freed themselves from household labor by hiring domestic servants or avoiding motherhood argued to institutionalize the dependency of other less privileged women. They did this through their support for pension programs' rules that enforced domesticity, encoded gender difference, and regulated the behavior of mothers. The result was a stigmatization of mothers who worked outside of the home and a national insistence on full-time, child-centered domesticity. Maternalists argued forcefully for the family wage and resisted policies that reconciled wage work and motherhood. Jane Addams, who had no children, expressed concern that "the day nursery is a 'double-edged implement' for doing good," which may also "do a little harm," because it could encourage women to "attempt the impossible" by becoming "both wife and mother and supporter of the family."[82] Even the NWP, despite its unshakeable support for women's right to work (whether they were married or single) dodged the social implications that arose when *mothers* exercised their right to paid employment. Mothers' pensions ultimately succeeded politically because they affirmed women's maternal role within the home, as well as the traditional division of labor between women and men. As the historian Sonya Michel has noted, it was during this era that governmental payments to poor mothers—for good or for ill—first became a social right for American women. Federally supported child care never attained that standing.[83]

Irwin challenged these prescriptive ideas about motherhood in two novels she wrote during the 1910s and 1920s. In *The Lady of Kingdoms* (1917) and *Gertrude Haviland's Divorce* (1925), she created an alternative archetype of strong, financially independent single mothers. Again she fundamentally challenged maternalist ideas that assumed "proper" mothers were married and dependent on male breadwinners. In both books, she depicts marriage as inhibiting and even cruel but motherhood as an avenue through which women experience rebirth and new meaning.[84]

The Lady of Kingdoms is a novel about two emergent New Women, Hester and Southward, who live in a conservative New England town during the 1910s and become radicalized. Hester is described at the novel's start as gaunt, sallow, unsteady, with a mother who demeans her at every opportunity she gets. In contrast, Southward is virile, slim, boyish, frank. Together they create a bohemian attic hideaway where they smoke cigarettes, exchange secrets, and recite their shared vow: "To see the world! To live our lives! Not to submit to the tyranny of things. To be friends, yet never to ask questions and to leave each other Free."[85]

Like Irwin, these two young women long for unconventional lives. "What do you consider the ideal life?" Hester asks Southward. "Travel," Southward responds. "Travel all the time. I want to see the top and bottom and both sides of this old world. . . . My idea of perfect happiness would be to join an exploring expedition. . . . Perhaps sometime after I'm old and all the ginger is gone out of me, I might settle down—and even marry. But not until there's nothing left." She wants to run locomotives, build bridges, or pilot airplanes. Hester, a local high school teacher, describes their hometown as "gone-to-seed—bleak, blank, stark, dead, a mere empty shell. . . . If I had my way I'd leave it this instant and not see it again for years. It's a grave-yard."[86]

Hester does leave Shayneford and throws aside gender convention and middle-class morality to become a single mother. The start of this rebellious novel finds her drawn to motherhood but uninterested in marriage: "I guess I'm the maternal type. I'm a breeder instinctively. I do love children. I would love to have a family—a big one. That's the only purpose matrimony serves in my eyes." When her feminist counterpart Southward Drake responds, "Any old female can be a mother and almost any old female is. I think I can do something better," Hester replies: "I love children. . . . And yet I suppose I shall never have a child."[87]

The catalyst for their emancipation is a group of young, urban, radical men and women who visit for a rural getaway, bringing new ideas in their wake. With this heterosocial group of socialists, reformers, and labor organizers, the two friends move to New York City, where the shackles of their narrow New England hometown begin to drop away. Southward speaks on street corners for woman suffrage and pickets with strikers on the lower East Side. Irwin colorfully portrayed Greenwich Village, where she lived in the decade, as "the only place in New York where people dress as they like, work as they like, live as they like, and love as they like," filled with bobbed hair Modern Girls, free lovers, and artists. The novel is in many ways a paean to New York, a city that Irwin loved.[88]

Irwin's heroine Hester accompanies her budding romantic interest, IWW member John Smith, to meetings where she hears youthful proletarians and Russian immigrants speak. Smith prescribes a reading list, and introduces Hester to people who might have come from Mars: Jewish settlement house workers, Irish American boxers, working people. One young socialist speaker's declaration of women's right to motherhood, and mothers' rights to autonomy and freedom from social judgment, deeply impresses Hester. "[We] . . . resent that phrase . . . *girl-mothers*. There are no distinctions between mothers. They are all mothers . . . Just that—*mothers*. The woman who brings a healthy child into the world is doing the state the best service she knows. Fatherhood is free. Motherhood is bound. Rewards and honours go with motherhood occasionally but only when convention has sanctioned it. They should go with it always. Our world has heaped two indignities on women. It has refused maternity to some and has forced it on others. People talk so much nowadays about the rights of women. There are only a few inalienable rights—one is the right to motherhood." Hester notes, "I thought of what she said—and thought of it—and thought of it—and thought of it. It haunted me."[89]

Along with her nonconformist notions about motherhood, Irwin also demonstrates in *The Lady of Kingdoms* her radical ideas about class. In the book, Smith offers a heartfelt soliloquy about the heroism of the socialist movement and his goal of a classless society. When Hester queries, "I don't understand the relations in society of all these classes to each other—labour—anarchists, socialists, reformers," he colorfully describes the world as a huge, dirty, toppling house with splitting walls and cracks in the roof. The upper story is filled with the rich—"all those who possess more money than they can ever possibly earn, more money than they know what to do with—the capitalist class, in short." The capitalists concealed the structure's decay by covering the walls with beauty— draperies, tapestries, fine paintings—as they talk, laugh, dine, wine, and dance. On the floor below is the middle class, who "spends all its time in mending the house, patching the ceiling so that it will not drop down on them, reinforcing the walls so that they will not fall in on them, keeping the frame together, in short, only by eternal and indefatigable efforts." And below this floor, with its tiny, chopped up rooms is the cellar where "in dark and muck, live the labouring class," who represent the hope of the future.

> They lie in the mud on their hands and knees, their very foreheads pressed into the slime. . . . The people in that cellar live and die in darkness and star- vation and suffocation and disease. . . . These men whisper rebellion into the ears of the people who hold the pillars of the house on their backs. Some of the men call themselves reformers. Some of them call themselves socialists. Some of them call themselves anarchists. . . . They are all urging these bound men to . . . rise up in their might, throw the pillars of the tottering old house off their shoulders and let it crash to the ground. . . . 'Working men of the world unite. You have nothing to lose but your chains.' I would rather have written those words than all Shakespeare.[90]

When Hester learns Smith is not free to marry her, she exhibits her newfound belief in unconstrained motherhood by determining to have a child out of wed- lock. Gaining the idea (and courage) from a childhood friend who has become a prostitute, Hester—a virgin, her face heavy with makeup—stands in Grand Central Station and selects a kind, boyish stranger to father her child. When she learns she is pregnant she is overjoyed, joins the woman suffrage movement, and pronounces to her abusive mother: "I've something within me that makes me independent of you and of anything that life can bring me. If my baby only lives a day, it will be worthwhile. . . . You can never hurt me again."[91] Although her mother initially rejects her as promiscuous and immoral, she changes her mind and travels with her daughter to San Francisco, where Hester gives birth to a twelve-pound son. The end of the novel finds Hester victorious and fulfilled in single motherhood.

Irwin's depiction of motherhood in *The Lady of Kingdoms* is radical: women can choose single motherhood, and that experience, and that relationship with infant and child, can liberate them. While public policy in the 1910s and 1920s placed unwed mothers outside the bounds of proper, or deserving, motherhood, Irwin championed the right to single motherhood. In doing so she challenged maternalism, which stigmatized illegitimacy and maintained the sanctity of the normative middle-class family, with a male breadwinner and a married female homemaker and mother at its core. Hester Crowell, who at the novel's start is "blank," is, by the end, very much alive. A twentieth-century Hester Prynne (the young protagonist of Nathaniel Hawthorne's *The Scarlet Letter*), Irwin's Hester too becomes an unwed mother. Whether she is punished as the colonial era Hester Prynne was—who was imprisoned, convicted of adultery, and sentenced to wear a prominent scarlet letter 'A' for the rest of her life—is unclear, since *The Lady of Kingdoms* ends with the birth of Hester's son. Reviewers took note of Irwin's heretical message, one writing in 1918: "Greenwich Village runs true to form in 'The Lady of Kingdoms,' the newest novel by Inez Haynes Irwin, [in which she] disguises a zealous dose of feminism under a veil of modern romance."[92]

Irwin also criticized maternalist ideas in her 1925 novel *Gertrude Haviland's Divorce*, and reaffirmed her pairing of modern feminism with financial independence and women's right to work. Irwin first published *Gertrude Haviland's Divorce*, dedicated to her deceased parents, serially in *American Magazine*, under the title "Discarded."[93] It is the story of thirty-two-year-old Radcliffe-educated Gertrude Haviland, who at the opening of the novel (set in 1913) has been married ten years, lives in an exclusive New England town, and is mother to three young children. Her single-minded dedication to motherhood has led her to neglect her lovely home, her physical appearance, and intellectual growth. Like Hester Crowell, her face is "curiously blank. Not the blankness which comes from unbearable tragedy or mental insignificance, but the blankness which scums the soul where the mentality is unstirred, the emotion untouched." The story opens with the mailman delivering a letter from her husband, informing her he is in love with another woman (who "completely filled the void left by your domestic absorption"), and requesting a divorce. Blindsided, Gertrude cries: "Is it possible that I have been deserted; that I am going to be a divorced woman? I . . . divorced? What am I going to do? What will become of me? Who will help me? Where shall I turn?"[94]

The feminist novel traces this "discarded" wife's journey to self-sufficiency, happiness, and power. She moves with her children to an old seaside farmhouse, where at first she is deeply depressed. When she discovers she is pregnant with her (soon to be) ex-husband's child, she is revitalized. She exclaims: "Now I'm going to have a baby that will be mine. All mine! All, all mine! Nothing of him about it! I shall be father. I shall be mother. I shall be its whole world. . . . The new life begins from this moment. From this moment the new woman emerges from the past."[95] She gives birth to a daughter, Joy, and begins to thrive—investing in houses, growing slender and vibrant, bobbing her hair, becoming a community leader, and—despite several men's expressed interest in her—determining she will never remarry.

When—his second wife dead—her ex-husband visits, he sees a woman he barely recognizes. He declares, "You *have* changed Gertrude! . . . You look so much younger. You've grown thinner—and then you've had this quiet country life . . . But there's something in your face that wasn't there before. . . . It's power. That's what it is—power. Your face has grown powerful." Finally freed to dismiss him, Gertrude burns the painful rejection letter—limp from much re-reading— that he had sent nearly a decade before. When Will comments, "The break did not break you," she responds, "On the contrary . . . it made me." She no longer needs alimony, since her income from the properties, combined with a community planning position, is more than enough to support the family. When her ex-husband describes himself as miserably unhappy and asks if she will remarry him, her victory is complete when she easily turns him down and realizes she is in love with the sensitive, feminist man next door.[96]

Gertrude's liberation springs in part from her newfound financial independence, which Irwin contended was critically important for women. Half seriously, Irwin described the divorcée in 1915 as "the most pathetic of all social dependents," a "pensioner on the bounty of a lost husband, a woman incapable of self-support." The fictional Gertrude Haviland initially discovers that her own attitude toward wage-earning left her unequipped to support herself and her children. "Now she became aware for the first time that she always entertained a sort of—not contempt—but indulgence, for the woman wage-earner. Normal women . . . did not have to consider such matters. They were taken care of." By the end of this feminist novel, Gertrude Haviland has learned how to take care of herself.[97]

In *Angel Island, The Lady of Kingdoms*, and *Gertrude Haviland's Divorce*, Irwin characterizes motherhood as most fulfilling if women experience it without men. Motherhood is profoundly freeing—it catalyzes women to tap their creativity, rebelliousness, and power: it is transcendent. It is marriage that stifles. Like Charlotte Perkins Gilman, Irwin believed that motherhood freed women to become social actors.

Yet, although Irwin celebrated unconventional motherhood in these compelling novels, she herself remained childless and seems to have felt both personal loss and social censure because she was not a mother. She once described maternity as "the great recompense" of marriage. The fact that she wrote so many books for children, including the popular *Maida* series, indicates a concern for and attraction to children. Had she been younger when she married Irwin, it is possible she may have chosen to have children with him.

CHAPTER 5

This Vast Laboratory

Modern feminism offered American middle-class women a double hope: meaningful work in the world and a resonant union with men. Stevens's friend Crystal Eastman, an attorney and member of her bohemian cohort, summed up the way of thinking neatly. The modern woman "wants money of her own. She wants work of her own." But the work she wanted had to be significant, interesting. She wanted a husband, home, and children, too. "How to reconcile these two desires in real life, that is the question." It is an intensely individualist, self-referential question, but as Christine Stansell has noted, it is a question also "keenly aware of the needs of all women." Was it possible that the goals of the nineteenth-century women's movement—education, political and civil rights, suffrage—could lead to the realization of both work and family? Could women aspire to the full lives most men automatically assumed as their right? How could women reconcile these two desires in real life? This question, first raised in the 1910s, was essential to twentieth-century feminism. It proved to be not quite answerable, although feminists like Doris Stevens and Lorine Pruette valiantly tried.[1]

The companionate marriage ideal of the 1920s offered one potential avenue. It drew on feminist beliefs raised in the nineteenth century and developed in the 1910s, including female sexual passion and an indictment of bourgeois marriage. Especially among a younger generation, this new marital ideal arose to great fanfare. Publicized by Ben Lindsey and Wainwright Evans in their widely read *The Revolt of Modern Youth* (1925) and *The Companionate Marriage* (1927), this model stressed marital sex for intimacy and pleasure, and deemphasized the parent-child relationship in its focus on the husband-wife couple. Lindsey and Evans advocated birth control, the right to divorce by mutual consent for childless couples, and training in marriage and parenting skills. They argued that strengthening marriage was the most effective way to restrain the oversexed younger generation.[2]

Most widely accepted among the educated, urban middle-class, companionate marriage became a prototype for a new conception of the American family as intimate, affectionate, nurturing, and egalitarian. Although criticized as "jazz marriage" and declared "nothing but free love" by the evangelist Billy Sunday, social scientists, journalists, and social workers helped spread the concept.[3] Modern feminists embraced companionate marriage, but as the painful experiences of Stevens and Pruette illustrate, many of them were ultimately disappointed. In 1924 journalist Ruth Hale described "the hope of the future . . . in the husband and wife walking side by side, equals, partners, friends, and lovers."[4] Six years later, in *Love in the Machine Age*, Floyd Dell grandly proclaimed that the destruction of the traditional Victorian family "has laid the basis for a more biologically normal family life than has existed throughout the whole of the historical period."[5] African American activists, journalists, and scholars also took up the idea of modern marriage.[6]

The companionate marriage ideal collided with earlier ideas Americans held about marriage. Early twentieth-century marriage law dictated and shored up difference by assigning and enforcing gender-specific roles and privileges. Marriage law also represented a racialized order, since anti-miscegenation laws prevented marriages between African American and white Americans.[7] Coverture, the legal doctrine from English common law that turned the married pair legally into one person—the husband—was deeply embedded in American law. Coverture meant that a wife had no right to legal avenues without her husband's consent and that upon marriage her assets became her husband's property, along with her potential earnings. In turn, the husband was legally responsible to provide for, protect, and support her; the wife was obligated to give her service, obedience, and labor to her husband.[8] After World War I, and especially after women won the vote, feminists increasingly challenged this patriarchal model.

At the same time, Americans were committed to marriages founded on love. In what one historian calls "a willful mystification," early twentieth-century rhetoric and popular culture represented marriage for love and marriage for money as polar opposites. Women who married for mercenary reasons were condemned; "true love," linked to new dialogues about sexual attraction and its importance in relationships, was glorified.[9] Sociologists Robert and Helen Lynd's analysis of Middletown (a thinly veiled Muncie, Indiana) concluded that a belief in romantic love as the only basis for marriage had persisted as a powerful icon from the 1890s through the 1920s.[10] Utilitarian marriages were considered un-American and influenced the ways social workers, settlement house reformers, and government officials perceived immigrants. The Old World tradition of extended family's involvement in the marriage choice, the centrality of class, and the dowry tradition ran against the modern American grain.[11]

Paula Fass has suggested that the sexual revolution of the 1920s was not a revolt against marriage but a revolution within marriage, characterized by the sexualization of love and the exaltation of sex.[12] This changed the way Americans thought about marriage. In *The Marriage Crisis* (1928), the sociologist Ernest Groves noted that "the pleasure principle" created outsized expectations that marriage could furnish individual satisfaction, which overshadowed all its traditional burdens. Movies, advertising, and music reinforced this message as they connected consent in marriage with awareness of the "magnetizing power" of sex. At the same time, divorce surged in Europe and North America; couples who married in the United States in 1880 had a one in twelve chance of divorcing. Those who married in the late 1920s had a one in six chance.[13] Conservative critics who argued that rising expectations would lead to divorce were proven correct: filings were increasingly based on lack of love, emotional intimacy, and companionship rather than cruelty, abandonment, or failure to perform gendered roles. The upswing in divorce was controversial: some blamed it on "the mood of the age," with its "yeasty unrest." Dorothy Dix, a journalist, explained, "people are demanding more of life than they used to. . . . Now . . . we see that no good purpose is achieved by keeping two people together who have come to hate each other."[14] By the late 1940s, attitudes had changed and divorce came to be a recognized fact of life in the United States.[15] But in the 1920s it was a heated topic, one about which everyone had an opinion.

The increased public focus on the importance of sex to happy marriages added to American wives' prescriptive burdens and in some cases led them to commit adultery. Marriage advice expert William Robinson stated unequivocally in 1912 that "every case of divorce has for its basis lack of sexual satisfaction." Slim volumes such as *How I Kept My Husband* matter-of-factly instructed early twentieth-century wives on how to give oral sex to their spouses.[16] Marital infidelity increased: one-fourth of husbands and wives surveyed in 1928 admitted having had at least one affair. Stevens's fears of her own sexual frigidity (an accusation lobbed at her by her first husband Malone) led her into the arms of an Italian soldier, and Pruette, too, turned to another man's bed in response to her husband's insensitivity.

The modern marriage ideal effectively undercut women's resistance by glorifying marriage as a mating of equals and comrades, which posed a challenge for early twentieth-century feminists. Enthusiasts not only urged women and men to marry but to do so at increasingly younger ages, since the growing public acceptance of contraception allowed for planning of parenthood. As Stevens stated, a man and woman married to form "a mating fruitful of joy and beauty and glamorous release."[17] But as her own mother noted on the eve of Stevens's first wedding, Doris avoided marriage for many years, and when she did marry it was with reluctance. The same held true for Pruette.

The companionate marriage ideal made it more difficult for ambitious women to choose careers over marriage: the modern feminist was expected to desire both. Louisa May Alcott spoke for an earlier generation when she stated in an 1868 article about "independent spinsters"—titled "Happy Women"—"I'd rather be a free spirit and paddle my own canoe."[18] In *New Girls for Old* (1930), social scientists Phyllis Blanchard and Carolyn Manasses concluded that a new generation asked of life not only marriage but a new kind of marriage, a modern union envisioned as a perfect consummation of both personalities.[19]

Pruette recognized the danger such an overemphasis on marriage held for feminism. "Back in the nineteenth century . . . the women who were kicking up a lot of dust about the suffrage question were almost always married, and happily married. And the ones who were not, gave no appearance of having lost everything that might make life tolerable. . . . They believed that a woman could do valuable and important things, married or not."[20] In contrast, twentieth-century feminists insisted the world was "arranged for people to go in twos." When Stevens wrote the older feminist Helen Archdale to inform her of her second marriage, Stevens described feeling like a waif when unmarried. Archdale's firm response indicates how far modern feminists like Stevens had moved away from the nineteenth-century tradition: "What you say about the beneficial effects of marriage on one's life rather puzzles me. Why should 'spinsterhood' be 'gray' or bachelorhood? Is it not simply tradition? Cutting out the physical, sexual intercourse part, out of which we all at some point must grow, is companionship, friendship, not at our disposal, at our acceptance when we will? What is the difference in marriage? The communion of friendship surely should be free of a sex basis—And why do you call yourself and why did you feel yourself to be 'a waif'? What constitutes being a waif? Lack of inner peace, lack of means, lack of friends, lack of a husband? I believe *only* the first of these."[21]

The *Nation* women who in 1926 explored the origin of their "modern" points of view described balancing marriage and career as their most perplexing challenge. Although some tempered the dilemma by marrying and not having children, the feelings of disappointment, guilt, diminished expectations, and compromise that white, middle-class feminists increasingly expressed throughout the 1920s and 1930s pointed to the impasse in which many found themselves. This conundrum, still unsolved today for many American women, has spawned an entire new literature and the interdisciplinary field of work-family studies.[22] In her bitter, eloquent, still sadly relevant 1931 essay "Why Women Fail," Pruette pronounced the risks ambitious women take when they marry. "The woman who wishes to be famous," she caustically advised, "should not marry; rather, she should attach to herself one or more women who will fetch and carry for her in the immemorial style of wives; women who will secure her from interruption, give her freedom from the irritating small details of living, assure her that she is great, and devote their lives to making her so."[23] Both Pruette and Stevens used marriage as a personal experiment and a laboratory for testing out how women could reconcile their desires for meaningful work and home and family. Their examples remind us of the deeply entrenched gender norms that connect house-hold labor and nurturance with women, and achievement and public ambition with men.

WE ALL WANT MARRIAGE: DORIS STEVENS

Stevens married the larger-than-life Dudley Field Malone in 1921, when she was thirty-four, much older than the average marriage age at the time. She postponed marrying until the successful completion of her suffrage activism and privately expressed doubt and hesitance as she embarked upon matrimony. She gave her parents and siblings only a few days' notice before the wedding, "so Doris would not have time to back out," her mother confided to a reporter.[24] The man she chose to marry was famous, influential, a left-leaning reformer, and a publicly recognized feminist. Malone, raised in a political, working-class, Irish Catholic household, became a renowned orator. He helped organize Wilson's successful primary and presidential campaigns, and when Wilson took office in 1913 he awarded Malone by appointing him third assistant secretary of state and later collector of the Port of New York. Malone and Stevens met in 1916 when she was leading the National Woman's Party's California campaign against Wilson's reelection and he was working to lure women voters over to the Wilson camp. When Stevens and other suffragists were arrested for picketing the White House the following year, Malone served as their attorney and eventually resigned his post in protest over the president's stance on woman suffrage. In 1918 he and socialist attorney Morris Hillquit defended *The Masses* against charges of con-spiracy to obstruct recruitment and enlistment in World War I. He went on to become a celebrated divorce lawyer.[25]

A gregarious, paradoxical man, Malone moved in glittering circles: he was drawn to glamorous, wealthy people as well as socialists and civil libertarians. His friends included luminaries from the worlds of business and the arts: F. Scott Fitzgerald, Charlie Chaplin, Gloria Swanson, J. P. Morgan, H. G. Wells, William K. Vanderbilt, William Randolph Hearst, and Gertrude Stein. He ran unsuccess-fully for governor of New York on the Farmer-Labor Party ticket in 1920. In 1925, Malone, along with Clarence Darrow and Arthur Garfield Hays, defended John T. Scopes in the famed "Monkey Trial," in which the Tennessee high school teacher Scopes was tried for violating the anti-evolution Butler Act by teaching Darwin's theory of evolution. Malone gave arguably the greatest speech of the trial in defense of academic freedom and the separation of religion from educa-tion. It was the first American trial to be broadcast on national radio.[26] Although Stevens and Malone were at that point on the verge of divorce, she sat by his side throughout the entire hearing.

Stevens had hoped their union would be all the "new" marriage was supposed to be—sexually sustaining, egalitarian, emotionally gratifying—but she found it instead to be degrading and solitary. She did all the modern things: kept her own name, refused to wear a wedding ring, used contraception, continued her career; but in an ironic twist, Malone—whose conviviality extended to women—took advantage of Stevens's open-mindedness to justify his infidelity and erratic behavior. "Modern women," Malone instructed Stevens, "must know that husbands and wives could not always go about together." "He told them all (the women he companioned)," Stevens remarked, "he had an extraordinary wife, who represented a new era or some such tosh as that." In a letter Stevens wrote Malone describing the first year of their marriage, which they spent in Paris—a well-deserved sabbatical for her—she expressed her incredulous disappointment and anger: "You show same restlessness—same nervous irritability, same reluctance to share any fun with me. . . . Nights out—too much drinking—Never know where you are—Dozens of dinners alone at home—My God in heaven—is it to be wondered at that a self-respecting, intelligent woman began to rub her eyes & wonder if this was to be her life." As she wrote him several years after their divorce, when Stevens sought her husband's company and a closer relationship, "you used to advise me to seek the companionship of other men. . . . Your answer was that there were men in Paris whose profession it was to please women."27

Malone's mental cruelty at times led to physical abuse. Stevens recorded the following violent incident in her 1924 diary: "[Dudley] came in . . . thumped me—choked me—knocked me down on the bed—kicked me black & blue on legs so was scarred for days—Kept saying 'I'll smash your jaw in.'" Two nights after this attack she recorded in her diary a poignant dream, in which—in order to please him—she mimicked The Little Engine That Could: "T. [Dudley] surrounded by balcony of people—I arrive & come toward him. He shouts to crowd 'Here comes my little wife—nice bitch she is.' In order to make crowd think he is festive, I smile . . . and answer as I come up an incline, 'Yes, here I am'—and make a funny noise like an engine puffing—kachow-chow-chow-chow." "Instead of filling our lives with beauty & union," Stevens declared, "you persist in mud slinging—brutality and vile names." Dudley refused to introduce Doris to his family, insulted her friends, and protested, "Feminism is all rot. . . . Your women are hard-boiled—iron-jawed." After he listened to Doris give a radio speech, Dudley commented that he was concerned that the audience would think he had married a woman with a lisp. "I spiritually blushed for that remark," she sadly stated. In a document in her papers titled "Mental Cruelty" Stevens wrote: "He frequently made remarks about my looks. I was strange looking. I looked like a man. I had a peculiar mouth. My eyes were badly set. I used to tell him I knew I was very plain as to looks, that I never pretended to compete with his beautiful girl friends, that I had no reputation for beauty, that I did the best I could with what personality and brains I had."28

Instead of submitting to Malone's abuse, however, Stevens took her own revenge. Her love affair and eventual marriage to tall, attractive Jonathan Mitchell signified her quest for the ideal male-female relationship, which she came much closer to realizing with him. Educated at Phillips Exeter Academy, Harvard, and Amherst, Mitchell was a journalist who in the 1910s and 1920s wrote for a variety of newspapers (including the *New York World*), served as a *New Republic* editor from 1933 to 1941, and went on to work for William F. Buckley's conservative *National Review*. He eventually became an anticommunist who published a political analysis of American foreign policy, *Goose Steps to Peace*, in 1931. Mitchell also worked with economists at Princeton's Institute for Advanced Study from 1941 to 1950, and later conducted research for the US Senate Subcommittee on Internal Security, which investigated subversive activities.[29]

Stevens's and Mitchell's conception of marriage advocated tangible shifts in gendered power relations. While most proponents paid lip service to gender equality, companionate marriage was still predicated on the assumption that the wife was economically dependent on, and thus subordinate to, the husband. Women wage earners were viewed as secondary workers in the family. Both Mitchell and Stevens questioned these suppositions. Mitchell wrote Stevens in 1924 (when she was still married to Malone) that, if they married, her career would come before his. "Best beloved," he wrote expansively, "I hope for so much. I have had an Atlas on the floor here, & we have made astounding trips. We have, or rather you have, written shelves full of astounding books. There have been blinding evenings when I listened to Dreka [one of his endearments for Stevens] rocking Madison Square Garden with enthusiasm & Red Revolution."[30]

Stevens and Mitchell endorsed a new marriage in which women could retain autonomy, realize their ambitions, reject (or choose) motherhood, and seek personal fulfillment. Men would support women's aspirations and career goals. Their correspondence in the decade before their marriage reveals a man desperately in love, willing to sacrifice almost anything to claim her as his wife. Mitchell's patience was, as he later stated, pushed to incredible lengths. For her part, Stevens believed she loved both Malone and Mitchell and vacillated for at least three miserable years over whether to divorce Malone. Drawn as she was to money and fashionable people, his fame and illustrious connections remained attractive until her loneliness became unbearable. She forlornly wrote Malone, "I was able through you to be taken to places where I wanted to be. I was taken right up to the doors of the glittering lights. And then I was not taken in. I was alone. And then I got a hate on the bright lights because they were always connected with some hurt." Stevens went through psychoanalysis to save their marriage, although she claimed her husband was the one acting "quite insane." She wrote Malone: "I faced social discussion of the fact that I had been pschyced [*sic*]—That wasn't easy. But I did even that. That you spurn. But a more loving person knows it is a self abusive & humiliating thing to do."[31] In his confusion Mitchell also visited a psychoanalyst, who advised him that decision had become impossible for Stevens and that he should not try to be "integrated & virile [and] high-hat." Putting his manliness aside, he wrote Stevens after this session: "The important thing is for me to be a calm and fervent lover of Dreka, and titles and crises don't matter. . . . Since I love you simply and freely, I shall always follow you."[32]

Utopian in their beliefs about marriage's potential, moderns drew on feminist ideas like individualism and autonomy, which some believed they could realize with a spouse. Stevens was close friends with Ruth Hale, who in 1922 founded the Lucy Stone League, which supported married women's right to keep their own names. By 1924 the league membership boasted five thousand married women who maintained their birth names in New York State alone. The credo of the league, as Hale told a reporter, was the belief that "My life is a whole thing to myself. Nothing that happens to me is greater than the thing that I am in my own right."[33] Yet privately Hale thought it might be impossible to realize individuality and independence in marriage. In a 1926 letter to Stevens, Mitchell described his visit with Hale the previous evening. He told her that Hale believed men and women could achieve the most harmonious relationship if they lived apart but near each other, and were not married. "Free love," he wrote, "she agrees is ruinous." Although he felt Hale's criticism was true of many marriages, he did not believe it would apply to theirs.[34] Stevens was not so sure. Once, when reflecting on how too much theory and too little action could lead to stagnation in a social movement, Stevens exclaimed: "It is like husband and wife, worn out contesting their theories as to the proper basis for the union. It is death to the union!"[35]

Modern marriage's intensification of male-female intimacy was connected to a loosening of other ties. While older women like Mary Beard and Inez Irwin perceived marriage as one (important) relationship among many, younger women in "companionate" marriages hoped their husbands could satisfy all their emotional needs. This interpretation foregrounded two isolated people in love, sidelining connections to friends, parents, and religious and other authorities. Nineteen-twenties youth questioned the veneration of mothers, close ties with siblings, and intimate female friendships.[36] "You're such a darling," Stevens wrote her lover in 1923. "Can you be a mother to me too? I never need a father but sometimes I need a mother."[37]

In his desire to marry Stevens and to realize marriage's feminist potential, Mitchell sent her descriptions of marriages that allowed freedom, self-governance, and ambition for both spouses. In a poetic passage that could have come straight from the pages of Fitzgerald's *The Great Gatsby*, published three years earlier, Mitchell jubilantly described to Stevens the "new" marriage, as he had witnessed it one Long Island September afternoon in 1928.

> It was just as the books said it would be, and generally speaking I like it. The house all done after "House and Garden," cocktails and wisecracks, everybody very liberal—approving Socialists, rough books, etc.

Inez Haynes Irwin in her late teens or early twenties (ca. 1890–1895), in a portrait taken in Cambridge, Massachusetts.

Inez Haynes Irwin in her thirties (ca. 1905–1910). Included in a scrapbook Heterodoxy members gave Marie Jenney Howe in 1920. Irwin inscribed: "Here's to Marie who in the midst of this strange universe and this cold city created a little world for us; a little world in which we could laugh and play; talk and make friends."

Mary Ritter Beard dressed in graduation cap and gown at DePauw University in 1897.

Charles and Mary Beard with their children, Miriam and William, on a picnic, probably on the shores of Long Island Sound, ca. 1915.

OPPOSITE PAGE: Mary Ritter Beard (on right) and unidentified woman at a tree-dedicating ceremony at Sequoia National Park, California, June 26, 1938. The three-thousand-year-old tree was dedicated in memory of Susan B. Anthony.

SUSAN B. ANTHONY

Max Eastman, Doris Stevens, and Jonathan Mitchell lying in the
woods in Croton-on-Hudson, New York, in a photograph taken
between 1925 and 1927.

Portrait of Doris Stevens at forty, in 1928, possibly at a convention at
Saratoga Springs, New York.

Doris Stevens and Alice Paul in the League of Nations Building in
Geneva, July 6, 1931. They are signing the Nationality Committee's
report asking for equality in women's nationality rights.

Lorine Pruette in 1919, when she was twenty-three.

Lorine Pruette in 1934, age thirty-eight. This was probably the publicity photograph for *Women Workers through the Depression*.

Well, it was the world you have and are creating, and although just a wee bit comic, very nice. Mrs. Cristophe announced she and her husband had decided they wanted to conceive a baby in the next month, in order to have it born in July, and were unmercifully razzed. Barring the Cristophes, who were very embarrassed and on the defensive, everyone thought babies terribly eccentric. The loud opinion was that they [were] nuisances. . . . Motherhood seemed to be in disrepute.

Miss Somebody—I think her name was Schaumeyer—was making more money than any of the rest of us, King second, probably, and then the men. There was, of a kind, real equality among us. The girls were recognized as peers or better. It was the sort of world I wouldn't mind being in. Kind of naïve about things we take as a matter of course. . . . But everyone physically very fit, very successful, very bright and truthful and having a good time. I suppose it would seem very American to foreigners. No traditions. A new world, especially for the girls, made by Dinsche [Doris] and her movements.[38]

Although a small, progressive group of intellectuals, activists, and artists were practicing companionate marriage in 1928, to most Americans it was anathema. Even the women's colleges, which earlier in the decade had offered courses to encourage women to combine home and career, by the end stressed an education that prepared students to be wives and mothers. Women's magazines, geared to the white middle class, reiterated the maternalist idea that the roles of mother and housewife were the only route to fulfillment and happiness. In the heady days after the passage of the Nineteenth Amendment, *McCall's* and the *Ladies' Home Journal* had run numerous articles defending women's right to work and to self-definition. By the late 1920s, such tolerance shifted to condemnation.[39]

Doris Stevens used her platform as an increasingly well-known leader of the National Woman's Party (NWP) to defend gender equality in marriage. She represented equal rights feminists who claimed an absolute right to work and who disagreed, at times vehemently, with maternalists and social feminists who supported the restriction of women's wage-earning in order to maintain the traditional family and/or the primacy of motherhood.[40] Her 1920 book *Jailed for Freedom* linked her to the radical suffragists, and in 1924 she spearheaded the party's Women for Congress campaign. By 1926 Stevens was NWP vice president and described the party as "the one organization in the United States standing for complete equality for women, including equal rights in industry."[41] She was arrested in 1928 for leading a group that attempted to present an international equal rights treaty to the delegates gathered to sign the Pact of Paris.[42] Stevens was in her thirties at the time, with a well-honed belief in the importance of civil disobedience, fashion, and publicity in any movement for social change. She readily took on the sticky topics of financial arrangements in marriage, including wages for wives. As an admiring reporter wrote in 1926 of Stevens's activism over the previous decade: "She has spent her time showing harnessed womanhood how to jump the traces."[43]

The Home as a Joint-Stock Company

Stevens's public advocacy for marriage reform coincided with the years of her difficult first marriage. When in 1922 she and Malone returned from their honeymoon, a journalist inquired whether marriage had changed her feminist views. Stevens responded that marriage had strengthened them. The reporter explained why Stevens had kept her own name: "[It] is not that she is so proud of her maiden name or that she considers it a matter of vital importance, but because she believes that the change in name hinders the freedom of thought and conduct of both parties to the marriage contract."[44] Stevens argued that women should "see the folly of being swallowed up in marriage—letting their husbands dominate them in everything, even in making his title their own."[45] To her credit, Stevens extended her marriage reform philosophy not only to professional women but to working-class women, full-time housewives, and mothers as well. She described her meeting in England with a Russian representative who discussed "the soviet of workers," elected councils formed after the Bolshevik Revolution, made up of manual laborers who were given certain powers of local administration. "I asked him," she noted, "if they had a soviet of mothers, and he didn't know what I was talking about."[46]

In fact, more married women—and mothers—worked for wages during the 1920s than in previous decades. In 1900, the typical female worker was unmarried and under twenty-five; in 1930 she was married and over thirty. Married women workers entered the workforce at five times the rate of other women in the 1920s and constituted 40 percent of the female workforce. They entered for varied reasons that included financial need, professional ambition, and a rising middle-class standard of living that demanded two incomes. One-third of these new workers were mothers with children under the age of thirteen. Still, fewer than 12 percent of married women in the United States in 1930 held paying jobs.[47]

Most married women worked so their families could make ends meet.[48] Race was a deciding factor in whether a married woman worked: during the 1920s and 1930s more than three times as many Black married women as white married women were in the labor force. Although African Americans and immigrant whites made up 57 percent of all working women, job segregation by race persisted. The only jobs open to Black and immigrant workers were in the garment industry as factory workers, or in domestic service.[49] Despite striking differences in work opportunities and treatment, all women encountered institutionalized discrimination and structural inequality in the workplace. These included a gender segregated workplace (where female workers were clustered in occupations considered women's work); sexual harassment, common in both white- and blue-collar jobs; obstacles to advancement; and pay inequity.[50] Employers assumed women would work until they married and had children, which reinforced the rationale for the dead-end nature of service and secretarial jobs. The belief that women joined the labor force to earn "pin money" strengthened employers' prerogative to pay them lower wages. It also gave public officials the justification for firing women workers who were viewed as casual members of the labor force.[51] Feminists like Stevens and Pruette, who were strong supporters of wage-earning women's rights, addressed these inequities throughout the 1920s and 1930s.

Linked to new ideas about marriage, the home was another site for 1920s experimentation. Stevens argued that household labor limited married women's abilities to "penetrate further into the social and productive life of the community." Although some believed innovative technologies would lighten women's domestic labor, Stevens understood that much more radical changes were called for.[52]

Like Charlotte Perkins Gilman before her, Stevens advocated the commodification of family-based work by suggesting it be removed from the home and moved into the labor market. Women who could afford to might purchase housecleaning services, child care, and restaurant meals. Stevens suggested structural solutions, rather than individual ones, to the work-family dilemma and envisioned women as leaders and professionals, performing in gender-blurred workplaces and homes. "World Tending toward Matriarchy, Declares Doris Stevens" trumpeted the April 1922 headline of a New York newspaper. "When the long-suppressed energies of women are released they will become strong and hard and men will say 'Oh, well, let them do it,'" Stevens avowed. "Women to-day want the earth and the whole heavens, the sun, the stars and moon as well." What was holding them back? More than marriage, it was motherhood, which "now is a life occupation unless a woman has immense means or great energy to follow other activities constantly."[53]

Relatively few 1920s feminists actually confronted traditional normative gender roles or supported women's need for economic independence.[54] For all her imperfections, Stevens was in that radical minority. Her farsightedness is captured in the small fact that, although sociologist Arlie Russell Hochschild has been credited with coining the term "the second shift" in her widely read *The Second Shift: Working Parents and the Revolution at Home* (1989), Stevens was using the same expression as early as 1926.[55] "The two practical things that stand in the way of woman," she wrote, "are the inadequate organization of her domestic service in the home, and the almost total lack of facilities for taking care of the young children who are too young to be taken care of by the state which now takes them in charge from nine to four for five days of the week. These two heavy tasks, house work and supervision of the young, are always facing the woman who would go out to work in the world. She has always to face the fact of a double shift. The task outside the home done, she returns to the home to perform a second shift of labor."[56]

Stevens rejected the culturally reinforced belief that finds it impossible to commodify women's labor because it is an expression of their love.[57] She was not afraid to ask: "What is a wife worth?" Stevens pointed out that wives were the only workers expected to labor for no remuneration, and she believed they had the right to own their own labor, for which they should be compensated. She noted that the federal census, which measures economic activity, discounted the value of women's household work by considering wives to be unemployed dependents. Still today, the only way domestic labor is counted in the US Census is when it is done by domestic workers who receive wages for their services.[58] Stevens declared: "The modern woman says: We have become so impressed with the importance of home and mother that we propose to do something about them. Even if we should do the wrong thing first, still we intend to try first one experiment and then another in this vast laboratory."[59] Stevens argued that wives and mothers should be compensated for their labor, either through federal stipends or wages paid by their husbands. Although many ERA enthusiasts opposed mothers' pensions, some like Stevens did support and strategically defend them in forums including *Equal Rights*, in testimony before Congress, and in a NWP 1928 pamphlet. Emphasizing the compatibility between equal rights and state support of children, their argument hinged on building the case for a gender-neutral approach.[60]

Stevens took this tactic in a 1924 debate with social feminist Alice Hamilton. She argued that if the ERA were passed, mothers, unemployed men, and veterans would continue to receive state and federal benefits. "Maternity legislation is designed to assist a special group of women under special circumstances," she stated. "It is not special legislation for *women*; it is for *mothers*. All women are not mothers. All mothers are not in constant need of maternity protection." Like workmen's compensation and soldiers' benefits, maternity benefits and widows' pensions would remain legal, she argued, because they were not based on sex, but upon the special needs of a given group under certain circumstances.[61] Stevens's feminist ideology recognized that mothering was work that benefited society and that women's legal equality was of critical importance.

Yet Stevens's support for husbands' payments to wives signaled, in historian Molly Ladd-Taylor's view, a private turn after 1925 in American feminists' approach to the problem of married women's economic dependence. Most feminists argued that labor force employment, not government programs, would address the economic vulnerability of wives and mothers, a depoliticization of motherhood.[62] Stevens supported both strategies. In addition to women's wage earning, she advocated state support of mothers in need as well as the importance of recognizing the economic value of women's household labor. A second way to do this was by an "experiment in the home," a marriage conceived as "a

joint partnership in the realm of finance as well as in the realm of the spirit."
Marriage should be recognized as "a business partnership" and the home as a
"joint-stock company." While the husband contributed capital earned outside
the home (money), the wife contributed labor capital (domestic service). Equal
partners, under this arrangement all profits accrued after expenses were met
would be divided between husband and wife.[63]

To assure both partners honored their end of the bargain, Stevens proposed
a legal contract of mutual support (like a pre-nuptial contract) be drawn up at
marriage. A divide-as-you-go policy would eliminate the need for alimony as well
as the "gold-digging" of some financially desperate wives, and would improve the
mental health and financial security of wives and mothers. "There isn't a business
partnership in existence," Stevens stated, "where one man could say to another 'If
you do your share of the work this year, you'll get a pearl necklace, perhaps, or a
little Ford runabout for your share of the profits!' Yet men say that to their wives
and expect them to like it!" "For those who work in the home, a contract form
of marriage should provide for economic independence," she declared in 1926.[64]
Returning to Omaha to speak before the women's division of the Chamber of
Congress the following year, Stevens criticized the Nebraska law that stipulated
that a woman's household labor belonged to her husband.[65] Further, the deroga-
tion of women's work in the home had a subtly pernicious effect when women
chose to enter the labor force. Carrying with them the psychology of the unpaid
work they left behind, women became so grateful to be paid at all that they
accepted extremely low wages.[66]

However far-sighted her analysis, Stevens was unable to realize her innovative
vision in her own unhappy marriage. Ironically, as she was writing and dissemi-
nating feminist theory about remaking marriage, she was struggling to break free
from her own abusive marriage. Her six-year "companionate" marriage ended in
heartbreak and bitterness. Malone refused to establish the financial partnership
she advocated, to her great disappointment and humiliation, and his extrava-
gance placed further strain on the marriage and led to his eventual bankruptcy.
He rejected as "an impossible experiment" Stevens's idea of establishing "a free
association" in which husband and wife came together "only when and if they
want to, retaining what is precious of love, affection, mutual esteem ... and lead
free and happy and guiltless-feeling lives ... functioning through themselves not
one through another."[67]

Although Malone insisted on his extramarital affairs, he objected to Stevens's
liaison with Mitchell and had her trailed by detectives. When they separated, he
stipulated that Stevens neither see nor interact in any way with Mitchell. Malone
remarked, "Whether the establishment, under your hoped-for Feminist regime,
of male mistresses like Mitchell, is to take the place of the old regime, is something about which you will have more information than I." When Stevens finally
ended the marriage she did so "to save my self from destruction." Malone made

nothing about the dissolution easy. One wrenching night in early summer, Stevens and Malone sat with their lawyers in Malone's office from 8:30 P.M. to 3:00 A.M., hammering out a divorce agreement. Stevens wrote in her diary on June 27, 1927: "Devastating evening. . . . It was without doubt the most torturing evening I ever spent or ever hope to spend. . . . It's done now and it's a sad and negative relief. I am empty." "The tears I've shed would make the desert moist," she scrawled a few days later. "May I never touch such a black bottomless pit again in all my life."[68]

The media reported the dissolution of their unconventional marriage with apparent pleasure. The *Omaha Evening Bee* gloated: "It was to be the ideal 50–50 marriage. Miss Stevens retained both her name and her place in a woman's party which is, right now, not only seeking equal privileges with men, but is also seeking to ban any special protection for women." The *New York Times* asserted that the Malone-Sevens marriage failed because of the impossibility of two persons of equally strong minds living harmoniously together. It is unclear whether or not Stevens asked for alimony. Although Mitchell stated decades later that "the New Woman in Doris, who wished her freedom, but was willing to pay for it" made her refuse alimony (to much editorial commendation), several letters she wrote her lawyer at the time suggest otherwise. Malone ultimately agreed to pay Stevens $25,000 (money he owed her), and she eventually collected half that amount.[69]

Although Jonathan Mitchell was eager to join Stevens in the modern marriage she envisioned, she vacillated between the two men for several unhappy years and tried to postpone Mitchell's desire to marry her. "I love you & want you & cannot be happy without you," Doris declared in 1923. "Perhaps I shall be brave enough to find a way." She described herself as "a weak shaky creature, scared & then scared some more." "I actually pray for strength & decisive conduct & hope as the Quakers say, 'Way will open,'" she wrote Mitchell. At the same time she wrote her husband, "There are roots which bind me to you in a hundred ways. Otherwise I should have gone long ago. . . . At times my head told me that unhappiness was ahead for me with you. But the heart was entrenched."[70]

Mitchell believed Stevens's hesitancy stemmed from her mother's unhappiness in marriage, but it was also connected to her growing realization of how difficult egalitarian marriage was for modern feminists to achieve. Mitchell recalled the first unresolved disagreement they ever had, when he urged her to speed up her divorce so she could marry him. "I remember her manner," he reminisced in the early 1960s, "which was that all men are difficult, and I was being—acting—like a man." "This incident raises the question," he added, "of whether Doris did not have a reluctance to be married. Her father and mother had loved one another, and it had been a happy family. But her mother had repeatedly told Doris that she regretted it." Stevens wrote Mitchell in 1927: "If I don't come leaping toward what seems quite simple to you—it's because I'm not a jumping leaper. But once I leap—I warn you—good heavens! How I land! Now it's time for you to be afraid." Four years later Mitchell scribbled in his journal: "Just a little, I was getting to have the feeling that marriage to you was in sight, & that it made no difference how we attained it. I still deeply believe we are mates, & that we will soon be married."[71] Mitchell grew increasingly anxious to marry Stevens. Although he later recalled them as being discreet, he recognized their liaison was widely known. He wanted to publicly claim her as his wife, and to build a home together. Although Stevens finally divorced Malone in 1927, she did not marry Mitchell until 1935, when she was nearly fifty.[72]

Not only did the advent of modern marriage finalize the dissolution of separate gender spheres, it also threatened women's access to the pleasures and rewards of motherhood. Despite Crystal Eastman's depiction of modern feminists' desire for work, husband, home, and children, the reality appeared more complicated. Stevens referred to herself more than once as a "childless mother." Although she stated that neither she nor Malone yearned for children, when he remarried three months after their divorce and had a son with his third wife, Stevens reacted with jealousy and regret. Her letter of congratulations was tinged with anger. "When I repeatedly expressed a desire to have a child by you," she wrote, "your answer was 'There are plenty of men who would be glad to have a child by you. Go and get one of them to sire it for you' . . . and again . . . 'If I ever have a child it will be by some ignorant peasant girl and no questions asked. The child will be mine.'"[73] An earlier letter Stevens wrote when she was thirty-nine and nearing the end of her childbearing years suggests her ambivalence. "I was given a stern lecture the other night," she wrote Mitchell, "for not having a child. Mr. Tebrick [her pseudonym for Dudley Malone] is full of the idea. It's not a novel one, of course, but a practical one in the existing fearful circumstances. Naturally I thought about it the rest of the night but without marked enthusiasm. . . . To date I'm still a childless mother—Can I trust my subconscious self? I believe so."[74]

Stevens worked on a manuscript, "Women in Industry," on an extended stay in Italy after separating from Malone. Wide-ranging and interdisciplinary, the volume drew on law, sociology, anthropology, economics, and international relations to construct a powerful case for women's financial independence, their right to work, and the need to eliminate protective legislation. In the preface, dated April 1927, Stevens boldly wrote: "Political equality was not nearly so dangerous a challenge to the masculine state as is economic equality. Dollars, distinction, delights of distraction menace the protector. The image of all women and so woman, potentially in possession of shining coins in pocket is a terrifying image to the male, always insecure in his false role of protector and master. Woman may walk away."[75]

In this manuscript, Stevens proclaimed her equal rights perspective, which reflected her affiliation with the NWP and her individualist, heterosocial feminist approach. Opponents of an Equal Rights Amendment (ERA) accused the NWP of cold class-bias and a limited view that represented the selfish outlook of rich women. Women's Trade Union League (WTUL) leader Pauline Newman recalled the years before laws limited working hours: "we were 'free' and 'equal' to work long hours for starvation wages, or free to leave the job and starve!" Former glove maker Elisabeth Christman expressed her desire to "put some of the 'equal righters' in a boiler factory or to work at the conveyor belt in a highly speeded-up mass production industry," to give them a sense of the realities of factory work.[76]

In "Women and Industry" Stevens ticked through arguments supporting protective labor legislation and dismissed them one by one. To the argument that male workers would gain protections if women gained them first, she responded, "Instead of the strong leading and pulling along the weaker with them, the weak are to lead the way in their weakness and the strong will profit by their gains." She compared this logic to military strategy that put the least valuable troops forward to take the first fire, and followed with the more precious troops later. To the belief that men's strength allowed them to tolerate harsh working conditions, Stevens responded that intelligence, not physical strength, led workers to avoid exploitation and that not all women were weak. She flatly differed with the notion that women's potential motherhood made them more vulnerable workers.[77]

Stevens disagreed that women workers needed protective legislation because their ranks were less unionized. "The theory that all men are organized and therefore do not need legal protection is plainly not true. If legal protection is called upon to protect the unorganized worker then let it say so and be written applicable to all unorganized workers," she argued. To those who insisted women were more difficult to unionize, Stevens retorted: "How shall we ever know, if we first say to them that they cannot be organized because they are transients in industry and will soon marry and leave it?" She cited a recent ruling by the organized trainmen of the Baltimore and Ohio railroad—signed jointly by the railroad and the union—that fired all married women clerks after a certain date, and refused to hire married women going forward. The NWP filed a complaint and suggested "that was a matter for themselves to decide," and queried "whose business but theirs it was in ethics or reason, to decide where women should work and how, the railroad officials were shocked into telling the truth. This is what in anger they revealed: Frankly ladies, this was one concession we could make to organized labor which wouldn't cost us anything."[78]

Stevens vehemently disagreed that women workers required shorter hours, special accommodations, took more sick days than men, were too physically weak to do jobs like core-making in foundries and lifting heavy weights, and should be prevented from entering certain professions altogether. A 1927 law, for example, prohibited women from becoming taxi drivers because such work posed "a hazard to their morals." Her indignation was greater still because women were expected to labor strenuously at home. She stormed: "Enter the reformer ... What do they offer? Women must have shorter hours in the workshop because they must attend to their 'natural' tasks when they get home." Stevens noted once again that as soon as these jobs were done for pay by men in the labor market, they were not only done as well and as "naturally," but men received wages for doing them.[79]

Stevens believed the family and state undervalued women's labor in the home. She thought that men—husbands and fathers—should share the burden or shoulder the costs of household labor; history has proven this egalitarian ideal to be elusive and a sticking point in contemporary married women's ability to succeed in the workplace.[80] Placing these innovative ideas within the context of women's historic struggle for freedom from male oppression, Stevens proclaimed in 1926:

> We have fought to own our own bodies, our own children, our own professions, our own thoughts, and now we fight to own our own labor in the home. This objection based on fear, was offered against women going to college, entering the professions, entering politics, entering the church. It is the objection of the dominant one to sharing power with the subordinate. We have always been met with men's reluctance to share power, reluctance to share money, reluctance to share the political state, reluctance to share the professions and trades. Now we are after the home—the last trench of the vested right of the male. It is stupid of men to resist—it always was stupid of them to resist and it still is. We will do it.[81]

THE CHARACTERIZATION OF HERSELF: LORINE PRUETTE

In *Women and Leisure: A Study of Social Waste* (1924), Pruette first stated her conviction that women and men share a psychological urge to activity, a human need that must be met by meaningful work in the larger world outside the home. "The characterization of herself," Pruette argued over her lifetime, was the only role for which the self-respecting modern woman should consistently strive.[82] She asserted that it was socially critical for women to realize a balance between life in the public and private spheres. Pruette advocated new structures in the workplace, home, and community to make this possible. These included part-time work for mothers, expanded child care facilities, collective kitchens, careers run from the home, the sharing of domestic responsibilities, and a "new" marriage based on mutual respect and affection. Privately, Pruette recognized the enormous difficulty of resolving the career-marriage dilemma. Her two marriages ended in divorce; her unpublished writings, especially her fiction, painted a much darker picture than did her public statements. This tension reverberated between her public proclamations as social scientist, writer, and feminist and her private, personal conclusions. Like Stevens, her conflicts prefigured those of a later generation.

Pruette blamed her initial negativism toward marriage on her mother. "My mother made one unhappy marriage," she wrote, "and consistently presented marriage to her daughter, to me, as the worst fate that could befall a woman." Pruette vowed in her youth never to marry, and to strive for a career "as much like a man's as possible," but later changed her mind. "I had begun to suspect that marriage could not possibly be as bad as I had thought it." When Pruette's first husband "hounded" her to marry him, she wrote her mother for advice. Mrs. Pruette's blunt response was that "in the beginning you felt you would die of happiness, when he took you in his arms, and then soon everything was terrible, the happiness was gone and you were pregnant, the most dastardly deed every done to woman by the man she trusted."[83]

Despite (or perhaps because of) her mother's admonitions, Pruette married fellow graduate student Douglas Fryer in 1920, when she was twenty-four. Like Stevens, Pruette set out to have a modern marriage. Insisting no man would give her away, she walked down the church aisle "quite alone," kept her own name, used birth control, and resolved to continue her career. Pruette stated that she married in part to break away from her mother's tenacious grasp. "When Douglas came back from the war, he said that he had determined that we should never be separated again. My heart sank. I had already refused to marry him, before he went to Europe. . . . Time passed . . . and here was Douglas on the doorstep. Well, I thought, I may as well marry him. That will be a nice agreeable way to escape from Mama and Tinnissee."[84]

Pruette's private conclusions grew out of her unhappy experiences as well as her evolving thought on the different psychological needs of men and women. When she married Fryer she had just finished her master's degree at Clark. When her mentor G. Stanley Hall learned of her plans to marry, he took the extraordinary step of writing her fiancé that Pruette had "a kind of genius" and should be "left free" to develop it. Fryer's response, Pruette later remarked, was that "this was an odd sort of letter, and that I might better help him write a report. And I did. I did." Despite her new husband's shortcomings, Pruette considered the first two years of their marriage (1920–1922), when she was a doctoral student and he was teaching, as a haven. "We played house. We studied. I taught while he studied," she recalled. But when their careers came into conflict, the marriage began to go rapidly downhill.[85]

Drawing on Adler's theories, Pruette came to believe that men had a basic sense of inferiority and psychological dependence that led to their need to dominate. After marriage "men appear to lose a large part of their capacity as adults," she dryly remarked.[86] Although she advocated companionate marriage, Pruette ultimately conceded that men's emotional dependence made such an egalitarian ideal impossible. This was reinforced by her marriage to Fryer, who, in the language of the feminist rebirth of the 1960s, she later labeled a male chauvinist.[87] In 1922, Pruette was contentedly teaching at Smith College and beginning her dissertation when—without consulting her—Fryer accepted a position at the University of Utah. She followed him to Salt Lake City where, cut off from friends, relatives, and feminists (she found the unemancipated Mormon women and the city's "pall of sexual guilt" depressing) and relying on her husband for all her emotional needs, she began to question her sanity. When in her despair she turned to G. Stanley Hall, he responded: "Are you not called upon to make a very great adjustment, and if you have the elevation of the soul to make it, won't you look back upon it in the future as the very greatest of your achievements, to make a virtue of necessity? . . . I think I am praying for you in the only sense I can pray." She noted later, "there was a little of the Puritan in him always."[88] After a devastating year, Pruette convinced a dean at New York University to give her husband a job. Returning to New York City was like coming home: "the conversations of students in the Columbia commons seemed like feasts of reason," she joyfully wrote, "and where if I was mad, there were others like me." When she applied for the position of dean of women at New York University, however, the same dean who hired Fryer turned Pruette down because she was married. "Suppose your husband got sick," he queried, "How could you do your duty by the students?" Incensed and never afraid to speak her mind, Pruette retorted: "Suppose your wife got sick. You'd be sorry, I'm sure, but you would still do your job."[89]

Pruette came close to near mental collapse, and worse, during these years. "Anxieties crowded [my] days," she later recalled, "the most fantastic anxieties, enough to make a psychoanalytical holiday." She fretted about her mother's perceived unhappiness, imagined horrific disasters, and felt smothered and trapped. At her lowest point, she later described in the third person, "she came to the verge of suicide, and it was like a hateful compulsion which might at any moment get the better of her. It was there, in any height, above water, or a high window, an almost irresistible attraction."[90]

Pruette believed Fryer's need to control her destroyed their marriage and symbolized power relations between husbands and wives in most modern unions. She began to question the naïveté and expectant sense of possibility with which modern feminists infused their new, shared lives with men. Although they shared the same profession and coauthored several articles, the camaraderie so evident in the Beard and Irwin marriages was obviously missing here. Fryer insisted on putting his career before Pruette's and denigrated her work. After she completed her Ph.D., published her dissertation to acclaim, and applied for a Guggenheim Fellowship, he secretly submitted an application. They were both rejected because he was not selected, and the foundation only offered married women fellowships if their husbands also qualified. "He always applied for anything which seemed suitable for me," Pruette later wrote. "Was he competing with me? I suspect so.

He had told me he knew I was smarter than he was. I was a better writer. If I were sitting in my room, reading a magazine, he would come in, say, well dear, you're not doing anything—will you rewrite this article for me? He thought reading was not doing anything! I did not agree."[91]

Preutte drew on both Freud and Adler's theories in constructing her thoughts on the masculine need to dominate as it was manifested in marriage. She playfully demonstrated this in an irreverent poem, "Book Blues," that she wrote in her late sixties. Pruette contended that, rather than women suffering from penis envy, men suffered from "penis anxiety," based on the "erratic behavior" of the male organ. Although a feminist critic and revisionist of Freud, Pruette accepted his contention that personality and adult neuroses are formed in infancy and early childhood. Yet she believed boys suffered more psychological anxiety and trauma than girls (which reverberated through adulthood) because of their more insistent need to separate from the female (their mothers).[92]

Pruette thought this weight of masculine dependence triggered women's psychological stress, endangered their success, and threatened the potential of the egalitarian marriage ideal. "Women fail," she wrote, "because they do not have to succeed; they fail because they lead contingent lives and depend for their satisfactions upon pleasing someone else; they fail because their men do not want them to succeed; they fail because they seldom have wives." No longer certain that, in the existing gender and marital structures it was possible for women to be fully realized human beings, she wrote: "the only role that the self-respecting individual can consistently maintain is not that of wife, mother, daughter, sister—but the characterization of herself. She has been too long, through the centuries, a creature whose life was bounded and determined by sex for her to be quite confident yet that she is finally and most importantly a human being and an individual entity. She cannot be a whole person if she hearkens too much to the claims of others that she should be a part of them. She cannot run very fast in the race that is still to the swift if she must carry the burden of a husband's jealousy of her work."[93]

THE MARRIAGE-CAREER DILEMMA

In a number of unpublished short stories, Pruette depicted the marriage-career dilemma as unsolvable. In her fiction all the successful career women are single and the plots turn around the female protagonist's choice between home/marriage/companionship and work/career/loneliness. In "According to Taste," a story about a single, professional woman and a housewife who trade places for a week, the husband advises the unmarried woman that "marriage is a job" that is "far from easy." Unless she is willing to give up her career she should not plan to marry. The protagonist in "Don't Look Homeward, Angel!" leaves her husband and their country home for her work as a poet. "Not for her to hope for: comfort, security and a dear companion; there was only . . . the torment and the joy of hearing always in her ears ineffable music which she would echo haltingly in words."[94]

Pruette believed that modern women's insistence on satisfying lives in both marriage and work might benefit men more than women. "Second Wife" (1934) is a short story about a woman who takes a job to help her husband meet alimony payments to his first wife. She concludes: "I can't do two jobs. It's true, I'm just an old-fashioned girl. As a modern woman, I'm a fraud. I've got to have a husband who will support me. How disgusting of me!" In "Not Magic in Mountains" the heroine refuses to carry the double burden of marriage and career. "I don't want to be a wife," she states. "I'm going to be a great actress, do you understand? And I can't do both. . . . That's all there is to it, really. That each of us is limited, can do so much and then no more."[95]

Why the striking contradiction between Pruette's private thought and public expressions about the career-marriage dilemma? Part of it stemmed from the anguish she suffered ensnared in its perplexities. From 1922 to 1930, as her marriage unraveled, Pruette found herself plagued with depression, claustrophobia, and anxiety. She later called those eight years, when she was twenty-six to thirty-four years old, lost to her. Fearing she was losing her mind, she consulted a psychoanalyst. When she showed him a poem she had written about the sun, he insisted it revealed that her depression would be cured if she got pregnant, and gave birth to a son. Outraged (having vowed never to have children), Pruette went home and wrote a story about a woman living under water where no one could touch her. She showed it to no one. Finally, on the verge of suicide, she visited a physician who diagnosed a severe thyroid disorder. Although she believed the medicine he prescribed cleared up her symptoms, it is surely more than coincidence that the year Pruette was cured of her depression was also the year she separated from her first husband, whom she divorced two years later. In 1932 she married educational theorist and painter John Woodbridge Herring. Two years later. that marriage also ended in divorce. A quarter century later, Pruette described marriage in a letter to a friend as "that state of hope forever unjustified, that state of grace never to be attained."[96]

In Pruette's earliest feminist work, however, most notably *Women and Leisure*, her stance on marriage and career was quite different. Influenced by Charlotte Perkins Gilman and Olive Schreiner, Pruette criticized female "parasitism" in the home and asserted women's right to self-expression through paid labor.[97] She described *Women and Leisure* as her first feminist outburst. As part of her research, Pruette interviewed 350 high school girls on their future life goals. When forced to choose between career and marriage, two-thirds chose marriage, but when offered a more flexible question about future aspirations, two-thirds chose careers. A full 50 percent opted for both marriage and career. Such seeming vacillation was not due to "inconsistency of desire," but to "the presence in the girl's life of two elements both of which demand consideration." Noting that girls of "undivided desire" would, assuming they could find husbands, form "the bulwark of contented womanhood," Pruette asked clear-sightedly: "what of . . . those who wish personal success as writers, singers, musicians, actresses, business women, nurses, stenographers, aviators, architects, explorers, teachers, scientists, who after dreaming of themselves at the moment of supreme success add that they also dream of a husband and babies, or that they hope to find some man who will be 'unselfish enough' to wish them to continue their careers?"[98]

Pruette declared that the Industrial Revolution threw women out of a job, and asserted that American society in 1924 was living by the mores of a preindustrial culture in its insistence that woman's place was in the home. While working-class women often held traditionally female jobs like food processing and textile and clothing production, Pruette argued—in a theme feminist and author Betty Friedan would famously reiterate four decades later—that middle-class women (those most likely and economically able to stay home) were leisured and unemployed, restless and bored. Pruette believed society inflicted a heavy burden on women, forcing them to "subdue or thwart" one part of their beings in order to satisfy the other part, while men reaped the benefits of both "an active life outside the home and a satisfactory home life."[99] If society did not allow young women fulfillment in love and work, such restriction could cause psychological distress and possibly full-scale rebellion. Most dangerous were the mixed messages young middle-class women received: while social mores dictated they stay home after marriage, popular culture, the media, and a rising standard of material expectations invested the career woman with glamor. Stevens struck a similar note in a 1927 speech, in which she attributed "illness and bad temper in women to inhibited desires, to the isolation of parlors and the dullness of kitchens." "Take a strong woman, full of ambitions," Stevens told her audience. "Turn her loose on any one person, and that energy is bound to be too intense. The amount of unhappiness caused by frustration is incalculable. And it is surprising the way women's illnesses disappear when they get into interesting action."[100]

Like Stevens, Pruette publicly insisted on women's right to full lives in both spheres. She advocated part-time jobs as a way for wives to stay professionally active and to enjoy some financial and personal autonomy.[101] Although she appreciated the obstacles (employers who might be troubled by mothers of young children working for them, recalcitrant husbands who liked wives at home, exploitative possibilities of overwork and underpay), Pruette maintained that part-time work was the wave of the future for both sexes. She urged private employers and the government to provide opportunities and incentives for job-sharing and pairing of workers. "Can home and career be combined?" Pruette asked in 1924. "Part-time work may be the solution," she answered.[102]

In contrast to Stevens and the NWP feminists she represented, Pruette supported protective legislation, was anti-ERA, and believed in women's difference from men. "Legal disqualifications are not necessarily or essentially an evidence of malice toward women," she asserted in 1925, "and wherever based on sound questions of protection of health or safety it is to be hoped that such social legislation may be increased." She disparaged what she considered modern women's individualist desire to imitate men, writing: "women are found doing their very utmost to negate their sex, and thinking that thereby they may advance themselves in their profession as well as further the cause of feminism in general."[103] However, she also invoked the language of equal rights feminism when she argued that women were human beings who deserved to develop themselves as autonomous individuals.

Pruette helped popularize a US Women's Bureau report that contended that protective labor laws did not harm women's employment prospects. The federal bureau, staffed by social feminists, rolled out the findings, based on interviews conducted in 1926 with 1,200 women workers in eight states. They concluded that women had gained much more than they had lost from protective legislation and stated that fewer than 60,000 women (out of more than eight million in the labor force) had lost jobs as a result.[104] Distilling the findings in *The Woman's Journal*, Pruette asked, "Are Working Women Handicapped by Protective Labor Laws?" and concluded, "The ghost of unfair discrimination is effectively laid. . . . Those cases where laws have been found to work any hardship are so few as to give comfort only to the most fanatic."[105]

Pruette's evolving analysis illuminates changing cultural attitudes toward women in the labor force, which in the 1920s appeared welcoming but by the Depression had turned hostile. Pruette seemed, by the 1930s, to be seeking a more flexible set of ideas about women's sameness or difference, as she shifted her argument to a stronger support for women's employment rights. She believed in women's right to work, and in the unfairness of the wage gap. She assumed mothers needed special protections, and should be responsible for the care of children. She asserted that legislation limiting women's hours actually led to the increased employment of women, since more women had to be hired because overtime was not allowed.[106]

Although the report did suggest that some women workers suffered from restrictive hours laws—pharmacists, for example—Pruette concluded that gender discrimination, not protective legislation, was to blame. "The public wants its pills made by men, or at least employers think this is true." Waitresses affected by state prohibitions of night work already faced discrimination, since "everywhere the first-class restaurants employed men, probably because employers and patrons prefer the service of men." Blasting wage inequities, however, Pruette exclaimed in 1929, "The fundamental importance of the double standard of wages for men and women cannot be overestimated. . . . Public opinion holds that women are cheaper than men and that they should be cheaper." In the same breath, she reiterated her opposition to the ERA and to NWP "radicals." She described a discord that arose between equal rights and social feminists at the 1926 meeting of the International Alliance of Women, clearly siding with the social feminists. "'If she wants protection, she is not a feminist.' So cried the ardent egalitarians at the international meeting of women suffragists held in Paris in 1926. . . . The extremists from England and the United States were a gallant, fiery band, insisting on no protection, no discrimination, and claiming the right of free women to fight their own battles without special privileges or special handicaps. They made the most noise, but the victory belonged to the women who held that certain protections should be established by law, for the sake of the health of the woman worker and the future well-being of the race."[107]

The onset of the Great Depression and the cascade of social policies that followed in the 1930s under Roosevelt's New Deal demonstrated the ways that gendered assumptions could limit women's access to full economic citizenship.[108] The scarcity of jobs illuminated deeply rooted assumptions about women's secondary status in the workforce and within marriage. New Deal policies reified the categories of male earner and female dependent and lent new support to the old economic underpinning of marital roles. According to one opinion poll, 89 percent of the American public in the 1930s thought married women with husbands should not work.[109] When this became clear, Pruette's advocacy for women's employment rights sharpened.

Not surprisingly, the companionate marriage ideal lost steam in the 1930s.[110] Both marriage and divorce rates fell in the decade, in part because both could be expensive undertakings. Despite the fact that women made up a quarter of the labor force by then, public concern about unemployment focused on working men. A rising outcry was leveled at wives with paid jobs. Many private and public employers—public school systems, for example—fired or refused to hire women who were married. Congress legitimized this with the passage of Section 213 of the Economy Act of 1932, which stipulated that in deciding how to reduce civil service personnel, married persons whose spouses also held federal employment should be the first to be fired. Numerous women lied or lived in common-law marriages in order to keep their jobs.[111] The optimism feminists had expressed about the potential of modern marriage was vanquished, and women's advocates were forced to backtrack to defend married women's right to work.

The NWP took the lead at congressional hearings held between 1932 and 1937 that challenged Section 213, and the Women's Trade Union League and the League of Women Voters joined them. The exigency of the situation brought them together despite their differences. Florence Barnes of the WTUL demonstrated this in her testimony in civil service hearings in 1935: "we are alarmed at the implications in the present law. Are we to come to a time when not a person's worth but the number of his dependents is to determine whether or not he shall work, and how much he shall be paid?" Speaking for the Business and Professional Women's Foundation, Dorothy Dunn asserted: "discrimination against married women is a blow to all women who work and to marriage itself, which would sweep from the ranks of workers all women whose only crime was their marital status."[112] Women's organizations of all kinds spent five long years lobbying to eliminate the offensive legislation.

During these backpedaling years, Pruette became a strong public voice for women's right to remain in the labor force. In *Women Workers through the Depression* (1934), a slim book summarizing an American Woman's Association (AWA) study, she built a case for women's financial need to work. The study surveyed 1,350 respondents, about one-third of the group's membership, to determine the effects of the economic crisis on professional women. This survey, which covered 1929 to 1933, focused on the typical AWA member—a New York City resident, forty-five years old, unmarried, well educated, with a track record in the workplace. "Never before," Pruette wrote, "have so many women had a direct stake in the economic system as today." Eleven percent of the women included were unemployed (for sixteen months, on average) and seeking work. Pruette estimated women's unemployment in New York City in 1931 at 13 percent, and 23 percent by 1934. She captured the rising disillusionment of a generation of women who had placed high hopes in paid work.[113]

Yet these urban, professional, predominantly white women weathered the Depression in creative and resourceful ways. Some returned to live with their parents, others drew on savings and investments, still others sought retraining, or leveraged hobbies into paying occupations. Since women workers had less to lose in personal and social status than male workers, they were more willing to do anything to stay afloat. She profiled over forty women who, after losing their jobs, demonstrated flexibility and resilience by finding new careers.[114]

Pruette made a compelling case for women's right and economic need— equally with men—to work for wages. "It is evident," she wrote of the AWA members profiled, "that such women have made a real investment in the occupational world." Arguing that marriage was no longer a guarantee of financial support, she also warned of the "fascist tendencies" in governments and nations that attacked married women workers. She pronounced the tendency of the government to "look with disfavor upon employing two persons from the same family" as exceedingly dangerous. She noted that, although only 19 percent of the women in the study were married, nearly half were wholly responsible for the support of others. "The notion that the woman worker is, at most, responsible for her own support and that she does not support others is one that has long been resented by women as unjust," she concluded.[115]

Like Stevens, Pruette never had children, a fact she, too, expressed regret about as she grew older. She blamed this on her mother, whose "strictures through the years made it perfectly clear . . . that never, no never, must I bear a child. It would have been a vast intolerable betrayal of my loved and hated mother." "If my mother had had a different obstetrician," Pruette asserted in mid-life, "it is quite likely that my own life would have been different. I would now be a graying haired mother, or grandmother, instead of a red-headed (rinses help) solitary female." However, her decision also appears to have been tied to her marital agreement with her first husband, who had made Pruette promise she would not have children. After they divorced, he remarried and in quick succession had five daughters with his second wife, a fact Pruette noted with irony and resentment. At sixty she wrote privately, "In that brief period of time when I had love, given and returned, [my] prayer was, 'give me a child.' I was not so lucky. So my immortality, so far as we know, has to concern the whole human race."[116]

Yet Stevens and Pruette were clear-eyed about the sacrifices professional women made for motherhood, and this surely influenced their own personal decisions. Pruette described childbearing as "a peculiar handicap from which there is no recovery. The time devoted to this will be irrevocably lost to the profession in which the woman is engaged." Ever creative and hoping to bend inflexible social structures, however, Pruette promoted small families, careful timing of pregnancies, as well as women's right to decide against motherhood. "For those women who feel no impelling urge toward maternity," she wrote, "and whose interests are entirely with their career, the problem very largely solves itself." Yet she continued to be a persistent marriage-career publicist. "More and more women are combining a career and a home," she wrote confidently. "More and more they are having to combine them if they are at all to enjoy the pleasures and the satisfactions of home life. A life plan must give room for both a vocational plan and an expectation of the normal love interests."[117] That she was never able to achieve this is one of the great ironies of Pruette's life, one that illuminates the nexus of contradictions early twentieth-century feminists who championed modern marriage found themselves facing. Like Pruette, Stevens ultimately concluded it would be up to a future generation to solve this quandary. She wrote Betty Gram Swing in 1946 about a daughter of a mutual friend: "Sally's generation will probably be able to carry out what ours only talked about—career & marriage."[118]

CHAPTER 6

To Work Together for
Ends Larger Than Self

The international women's movement was another site of feminist experimentation in the 1920s and 1930s, and both Doris Stevens and Mary Beard led organizations in these years that were global in scope and grand in vision. An investigation of the Inter American Commission of Women (IACW), which strove for equal rights in international laws, and the World Center for Women's Archives (WCWA), which advocated the preservation of women's historical documents, highlights innovative feminist efforts and challenges in these years. The IACW was an international panel charged with investigating proposed legislation affecting women's status in the Americas. Stevens chaired the commission from 1928 to 1939. The WCWA, which Beard co-founded in 1935 and led until 1940, was to be a gathering place and clearinghouse of women's historical documents. Both organizations ultimately fell apart because of lingering suffrage rivalries, different conceptions of feminism, racial tensions, larger world events, and Beard's and Stevens's own personal fatigue and age. Although in the short run both organizations failed, their founding visions lived on, and many of their objectives were ultimately realized. Through the organizations they led and the ideas they represented in the 1930s, Beard and Stevens carried feminism forward. The 1930s marks the midpoint of their feminist activism, and was the decade in which both women achieved the height of their public influence.

Like Mercury Poised for Flight: Doris Stevens

The 1930s were personally difficult for Stevens, but they were also years of public recognition and independence. Stevens was forty years old in 1928 when elected the first chairperson of the IACW. Although formally under the aegis of the Pan-American Commission and representing "no political party in any country and no one point of view," the commission was a National Woman's Party (NWP) satellite during the eleven years Stevens directed it. Through Stevens's IACW leadership the party put its equal rights credo before an international audience.[1]

International feminism was attractive to the NWP for a number of reasons. It carried on the tradition feminists had established during World War I when they worked for suffrage and peace on an international scale. Party members identified closely with English feminists, whose militant tactics had inspired their own suffrage activism. Despite their reluctance to embrace the priorities of African American women at home, the party consistently—and paradoxically—held that feminism should not be limited by national boundaries.

International feminist organizations replicated the same global hierarchy that existed in the 1930s.[2] Pre–World War I transnational women's organizations originated in Europe and "neo-European" countries like the United States, Canada, and Australia, and women who joined were predominantly of European heritage. One exception was the International Council of Women of the Darker Races, founded in 1920 by the US-based National Association of Colored Women, which strove to draw attention to racial discrimination as a global phenomenon.[3] The International Council of Women, the International Suffrage Alliance, and the Women's International League for Freedom considered "Western" societies the peak of progress and "Eastern" societies repressive and backward.[4] Women heading these organizations viewed western and northern Europe and the United States as the core, southern and eastern Europe as a semi-periphery, and Latin America, the Middle East, Asia, and Africa as the periphery of a feminist global hierarchy.[5] This perspective led to the image of European-descent women in the lead for women's global rights, helping out their more oppressed sisters.

As colonized countries began to gain their independence, however, diverse voices around the world rose to challenge imperialism within international women's organizations. Women in Latin America, the Middle East, Asia, and Africa questioned assumptions about European supremacy and insisted on speaking for themselves. As a result, in the 1920s and 1930s international women's organizations added branches in Chile, Brazil, Egypt, India, Jamaica, Palestine, Haiti, Japan, Peru, Bermuda, Cuba, Puerto Rico, Turkey, Mexico, Tunis, and South West Africa. By the late 1930s, "international" assumed a new definition as women gazed not only across the Atlantic but around the globe.[6]

The NWP joined international feminism after World War I and pushed forward in the global arena their singular feminist vision. Party members believed women might succeed where men had failed in making the world more peaceful and egalitarian.[7] NWP members wanted to be vigilant about international decisions made by governing bodies of men, which affected the rights and status of women. "Since the beginning of time, men with the best of intentions . . . have been writing laws for our good," Stevens stated. "Since the beginning of time, brave and valiant women have been abolishing these same laws."[8]

Alva Belmont was committed to the idea of international feminism, and her funding was influential in the direction the party moved in the post-suffrage years. Belmont told an NWP audience in 1923 that "the day may not be so far distant . . . where [women] will set up a woman's government by women for women and children and humanity in general."[9] The separatism of this vision, reminiscent of Frances Willard's 1890s image of a Republic of Women, was emblematic of the paradox NWP feminism embraced in the post-suffrage years.[10] Their equal rights stance insisted women were "the same as" men, yet they stressed female solidarity and assumed a self-consciousness of gender "difference." Belmont's imperious treatment of other women, from the African American suffragists she purported to assist in the 1910s to her reliance on Stevens, stood as an ironic testimony to her rhetorical, disingenuous use of the term "sisterhood."

The NWP's post-suffrage struggles illuminate some of the organizational feminist challenges that arose after the heady victory of the Nineteenth Amendment. The racial tensions that had run through the suffrage movement were still in evidence. As early as 1920, Alice Paul's single-minded focus led her to overlook the racial discrimination that kept some women from exercising their right to vote. As they had feared, even if they could register Black women were forced to wait in long lines, to document tax payment and property ownership, and even to take "educational tests" to prove their intellectual capacity. When they challenged Paul to speak out, she equivocated, insisting mistreatment at the polls was a race issue, not a women's issue.[11] This disagreement came to a head at the 1921 NWP convention to commemorate suffrage pioneers. Mary White Ovington, president of the NAACP and member of the NWP Advisory Council, asked Paul to organize a committee dedicated to investigating the inequities affecting African American women.[12] Paul declined, provoking a range of responses. NWP field secretary Addie Hunton, who was African American, proposed that a deputation "ask for a hearing during the convention and at the same time have groups picketing the convention the entire time it is in session." She believed this strategy would offer "a very positive challenge to the Woman's Party to uphold the principles upon which it is founded."[13]

When Paul got wind of this, she asked clubwoman Hallie Q. Brown to read a resolution on the subject of Black women's suffrage on the convention floor. Hunton was skeptical: "Miss Paul, I fear, is not a bit interested in the question of suffrage as it relates to the colored women, and I am afraid she has given us the opportunity of having you [Brown] before the Resolution Committee, because she knows that it will be a nice burying ground for anything that we want to do."[14] Mary Church Terrell, president of the National Association of Colored Women, led a group of sixty African American women to visit Paul three days before the convention. Paul continued to vacillate, causing Terrell to exclaim that she "displayed the most painful lack of tact I had ever seen."[15] In a sharply critical article, "Alice Paul Pulls the Strings," *Nation* journalist Freda Kirchwey commented: "Miss Paul was indifferent to this appeal . . . and resented the presence of the delegation."[16]

Concerned about negative publicity, several white officers apologized to Hunton and pleaded with her not to bring the Black women's resolution to the convention floor. Hunton refused to back down, and the resolution was read. It stated in part: "[Black women] have . . . come today to call your attention to the flagrant violations of the intent and purposes of the Susan B. Anthony Amendment in the elections of 1920." Although the resolution failed to pass, African American women won a victory by getting it on the convention floor and put the NWP on record refusing to take up the issue of Black women's disenfranchisement.[17] Florence Kelley, an NAACP and NWP Advisory Committee member, stated that the party had "welshed on the Negro question" and passed up the opportunity to launch "one of the most hopeful events thinkable for this new year."[18]

Paul claimed she had to keep her concentration squarely on the passage of gender-based equal rights legislation. She refused to acknowledge that the law affected women differently, arguing that legal discrimination created a shared experience that unified women across racial and economic differences. In addition, she contended her responsibility was to hold the party together by avoiding internal dissension.[19] Her insistence on treating sexism as primary reflects the assumption that women's experiences are informed first and foremost by gender oppression. Although Paul was anxious to appease white members, the incident alienated supporters and helped precipitate a steady decline in membership.

At the same time that African American members challenged the national agenda of the NWP, the party was at work striving to build international connections, with Stevens in the lead. As chair of the NWP Committee on International Relations, she was present at the sixth Pan American Union held in Havana, Cuba, in 1928, where the Inter American Commission of Women was created. The Fifth International Conference of American States (Pan American Union), held in Santiago, Chile, in 1923, had passed a resolution to include women's rights on the agenda of future conferences. Cuban women, leaders in attaining legal reforms and at work on numerous feminist fronts, then took the floor and proposed the creation of a women's organization within the Pan American Union. The resolution recommended that countries of the Americas strive to educate women and eliminate sex-based constitutional and legal limits.[20]

Doris Stevens, Jane Norman Smith, Valentine Winters, and Puerto Rico's Muna Lee represented the NWP at the 1928 Conference. Not only did three of the "battalion of four" face a language barrier, they knew very little about international treaties. "As to the treaty-making powers of the various governments . . . and . . . [the] manifold complexities of international machinery, the chairman," Stevens wrote of herself, "might as well have been in the cradle."[21] Nonetheless, they came with Paul's freshly drafted Equal Rights Treaty in hand, modeled on the ERA, which required governments to bring their laws into compliance with the equal rights principle. Article 1 read: "The contracting states agree that upon the ratification of this Treaty, men and women shall have equal rights throughout the territories subject to their respective jurisdictions."[22] Stevens exuberantly wrote Jonathan Mitchell from Havana: "It is wonderful to work in a country where women are such tremendous news. . . . Everyday on every one of six Spanish papers we are taking everything from headlines to prominent columns. . . . The Latin American men are so much quicker so much more sensitive than our fish that we expect results from them but not from ours. Every one of the men we speak to whether for or against are captivated by our treaty idea."[23]

On February 7, 1928, the final act of the conference was to create the IACW, resolving, "That an Interamerican Women's Commission be constituted to take charge of the preparation of juridical information and data of any other kind which may be deemed advisable to enable the Seventh International Conference of American States to take up the issue of the civil and political equality of women on the continent."[24] A panel of twenty-one women established to study the status of women in Central and South America, the Caribbean, and the United States, the commission was also to investigate all proposed legislation affecting women. Stevens was elected its first chair, a victory for the NWP and a tribute to her own leadership abilities and tactical genius. Drawing on skills developed in the suffrage movement, the NWP feminists with others succeeded in getting six countries to endorse the inclusion of the Equal Rights Treaty on the agenda of the next Pan American Conference, to be held in Montevideo, Uruguay, in 1933. "Our treaty proposal was heard amidst mingled astonishment and admiration," Stevens stated at a League of Nations banquet upon her return, "astonishment at its comprehensive nature, and admiration for our courage in asking so much at one time."[25] She grandly described the conference as a "great and historic occasion," where "international feminism was born."[26]

Cuban women did not yet have the vote in 1928. On their visit that year, Stevens and other NWP representatives organized a Havana march to protest Cuban women's disenfranchisement. In the 1920s Cuban feminists drew on motherhood as the cornerstone of a women's revolution and argued that women's roles as wives, mothers, and guardians of morality made them deserving of additional power and rights in both the family and state. Between 1927 and 1933, the government of President Gerardo Machado was marked by public opposition, violence, and political chaos. Cuban suffragists joined forces with the revolution and, using votes for women as a symbol of potential Cuban democracy, helped bring down Machado's repressive regime in 1933, and won the suffrage that same year.[27]

Many North American feminists were dismissive of Cuban women's efforts to win the suffrage. At the 1926 Inter American Women's Congress in Panama, the North American delegation abstained from voting for a resolution that would bring woman suffrage to all American nations, arguing that Latin American women were not sufficiently prepared to vote. In 1929, Carrie Chapman Catt, then director of the Women's Struggle for World Peace and Friendship with South America, described Latin American women as "a threat to friendly and peaceful relations between the United States and South America."[28] Although the reason for this strong declaration is unclear, Catt apparently felt Latin American women had not fought for the vote long enough to understand the responsibilities of enfranchisement. Cuban feminists were disappointed that other Latin American countries, particularly Argentina, sided with the United States in opposing their suffrage. Stevens, whose relationship with Catt was strained at best, brought a fresh pro-suffrage position with her as IACW chair, representing a welcome softening of the North American view.

NWP members in the United States were thrilled with the organization's movement into international feminism. They compared the effect the Pan American conferences had in the Western Hemisphere with that the League of Nations had in Europe and believed Pan American states that approved equal rights would pave the way for the rest of the world. Stevens claimed that the significance of the Havana accomplishments was that women's human rights would be restored, and that "in this hemisphere no longer will international law be written by men only, passed upon by men only, and enforced by men only."[29]

One of the first tasks commission members undertook was the arduous job of researching the disparities in the laws applying to gender in their respective countries. Word by word the members, who together spoke and read a number of languages, went through the twenty-one constitutions, civil codes, and judicial decisions pertaining to women. Stevens confided in a letter: "We are making a digest of all the laws relating to the status of women in the 21 Republics of this hemisphere. It is a sad & melancholy task. Some of them are intact as they were written in Spain in 1200. But it will be an invaluable compilation, as nothing of the sort has been done."[30] When they were finally completed, the notebooks of legal discrimination became known to feminists as "the Black Books" because of the "sins against women" they contained.[31] Whether they were used by policy makers in the twenty-one nations is unclear, but they were rich repositories for activists to draw upon in their efforts.

In August 1928, Stevens led a group of nine—including French lawyer and International Council of Women member Maria Verone, French Alliance leader Germaine Malaterre-Sellier, and British feminist Lady Margaret Rhondda—to the gathering of male plenipotentiaries who had come to sign the Kellogg-Briand Peace Pact at the French president's summer château in Rambouillet, a Paris suburb. After their request for a hearing on the Equal Rights Treaty was ignored, the deputation gathered at the chateau gates and unfurled a banner demanding equal rights. The women were promptly arrested by the French police, who tore up their petition and escorted them to the station. Their civil disobedience garnered a deluge of publicity, both positive and negative. Hearkening back to

Stevens's 1917 arrest and imprisonment for suffrage activism, *Equal Rights* ran a front-page photograph of the women at the police station under the headline, "Jailed for Freedom." Stevens reported being "screamed at, yelled at, scolded, bullied somewhere along the line by practically every colleague with whom I was attempting to work." At the same time she proclaimed the event "brilliant" and stated immodestly to Paul, "our methods [are] so far ahead of European methods," despite the fact that NWP feminists had learned the radical tactics they successfully employed in the suffrage struggle from British suffragettes.[32]

Their arrests stirred French women to organize a protest rally, at which Stevens declared: "This humble event at Rambouillet became the world's forum. All the world knew the following day about the Equal Rights Treaty. They told us we lacked tact. Of course, we lacked tact. We are in revolt."[33] Belmont was one of the colleagues opposed to this attention-grabbing tactic; she called the protest "foolish," while another American former suffragist thought it "lovely."[34] Jonathan Mitchell wrote Stevens jubilantly: "You're a very famous person. You are, I think, the best newspaper figure among American women. You are the acknowledged head & front of the women's movement. . . . You've been taken to the heart of the nation for what you've done. You are our Doris, you are an American girl, & we Americans love you."[35]

Although prone to hyperbole, Mitchell did not appear to be exaggerating. Europeans who followed the women's movement were curious to know more about Stevens. One writer to the British feminist weekly *Time and Tide* inquired: "Who is this Doris Stevens? . . . Is she old or young? What is the secret of this power she seems to possess to make things happen?" In October 1928 the publication ran an article, "Doris Stevens: An Apostle of Action."[36] Its editor Rhondda firmly believed the NWP was the keeper of the flame of radical feminism the English suffrage movement had bequeathed to the languishing US movement during the 1910s. "I am absolutely clear," she wrote Stevens in 1928, "that the torch of the militants which has been handed from one side to another of the Atlantic during the past century is now in the hands of the Woman's Party and I would follow you if I were the only woman in Europe to do it—But I shall not be the only woman."[37]

Stevens's brilliance as an activist sprang from her ability to speak with eloquence and passion and to capitalize on the symbolism of events that would become historic. The same gifts that made her a suffrage leader—her personal magnetism, political savvy, and unconquerable energy, her natural ability to lobby, fund raise, and organize—made her an effective international leader. Rhondda wrote Stevens admiringly the day before her 1928 arrest: "Your powers are only just short of magical. . . . I've never seen any organizing in the world to begin to touch it—it's that capacity for throwing the whole of your self into one channel, rushing towards one aim; I think theres [*sic*] nothing left of you to see, or hear, or think except towards what you mean to get—& you can yet continue to think clearly, & keep your mental & nervous balance—it's almost unbelievable—a kind of absolute self-immolation."[38]

By many accounts, Stevens's energy was invincible and her vision passionate. She asked no more of others than she asked of herself. A French colleague wrote: "Doris Stevens . . . is an idealist, sincere, generous, ardent. One feels she has given up everything—comfort, pleasure, personal work, happiness—for the great cause she has set her heart to—the freedom of women . . . we hardly dare to mention such things as food or sleep, as she never did herself. She seemed to be living on air and Feminism."[39]

Not surprisingly, Mitchell waxed eloquent in his congratulatory letter, writing, "Rambouillet was Armageddon. That was a great creative act. It was a poem of action, to which women, at least in America . . . are going again & again for refreshment, as people go to the Acts of the Biblical apostles." He told Stevens that she belonged to history, and that she had been able—"in four days of tremendous flashing work"—to raise the status of women, something the NWP had been striving to do over many long years. He commiserated with her over Belmont's disapproval: "I don't like to write about Lady B. Everyone who hears about her will be honestly shocked. Because people thought she loved you, women liked her. But for you, she is just nothing—a fat, awkward, rich, asthmatic old woman. She must know no one thinks she is fit to touch your shoes, except that she loves you. . . . I'll bet it's literally true Mrs. Belmont needs you far more than you need her money."[40]

Characteristically, Stevens threw her formidable energy into international feminism during the eleven years she headed the commission. After her arrest she traveled to Geneva, where she successfully lobbied the League of Nations, asking the new delegations to the Hague Conference on the Codification of International Law to consider women's issues. She helped found the Open Door International in Berlin in 1929, whose purpose was the emancipation of the woman worker, and whose eleven-point manifesto strove to ensure women the right to paid work regardless of gender, marriage, parenthood, or childbirth.[41] At the same time, she entered a Ph.D. program in political science, with a concentration in international law and relations, at Columbia University. Admitted in the summer of 1929, Stevens combined her graduate studies with her IACW leadership, remained enrolled between 1929 and 1931, but never completed the degree. She was invited, as a visiting professor, to give a series of lectures on international law at the University of Havana. In 1931 Stevens became the first woman to be elected into the prestigious American Institute of International Law, taking the seat formerly held by Theodore Roosevelt's secretary of state Elihu Root. Soon afterward, a syndicated newspaper column offered "A Good Intelligence Test" in hundreds of American newspapers: it was a series of questions about Doris Stevens. An *Equal Rights* article on Stevens declared, "Havana, Paris, Berlin, Washington, are merely stepping-stones in the career of one who has again proved to the world the firm solidarity of Feminists." She was described elsewhere as "like Mercury poised for flight."[42] Privately, she admitted exhaustion.[43]

At the same time that she experienced professional success, Stevens suffered a series of personal losses. Her parents died within two years of one another: her father in 1930, her mother in 1932. Alva Belmont died in 1933. Stevens's enigmatic relationship with Belmont was intertwined with her feminist activism, and it influenced her rapport with Alice Paul. The triangulated relationship between Stevens, Paul, and Belmont appears to have been stoked by Belmont, beginning in 1927. She told Doris that year, in confidence, that Paul had blackmailed her into paying Paul one thousand dollars a month. When Stevens came to Paul's defense, Belmont replied sharply: "Don't defend her. I know what I'm talking about. Besides she is not your friend. She does not approve of you."[44] Belmont also told Stevens privately that she would be repaid and recognized for her hard work and services by a legacy after Belmont's death. Stevens wrote in her diary on July 18, 1927, during a visit at Belmont's chateau: "had important conversation with Mrs. Belmont on morning walk. We have made agreement—she has promised to put me in her will because of all I have done for her—I am greatly relieved—said I could do law later—after she was gone—very sad—she is angry at Miss Paul." Belmont insisted Stevens tell no NWP members she was included in her will because it might cause hard feelings. The only person Stevens shared this with was her mother, "when she complained that I had so little time to spend with her in her declining years, explaining to her that I had a duty to fulfill to Mrs. Belmont."[45]

Despite Stevens's increasingly heavy schedule, Belmont called upon her for tasks both large and small. In June 1930, when Belmont traveled to Aix, France, for her health, she asked Stevens to accompany her. When Belmont abandoned this idea, she invited Stevens to come live with her at her Paris chateau and from there she directed Stevens's work through August, September, October, and part of November. In much of her international activism, Stevens followed Belmont's direction: "'you will represent me,' she said—her favorite phrase."[46] Although increasingly fatigued and suffering from chronic stomach problems, Stevens carried on her labor with the commission (for which she was not paid), occasionally receiving checks from Belmont. Being so closely associated with Belmont and Paul at times proved a stumbling block to her international efforts.

By 1930 Belmont's health had begun to fail. Then seventy-seven, she was alarmed to find her body weakening and leaned more heavily on Stevens to represent her in feminist work. In an April 5, 1929, letter Belmont exclaimed, "I am so proud of the work you are doing for us and the great name you are making for yourself. At last we are to have what we deserve, as you say it is coming so fast now, and oh! How we have worked for it." Belmont continued: "During the long hours of the night when I do not sleep, I realize what I am unable to do out here, it is dreadful to grow old, to know that the body stops the will. I never expected this." She tucked a $500 check into the envelope, instructing Doris, "I want you to use [this] for yourself alone do not mention it to the Party, it is for your personal use not for them."[47]

It is difficult to understand the personal sacrifices Stevens made for Alva Belmont. They went beyond her hopes of receiving a large inheritance, but had to do with Stevens's passionate dedication, which Belmont shared, for achieving equal rights. Stevens put family, friends, health, and financial security in jeopardy in her zealous commitment to the cause. Some have suggested that Belmont functioned in part as a mother figure for Doris.[48] In May 1930, when she wanted Stevens to stay near her in Paris and arrange lunches, teas, and press conferences to publicize their successful work at the Hague, Stevens did so, even though she was anxious to return to the United States because her seventy-year-old father was ill. "Mrs. Belmont said she was so lonely and was so eager to have me stay, that I risked staying and got back home only to receive a telegram a few days later summoning me to my father's funeral." In some of their correspondence, Stevens almost sounds like a kept woman: on December 26, 1930, Belmont wrote: "What would we do without you and Miss Paul? Don't work too hard. Manage to have *some* fun. I enclose my check. Take it and go on a spree. In the past you remember we *did* have sprees?"[49] In 1931 the Alva Belmont House, donated as the new NWP headquarters, was dedicated in Washington, DC, and Stevens spoke in a nationwide broadcast on behalf of Belmont. In June of that year, as Belmont volleyed numerous letters demanding Stevens take on other IACW tasks, she ordered her to attend a League of Nations Women's Committee meeting in Geneva, and then insisted she and Paul visit her in France.

In a long memorandum describing her complicated relationship with Belmont, Stevens described a ten-day visit to her French chateau in August 1931. Paul was there as well for a few days. Stevens chronicled, "I rode with her, read to her, played cards in the evening, inspected her playground, visited a little French child whose upkeep she had undertaken, etc. She seemed to me very ill, although very valiant about it." At a final tea alone, Belmont offered Stevens a rose from her garden, talked about death, and asked Stevens that Belmont's son William have a monument to her erected. Belmont described exactly what she wanted, a heroic figure of herself in the open air in Washington, DC. She envisioned the monument containing a bas relief depicting the Washington-based activism of the final phase of the suffrage movement—riots by the police and the mob, women arrested for picketing President Wilson, women being loaded onto patrol wagons. "In short," Stevens recalled, "she wanted cut in stone the sacrifices which so many women had made in going to prison for this idea." They parted in tears; it was the only time Stevens saw Belmont weep.[50]

At the same time, her mother's remaining years were limited. Doris's family correspondence suggests that, although not often physically present, she served as the arbitrator and leader, lending money, dispensing advice, and offering emotional support to her three siblings and their parents. Her brother Henry wrote in December 1932, after their mother's death: "As you say mother's going alone was a terrible thing. . . . Doris you say you are sorry you could not do better in 1932. Well you were always thoughtful when you had it. And would send money to Ma. And I give you credit for all what you did, Doris."[51] A friend— probably fellow NWP member Vivian Pierce commiserated, "Of course it is really tragic that you did not get out. I know how awful it must be to think you could have done more. But she was always so tremendously moved by your life, and I am sure she understood."[52]

Stevens was a workaholic who pushed herself incessantly. She was so over-wrought at the start of her international labor that she lost sixteen pounds and recorded her weight in October 1928 as only 116. Mitchell urged her to toil less and to take care of herself: "I know that you will be at your headquarters conscientiously, like a good child, & infinitely touching, working until all hours over every little detail of what other people won't do. And I beg of you, heart of my heart, please let even little things be undone, rather than exhaust yourself. . . . But I write this despairingly. You will give of yourself, probably, as long as you can hold your head up."[53]

In May 1932, Belmont suffered a stroke, followed by a second several months later, and died in early 1933, setting off a dramatic chain of events in Stevens's life. Along with Paul, Stevens played a central role in the ceremonies surrounding the funeral. After a short Paris service Belmont's body was brought to New York on board the SS *Berengarian* and met dockside by an NWP honor escort headed by Paul and Stevens. An additional forty party members stood watch beside the coffin until the service began. Held on February 12, 1933, in Saint Thomas Church, the funeral—which Belmont had painstakingly planned—was attended by fifteen hundred mourners, including two hundred NWP delegates wearing the suffrage colors gold, white, and purple.[54] Stevens was one of twenty honorary pallbearers and delivered the eulogy, stating generously, "There is not a woman living today who is not nearer the benefits and beauties of freedom because of Mrs. Belmont."[55]

After Belmont's death, Stevens's relationship with Paul soured even further. Although Stevens had "affectionately" dedicated *Jailed for Freedom* to Paul in recognition of her "brilliant and devoted leadership," she was tiring of what she perceived as Paul's increasingly tyrannical leadership.[56] Some of Paul's behaviors suggest she resented the publicity Stevens attracted, even though Stevens drove herself largely on behalf of the NWP. Years later, when she and Paul were at odds over the ERA strategy, Stevens recalled, "this is not the first time she has blown up about my getting press attention without seeking it." Stevens wrote a colleague in confidence:

An incident in Geneva comes to mind—I think it was as far back as 1931,— which first shook my naïve belief in the legend of her [Paul's] great and saintly indifference to recognition. I had been in the hotel only a few moments when Clarence Street of the NYTIMES appeared and told Paul he was there to get a statement from me about my mission in Geneva. She produced me and I gave him something. Scarcely was he out of the hotel headquarters which she was in charge of when she let go with "How does it happen he comes for a story from you? I have been here for __ months (I forget the number) and he's never come for one from me!" I told her he had told me that his NY editor had cabled him to get a statement of so & so many words from me. Still incredulous, she asked, "Do you know him?" I told her I had never seen him before in my life. She was so unhappy it was embarrassing.[57]

In addition, Stevens believed Paul convinced Belmont to leave her out of the will. In a private memorandum Stevens wrote in 1933—described by Belmont's biographer as "an angry and self-pitying description of what it was really like to be Alva's surrogate militant suffragist daughter"—she commented: "She [Paul] knew I was the personally preferred and better loved one in relation to Mrs. Belmont and this had concerned her more than I could ever have dreamed possible."[58] Doris's sister Alice wrote her kindly: "Hope this finds you reconciled about the Belmont will. I have thought about it so often and know just how you must feel.... If only the reporters would have a heart for your sake. You & father were alike in the money proposition. The only value it had was for the things it would buy."[59]

Belmont had left Stevens $50,000 in an earlier will, but to Stevens's dismay Belmont changed her will.[60] When Stevens discovered this she sued the estate, claiming she had served as the older woman's alter ego for eighteen years. Paul was not included in the will either, but the NWP received $100,000. Party members rushed to repair the widening rift between Paul and Stevens.

Despite these efforts, in August Stevens attended a hearing where she made her claims on Belmont's will; the following year she received $12,000, which may have been a private agreement worked out between Stevens and Belmont's three children.[61] Writing her close friend Sara Bard Field, Stevens tried to explain why the revocation was so upsetting: "It would take Freud himself, and I doubt if he could explain it adequately, to know what emotions which had gone into our odd relationship for so many years had been violated by her public repudiation of me."[62]

Belmont's biographer suggested Stevens was unaware Belmont had made her legacy conditional on Stevens postponing her graduate studies, but Stevens's relationships with men may also have been a concern. Belmont changed her will in 1931 when Stevens failed to visit because she was taking her doctoral qualifying exams. When she did arrive, Belmont thought she behaved badly. She may have been referring to her flirtations, highlighting their ongoing conflict over this topic.[63] Belmont's attitude toward men, despite (or perhaps because of) her own two marriages, was hostile. When Stevens's marriage to Malone was falling apart, Belmont warned her that men were not to be trusted. Paul confided to Stevens that Belmont was disturbed by Stevens's heterosocial lifestyle, "having been told," Stevens exclaimed, "that while I was in Geneva I 'went out with men!'" Belmont viewed men as a distraction to feminist work, while Stevens—like other modern feminists—considered her interactions with men an important part of her strategy as well as her definition of feminism.[64]

EQUAL RIGHTS DEBATE IN THE GLOBAL ARENA

Despite the death of Belmont and the rivalry between Paul and Stevens, the work for equal rights continued. Stevens's unyielding support of identical laws for women and men, which put her at odds with maternalist thinkers and US social feminists, also affected her international work. Laws regulating women's labor were a global issue because of the international ties of the socialist and trade union movements and because governments, concerned about wage competition on the world market, increasingly collaborated to set consistent standards. The founding of the International Labor Organization (ILO), a body established as an agency of the League of Nations in the Treaty of Versailles, testified to the transnational character of labor issues in an increasingly globalized world.[65]

The tense state of domestic affairs exploded at the International Suffrage Alliance's 1926 meeting, when the alliance considered the NWP's application for affiliation. The alliance consulted with the League of Women Voters (LWV), the only American affiliate at the time, on the advisability of admitting the NWP. The LWV executive board not only voted unanimously against admission, but filed a protest, claiming the NWP did not educate women as citizens, was not organized into branches throughout the United States, and was a "party" that engaged in partisan politics. Catt worked behind the scenes, warning that the NWP's "presence in the Alliance may well lead to the withdrawal or alienation of other organizations."[66] Placed in this awkward position, the alliance board relented and voted against admitting the National Woman's Party. Although the party protested and was backed by British feminists, it was not admitted. Party member Crystal Eastman dubbed this "The Great Rejection; Part II." Stevens— who was on the spot—cabled Alice Paul, who counseled prudence: "I feel that unless we are ready to carry on [the] international movement ourselves," Paul replied, "we ought to support those doing it and not be responsible for splits in their ranks."[67]

Along with the delicacy of maneuvering in global feminist waters shared by the LWV, Stevens and Paul had to be careful not to step on the toes of feminists outside the United States who had long worked on married women's nationality rights, a cause they also embraced. Rhondda had warned Stevens of this as early as 1928:

> To go to the Hague waving an Equal Rights Treaty is one thing . . . to go there asking for Nationality for Married Women is quite another. The Equal Rights Treaty is a new idea it is your patent—it is nobody else's program. . . . But Nationality of Married Women is already the program of the International Suffrage Alliance. . . . There is another thing—obviously you and Miss Paul have got the plan on your minds and you are putting the work research etc. into it—Now if when you come to the International part of it you lead as feminists (who just chance to be American) all will be well—But if you do it as if *America* is leading it will be hopeless—No one country cares to be lead by any other. . . . As it happens America is so thoroughly on Europe's nerves just now that the mere thought of having America lead her kindly to the Promised Land would make any European country forego any promised land.[68]

The high point of Stevens's IACW leadership was the adoption of the Equal Nationality Treaty at the 1933 Pan American Conference in Montevideo, Uruguay. The treaty, crafted by the IACW, proposed to make the law on nationality identical for men and women, which would guarantee the right of married women to nationality independent of their husbands and the right of mothers, equally with fathers, to transmit nationality to their children. The nationality of married women, a topic addressed as early as 1905 by the International Council of Women, was the first issue the IACW had researched. Married women's nationality took on a new urgency after the First World War, when wives could find themselves enemy nationals in their countries of birth. After the war, some women discovered they were stateless—their countries did not recognize their nationality, nor were they granted their husbands' nationalities.[69] In 1928 there was no legal uniformity on nationality: in the United States, a woman who married a foreigner kept her citizenship only if her husband was also eligible to be a US citizen. In other countries all women who married men of different nationalities lost their citizenship and gained that of their husbands. "We note that in nearly all these conflicting types of laws on nationality there is one outstanding attribute," Stevens stated, "women are discriminated against." The Equal Nationality Treaty was unanimously endorsed at the first IACW conference in 1930.[70]

While in theory dueling women's groups supported equal nationality, the topic became a point of contention between equal rights and social feminists. Although the LWV had worked throughout the 1920s and early 1930s for congressional bills to remove nationality discrimination, league members feared the NWP would take all the credit if this treaty passed. Married women's nationality was on the agenda of both the 1930 Hague Conference on the Codification of International Law and the League of Nations Assembly; the International Alliance of Women had also passed a resolution advocating women's nationality remain independent of their husbands' nationality.[71] Social feminists and equal rights feminists were openly hostile to each other at the Hague conference. League president Maud Wood Park and Wisconsin LWV member Mrs. Pitman Potter spoke at the hearings, as did Stevens. Despite an impressive demonstration in support of independent nationality—including a parade of women in vibrantly colored dresses and sashes symbolizing the status of their countries' nationality laws—the conference concluded by recommending that a wife's nationality remain dependent on that of her husband. Out of forty-one countries present, the United States was the only one that refused to sign the discriminatory Treaty on Nationality. Stevens declared that the conference "outraged the dignity and integrity of women the world over." It was the same issue at stake, "whether women shall be treated as human beings or again, continuing and repeating the errors of the centuries, be treated as a special group."[72] In their anger, women's groups opposed the ratification of the entire convention but to no avail, and shifted their attention to the League of Nations, where they lobbied against ratification of the nationality convention.

The IACW joined forces with a new committee, convened by British feminist Chrystal Macmillan in early 1931, that supported their stance on identical laws on nationality. This International Committee for Action on the Nationality of Married Women successfully lobbied the League of Nations to add nationality to the agenda of the next assembly. Composed of representatives from six international women's organizations, this new group, which also appealed to socialist and working-class women, worked to urge delay of the ratification of the nationality convention and to stipulate that any later convention would recognize equality of the sexes in matters of nationality. The LWV, still holding out for special legislation, caved to mounting pressure and invited nine international women's organizations to create a Women's Consultative Committee on Nationality. Its first report strongly opposed ratification of the Hague Convention (whose Nationality Treaty discriminated against married women) and demanded that distinctions based on sex be abolished. But feminist agreement stopped there. Members broke into two camps, half supporting equal nationality, embodied in the proposed Equal Nationality Treaty (the IACW was in this camp, arguing for identical laws on nationality for men and women) and the other insisting on independent nationality, which called for laws that would allow women the right to choose which nationality—their own or their husbands'—they would adopt.[73]

The disagreement among US women's organizations greatly hindered the chances of the successful passage of the Equal Nationality Treaty. At the end of 1932, the League of Nations Assembly, fed up with organized women's inability to speak with a united voice, recommended ratification of the controversial Hague Convention. At the Montevideo Pan American Conference in December 1933, NWP and LWV feminists continued their standoff. Largely because of LWV lobbying, the United States reversed its earlier position and opposed the Equal

Nationality Treaty. Sophonisba Breckinridge, US representative to the conference and league member, wrote former league president Belle Sherwin that the women's meeting at the conference was confused and disorderly. She hoped the IACW would be disbanded and that Latin American women "who do not share the characteristics of the leading members of the Woman's Party" could be reorganized. Stevens recognized this attack and cabled the president of the American Society of International Law: "delegation opposing continuance present Chairman commission.... What price diplomacy is this? ... United States only delegation attacking me because of association Woman's Party.... Future commission being sacrificed to insane private grudges which have nothing to do with me nor with great principle."[74] Sherwin justified her overreaction in a letter to a fellow league member: "the League of Women Voters is always on the defensive in respect to the action of the NWP."[75]

The hostility of the nationality dispute carried the animosity fueling US feminist conflicts into the global arena and further accentuated disagreements over maternalist ideas versus equal rights. Although women's groups were close in their beliefs about the need for equitable legislation on women's nationality, the personality clashes, leadership struggles, and lingering bitterness over the suffrage movement left its mark. Paul's demeanor, particularly her overbearing manner, combined with a perception that she was trying to control the Consultative Committee and to encourage Equal Rights International to focus on the nationality question, also estranged women throughout the movement. Stevens recognized this as well, noting, "in order to work with Miss Paul, one has to surrender all. She is a leader who accepts no one who holds reservations."[76]

Despite the initial resistance of the United States, all the American republics except Costa Rica and Venezuela signed the Equal Nationality Treaty at the December 1933 Montevideo Pan American Conference. (After seventy-two hours of vacillation, the United States signed it.) This was a major victory for the IACW as well as the NWP. "Equal nationality in itself is a small gain," Stevens stated. "But winning it for women by treaty is not. A precedent for international action on behalf of equality was established from which we need never retreat." The fact that it was signed during a worldwide depression made the treaty even more significant, Stevens believed. "Only by such international action can women feel sure that their rights will not be wiped out, overnight, by some sudden economic or politically reactionary pressure," she declared.[77] Stevens stated at a victory dinner: "this treaty is a great thing for women ... because it represents what women themselves want. It is not men's idea of what women ought to want, nor men's idea of what would be good for them. . . . Women must depend upon themselves to get equality. No group in the community with lesser rights was ever given liberty by those who had greater rights." Women at the conference walked away with another prize as well: four countries—Uruguay, Paraguay, Ecuador, and Cuba—signed the Equal Rights Treaty.[78]

Despite their shared commitment to legal equality, Cuban and Latin American women viewed the conception of equality differently than American feminists did. In Cuba social groups, rather than individuals, held power, and they struggled for equal rights as group members. Cuban women were granted equal status before the law, but it was simultaneously recognized that as mothers they required special protections. The fact that Cubans and other Latin Americans viewed women as at once equal with and distinct from men allowed an equal rights law to pass with little controversy about whether it would affect laws that protected mothers and women workers.[79] Nonetheless, Stevens was rightly proud of the IACW's accomplishment. Even her ex-husband Dudley Malone generously telegrammed her: "Xmas blessings Congratulations brilliant achievement Your life's ambition."[80] NWP feminists were ecstatic and confident. "Just two days remain before this memorable old year of 1933 will pass into history," *Equal Rights* editorialized. Six months later assurance still reigned supreme; an *Equal Rights* editorial proclaimed: "We cannot believe that ratification of the Equal Rights Treaty can be any longer delayed, once the Equal Nationality Treaty is written into international law. And then what possible other step can there be than that the Equal Rights Amendment, sprung full-fledged like Minerva from the brain of Alice Paul, Founder of the National Woman's Party, will be written into the Constitution of the United States?"[81]

The IACW's resounding success made Stevens something of a celebrity. She shared the limelight with Paul, author of the treaty and chair of the commission's committee on nationality. A *Baltimore Evening Sun* editorial described Stevens and Paul as "two ladies who are lavishly endowed with grit, stamina and the will to success." Dr. James Brown Scott, president of the American Society of International Law, pronounced them benefactors of the human race and proposed a bronze likeness of the pair in Washington, DC—"the one looking straight forward, the other with head in the air, and the hand of each upon a laurel wreath."[82] Meanwhile, the personal relationship between the two women continued to spiral downward.

At the same time, others within international women's movement circles criticized Stevens for what they considered her unrestrained heterosexuality. A Brazilian International Alliance of Women member, Bertha Lutz, who was unmarried, expressed her repugnance at Stevens's IACW lobbying tactics, which she believed relied on flirtations with male government representatives to the Pan American Union. Lutz labeled Stevens a "nymphomaniac" and accused her of "paying the mexican delegates in kisses . . . [and] luring the Haitians with a French secretary she has." Lutz, who called herself Carrie Chapman Catt's "daughter," dubbed Stevens a "sex-mad psychopath" and a "mentally deranged woman." Stevens did apparently pursue flirtatious relationships with several Latin American male diplomats during these years. There is no firm evidence of this in her papers, however, and it seems surprising, given the romantic letters Mitchell was routinely writing Stevens during her trips abroad. It is possible that Stevens's interactions with male diplomats were both politically strategic and another demonstration of her belief in sexually liberal relationships. She was unmarried at the time. Whatever the true story, Stevens's behavior displeased feminists who did not share her liberated views or her vision of a gender-integrated world. At the 1937 Buenos Aires conference, Lutz exclaimed that Stevens put "all women to shame."[83]

Generational strain simmered in international feminism around those who clung to the homosocial world, and those who embraced the cultural shift to heterosociality. Feminists who went too far were harshly criticized. As Leila Rupp noted, "unorthodox heterosexuality crossed the line of respectability in a way that women's same-sex relationships did not and as a result met with disapproval."[84] Stevens was known in the movement as a vocal advocate of both working with and playing with men. For some of the old guard, this was unacceptable. These tensions around women's personal lives and behavior and political choices added to the national, class, and racial differences already brewing within women's organizations.

Despite their optimism, NWP members never saw the Equal Rights Treaty passed, nor would the Equal Nationality Treaty be written into international law for more than two decades. Although the NWP worked throughout the 1930s to move the Equal Rights Treaty through the League of Nations, the protective legislation issue and the NWP-LWV animosity effectively prevented it. According to Paul, the party's strategy was to get the Equal Rights Treaty on the agenda of the League of Nations' assembly, gain as many endorsements as possible from international women's organizations, and turn to individual countries to build support for ratification. But Paul's lack of social capital prevented her from gaining support, and Stevens also raised a few hackles. An NWP colleague wrote Chrystal Macmillan, "Feminists could accomplish almost anything they want in the way of equality legislation if they could unite."[85] But they could not. When the IACW did get the treaty on the agenda for the 1935 meeting, LWV delegates, led by Women's Bureau chief Mary Anderson, drew up a protest to be circulated among League of Nations delegates. Claiming the treaty was harmful and impractical, their strategy succeeded. The league recommended further study and assigned protective legislation to the International Labour Office for research.[86]

Franklin D. Roosevelt's 1932 election and the unfolding of the New Deal in 1933 and 1934 had important implications for transnational feminist work, because it brought into power an influential group of social feminists who opposed the equal rights stance of the NWP. Many of these feminists knew each other from Progressive-era social welfare activities as well as the suffrage campaign and identified as social reformers rather than feminists, which they associated with the NWP and the ERA.[87] Eleanor Roosevelt was the foremost member of this New Deal political sisterhood.

Although by mid-decade advocates of protective labor legislation found themselves standing increasingly alone, the power of this women's network prevailed to block the Equal Nationality Treaty and the Equal Rights Treaty and to remove Stevens from her position.[88] "There was practically no support to the [LWV] point of view outside the U.S. delegation," noted its representative to the 1935 Alliance of Women Congress. The rise of Hitler and Mussolini and their passage of laws limiting married women's right to work made European women especially afraid of seeing their economic opportunities threatened. Grace Abbott, American delegate to the ILO and chief of the Children's Bureau, wrote a private report to American feminists in 1935 in which she stated: "While we have felt some of the fear of those in the U.S. . . . I was surprised to find out how serious European women feel the situation to be." Although she believed the Equal Rights Treaty had little chance of passage, she warned that the Open Door International, the German-based organization that supported women's right to paid work despite maternity or marriage, had been urging that women stand together and consequently "some [women] who favor industrial legislation have concluded that at this time they ought to stand for the 'Equal Rights' Treaty."[89]

The women's network began making plans as early as 1935 to have Stevens removed as chair of the IACW. Mary Winslow of the Women's Trade Union League (WTUL) began maneuvering behind the scenes to expel Stevens a full year before the eighth Pan American Congress in Lima, Peru. Mitchell heard rumblings of this and warned Stevens: "the Trade Union League [is] actively and deliberately lined up to oppose you." He continued: "if these hatchet-faced bitches [raise] a hand against you, [you'll] wallop them." Friend of Eleanor Roosevelt and director of the Women's Division of the Democratic National Committee Mollie Dewson worked to get a woman supportive of protective legislation in the US delegation to the Pan American Congress. Winslow and others drafted a resolution, approved by President Roosevelt and supported by the US delegates, which advocated women's rights but also defended protective legislation, a stance in opposition to Stevens's.[90]

The LWV and their allies successfully colluded to replace Stevens as chair with a US State Department appointee. Winslow's name was in the running, as well as Women's Bureau head Mary Anderson and the WTUL's Elizabeth Christman. The NWP faithful responded vigorously. They lobbied Congress and even convinced Senator Edward R. Burke of Nebraska, Stevens's home state, to introduce a Senate resolution to prevent her removal. Whatever Paul's personal opinion of Stevens, party leaders publicly supported her.[91]

The NWP also protested to the governing board of the Pan American Union, but to no avail.[92] On February 1, 1939, the State Department announced Mary Winslow's appointment as new head of the IACW. Soon after, Marguerite Wells, president of the LWV from 1934 to 1944, wrote Winslow that although Stevens had the endorsement of the *New York Times*, she was "on the way out, both as a personality and the leader of her particular cause, but she may make quite a struggle getting out." Wells suggested the LWV do some serious lobbying and advised: "Don't let the people in Washington get discouraged—we had Doris on the run once—we can get her there again. I don't see why the whole thing can't be handled by clever administrative rulings and appointments. You must get the Pan American Union to get over being intimidated by Doris. It's a bad habit people have. She is vulnerable in certain spots."[93] When, in 1940, the IACW was reorganized and a Latin American woman appointed chair and Winslow US representative, the NWP had no grounds for a lawsuit because the Pan American Congress, not the US government, had appointed Stevens.[94]

Stevens was understandably bitter about her loss of the commission. Rather than blaming it on conflicts among feminists, she held Eleanor Roosevelt responsible and launched a vendetta against her. Stevens clipped and filed articles on Roosevelt's "Red Activities" and publicly opposed all the social welfare policies of the New Deal, as her own politics took a decided turn to the right. She stated in a 1941 letter that the story as she understood it had never been told, including the many people involved, both in and outside of government, and the smear campaign and name-calling. She described a First Lady who was controlling, out to get her, and duplicitous, noting "her final desperate tactic of getting the State Department . . . to paint me a fraud of ten years and say I had never been a member, the U.S. had had a 'vacancy' all that time . . . etc, ad nauseam." Stevens continued: "The press reported it a dispute in feminist ideology. This was utterly ridiculous and I knew it. Her [Eleanor Roosevelt's] ruthless methods to get control of the IACW were of a piece with her long career of allying to her personal following every group she could lay hands on: the League of Women Voters, heretofore non-partisan with a strong Repub. bias, the Women's Trade Union League, of socialist and old progressive beliefs—etc."[95]

After 1940, social feminists took over the NWP's leadership in Latin American feminism and the IACW became an educational, rather than activist, commission. "Our old friends of the L.W.V. are at it again headed by that busybody: Mrs. R.," a sympathetic friend wrote Stevens. "To pass the Commission over to the other Camp must be more than you can bear."[96] And perhaps it was. In the years to come Stevens grew less hopeful and increasingly dispirited, both about women's organizations and the future of American feminism. A 1942 letter she wrote Eleanor Roosevelt, after the First Lady was forced to step down from the Office of Civilian Defense due to the awkwardness of her holding a federal position (although unpaid), revealed how Stevens's own dismissal still stung. "I have just heard your broadcast . . . in which you gave vent to your feelings concerning your removal as Assistant Director of OCD. Permit me to say that, as you will appreciate, probably no one in the United States understands more fully your sense of outrage nor can measure more precisely your resentment at such treatment."[97]

We Must Do Everything at Once: Mary Beard

During the years Stevens was fighting for women's equal rights in the contentious international arena, Mary Beard faced her own challenges trying to bring US feminists together as she shared her evolving philosophy with both factions. The deepening economic crisis influenced Beard's feminist thought. Increasingly through the 1930s, she equated feminism with individualism and envisioned a new kind of movement that was collective in spirit and humanist in vision. In 1932, she stated that a disaster had overtaken "rugged American feminism," and declared: "Everything had looked so promising to feminists until the 1930s. . . . As long as the *laissez faire* philosophy to which the creed of equality was attached could maintain its economic basis, women did good tail-flying. But the man's kite was always in danger of falling . . . women, racing in the rear, were lamentably blind to the perils ahead." Beard believed women ought to forget about men and their perquisites and concern themselves with creating a better civilization. The equality feminists coveted was in Beard's opinion "equality in disaster"; she advised women to replace their demands for "the prerogatives of men" with new ideas which would lead to "a more equal distribution of wealth and a stable economy for all."[98]

Beard's challenge to equal rights feminism alarmed NWP members. Party leader Jane Norman Smith wrote Stevens in 1932, "If you will read Mary Beard's article in November's 'Current History,' you will see how she is trying to lead women away from the idea of continuing to press for equal rights, and get them thinking about taking leadership in constructive work toward a new social order." Beard's imprint was on the International Congress of Women, held in Chicago in 1933, whose theme was "Our Common Cause—Civilization." "I am very fond of Mary," Smith wrote Stevens, "but I don't agree with her point of view regarding equal rights." In another letter to Stevens, Smith described the shortcomings Beard saw in equal rights feminism and suggested that her ideas were influential.

> Women leaders are being led far away from the Equal Rights for Women idea. This is what one said to me: "The Equal Rights" program is as much out-of-date as a woman's program as any other program launched 84 years ago. If prosperity had continued, perhaps that program could have been followed to a certain extent. Now, that everything is tumbling down on our heads & the 'best minds' realize that the competitive system in industry has been a ghastly failure . . . doesn't it seem silly for women to continue to try to patch up an outworn system by asking for the right of women to compete on equal terms with men; that women must abandon

an equality of opportunity campaign & bend their efforts toward creating a
better civilization—Otherwise, we shall have a Stalin or a Mussolini, & where
will women find themselves under either regime? A new order, as visioned by
these women, would provide equal opportunity for women (As they are all
protectionists, I have my doubts).[99]

For her part Stevens, who in the early 1930s still adhered to Alice Paul's single-
issue approach, found Beard's interest in collectivism and her holistic vision dis-
turbingly similar to communism. Beard wrote Harriot Stanton Blatch in 1934
and described a long evening she spent with Stevens in Washington. "She insisted
that a feminist can and must do one thing at a time," Beard noted. "She maintained that I should work for Communism. 'But I am not a communist,' said I . . .
I believe that we have to do everything at once."[100] Beard related her broad view to
her conviction that equal rights feminists lacked strategic foresight in their post-
suffrage battles. Why fight for equal access to the professions, higher education,
and politics without questioning the masculine individualism of these arenas,
without trying to reshape them?[101]

Beard's opinions also set her at odds with more conservative women's groups
than the NWP. The deliberative, educational approach of the League of Women
Voters annoyed her. She contended that women had served with men in the public sphere for centuries and ought to enter the political arena immediately. Her
shared belief with Charles Beard that the United States should remain neutral in
the rising conflict in Europe was in disagreement with some moderate women's
groups. At mid-decade, her views on US neutrality coincided most closely with
women in the National Council for Prevention of War and the Women's International League for Peace and Freedom. She remained in close touch with peace
activists throughout the 1930s.[102]

Beard had a vision different from that of either NWP feminists or women in
more middle-of-the road women's groups. She believed a new feminism could
emerge in the twentieth century. This feminism would not be based on the idea of
men's historical subjection of women which, referring to the "Declaration of Senti-
ments," the document signed by attendees at the first women's rights convention in
Seneca Falls, New York, she called a "false theory which dominated the women of
1848," but instead would show women the way to take the initiative in social leadership. This feminism would be "less imitative than the old, more constructive and
less acquisitive (therefore destructive), indicative of feminine concern with political economy as a whole as the old feminism was not, and in its collectivist vision
betraying its realistic roots." She sketched out this conception in a model syllabus
she prepared at the invitation of the American Association of University Women in
1934 entitled *A Changing Political Economy as It Affects Women*.[103]

Although Beard did not support the Equal Rights Amendment, she remained
publicly silent until 1937, when she published an eloquent letter intended for

both feminist camps. In it she expressed her dismay at both sides' agendas and described her own image of what feminism could become. Although reluctant to "hurl herself into the factional fray," Beard wrote it due to a misunderstanding which had arisen over her connection with the Women's Charter, a document written by a Committee of Five Hundred against the Equal Rights Amendment, which asked for "complete freedom for women" but also supported gender-specific labor legislation.[104] Invited to a conference on the proposal for a broad review of women's position in the summer of 1936, Beard was asked to consider the charter, which supposedly combined the desires of all leaders of women (but was opposed by ERA proponents). Critical of the contradictory draft she read there, Beard never signed it or any other version. However, the press linked her name and that of the WCWA to the Women's Charter, much to Beard's dismay and anger. To set the record straight, she asked Mary Van Kleeck, chair of the Women's Charter group, to write a letter to the *New York Times* disassociating her name with the Charter, and Beard wrote a powerful letter to the readers of *Equal Rights*.[105]

In the letter, Beard criticized equal rights feminists for "[running] the risk of positively strengthening anachronistic competitive industrial processes; of supporting, if unintentionally, ruthless laissez faire, of forsaking humanism in the quest for feminism as the companion-piece of mannism." Although she believed that the "woman's bill of rights" was long overdue, and "should have run along with the rights of man in the eighteenth century," she found the ERA unworthy as a goal in and of itself. Even if it became an amendment to the US Constitution, "It would be so inadequate today as a means to food, clothing and shelter for women at large that what they would still be enjoying would be equality in disaster rather than in realistic privilege." Although Beard found it emotionally hard to appear unsympathetic with NWP members, for whom she felt "affection and high regard," she wrote, "I could not throw my heart and energy into the mere struggle for equality on a basis of laissez faire in the twentieth century."[106]

However, Beard disagreed with ERA opponents as well. She shared their concern about the regulation of working women's wages and hours, but believed they also were too complacent in their acceptance of capitalism. "The minimum wage implies a wage," she wrote, "and leaves out of account the millions of unemployed to whom a wage at all is sheer utopia." This view represented "too sentimental, an acceptance of capitalism" and was consistent with "the economic rule of a plutocracy." Furthermore, "Protectionists'" ideas about women's difference from men, which often centered on maternity and women's role in the home, were too traditional for Beard's taste. "Sex protection . . . embodies the objectionable idea of dependence. Equality leaves out of account the objectionable mores of 'free' men," she stated, illustrating her disagreement with both sides.[107]

Both flanks of the ERA controversy did raise some legitimate points. The anti-ERA contingent was probably correct that those in favor of the amendment concerned themselves more with the fate of middle-class rather than working-class women. The pro-ERA forces seemed to have been correct when they argued that protective legislation actually hurt women. Especially by the late 1930s, when the right to bargain collectively in labor unions had been achieved, and the 1938 passage of the Fair Labor Standards Act provided protective laws for both sexes, the reasons for opposing the amendment no longer existed. By the late 1940s, most major women's groups laid aside organizational and personal antagonisms to support, or, at least, stop opposing, a federal equal rights amendment.[108]

Beard's personal vision placed women in the position of social and moral leaders. She spoke of women demanding "decency of life and labor all round and security if possible to attain," of valuing humanity over "money profits and dictatorial power," and working for "a set-up in every industry" that would provide "a high minimum of labor reward without discrimination of sex." She believed women could bring something different to leadership, that women were challenged "as never before to work together for ends larger than self," and that they were meeting that challenge.[109]

Some feminists, however, were openly skeptical. Jane Norman Smith, who had been NWP chair from 1927 to 1929, wrote Stevens about Beard's ideas: "The statement was made . . . that now women should . . . stop talking about 'discrimination' against them, and boldly step out and take leadership; that they have the power, if they can be made to realize it . . . I asked one of these women how they expect to use the power of these five million women, for, after all, discussion is one thing & action & results something else. 'That will have to be worked out,' she said."[110]

In the second half of the decade, Beard found an avenue through which she believed women could realize their leadership potential and remake the world. The World Center for Women's Archives, which began in 1935, was to be a gathering place and clearinghouse of women's historical documents. Its mission was to make a wide variety of women's materials available to researchers and the community, with the hope of securing "a more balanced picture of humanity in the interests of historic truth." Its political goal was an educational revolution. Beard believed once women learned about their own historic importance, they would become the "creative leaders in the vanguard" she so wanted them to be. She believed the international archive could influence the future of US feminism and politics by educating women about their leadership and agency in the past.[111]

Hungarian-born Rosika Schwimmer, a feminist and pacifist well known in radical and reform circles, initiated the idea of the "Great Women's Archives." Near the turn of the century, Schwimmer had begun to compile an extraordinary collection of materials. She fled to the United States as a political refugee in 1921, and the valuable documents she brought with her by this time included pamphlets, leaflets, letters, and books on the Neo-Malthusian League and the birth control movement.[112] When the US government denied her citizenship in

1929, her desire to keep the materials intact led her to write American feminists in 1935 with a proposal to create "an international feminist-pacifist archive." Harriot Stanton Blatch and journalist and writer Dorothy Dunbar Bromley suggested she talk to Beard, whom Schwimmer already knew through the International Woman Suffrage Alliance. Beard was a logical choice because she was one of the few American leaders who maintained friendly relationships with both equal rights and social feminists. She was also a women's history scholar of growing reputation. After their first conversation Schwimmer wrote Beard: "It was quite rejuvenating to meet again someone who possesses a fiery spirit and intellectual superiority,—something that has become so rare in the ranks of feminists."[113]

Beard immediately set about recruiting sponsors and donors; she sent copies of the archives proposal to the League of Women Voters, the National Federation of Business and Professional Women, the American Association of University Women, First Lady Eleanor Roosevelt, and writer Ellen Glasgow. She appealed to old friends from her suffrage days, writing one: "we might recapture the feminine imagination for a woman movement on a grander design, revive some of the old indomitable spirit which centered around the Old Cause, and regain a united front directed toward peace and creative enterprise. It is worth trying, isn't it?" Although initially hesitant, Beard did write Alice Paul who, along with nearly everyone else Beard contacted, including Irwin, Stevens, and Pruette, agreed to support the new women's archives. Beard asked Irwin to serve as national chair, and she readily accepted. Beard wrote Florence Kitchelt, who in the 1930s was an LWV member, "I wonder whether you have noted in the sponsor list that it includes every suffrage faction leader—the first thing to draw them all in as far as I know."[114] She declared to Lena Madisen Phillips, attorney and president of the National Federation of Business and Professional Women's Clubs, in November 1935, "All the sects of feminists, now including Doris Stevens, are ardent for this thing." She wrote Stevens: "We are making headway. The thing looks good. It cheers me to have your approval. . . . I'll keep you in touch with 'progress.'"[115]

The archives' motto was a phrase written by French historian Fustel de Coulanges, "No documents, no history." Beard wrote Dorothy Porter, Howard University librarian, who agreed to collect African-American women's materials: "Papers. Records. These we must have. Without documents; no history. Without history; no memory. Without memory; no greatness. Without greatness; no development among women." Beard believed the documents should represent women in all their diversity, particularly in regard to race, class, and profession, signaling her commitment to combine internationalism with inter-racialism. Desired materials ranged from letters to speeches to housewives' budgets: "material which brings the ghost to life."[116]

Beard hoped preserving their documents would lead women to an understanding of their importance in history and to a discovery of role models who could inspire them to distinction. "Thoughtful men do this in connection with men. Women have not yet understood the necessity of doing the same with respect to themselves." Beard told a reporter in 1936:

> Something happened to American women to make them feel like little girls instead of adults. . . . To be great one must live in the shadow of greatness. . . . Under the sway of formal history writing and teaching in our day women only are supposed to have cast the shadows which inspire greatness. The height of woman's ambition thus becomes the desire to attain heights reached by men . . . In this interest of historic truth, and in part for the dignity of women, factual data . . . must be rescued from oblivion, preserved from destruction, and made available . . . Unless time is taken by the forelock and provision made for their preservation, it is conceivable that the records of women in the modern age will disappear.[117]

Beard imagined the archives as a way to link feminist theory and activism, which might also evolve into institution building, including the nucleus of a women's college as well as think-tank and Center for Research on Women. She wrote in a 1935 letter: "If . . . from such a place could go forth the demands and the protests, issued by a watching committee with its power increased by its wealth of data at its hands, then possibly the woman's culture could be integrated into the study of culture in the large and all our common intelligence enriched. Such is my dream anyway." Writing Schwimmer, she excitedly exclaimed, "we might set women on fire. A weekly seminar. Effective persons to do the talking. Women educating themselves since no one else can do it for them."[118]

By 1936, when Eleanor Roosevelt endorsed the WCWA, Beard found herself at the center of a flurry of public attention. In February and March the *New York Times*, the *Chicago Tribune*, the *Washington Herald*, and the *Boston Traveler* all featured articles on the women's archives. She wrote Schwimmer: "The truth is that my phone bell, my door bell, and my fan mail have been so compelling since I went to Mrs. Roosevelt's press conference last Monday morning that I have had no single half hour in which to report events to you." Apparently, Schwimmer willingly stayed in the background because of her controversial antiwar views.[119]

Yet a strain was beginning to develop between Beard and Schwimmer. Beard felt Schwimmer was proceeding too rapidly and focusing more on style and publicity than substance. Schwimmer was dissatisfied with the way women were chosen for the national board and was particularly unhappy with the New York women involved in the project. Beard tried to appease her: "Dear Mme. Schwimmer, you must know that we all hold you in high esteem. My interest in you and my affection for you have never changed. I have been so delighted that we could find women capable of carrying out the grand idea which you formulated for an Archives Center."[120] However, she also reminded her of her own contributions: "I believe you should be not-a-little content at the way I got behind your idea and then got other women behind it—women of the kind who really push it along to realization. You and I could have spent the rest of our lives picking and choosing purely intellectual, spiritual, feminists and pacifists as the guarantee of THE IDEA in its perfection. But we should have no outcome, I fear, if we undertook that fine work of selection by elimination. As it is, a widely representative group, several with national and international reputations, representing peace, feminism, labor, the three major religions, racial and civic work and the arts, has been brought together." Despite Beard's efforts, Schwimmer resigned from the project in April 1936. Years later, Beard described Schwimmer as "a very great woman" who was "terribly difficult" and "so self-sure that she wrecked some movements by her will to dominate."[121]

Schwimmer's departure freed Beard to expand the archive's original focus on white, middle-class pacifist and feminist materials to an eclectic, diverse assortment of women's sources. Documents were collected under the categories of Native American, Catholic, Jewish, working, immigrant, and rural women. Aiming for an all-encompassing multicultural history, Beard—whose range had long extended beyond the borders of the United States—assigned researchers to projects on women in Asia, Australia, Latin America, Canada, Central Europe, India, the Arab nations, and the Far East.[122]

Beard pressed on alone as WCWA leader, and her feelings ranged from high-spirited optimism to flat discouragement. She wrote one supporter, "Women are challenged as never before to work together for ends larger than self. I like to use the phrase The New Feminism, in this connection." She continued to receive a great deal of public recognition. She was featured, with thirteen other women, in the *New York Sun's* yearly list of the outstanding feminists of 1936. In the spring of 1937, Beard spoke at the convention of the Association of American University Women, gave the keynote speech at Mt. Holyoke College's one hundredth anniversary celebration, and lectured before the National Education Association.[123]

Still, by 1938, the Women's Archives movement began to experience increasing difficulties. Beard, sixty-two, was growing tired. Aside from running the WCWA, she was also collaborating with her husband on *America in Midpassage.* Charles Beard had limited hearing by then, and Mary assisted him closely in his 1938 testimony before the Committee on Naval Affairs of the US House of Representatives, in which he argued against raising naval expenditures. Mary wrote philanthropist and NWP member Miriam Holden, "If [the WCWA] has to be built up any longer around me who started it, then it must mean defeat. I simply cannot at my age and with my burdens carry this one as my sole responsibility. If the Center does not grip other women as it grips me, then there is not enough belief to make it a reality."[124] Furthermore, fundraising was proving challenging, and there were internal dissensions among board members that culminated in a walkout by the New York board in late 1938.

Despite the fact that Beard rightly took pride in her ability to attract a diverse coalition of women and organizations, the alliance was still a shaky one.

Particularly in regard to suffrage documents, the women who had remained with the more conservative NAWSA in the 1910s were reluctant to hand their precious sources over to an organization they suspected was run by NWP cronies. When invited to a meeting to help organize a WCWA state branch, one Massachusetts LWV member hastily wrote Catt: "I sensed that perhaps 'our' group might not want to turn over to this new committee the personal collections we have been treasuring. Is the Women's archives Committee definitely connected with the Natl. Woman's Party?" When Catt was approached to donate her papers, she responded coolly, "I am unable to help anywhere along the line . . . I cannot contribute and I cannot send names of wealthy women who might be interested." Alice Stone Blackwell, who did lend her name to the WCWA sponsor list, declined to give her own papers (although she donated her mother Lucy Stone's volumes of *The Woman's Journal*), and later renounced her association. Beard wrote her in a placatory letter: "It has grieved me very much that the proposed World Center for Women's Archives seemed spoiled for you by the personnel in part. But the attempt has been made to make the collection of materials widely representative and it seemed wise therefore to have all groups and interests among women identified with the leadership. . . . It would be a very specialized set of archives if only one or a few feminine attitudes toward life and labor were assembled, you will agree I am sure."[125]

Beard's belief in the activist potential of history was central to her mission for the archives. She was unshaken in her commitment to building an African-American collection as a weapon against racism. Acutely aware that Black women had been erased from the historical record, earlier in her career she had approached both Mary McLeod Bethune, an educator and founder of the National Council of Negro Women, and Lucy Diggs Slowe, the first African-American woman dean at Howard University, about historical projects. In addition, Beard had been a consultant to an initiative encouraging history in Black colleges and organizations. At the 1938 convention of the National Council of Negro Women (NCNW) the WCWA proposed a collection of African-American women's documents for the archives. Council President Bethune appointed a chairperson to head the Negro Women's Committee, which began its collecting from NCNW headquarters in Washington, DC.[126]

Despite mounting obstacles as the decade drew to a close, the women's archives movement still knew moments of optimism and triumph. An enormously successful fund-raising luncheon in Washington, DC, in March 1939 drew nearly five hundred women, including Eleanor Roosevelt, Frances Perkins, Fola La Follette, and Emily Newell Blair. Beard noted with satisfaction that the wives of several Supreme Court justices were present, as well as four African-American women.[127] In a May 1939 letter, Beard appeared jubilant: "this Archives thing is becoming tumultuously important. The radio clamors for stuff. The country is excited. College presidents galore are lining up with us. The gals are getting assignments to study women in history. Groups are forming here and there to back up the project."[128] Indeed, more than thirty college presidents endorsed the project; branches were established in Connecticut, Indiana, Michigan, New Jersey, Pennsylvania, and Washington, DC. Many women's leaders pledged their support, and an impressive group of documents had been collected.

A number of events occurred in 1940, however, which led Beard to resign in June and the Women's Archives to dissolve three months later. Some were internal to the organization and others were major world events. One internal issue focused on race. The African-American women who Beard recruited to collect Black women's documents were a Washington, DC–based group that included Mary Bethune; Howard University librarian Dorothy Porter; Sue Bailey Thurman, the wife of Howard University's dean; and two past presidents of the National Association of Colored Women, Mary Church Terrell and Elizabeth Carter Brooks. The WCWA bylaws required members to join a local branch, but the white members of the Washington unit, reminiscent of white American suffragists two decades earlier, would not allow the "Negro Women's Archives" group to join. It is not clear whether the African-American women were aware of this. Beard decided to sidestep the situation by asking the Black women to work directly with her on the archives and bypass the Washington, DC, group altogether.[129]

Miriam Holden, a white WCWA board member who had worked for racial justice through the NAACP and Harlem organizations, accused Beard of turning her back on racism. Beard wrote her, "It is all a question as to whether we should run the risk of an awful row over a minority which might ruin WCWA. The most delicate diplomacy seems to be required." Holden wrote Beard, "To me the way we handle it [the Negro matter] is just about as important as whether we continue to have an archive center or not." Beard responded, "Then on a Negro issue, which does not have to be made an issue but can be taken care of so well that the Negro women will be the great gainers, you would let all this die? How do you know that in doing that and feeling that way you are doing anything for the Negroes? What reason have you for believing that you are a better friend to them than I am?"[130]

In addition to racial tensions, the class-based contradictions embedded in Beard's conception of the WCWA became an issue. The archives project could not survive without donors, so she sought to attract prominent, wealthy women to contribute their papers, which she knew would bring publicity and prestige. At the same time, Beard wanted to collect the materials of laborers, the poor, and the working class. When she was criticized for soliciting Alva Belmont's papers, Beard responded that they could "not be left neglected if the true and comprehensive story of the winning of the vote is to be on record."[131] Whether the irony of her own departure from the NWP three decades earlier in protest over their decision to hold the convention at Belmont's Newport mansion—for the same purpose of attracting affluent, high-status women—occurred to Beard is unclear. Her inclusive view of the archive's collections demonstrated her sincere desire to assemble a rich, representative group of documents. At the same time, it created an apparent conflict of interest that dissuaded some potential supporters.[132]

In addition to internal tensions and financial worries, America's entry into World War II delivered the final blow to the archives' survival. Hitler's invasion of Denmark, Norway, Holland, Belgium, Luxembourg, and France, which began in the spring of 1940, moved most American noninterventionists to support entry into the war. Charles Beard's *A Foreign Policy for America*, published in 1940, in which he restated his belief in American neutrality, was greeted with harsh criticism. American women's support for the war seemed to disprove Mary Beard's thesis about women's essentially pacific nature. With some optimism she had written the year before: "I hope you are well despite the horrors of a world at war and more widely war-minded. . . . It seems more important than ever, to me, for us to try to uphold such a movement as this [the women's archives] when human and intellectual values are in such jeopardy even in our USA." But unable to sustain it any longer, Beard resigned from her creation. She wrote Florence Kitchelt, "We have had to close the office of WCWA—&—we are going out of business. A WORLD ORDER or a World War seems to engage EVERY-WOMAN's attention now. You will understand my—our sorrow at this demise. We consider it a war casualty."[133]

Some supporters were infuriated by Beard's decision. Miriam Holden complained to another board member, "How can anyone walk out on their own project so calmly and so freely I just can't imagine. Apparently no sense of responsibility to us or the people who have sent their precious archives." Yet Holden clearly was unaware of how Beard had agonized over the state of affairs.[134]

When her cofounder, Schwimmer, learned that the WCWA was folding, she wrote Beard, "I have buried many dreams in these last decades. The World Center for Women's Archives goes now with the lot." Beard responded with persistent hope: "I have tried for five years to *force* the Archive into existence, my faith matching your dream. Now, I realize that more groundwork must be laid—the reality. But I am also convinced that your-my dream of a great Women's Archive is not lost . . . I am confident that the work will go on." And, in the long run, she was correct.[135]

CHAPTER 7

Feminism as Life's Work

Inez Irwin, Mary Beard, Doris Stevens, and Lorine Pruette carried feminism forward in new sites of experimentation in the years after the 1920 suffrage victory. These sites included sexuality and relations with men; marriage; work and financial independence; and the National Woman's Party. How they did this, and the myriad of challenges they encountered along the way, is the story I have tried to tell in this book.

As these four women's lives vividly illustrate, being "modern" raised new challenges for feminists. These women lived through a time of dramatic transition in the US women's movement, as it moved from the separatist culture of the nineteenth century to the gender-integrated world of the twentieth. Modern women stressed female incorporation into a male world and optimistically sought parity with men in all the spheres of life. This attitude brought with it new opportunities as well as new hazards. The new point of view toward men, marriage, children, and jobs; the desire for heterosexual love as well as paid work—these were all difficult to realize in light of the realities and stresses of the female life cycle, as well as still-existing patriarchal attitudes.

In sexuality and their relations with men, modern feminists sought to create new, transcendent relationships that would symbolize the possibility of partnered, equal human beings. They tried to remake marriage as sexually intimate, companionable, and egalitarian. They strove for gender equality in the workplace and envisioned paid work and financial independence as ways to avoid domesticity and to define the self. They reached into the inner reality of their own lives, and in striving to understand and change them, created feminist theory and inspired feminist activism. They suffered in the process.

Like early twentieth-century sex radical ideas, the idea of modern marriage held important implications for American feminism. By glorifying marriage as a mating of equals and comrades, the modern ideal effectively undercut women's resistance to marriage. Ideals of modern marriage actually made it more diffi-cult to balance work with marriage and placed tremendous weight on the mari-tal relationship. Of her generation of women who were young just after World War I, Pruette wrote: "Out of the temper of the times they arrogated to them-selves all conceivable roles, wife, mistress, mother, career girl, they were going to give up nothing, to seize all of life in their demanding and competent hands. They often showed a valiant spirit and they took a considerable amount of pun-ishment, carrying their double and triple loads. . . . They had an odd code of gallantry, of being little gentlemen, and freedom was the word which answered every doubt or difficulty." As these bold free spirits approached middle age, "the time of stock-taking, the period of appeasement of dreams," Pruette described them as voluble in their discontent.[1]

Yet despite the difficulties, all four women examined here defended married women's right to work for wages and proposed innovative strategies to make this possible. Stevens was in the radical minority of 1920s-era feminists who confronted traditional understandings of women's "instinctive" care-giving skills and temperament and invoked the term "the second shift" as early as 1926. She argued for an egalitarian arrangement in dual-earner families and advo-cated state payments and wages for wives. She anticipated feminist theorists of the 1960s and late twentieth century who wrote on housework as a politi-cal issue as well as the financial vulnerability of wives. The workloads some early twentieth-century women carried as they strove to put their theories into practice made Pruette state, "we cannot hope to have everything, that is the hard and bitter truth at the basis of our discontent."[2] Both she and Stevens ulti-mately concluded it would be up to a future generation to solve the quandary of career and marriage. Yet their perseverance and courageous defiance of rigid early twentieth-century gendered stereotypes contributed to social change that has trickled down to our own time.

Their struggles prefigured the conflicts of a later generation. Highly educated, privileged, and elite, their lives and difficulties captured the conundrum of what "being modern" meant for many white, middle-class, professional women in the early years of the century. The dilemmas they encountered are still with us. As Anne-Marie Slaughter wrote in her controversial 2012 *Atlantic* article, "Why Women Still Can't Have It All," "Women of my generation have clung to the fem-inist credo we were raised with, even as our ranks have been steadily thinned by unresolvable tensions between family and career, because we are determined not to drop the flag for the next generation. But when many members of the younger generation have stopped listening, on the grounds that glibly repeating 'you can have it all' is simply airbrushing reality, it is time to talk."[3] All these decades later, the feminist credo that modeled full lives on the ideal of male achievement in the public sphere has still not successfully transformed greedy, inflexible workplaces or a culture that devalues children and care giving.

Modern women's new ideals coincided with the diminishment of the public women's movement from a mass, heterogeneous movement in the 1910s to a smaller, contentious one. Precipitated by the National Woman's Party's 1923 proposal of an Equal Rights Amendment to the US Constitution, feminists divided over the ideas of gender "difference" versus "sameness." Protective legislation that benefited working women and mothers in the labor force became a bone of contention among warring feminists. In addition, a rising anti-feminist climate in the country at large made all advocates of women's rights suspect in the 1920s and 1930s. Simultaneously, a younger generation found feminism increasingly unfashionable.

In many cases, feminism was literally their life's work. This was true of Irwin, Beard, Stevens, and Pruette. Between them they devoted 230 years to women's causes. All four women lived long lives, and remained as physically and mentally active in old age as they were able. With barely a pause they worked steadily on a variety of fronts from the 1910s to the mid-1950s in Beard's case, the early 1960s for Irwin and Stevens, and the 1970s for Pruette.

Like the energetic, long-lived first generation of women's rights leaders whom they followed, these twentieth-century American feminists were sustained by their optimism, indignation, deep belief in their goals, skills at organizing and institution building, and their stamina. During what have been called "the doldrums" and "the bleak and lonely years" of the US women's movement—1945 to the 1960s—these women persisted. They considered themselves heirs of the suffrage movement and guardians of a long feminist tradition. Leila Rupp and Verta Taylor's description of American feminism in these years as a "link in the chain stretching from the early women's rights movement of the 1840s to the women's movement of the 1980s" is fitting, and that chain continues to extend into the twenty-first century.[4]

American Feminism, 1940–1977

Dramatic world events in the 1940s once again sidelined American feminism. The United States joined World War II on December 8, 1941, the day after Japanese pilots attacked the American naval base at Pearl Harbor. In August 1940 Irwin, who in the 1910s had witnessed war's devastation up close, wrote Maud Wood Park: "One can only discuss this present situation in clichés. One has no adjectives left, no comments. My tired imagination no longer thrills to the lure of trying to think to what death I would submit Hitler if I could only get my hands on him. Perhaps it is my Indian ancestry but I can think of several pretty painful methods." In December of that year, Irwin sadly observed that "the malign and sinister happenings of every day" were scarring the country's youth.[5] The United States' declaration of war against Germany, Japan, and Italy launched a huge military mobilization that pulled the country out of the Depression and sent sixteen million young men and 350,000 women into the military.

Like most wars, this one opened up new work opportunities for women, who eagerly filled jobs left vacated by men. Women found employment in occupations previously closed to them: on assembly lines, in defense industries, as toolmakers in shipyards, as switch operators on railroads. By 1944, nineteen million women were in the labor force, 72 percent of them married. Still, employers, unions, and the government viewed this as only "for the duration," and expected women to return home after the war (although two-thirds of them were employed before it began).[6] By 1944, Irwin believed that in order to save the world from self-destruction, women would have to seize leadership from men. Declaring war was "man's game," she said, "this succession of wars has become so serious that we women are going to be obliged to do something about it unless we want to live in a world without men."[7] In April 1945 Hitler committed suicide, and in May Germany surrendered, formally ending the war in Europe. In August, American fighters dropped atomic bombs on the cities of Hiroshima and Nagasaki, incinerating over 100,000 and causing Japan to surrender. Three months later Irwin stated that, although she had always wanted to live forever, the invention and use of the atomic bomb had reconciled her to death. "I cannot seem mentally to cope with that problem and the situation fills me with horror," she explained. Similarly, Pruette finally knew she was old when she refused to try to understand "the Einstein formula."[8]

The war diverted the American feminist movement, as did a new incarnation of mother blaming that led to the 1950s resurgence of prescriptive domesticity. Journalist Philip Wylie's 1942 *Generation of Vipers* coined "momism" to depict the ways mothers undermined their sons' confidence and independence. The dominant discourse linked the family—cared for by a full-time mother—to democracy and considered women's return to the home as a return to normalcy.[9] Although some feminists, including elected representatives, lobbied Congress to expand government support for child care centers, the postwar forces pushing women back into the home were inhospitable to women's rights. American feminists recognized this. In November 1945, a National Women's Party (NWP) member wrote Alice Paul, stating that if women wanted to return to their kitchens it was fine with her, but she would feel differently if it was caused by "an underground movement put forward by the N[ational] A[ssociation of] M[anufacturers], etc." Stevens wondered in 1946 if "those who were living at the beginning of the last Dark Ages . . . knew the darkness had descended!"[10] At the same time, a new generation of labor feminists dedicated to wage-earning and women's economic citizenship emerged and offered a variant vision of women's equality. Like the social feminists they followed, they were at odds with the NWP's individualistic brand of feminism.[11]

Still, the NWP played a central role in the women's rights movement after 1945. It stuck to its laser-like focus on the ERA, doggedly lobbying year in and year out for the amendment's introduction in Congress. By the 1930s the ERA had gained the endorsement of professional women in the National Association of Women Lawyers and the National Federation of Business and Professional Women's Clubs, which gave it a boost.[12] Although introduced in every Congress since 1923, not until 1946 did the Senate vote on the amendment. Hopeful about its passage, NWP members courted congressional sponsors, struggled to keep the amendment in both party's platforms (Stevens played a key role in convincing the Republicans to include it in 1940, and the Democrats followed suit in 1944), and lobbied other groups. Despite their stalwart efforts, the amendment did not successfully pass both houses of Congress to be sent to the states for ratification until 1972.[13]

Historians have characterized the story of the National Woman's Party after 1945 as a narrative of decline and survival. Its membership shrank, it failed to enlist new, youthful members, serious internal conflicts weakened it, and its reputation was increasingly linked to "amusingly eccentric and anachronistic old feminists." At the same time, the party nourished and sustained a women's community, and in the Washington DC, headquarters of the Alva Belmont House provided a feminist space and surrogate home for some members.[14] Despite its diminishment, the party's national influence extended well beyond its tiny size, influencing the distinctive character of the women's rights movement in the twenty years after the war ended.

The party did have a stormy history in these years, related to its leadership and the closed nature of the group. Alice Paul continued to stir controversy and conflict. In 1942 she resumed the title of chair, which she had not held since 1921. Three years later she announced she would not run again, and the selection committee nominated Anita Pollitzer. Stevens helped organize a small dissenting group, the Coalition Council, which opposed Pollitzer's candidacy and, protesting the lack of choice, fielded an alternate slate of officers. When Pollitzer handily won, the Coalition Council hardened into a true opposition force, challenging both women's leadership and—referring to Pollitzer as Paul's handmaiden—cynically dubbed them "the two A.P.'s."[15]

Stevens played a leading role in a 1947 legal battle over the name, leadership, and assets of the NWP. While the Coalition Council allegedly disapproved of Pollitzer because of her involvement in a conflict between the New York City party branch (which she headed) and the New York State branch, for Stevens the altercation offered an opportunity to publicly repudiate Paul. The depth of her hurt over what she considered Paul's earlier betrayal is clear from a 1942 letter she received from Lucy Burns, who had co-founded the Congressional Union and National Woman's Party with Alice Paul. Burns advised Stevens to forget the past, toughen up, and leave the party behind as she moved forward in her life. "I am really sorry. But it is almost the rule in dealing with 'organizations.' One needs a long spoon in supping with them."[16]

Stevens extricated herself more and more from the NWP, noting in 1944 that she had not visited headquarters more than a half dozen times over the previous decade. "The elite are all gone," she complained. "Those who remain were never my cup of tea. Sodden as they now are with sycophancy, they appear poison." Stevens objected to Paul's hierarchical, top-down style and her limited vision and agenda. Jeannette Marks, who had been a long-time Mount Holyoke professor and NWP member described the NWP in 1946 as "that mill of autocracy" and praised Stevens's desire to breathe new life and democratic leadership into the party.[17] Although Stevens reluctantly joined the conflict, she eventually became a leader of the opposition group, along with disaffiliated attorney Laura Berrien and long-time *Equal Rights* editor Anna Kelton Wiley, who felt underappreciated by Paul. Stevens wrote bluntly in June 1946 that she had "joined with others to . . . throw out Paul and her goons and get a safe, neutral chairman who will not destroy what is left of the party."[18]

At the national council's September 1946 gathering, Stevens and her fellow mutineers proposed reorganization and insisted upon a convention. When Paul and Pollitzer walked out, the opposition used a constitutional provision they claimed authorized ten council members to call a gathering without the chair's approval, and held a meeting in October. When Stevens's group scheduled a convention for January 1947, Pollitzer announced a different date, and the situation escalated. Stevens's supporters went ahead and held what their opponents called the "Rump" Convention, where they selected Sara Whitehurst, a Baltimore feminist and General Federation of Women's Clubs member, as chair. By the end of the month the party had two different sets of officers. Stevens and her allies visited headquarters and found a male detective barring the door. Infuriated, they pushed their way into the building, scuffled, and eventually filed two lawsuits. The first was over the name, leadership, and assets of the NWP; the second requested an injunction against the closing of Belmont House.[19]

After this internal skirmish, disaffiliated party members increasingly criticized Paul's domineering leadership, her alleged misappropriation of funds, and her inability or unwillingness to draw fresh blood into the organization. In an April 1947 letter, Stevens and her colleagues complained to Paul that, from the time of her return as chair, "you surrounded yourself with a small clique, and to question your imperious will even mildly was to provoke the clique's attack."[20] Despite Jeannette Marks's subsequent attempt at reconciliation with Paul, Whitehurst resigned as chair in June of that year. The group eventually lost both legal cases they filed against Paul and the NWP. The following month, when Paul recommended the group split, Berrien and Stevens circulated an open letter to Paul, which was even more pointed: "You have made it clear that you consider yourself and the small group around you an *elite* with superabundant intellect and talents, and consider us, in contrast, the common folk, although you were generous enough to say that some of us, at least, would attract 'thousands and thousands' of women. Thus, these two parts of a whole would march forward, you providing the brains, and we, the busy, but witless, hands and feet."[21]

Paul's supporters accused Stevens, Berrien, and their followers of everything from jealousy, greed, and anti-Semitism (Pollitzer was Jewish) to fascist involvement and communist infiltration. In a malicious letter that illustrated the bitterness of the dispute, Stevens called Paul "the high priestess of the National Woman's Party" and "a venomous specimen of the snake pit."[22] Incredibly, party officers eventually turned over information about the schism to the FBI and the Committee on Un-American Activities of the House of Representatives. This was bizarre on a number of fronts, not least because both Stevens and Berrien, along with Paul, eventually became strident McCarthy supporters. There is no obvious evidence that basic political differences separated the two sides in this dispute. One NWP member described the schism as simply "another of those things that happen in [the] history of movements."[23] For Stevens, however, it was a culmination of the decades-long resentment she held over her difficult relationships with Belmont and Paul, as well as her sincere desire to see the NWP as once again the vibrant, innovative, courageous organization it had been during the suffrage years. After twenty-four years as a member of the National Council of the National Woman's Party, Stevens left the organization in 1948.[24]

The clash had serious consequences for the party, resulting in many resignations and leading to another internal struggle in the 1950s, which further weakened it. Never a mass organization, the NWP lost membership quickly after 1920. By 1945 it claimed a general membership of 4,000, which increased to 5,500 in 1953 but dwindled to 1,400 in 1965. By the end of World War II, the NWP functioned almost entirely on the national rather than on the state or local level. Although the group periodically discussed the membership problem, the leadership preferred to keep the organization small and elite. Paul believed a small cadre of women working to get existing women's organizations to endorse the ERA would be most effective. As death thinned the ranks and few fresh recruits joined, the leadership kept the membership figures secret.[25] Still the party deserves credit for an important feminist achievement in these years. With the support of conservatives and over the opposition of liberals, African Americans, and labor unions, the NWP played a central role in having "sex" added to the Civil Rights Act of 1964, now recognized as an important milestone for women.

Historians have portrayed Alice Paul as an unapologetic martyr who devoted her life to overcoming women's culturally ascribed roles and the one twentieth-century individual chiefly responsible for building momentum to win policies to give women full political and legal equality.[26] More recently, scholars have credited Paul with establishing the first successful nonviolent campaign for social reform in the United States. The dramatic visual campaign she led as part of the suffrage movement—which went beyond writing and speaking to include cartoons, photographs, parades, boycotts, car and train trips, picketing, and hunger strikes—invoked the communication possibilities of a new century. It was intended "to engage, to shock, to thrill, to shame, to pressure, and to convince."[27] At the same time, Paul's class and race elitism is recognized, as is her individualist approach to equal rights, her cultivation of a small cadre of upwardly mobile society women with financial resources to keep the NWP afloat, and her belief that women were the same not only to men but to one another.[28] Despite the fact that after decades of loyalty Stevens turned against Paul, Paul had a deep, profound influence on Stevens's thought and activism. Paul was unarguably a central figure in the American women's rights movement of the first half of the twentieth century. She died in 1977, the same year that Pruette died.

While Stevens was entangled in party quarrels with Paul and others, Beard, true to form, tried to steer clear and focus on her scholarship. She continued to write nearly to the end of her life. She published her most important book, *Woman as Force in History*, in 1946, at the age of seventy. In it she further refined her critique of nineteenth-century feminists' emphasis on women's subjection, arguing that this stemmed from a flawed reading of women's status in English common law. She once again criticized capitalists, politicians, and careerist women, as well as the US women's movement. Not surprisingly, the reviews were mixed. One female reviewer queried why, when Beard herself had attained marriage, an equitable relationship with her husband, children, and intellectual work, did she sound "so cross"? An *Independent Woman* editor called the book a "hellish thing," while others rejected her thesis of woman's force in history. A male reviewer wrote that "Mrs. Beard misses the heart of the historical problem, which is that equality for women is a chimera when the material foundations for it are lacking."[29] By the next year, Beard was dismayed at the book's sales. Although it did go into a third printing in 1947, she considered the 7,500 sold "a wash out" in comparison to the tens of thousands of Ferdinand Lundberg and Marynia Farnham's virulently anti-feminist *Modern Woman: The Lost Sex* that the public snapped up. Lundberg and Farnham described feminism as a "deep illness," caused by neurotic, male-imitating women who wanted to destroy the family. By 1949, Beard was even more incensed by Simone de Beauvoir's *The Second Sex*, which Beard believed portrayed women as victims rather than agents, was ahistorical, and "perfectly ridiculous," yet it captivated college women in a way that *Woman as Force in History* did not.[30]

The anticommunism of the late 1940s and early 1950s troubled Beard, as well. Triggered by the Cold War and a nuclear arms race, US postwar foreign policy shifted to focus on containment of the Soviet Union. From 1950 to 1954, a Republican US senator from Wisconsin, Joseph McCarthy, incited an anticommunist furor, accusing the government of shielding communists within its ranks.

McCarthyism dismayed Pruette and Irwin as well, although Stevens was by then a strident anticommunist. Pruette stated presciently that she hoped Joe McCarthy would be relegated in history to "the buzzing of a not very bright gnat." For Beard, the condition of the world fueled her continuing fight for justice. In 1950 she stated, "If one doesn't get bogged down mentally by the horrible state of the world, if one can believe that it is still worth while to work at truths of life as truths of history, there is a vast amount of work to be done." By the end of the year, however, she was deeply discouraged. She wrote of the "dark hour of history" and sadly confided to a friend, "I am sick enough at heart to prefer the regular silence of my days now. There is no value in anything I might say and I have ceased to be the chatterbox I was for so long, so long."[31]

By the politically conservative 1950s, when Beard's ideas about history and its relevance to social change had lost resonance with scholars, the public, and feminists, she grew increasingly irritable and found it harder to find intellectual comrades. In her critical swath she included famed anthropologist Margaret Mead, whom she had once admired; social scientist Karen Horney, whom earlier she had praised; and novice women's history writers Alma Lutz and Elizabeth Dexter, participants in Radcliffe's first women's history seminar. Beard found Lutz's *Created Equal* two-dimensional, focusing more on Elizabeth Cady Stanton's equal rights stance than on her critique of cultural attitudes, "her sharp analysis of Woman, Church, and State," which Beard admired. She dismissed Dexter's *Career Women in America* for its undying "careerism," much as she did the "Dumb clucks" of the American Association of University Women, whose "'packaged thinking' seem[s] never to burst a package."[32]

In old age, Beard found fulfillment in her children and grandchildren, her research and writing, and her love for nature. "Days with my fine and precious grown children," she wrote a confidante in 1951, "are indeed golden days." However, she also informed Florence Kitchelt, who lamented her loneliness without children, that "children are not the absolute answer to problems of old age." "I . . . have joy in Nature," she wrote in 1953, and on Easter day 1954 Beard declared, "spring gets into my blood and makes me as happy as I could be alone."[33] Beard lived in the New Milford, Connecticut, home for seven years after Charles's death, and wintered with her son in Tucson, Arizona. In 1953 she wrote a friend that she had recently fallen several times and that her right hand was "apt to fail" on her. Her handwriting in the last several years of her correspondence is tiny and nearly illegible. Her daughter Miriam, who lived in a house on the Beard property, insisted on coming over "for fear that I," Beard wrote, "with my domestiques away on their days off, might confront a Marauder." "I have to save some energy," she wrote a friend in 1955, "and people . . . refuse to let me. . . . I am too old—at last."[34] She also published *The Force of Women in Japanese History* (1953) and her final book, a tribute to her late husband, in 1955. Although after she finished *The Making of Charles A. Beard* she complained of "lightheadedness" and resolved to do her best "to achieve a stronger mind," she still determined to keep working. "I sound very good, don't I?" she wrote friends in 1955. "I am partly good—part of time, pray believe me."[35]

Beard faced her final years with the dignity and sense of humor that characterized her.[36] She visited her son in August 1955, became ill in the autumn, and never returned home. In 1956 William took over his mother's correspondence. He wrote a close friend, "Mother is rolling along in her 80th year in good spirits. . . . She eats heartily and likes to joke still . . . [but] her memory is not always very clear." He noted that she had a twenty-four-hour nurse and "carries on somewhat unpredictable conversations." On Beard's eighty-second birthday, August 5, 1958, William wrote a family friend that she was "quite weak but very brave indeed, and takes age as calmly as anybody could possibly do. She never complains and is altogether wonderful." Beard celebrated that final birthday in bed, dressed up, with a cake, flowers, and cards (sadly, only eight friends remembered her birthday), and died five days later. Her death was, according to her son, sudden and peaceful. She was cremated; her funeral was held in Phoenix, Arizona.[37]

Although Beard died before the revitalization of the women's movement, Stevens lived long enough to recognize its beginnings. During the 1950s, Stevens returned to her early interest in songwriting, and continued her feminist activism via other channels than the NWP, including serving as vice president of the reestablished Lucy Stone League. The league was discontinued in the 1930s but revived in New York City in 1950. Strident to the end of her life in her insistence that women demand leadership positions, Stevens never hesitated to talk about power, how women could get it, and how they should use it. Later in the decade, she gathered her papers to deposit at Radcliffe, and reconsidered the arc of her career. In 1959 an Oberlin representative queried Stevens, asking for a succinct description of her life's work for the alumnae catalog. "Would the following designation be satisfactory," he inquired—"Author, publicist and organizer for Women's Rights?" True to her activist and keen public relations instincts Stevens suggested instead, "Publicist, organizer for women's rights, author."[38]

Although ill at the time, Stevens was attentive to feminism's nascent rebirth, which was beginning to glimmer. In 1961, just a few years too soon, she proposed that *Jailed for Freedom* be reissued. "The time has rolled around," Stevens wrote her original publisher, "when my book, which is a primary source of the story of women, should be made available to the oncoming generation." *Jailed for Freedom* was not reprinted until 1976, however, thirteen years after Stevens's death, and quickly went out of print. It was reissued in 1995, to commemorate the seventy-fifth anniversary of the ratification of the Nineteenth Amendment, and is still in print.[39]

Jonathan Mitchell—with whom Stevens achieved the companionate marriage she advocated for so long—cared for Stevens in her final years. She suffered the first of several heart attacks in 1960, when she was seventy-two. In 1961, her brother Ralph wrote Mitchell: "Both you and Doris have had a long drawn out battle . . . I do not think there is anything more you could have done, and you certainly do not have to apologize for what might have been averted. I think you should write a book on what to do in care of heart attacks." Doris Stevens died of heart disease on March 22, 1963, at age seventy-five. She was buried in Evergreen Cemetery in Portland, Maine. After her death, Stevens's brother wrote Mitchell: "We deeply appreciate the hard time you must be having to adjust yourself to the loss of your beloved wife. . . . I have never known anyone who was so devoted to his wife as you were to Doris."[40]

Like Beard and Stevens, in her later years Irwin continued to be active in feminist circles and kept writing. She published twelve books between 1940 and her death in 1970, including two mysteries, *Many Murders* (1941) and *The Women Swore Revenge* (1946).[41] Her children's books, launched in 1909 with *Maida's Little Shop*, represented the bulk of Irwin's literary output in the 1940s and 1950s, when she published ten volumes in the series. She closed the series (and her long writing career) with her final book, *Maida's Little Treasure Hunt* (1955), at seventy-five.[42] Irwin continued to serve on the NWP board in the 1940s, and with Alma Lutz and Edith Houghton Hooker was a contributing editor to *Equal Rights* in 1941. Demonstrating her generosity of spirit and unending loyalty to Maud Wood Park, in 1943 she helped organize a celebration of the twenty-third anniversary of woman suffrage, held at Radcliffe, which honored Park.

Irwin—who "prided and preened" herself on her family's longevity—lived to be ninety-seven and devoted her twilight years to ordering her papers and remaining as active as she could. After Will Irwin's death she retired to their summer home. Although troubled with weight gain, at sixty-seven she still swam in the ocean daily. "At seventy-two years of age," she wrote Park in 1945, "I, too, am beginning to take stock of things and get ready for that great move which is death. Everything that I can send to the Radcliffe Archives is going there." She continued, "I wish I could summon up the faintest film of a belief in a future life. But I can't. Occasionally I do reflect that birth is a marvelous thing; death might also be marvelous." Thirteen years later, however, she described death as "surely the blackest, iciest catastrophe in all life."[43] In the 1950s, after Park died and when Irwin was in her mid-eighties, she corresponded with Park's biographer and read and commented on the manuscript.[44] She also labored over her own autobiography, "Adventures of Yesterday," which she successfully completed but for unknown reasons never published.[45]

Irwin's late letters, still written in her round, childlike handwriting, poignantly and with valiant humor describe the physical and emotional hardship of growing old. "Your letter fills me with that despair to which old age is occasionally susceptible," she wrote a friend in 1958. "You are . . . so busy on important things. But eighty-five years of age . . . is not seventy-five years or sixty-five years or fifty-five years. Alas and alackaday it takes its toll of one's vitality." The next year she complained of "a frightening eye condition" and "a general weakness throughout." "It is my considered opinion," she proclaimed wittily, "that being eighty-six years of age is enough for one woman to stand and is sufficient punishment for anything the said woman may have done." Irwin did live to witness renewed public interest in her ideas and writing. *The Story of the Woman's Party, Angels and Amazons*, and *Angel Island* were all reprinted during the feminist resurgence of the late 1960s and early 1970s. Irwin died of arteriosclerosis in a Norwell, Massachusetts, nursing home on September 25, 1970. Her *New York Times* obituary headline simply read: "Inez Haynes Irwin, Author, Feminist, 97."[46]

———————

Women's activism in the years after World War II profoundly changed US society. The civil rights movement challenged long-held assumptions that racial segregation and democracy could coexist. The movement to end racial discrimination stimulated a cascade of reform movements, including liberal feminism, whose advocates founded their own organizations that pressured the government to outlaw gender discrimination. At the same time women entered state, local, and federal government and the political parties to work on change from the inside out.[47] Betty Friedan's *The Feminine Mystique* (1963) blasted the icon of 1950s domesticity, the culmination of the glorification of marriage that the companionate marriage ideal had first set in place. Major legislation emerged from liberal feminism, including the Equal Pay Act of 1963, Title IX of the Education Amendments of 1972, and the Women's Educational Equity Act of 1974.[48]

The historian Sara Evans vividly described the "second wave" of American feminism as "a tidal wave of feminism that washed over the United States and changed it forever."[49] Late 1960s feminists challenged the social construct that equated heterosexuality with normality and marriage with fulfillment. The lesbian-feminist movement celebrated the "Woman-Identified Woman," and confronted the homophobia of American culture and the women's movement itself. Radical feminism, rooted in the student New Left and Black Power movements, also emerged during the late 1960s. Radical feminists rejected government reform as a method for creating gender equality and instead emphasized sexuality and private life. Disenchanted by their treatment by male peers in the anti–Vietnam War movement and the New Left, radical women's groups created a groundswell of diverse organizations that articulated new theories of female oppression.[50] Anti-racist white women, led by Jewish women and lesbians, strove to understand how white privilege had prevented women's cross-race alliances and aimed to articulate a new politics that would consider white women's position as both oppressed and oppressor.[51]

Like white women, Black, Latina, Chicana, and Asian American women also organized, often in response to the sexism of their male peers.[52] The Combahee River Collective, formed in 1974, expressed the tension African American women felt as they moved between Black Power and women's liberation movements.[53] Latinas discovered feminism through women's experiences in the 1960s Chicano movement, centered in the Southwest and California. Asian American feminists emerged in 1970s San Francisco and New York, calling for, among other things, a defying of the cultural codes that encouraged them to be silent.[54] They all drew on some of the ideas that had circulated among earlier generations of feminists.

The youngest of the four women examined here, Lorine Pruette was the only one still alive (or well enough) to actually witness this feminist rebirth and to experience her own rediscovery. She had continued her work as a visiting professor and psychotherapist, opening a private therapy practice in Ossining, New York, for troubled children, adolescents, and their parents in 1946 (at age fifty), which she ran until 1954. Between 1954 and 1956, Pruette conducted group therapy with mothers of mentally disabled children at New York Medical College. She grew interested in the psychology of aging. "I hope we approach the matter of aging," she stated in 1964, "with a mature philosophy—a crystal chandelier philosophy rather than one of depression and defeat—Keep alive at keeping busy through something worthwhile and pleasant." She took her own advice: during the 1960s, then in her late sixties, Pruette worked to establish what she hoped would become an internationally recognized crafts school in the Smoky Mountains town of Gatlinburg, Tennessee, where retirees could "find a new way of life," but it never materialized. In 1963, after "many years among the Alien Corn," Pruette returned to her hometown and was named special lecturer in psychology at the University of Chattanooga, which she had attended as an undergraduate a half century before. Again, she opened a therapy practice, despite the fact that she was approaching seventy.[55]

Because she was old and ill at the time, the American feminist renaissance was, for Pruette, bittersweet. Pruette believed she was a feminist ahead of her time; that, she concluded, was a mistake, but one "cosseting to the ego."[56] She stated that Kate Millett said much the same thing she had said forty years earlier. The only difference was that Millett made $75,000 on her 1970 bestseller *Sexual Politics* (and in Pruette's opinion was a dull writer to boot), and she herself made little on *Women and Leisure* (1924). Both were originally Columbia doctoral dissertations—Pruette's in psychology and Millett's in literature—that hit a public nerve and made their way into American debates about sexuality, gender roles, and feminism. Millet's book, which historians believe put radical feminism on the cultural map, drew on literary criticism and feminist theory to argue that generations of American women had learned about female sexuality from male novelists, who characterized women as sex objects.[57]

Pruette became the subject of scholarly interest during the last decade of her life. In 1974 Sherna Gluck of the Feminist History Research Project in Topanga, California, commissioned oral histories with eight feminists active between 1900 and 1930. Lorine Pruette was one of the women she arranged to be interviewed. Although Pruette agreed to the initial conversation, exclaiming, "Delighted to find that now I am a classic!" after the first session, irritated at the number of questions, she flatly refused to do any more. She acerbically wrote Gluck: "I agreed to do an hour and a half recording. Put me in bed. I'm 78 years old, sickly, had to impose on a very busy man who drove 30 miles to do the recording and 30 miles back.... I'm not going to talk into [the tape recorder] on How I became a Feminist. Sorry." Consequently, she is not included in the 1976 volume that resulted, *From Parlor to Prison: Five American Suffragists Talk about Their Lives.*[58] Later that year, Pruette was interviewed for the *Chattanooga News-Free Press.* When asked, "What is success?" she responded: "Success is the realization of as many of your potentialities as possible. There was a time when women didn't think they had any potential ... all they thought about was babies, babies, babies. We've had great improvements in my lifetime." But, when asked if she considered herself a success, she stated, "I was ahead of my time. I didn't make any money on my first book [*Women and Leisure*]. Now, women are 'in' and it's in its second printing. No, I don't think I'm a success. I wish I had written more novels."[59]

Pruette tried to intervene in the emerging academic narrative of the history of American feminism in the twentieth century. She seemed to read everything she could get her hands on, including the new women's history scholarship that grew out of the feminist movement. One of the books was historian William O'Neill's important 1969 *Everyone Was Brave: A History of Feminism in America*, in which he criticized early twentieth-century feminists for their limited vision and unwillingness to take on marriage and the family. Pruette, who knew this was untrue, was incensed.[60] When the sociologist Alice Rossi published *The Feminist Papers* in 1974, Pruette wrote her to protest Beard's omission from the book. Rossi responded that she had originally planned to include Beard in her compilation of early twentieth-century feminist writings, but had to eliminate her due to length constraints. "I certainly share your admiration of Mary Beard," she wrote Pruette.[61] Pruette sent her own fine 1931 essay "Why Women Fail" to the fledgling feminist magazine *Ms.* in the early 1970s, which declined to print it.

In her later years Pruette returned to the writing she had set aside, including a book manuscript on women's health that predated the resurgence of the women's health movement. "After years of being bogged down in everybody else's horrors, psychotherapy," she wrote irreverently in 1962, "I have determined to go back to writing about my own miseries." Like the Boston Women's Health Book Collective that published the best-selling feminist guidebook *Our Bodies, Ourselves* in 1973, in "My Life among the Doctors" Pruette insisted on women's right to understand their bodies and to exercise agency in their own health care.[62] A self-avowed patients' rights activist, Pruette penned her manuscript as a salty, funny, feminist guide for women on how to choose and interact with male physicians (female physicians she believed were all excellent). "If he bullies you, leave him," she advised, "If he tells you you are an emotionally unstable woman, leave him. .... If he tells you your miseries are all in your mind, leave him. If he tries to 'psychoanalyze' you, leave him." Unfortunately, none of Pruette's later submissions were accepted; her last publication appeared in 1941.[63]

In her late, unpublished essay "The Making of a Feminist," Pruette described her reactions to the revitalized women's movement, positioning her own ideas in relation to new theoretical voices. She supported much of the agenda of liberal feminism and even more of the tenets of radical feminist thought that (re)emerged in the late 1960s and early 1970s. Like her intellectual followers, Pruette consistently argued that the private sphere of home and family was saturated with gendered power relations, and thus with politics. "Radical feminism," as political theorist Moya Lloyd has written, "contested and transformed what could be thought of as a political issue. It *politicized* sexual relations (including prostitution and pornography), sexual orientation, the body, abortion, and reproduction."[64] Or, as the radical feminist slogan put it: "The personal is political." Pruette had begun politicizing these issues as early as the 1910s, and all four of the women highlighted here used their lives as sites of feminist experimentation.

Yet, dependably rebellious and iconoclastic, Pruette also found tenets of radical feminism with which to quarrel. She approved of the "Women's Lib" ideas of equal pay for equal work, the outdatedness of the conventional marriage ceremony, and of keeping one's name after marriage. She considered male chauvinism a valuable term; "naming a thing is a very important element in one's thinking," she astutely observed. Yet she could not relate to women's anger at being excluded from men's clubs or being considered "sex objects," although her response here was contradictory to some of her other statements. She suspected feminism late-1960s style was characterized by "man-hating." A book like Shulamith Firestone's *The Dialectic of Sex* represented "violent abrasive[ness]."[65]

Like Millet's *Sexual Politics*, Firestone's book was published in 1970 when Pruette was seventy-four, and became another seminal text of the rejuvenated women's movement. In it Firestone synthesized the ideas of Freud, Wilhelm Reich, Marx, Engels, and de Beauvoir and argued that women's inequality was linked to their biology, specifically pregnancy, childbirth, and child-rearing. She proposed women seize the means of reproduction and suggested cybernetics as a method in which human reproduction could take place in laboratories rather than within female bodies.[66] Pruette's objection to *The Dialectic of Sex*, coached in her psychotherapist's concern for the "frail male ego" and masculine sexual potency, once again hearkened back to her childhood position in the triangle of her powerful mother, her browbeaten father, and herself. It also echoed the strong messages she absorbed as a young graduate student from G. Stanley Hall and her lifelong, paradoxical feelings about sexuality. Although she chose not to acknowledge it, like Firestone Pruette argued that the nuclear family largely prevented women from realizing full, creative lives.

Of the four women, Pruette was the only one still alive when the landmark court case *Roe v. Wade* legalized abortion in the United States in 1972. She was staunchly pro-choice, criticizing in 1973 a Tennessee panel of physicians who proposed a state law outlawing abortion. Pruette drew on the new feminist language to write bluntly: "Like most of his colleagues, Dr. W. Powell Hutchison is a chauvinist. He feels that the wisdom of the physician must decide who has an abortion. There is no recognition that the woman's body belongs to her and that it should be her decision to bear or not to bear a child."[67]

Neither Stevens nor Irwin lived to see the renewed ERA battle, which provided a focal point for American feminist mobilization between 1972 and 1982. Had they been alive and able, they would surely have been at the center of the struggle. In March 1972, two years after Irwin's and nine years after Stevens's death, the ERA passed the US Senate by eighty-four to eight, fifteen votes over the two-thirds required for constitutional amendments. Scholar Jane Mansbridge has argued that, although it was unlikely the Supreme Court would have used the amendment to bring about significant changes in the relations between men and women, both sides of the reincarnated ERA debate argued that it *would* produce such changes. Like Americans earlier in the century, Americans in the 1970s and early 1980s did not want significant changes in gender roles: not in the workplace, home, or in other institutions. Legislators in borderline states feared the ERA might lead to such drastic changes, and voted against it. Both proponents and opponents exaggerated its potential influence, proponents arguing the amendment would send women military draftees into combat on the same basis as men, opponents insisting that all bathrooms would become unisex and that the amendment would hurt homemakers by weakening family law that distinguished among family members based solely on their sex. Much like ERA champions earlier in the century, 1970s pro-ERA feminists embraced a philosophy that called for full equality with men, not for equality with exceptions. Had they been able to craft and disseminate a synthetic model of feminism that stressed "equality in difference," it is possible that the ERA might now be law. Instead, unwilling to compromise, both sides staked out equally radical positions. Adding to this ideological impasse was a conservative backlash against feminism accelerated by the rise of the New Right and Ronald Reagan's 1980 election to the presidency, which sounded the death knell for the passage of the ERA in the twentieth century. Although a majority of Americans reported favoring the amendment, the ratification deadline passed on June 30, 1982, with only thirty-five of the needed thirty-eight states.[68]

Pruette, who lived to be eighty-one, was—like the other women in this collective biography—also subjected to the indignities of old age. Diagnosed with diabetes in 1966, even as an old woman she candidly plumbed her own experiences for the benefit of other women. She drolly wrote a publisher, "Last year it was discovered that I have diabetes, and that is quite a thing to have. Since it happens most to middle-aged fat ladies I should think a personal account might go to the women's journals." A 1968 photograph shows her using a cane and having gained a great deal of weight; she described herself that year as "somewhat crippled." The following year Pruette's eyes were operated on for glaucoma, and her eyesight became limited. "Looking for a book on a table," she wrote a friend, "I have to go over the table, about like a pig hunting truffles." In 1970 she sold her house and relocated to an apartment building for senior citizens. As she grew increasingly unable to care for herself, she moved into a nursing home in 1973. "I have never asked for a Special Diet," Pruette tartly wrote the visiting nursing service. "I find it definitely a superderogatory bit for you to propose to 'safeguard' me.... Should I eat a sweet bun instead of giving them to the yardboy, no one would sue Senior Neighbors." "Everything exhausts me," she declared later that year.[69]

Like Stevens and Irwin, Pruette organized her papers to donate to the Schlesinger Library at Radcliffe, and pondered death. "We must accept the disintegration of this complex of bone, muscle and nerve," she wrote. She awoke several nights as an old woman crying out, "Immortality, that's what I want," and regretted she had no children to carry on her "bit of protoplasm." Several years before she died, Pruette had a nightmare in which no one came to her funeral. She died in the Alexian Brothers nursing home in Chattanooga, Tennessee in 1977.[70]

FEMINIST LEGACIES

Irwin, Beard, Stevens, and Pruette were feminists in a period that has largely been relegated to the backwash of feminism's high tide. Their creative ideas and committed lives offer important insights into the history of feminism in the United States in the early twentieth century. Three of them were prominent figures in the woman suffrage movement and demonstrate the diversity of philosophy that fueled the final generation who pushed the movement to victory. Although allied with the tiny militant wing of the 1910s movement, their varying perspectives on the ERA debate, which took up so much feminist attention and energy in the 1920s and 1930s are instructive, as are their responses to maternalist ideas, another wedge issue in the US women's rights movement in these years.

Inez Haynes Irwin attempted to synthesize the ideas of gender equality and difference, to advocate for both women's right to equity in the labor market and their entitlement—as mothers and wives—to the protection of gender-specific legislation. She rebelled against the social conventions that tied women to the home, yet in her feminist fiction she crafted a subversive reconceptualization of motherhood as a route to liberation and self-actualization, as well as a force for social change in a masculinized world. A dedicated NWP member, Irwin supported the ERA and placed her trust in women's individualism, personal liberty, and self-definition. She stressed women's potential as autonomous human beings rather than as wives, mothers, or daughters. She wanted to see women, as she stated in 1916, "with their hands literally on the machinery of the world."[71] Her shorn winged women in *Angel Island* represented her fears of men's attempts to tie women down, to ground and immobilize them. In *Angels and Amazons*, she praised pilot Amelia Earhart—"a girl eaglet winging her impetuous ways over the vast deeps"—as "a supreme proof of woman's equality in nerve, mechanical skill and courage."[72] At the same time that she advocated women's literal and metaphorical freedom to fly, Irwin was drawn to the concept of maternalism, which she reinterpreted to her own feminist vision.

As cofounder of the College Equal Suffrage League in 1900, Irwin helped funnel fresh energy and young recruits into the moribund American woman suffrage movement. Deeply inspired by the women she considered the nineteenth-century giants of the movement, she appreciated her access to higher education and expressed her gratitude through her suffrage activism and in her writing women's history books. A labor organizer and IWW supporter blacklisted in the communist backlash years, she envisioned woman suffrage as an inclusive movement that addressed class as well as gender, and reached across differences to bring women together. Her militancy and rebellious spirit led her to join the Congressional Union/NWP in the intense final years of the suffrage movement. She proposed activist tactics to secure the vote, including a suicide pact among suffragists (which was not implemented) and the labor union model of picketing the president of the United States (which was successfully implemented in 1917, and may have helped turn the tide in the long struggle). Her resilient, devoted friendship with Maud Wood Park demonstrates her ability to rise above the rancor that churned between the National Woman's Party and the League of Women Voters in the post-suffrage years. Irwin unabashedly admired certain women who opposed the NWP's equal rights agenda. Although a few of Irwin's books are still in print, her feminist leadership, radical ideas, innovative fiction, and the large spirit and joie de vivre she brought to the early twentieth-century women's movement have been largely overlooked.

Mary Beard's insistence that women had played a central role in history and that their lives, experiences, thought, and social contributions must be incorporated into the mainstream of historical writing bore fruit in the revitalized interest in women's history, now a rich and prolific field of academic inquiry. She labored to make a diverse assortment of women's documents available to the public and scholars in order to secure "a more balanced picture of humanity in the interests of historic truth" and highlighted women's roles in the family as a legitimate, neglected area of inquiry.[73] She believed feminism should be collective in spirit and humanist in vision, and was a bridge builder during decades in which the tensions of the suffrage movement were still palpable. Her World Center for Women's Archives drew in leaders from every feminist faction, including the three other women profiled in this book. Beard's vision of feminism was interracial, cross-class, and transnational. In her writings she argued that the historically feminine—which she equated with impulses toward humanism, collectivism, and maternalism—were the only antidote for a twentieth-century culture hurtling toward materialism and destruction. She advocated a translation of women's nurturing and domestic skills from the private to the public sphere. Her sympathies with the working class and her contempt for the individualism and male imitation she believed professional women represented led Beard to devalue the very real dilemma some middle-class twentieth-century women faced, of how to achieve fulfilling lives in both spheres. Beard pinned her hopes on a new feminism, one that included equal rights and difference, rooted in women's understanding of their past.

Although she did not live long enough to see the rise of the New Left, civil rights movement, antiwar protests, or women's liberation, these movements were accompanied by the rewriting of social and cultural history by scholars who, like Beard, recognized the connection between research and social beliefs. As the historian Julie Des Jardins has noted, Beard's archive project in particular "articulated her plan for combining historical learning with women's activism, idealist thought with grassroots action, and feminist theory with social practice."[74] She believed education should motivate and inform social change and that historical research could lead to social reform. Beard's 1934 women's history syllabus posed questions that demonstrated her understanding of the intersectionality of race, class, and gender, a concept still at the center of scholarship being written in the early twenty-first century. She was persistently ambivalent about women's haste to embrace the male career model, which at times placed her at odds with her modern peers. She believed that rather than fight for equal opportunity, women should reshape the masculine system and serve as social and moral leaders. Although Beard's World Center for Women's Archives dissolved in 1940, the sources collected today form the center of two important archives of women's documents: the Schlesinger Library at Harvard University and the Sophia Smith Collection at Smith College.

Through her feminist leadership, Doris Stevens fought for the political and legal rights of women and the importance of female representation in the writing of the laws, treaties, and conventions affecting their status. As head of the Inter American Commission of Women, she brought the equal rights philosophy of the NWP before an international audience. She was a gifted, self-sacrificing organizer, described memorably by one fellow activist as "living on air and Feminism," and by an admiring journalist as "like Mercury poised for flight."[75] Stevens loved mapping out political strategy and drew energy from a challenge. This is what kept her going through decades of travel, lobbying, public speaking, and acts of civil disobedience. She recognized the importance of a women's movement that was associated with youth, modernity, and pressing issues of the day. She complained that the 1940s NWP failed to keep abreast of the changing times, dubbing Paul and her loyalists the Conservative Group and describing her own clique as "the people who want a little more 1945 and a little less 1920 and before in our propaganda."[76] Stevens's enigmatic twenty-year relationship with Alva Belmont and her split with Alice Paul in the 1930s provide further insights into the history of the NWP and its two controversial leaders.

There has been renewed interest in Stevens's life, particularly in her radical suffragism during the 1910s. The new edition of *Jailed for Freedom* published in 1995 garnered attention, and the book—which she wrote at twenty-eight—is the product most firmly connected to Stevens's legacy. The actress Laura Fraser portrayed Stevens in the popular 2004 HBO film *Iron Jawed Angels*, which highlights the dramatic final years of the woman suffrage movement in the United States.[77] The sentimental ballads Stevens wrote invoking her childhood memories of Nebraska met with some success in the entertainment industry.[78] In her final years, Stevens encouraged the establishment of feminist studies as a field of academic inquiry in American universities and tried unsuccessfully to establish a Lucy Stone Chair of Feminism at Radcliffe College. Twenty-three years after her death, Stevens's desire was realized when Princeton University announced in 1986 that her estate, through the Doris Stevens Foundation, had endowed a chair in women's studies. Today the annually rotating Doris Stevens Professorship in Women's Studies attracts senior scholars with a distinguished history of publications to the once all-male Ivy League institution. Stevens stipulated that selected scholars be social scientists, but she hoped they would be experts in one of her own fields of study and activism: political science, sociology, and international studies.[79] Her work in international feminism continues in the global feminist movement, although contemporary organizations are more attuned to power relations resulting from race, class, and political location. She would be delighted with the founding of UN Women, an umbrella organization for women's issues in the United Nations, currently headed by Michelle Bachelet, former president of Chile. Stevens's goal of gender parity in political bodies in the United States and other countries has yet to be realized. In the United States in 2013, women constitute only 15 percent of bodies that write laws that affect their status.[80]

Social scientist Lorine Pruette argued in lectures, articles, and books written and delivered over decades that it was possible and socially critical for women to enjoy meaningful, productive lives both as wives and mothers and as wage earners. Her 1924 book *Women and Leisure: A Study of Social Waste* was widely read and made her a feminist spokesperson as well as a barometer of the younger generation. In her advocacy of part-time work and job sharing as ways for mothers to maintain standing in the labor force, she was ahead of her time. Pruette drew on Freud's and Adler's theories to construct an argument for men's and women's differing psychological needs and anticipated late twentieth-century feminist theorists like Dorothy Dinnerstein, Nancy Chodorow, and Carol Gilligan in her belief that boys (and men) suffered more anxiety and psychological trauma than girls (and women) because of their stronger need to separate from the female (their mothers).[81] Her linking of politics and gendered power relations within the private sphere of the home and family is an early example of radical feminist thinking. Her 1931 statement on "Why Women Fail" captured an essential part of her intellectual legacy, one that holds that women, like men, deserve to be fully realized human beings and that fulfillment for both sexes includes love and work. Yet Pruette opposed the ERA and in the 1920s viewed NWP members as fanatics and ideological purists. Her evolving analysis of women and work responded to broader social attitudes toward wage-earning women in the United States, which in the 1920s appeared welcoming but by the 1930s had turned hostile. During the depression she built a case for women's financial need to work and depicted women workers as committed, permanent members of the labor force.

Three of the four women were drawn to feminism partly in rebellion against the pronatalist ideas and prescriptive notions of mother and home that dominated thinking about female gender roles in American culture between 1890 and the 1930s. As scholars have argued, maternalist ideas ultimately enforced domesticity, encoded gender difference, and regulated the behavior of mothers. Maternalist thinking separated "fit" mothers (white, native-born, married, and stay-at-home) from "unfit" mothers (African American, immigrant, wage-earning, unmarried, or divorced). Beard criticized these normative ideas, and Irwin struck back against them as well in her defiant creation of fictional mothers who were strong, financially independent, and single. She depicted marriage as inhibiting and punishing, but motherhood as an experience that could offer rebirth and a path to personal power. She advocated the rights of all women to become mothers, as well as mothers' rights to autonomy and freedom from social judgment. She rejected the ideal model of the middle-class family, with male breadwinner and married female homemaker and mother at the center. Both she and Beard demonstrate that one could advocate maternalist ideas (and gender difference) in ways that were provocative and even radical.

———

By fighting for women's right to be treated the same as men under the law, in their domestic and international work the NWP questioned the constitutionality of labor laws that recognized women's distinct experiences as workers. Equal rights feminists believed that women's rights as individuals without regard to family or marital status was the most effective way to approach legal and social determinants of women's opportunities and status. Tied to the tradition of liberal theory rooted in individual rights, equal rights feminism equated economic independence and political participation to the requirements for full citizenship. The NWP argued that special labor laws categorized all women as weak and helpless, and set them aside as a special protected class. They carried this belief into their 1930s international feminist organizing, when they advocated an Equal Nationality Treaty and an Equal Rights Treaty. Labor historian Dorothy

Sue Cobble has argued for the acknowledgment of multiple forms of American feminism, including labor feminists who appear in some historical narratives as antagonists of feminism. Because labor feminists opposed the ERA, fought to retain sex-based state labor laws, and did not pursue an equal rights legal strategy, some have depicted them as holding back the movement.[82] Beard and Irwin supported the labor feminist stance and were solid, lifelong proponents of feminism. Their examples support Cobble's contention that there have been multiple forms of American feminism, including those that are primarily grounded in class analysis.

The dispute over gendered labor laws, which fiercely divided women's rights advocates in the 1920s and beyond, raised a number of unresolved issues that remain at the heart of current equal rights debates. These contemporary issues include women's responsibility as primary caretakers and women's unique health care needs and are relevant to pay equity strategies, work and family policies, and divorce law.[83] Since 1980, when increasing numbers of women experienced results of gender-neutral legislation like joint custody and no-fault divorce laws, some feminists have criticized strict adherence to a doctrine of egalitarianism, arguing that women suffer from such legislation.[84] While sex-based state laws may have been used to restrict women's prospects and pay, gender-neutral laws are not always in women's best interests and may in fact be used against them.[85] Beard and Pruette would have concurred. Women's lives, they believed, were more complex and burdened than men's, and until men shared in childcare and domestic labor and women shared in economic privilege and political power, no court could legislate equality. All four women at times advocated a flexible interpretation of gender equality that included some room for gender difference. This points to the complex views held by twentieth-century American feminists.

These modern feminists, who were different in some ways, found much common ground on which to stand. All four were agnostics, or had unconventional religious beliefs. Pruette wrote, "I would be easier with my various miseries if I thought God in a White Coat was seeing all and knowing all, even if he wasn't doing anything. But as a hardened skeptic and French Huguenot, doubting most authority, I just can't see God wearing a white coat. . . . My God is much more august and concerned with deeper meanings." In one of her short stories she depicted God as a lecherous old man. Beard referred to God pan theistically as "the skyfather," "the Chief of the heavenly horde of thunder and other goods." "It has been too difficult for mortals to accept and follow Christ's doctrine of Love," she stated in a more serious vein, "but the doctrine has imperishable values, I hope." In a similar vein, Irwin stated that she believed in neither the "pre-life" nor "after-life." "It is my tragedy that I have never had an innate 'faith' of any kind," she wrote in her autobiography. In 1909 she had written a letter to *Collier's Magazine* signed "An American Woman," in which she gave her opinion on why churches had failed. "That letter simply raised hell," Irwin wrote Park. "Letters from shocked and hurt divines came in by the bale and boat-load. . . . It was soon borne in upon me that I was a PERNICIOUS INFLUENCE. I would have provided the rope for my own lynching. Gee, it takes a man of God to soak you in the back, doesn't it? They insinuate everything except that I'm unchaste."[86]

All four lived to see the world twice torn apart by war. Ultimately they each linked feminism with pacifism and believed women could make the world a more peaceful and, in Beard's term, "civil-ized" one. In their shared belief that women were essentially more pacific in nature than men, they reflected the values of care, nurturance, and morality that maternalists attached to mother-hood. Through her transnational activism, Stevens had proved to the world, a 1929 article proclaimed, that "the firm solidarity of feminists" would lead to "the peace of nations." In 1920, when she visited the Reines battlefield in France, she had written in her diary: "Heaps of wire, shrapnel, debris. . . . Here & there a piece of uniform—a shoe. . . . Human dung heaps . . . [I] suddenly realized that this was how the beautiful youth of our generation lived & died." "What an indictment on the way man has managed the world!" she exclaimed. Stevens believed women would be more successful in establishing peace than would men but scorned any attempts to involve the government in the effort.[87] In 1949, Stevens joined the Women's Peace Party, which had been founded in 1915 and first chaired by Jane Addams.

When Franklin D. Roosevelt proposed his New Deal cabinet, Pruette suggested he instead inaugurate "a *real* New Deal," a cabinet made up of women, whose "broader social viewpoint" and concept of social justice could help steer the world away from militarism. "Rename the War Department the Peace Department and put an intelligent *pacifist* at its head," she urged and suggested Hannah Clothier Hull, president of the Women's International League for Peace and Freedom, for secretary of the navy. For secretary of state Pruette nominated her friend Mary Beard, whose "sense of humor would prevent the least of her subordinates from hastening abroad a silly organization's protest against a scientific genius' political views—as Henry L. Stimson's State Dept. did in the Einstein visa tragic-comedy. Nor would Mrs. Beard spurn the obvious thing, such as recognizing Russia."[88]

At times the lives of these women proved challenging and painful. Irwin provocatively explored and celebrated unconventional motherhood in a series of feminist novels she wrote in the 1910s and 1920s, yet she remained childless. She lost her mother to suicide and periodically returned to this theme, at times connecting it to social protest, at other times weaving it into her fiction. Pruette was a tireless public voice for women's right to work and family, yet her own two efforts to achieve this failed, and her unpublished writings, particularly her fiction, paint a much darker picture of the possibility of attaining both. Pruette struggled with depression, suicidal thoughts, and restlessness. "Once when I was in a rather bitter depression I sometimes stayed at a small shabby hotel in mid-town New

York," she wrote. "Tiny rooms, a tiny window staring at brazen—or aluminum—skyscrapers. A postage stamp sky. I was troubled, even haunted, by the feeling that I should have to climb out that narrow window and plummet down to the distant sidewalk. It was not that I wanted to spatter my brains out. What I wanted was—to *git* out." She described "the wall of glass" she met, which she portrayed as "very thick, powerful, but crystal clear glass, with me on this side, and all life, all joy, all functioning on the other side." She concluded with an image eerily evocative of contemporary writings about women's struggles to break through the Glass Ceiling, the invisible barrier that keeps them from rising to higher positions in workplaces. "Of course," Pruette concluded, "I never get to the top or over to the other side, where the grass grows green."[89]

Pruette suffered from both loneliness and an indelible fear of being trapped by marriage and domesticity. A second keynote in Pruette's life was making herself do things she didn't really want to do. "I agree with Papa Sartre," she wrote, "that we *do* choose. We choose according to our own patterns. A pattern of illness. A pattern of loves. Of marriages. Of undertakings; Henry James, much wiser than his psychologist brother called it the Figure in the Carpet. Uncle Adler called it Das Lebenstyle." Considering that she had married two men "when I had wanted to marry neither," she concluded, "Here was my Lebenstyle. Don't fight; don't argue; just slip around Robin Hood's barn."[90] The intense pressure to marry and live heterosocial lives that Pruette and her contemporaries felt during the 1910s, 1920s, and 1930s may have motivated her to marry against her will and contributed to her unhappiness and disenchantment. Leila Rupp's suggestion that sexual radicalism had a profound influence on the women's movement after 1920 is worth reconsidering here.[91] Rupp argued that the ambivalence and conflicts that women like Stevens experienced in response to early twentieth-century ideas of sexual liberalism and heterosociality were of great consequence. They signaled a crisis in American feminism as significant as that caused by the loss of a unifying goal after woman suffrage was won. Pruette's life directs us to the same conclusion.

Like Pruette, Stevens suffered episodes of depression, especially after she lost the IACW chair, as Jonathan Mitchell stated in a 1963 oral history. "After 1940," he remarked, "[Doris] had her depressed periods, when—before I was aware of what was happening to her, we had spells of silence, and bitter words."[92] Lucy Burns wrote her in 1942, evidently responding to a letter in which Stevens had asked for guidance on what she should do next. "I feel as if I understood and felt your situation inside and out," she wrote. "But when it comes to a solution on any suggested course, I pause very cautiously. . . . I choose peace, poverty, and the quiet life. . . . But you are quite a different person—more restless and dynamic, and much more socially minded. And you have no turn for poverty— . . . Might it not be a good idea to get in touch with Mary Beard?"[93] Beard was also eminently sane, probably another reason this friend suggested that Stevens consult with her in her moment of need. But Beard, too, at times faced her own demons as she tried to reconceptualize feminism in a fractious, unreceptive age.

———————

Karen Offen has convincingly argued that in order to accurately define feminism, scholars must consider its historical development as well as its use in a variety of cultures. An understanding of the term "feminism," she states, "must be not only historically sound but comparatively grounded in order to be conceptually illuminating." Evidence suggests, she contends, that feminism is represented by "two historically distinct and seemingly conflicting modes of argument," which she calls relational versus individualist approaches to feminism. Viewed historically, arguments that have drawn on relational feminism have proposed a gender-based but egalitarian version of social organization. Relational feminism represents the prevailing line of thinking before the twentieth century throughout the Western world and until the later twentieth century dominated feminist debates throughout Europe. Relational feminist arguments considered a companionate male-female couple as the basic unit of society and emphasized women's rights as women (defined by their childbearing and/or nurturing capacities) in relation to men. "It insisted on *women's* distinctive contributions in these roles to the broader society and made claims on the basis of these contributions," Offen writes.[94]

In contrast, individualist arguments considered the individual, without regard to sex or gender, as the basic unit of society. Drawing on abstract concepts of human rights and valuing the quest for personal independence or autonomy, the individualist feminist tradition downplayed all socially defined roles and minimized attention paid to sex-linked qualities or contributions, including childbearing and childrearing. Individualist feminism has deep historical roots in European culture and reached its most expansive development in Anglo-American thought. Significantly, though, there are instances of Anglo-American feminism that reveal relational modes of argument existing side-by-side with individualist approaches.[95]

In Offen's view these two approaches to feminist thought are more productive than the "varieties" of feminist thought interpretation, many of which are ahistorical. Her analysis is useful in considering the diverging, and at times contradictory, thought of these four women. Individualist feminist approaches have particularly served the quest of single women to justify an independent, non-family-based existence in a patriarchal world. The emergence of a large group of emancipated single women in the nineteenth century was connected to a rising middle class that advanced prosperity and industrial competition in Western societies. Individualist feminism (which I have called equal rights feminism) has stressed the importance of achieving the ERA, dismantling occupational segregation, and addressing gender-based educational inequities. The American public most often understands feminism as individualist feminism, which is responsible for much of the antagonism toward feminism, especially among women who have chosen to be full-time wives and mothers.[96]

Stevens and Irwin were firm disciples of equal rights, who also cared a great deal about the family as a social unit. Stevens believed women should be compensated for housework and care giving; she also contended they should compete equally with men in the labor market. At the same time, she believed women should organize and agitate as women. Beard acknowledged this shared conviction in a 1937 letter to Stevens in which she applauded her for believing women were foolish to represent themselves as neutral "human beings, neither man nor woman."[97]

In her fiction, Irwin depicted motherhood as liberating and supported government stipends to mothers that would allow them to stay home with their children. Simultaneously, she worked to open doors in education and the professions to women. In their restive rejection of domesticity, both Stevens and Irwin wanted something more for women: financial independence, creative and autonomous lives, the opportunity to lead, not just in single-sex institutions but alongside men. They rejected culturally prescribed, gender-based roles at the same time that they recognized the value of motherhood. Offen has argued that individualist and relational feminism are not always in opposition. "Relational feminism could and did incorporate demands for women's right to work outside the household, to participate in all professions, and to vote, alongside demands for equality in civil law concerning property and persons."[98] In Offen's interpretation of historical feminism, Irwin and Stevens were at the same time both individualist and relational feminists.

The same can be argued for Beard and Pruette, who consistently opposed the ERA and—in the relational feminist tradition—believed in biological and cultural distinctions between the sexes. They explicitly acknowledged differences in men's and women's gendered functions in society. They supported women's occupational advancement and economic independence, and of the four, Pruette most adamantly defended women's right to self-realization. She was also the one who spent much of her life as a single woman and most clearly articulated the ramifications of the loss of the earlier separatist female community. Offen notes that the ideas of nineteenth-century French feminists, who were primarily relational feminists, culminated in the paradoxical doctrine of "equality in difference," or equity as distinct from equality. She described other nineteenth-century feminists, like Sweden's Ellen Key, who neither fit within the "equal rights" or "autonomy" models, and suggests that this mode of "bi-valent" argument had important influence in developments throughout Europe and the rest of the world.[99]

Especially between 1920 and 1940 in the United States, the aims and goals of relational (what I have called social feminist) approaches and individualist (equal rights) approaches appeared increasingly irreconcilable. The very real hostility, backstabbing, jealousy, bickering, and refusal to work together that characterized both groups is not a proud legacy of the history of American feminism. Yet these four women's experiences suggest that lingering suffrage antagonisms may have driven feminist discord in the post-suffrage decades more than unyielding ideological conflicts did. Much to Beard's dismay, individualist feminism gained momentum in the 1920s as birthrates fell, women experienced unprecedented professional success, and the economy boomed. The strong anticommunist reaction to the 1917 Russian Revolution coincided in the United States of the 1920s with a downplaying of sex differences among feminist intellectuals and the diminishment of the notion of separate spheres.[100] Attacks on this individualistic form of feminism included a rejection of it as male-imitative (Beard), unwomanly (G. Stanley Hall), and male-hating (Pruette). Beard rejected Simone de Beauvoir's existentialist thesis, which interpreted "the feminine" as a cultural construct and posited the male model as the ideal. Until the time of her death, de Beauvoir's ideas were more popular in English-speaking countries than in her own.[101]

Wendy Sarvasy has offered another valuable way to conceptualize post-suffrage feminism, a synthetic model that moves beyond the difference/equality split (or the relational versus individualist approaches) to favor a more comprehensive vision. Such a vision, she has argued, suggests a post-suffrage feminist theoretical process striving to reconceive gender equality. Although American women vigorously disagreed on how to achieve formal equality with gender difference after 1920, Sarvasy concluded that these synthetic feminists (some of them NWP members) formulated creative solutions that addressed the conundrum head on. "[They] showed how unequal power relations turned biological differences into socially constructed, substantive gender inequalities; they formulated public policies based upon a new conception of gender equality to alleviate these substantive inequalities; and they sought to use the emancipated aspects of women's different experiences and outlooks to create a more egalitarian political and social environment."[102]

Sarvasy argues that some early twentieth-century feminists intended to use public policy as a vehicle for creating a new synthesis of equality and difference.[103] She also notes how scholarly and popular treatments of these historical feminist debates have often taken sides and blamed the other for contemporary social problems. Critics have held pro-ERA groups accountable for the country's failure to develop a comprehensive family policy and accused proponents of labor legislation of creating today's gender-segregated labor market. Acknowledging this, Dorothy Sue Cobble has called for "a reconstitution" of feminism as "an intellectual tradition and as a present-day politics." Citing the historical amnesia from which current critics of feminism often suffer, what is needed, she argues, is to "acknowledge multiple forms of American feminism and move beyond the 'equal rights teleology' that shapes the narrative of twentieth-century feminist history."[104]

Feminists continue to be ridiculed, vilified, scorned, and misunderstood. In an opinion poll taken in 2000, 85 percent of Americans stated they believed women should have equal rights. Yet that same year, when asked if they were feminists, only 29 percent of Americans in another poll answered in the affirmative.[105] In 2013 feminism is still equated with individualism, man hating, the decline of the family, as well as the rise of conservative women in American politics. Three-fourths of Americans polled in a 2010 survey said that the nation had "more important issues to fix" than gender equality.[106] Why do these ideas continue to reverberate with such intensity? Historian Estelle Freedman persuasively argued that fear of feminism runs deep. "No matter how insightful its politics," she writes, "feminism feels deeply threatening to many people, both women and men." In its potent critique of social institutions like marriage and the family, power relations between women and men, and sexual and racial relationships feminism, Freedman writes, "exposes the historical construction, and potential deconstruction, of categories such as gender, race, and sexuality."[107] But Freedman also argues that there is no turning back, that with great struggle on the part of both women and men, feminist ideas remain part of the political landscape.

FEMINIST WAVES

Historians and scholars have challenged the wave metaphor that charts the history of women's rights in the United States, questioning its adequacy to portray fully the diverse movements that make up American feminism, past and present. "The concept of waves surging and receding cannot fully capture these multiple and overlapping movements, chronologies, issues, and sites," Nancy Hewitt writes.[108] The wave metaphor is convenient because it is understandable to a general audience; it has been widely publicized, is manipulable and fluid, and can be used to illustrate the ways that multiple sources of energy contribute to the whole. Hewitt suggests that the wave analogy distances current women from their feminist forerunners: it is a way of saying that *we* are better; *we* will be different.[109] Such narratives, Hewitt notes, assume that each wave improves upon the last. "The feminist learning curve is thus foreshortened," she concludes. The existing wave model of US feminism has also been critiqued for whom it leaves out, both racially and generationally, and what it leaves out in terms of content. "The script of feminist history," Hewitt remarks, "that each wave overwhelms and exceeds its predecessor, lends itself all too easily to whiggish interpretations of ever more radical, all-compassing, and ideologically sophisticated movements."[110] Melody Berger illustrates this in her statement: "People will ask me if I identify as a Third Waver, or if I think that my generation is part of a new wave, a post-Third Wave, a Fourth Wave, if you will. My answer: 'Good God, we don't need another wave.'"[111]

Some scholars believe the periodization of the US women's movement in terms of mass activist movements obscures the historical role of race in feminist organizing. Kimberly Springer states: "If we consider the first wave as that moment of organizing encompassing woman suffrage and the second wave as the women's liberation/women's rights activism of the late 1960s, we effectively disregard the race-based movements before them that served as precursors, or windows of political opportunity, for gender activism." But she also suggests that, rather than abandoning the wave model we reconceptualize it to include women of color's resistance to gender violence and other oppressions.[112] Springer states that scholars were doing just that, as they began to insert narratives of Black women's gender activism in the historical records of the civil rights and women's liberation movements from the 1980s into the early twenty-first century.[113]

A few critics of the wave model have suggested it be replaced by a generational approach. Karl Mannheim offered a classic definition that interpreted generations as identities of location. "The social phenomenon of 'generations,'" he wrote in 1959, "represents nothing more than a particular kind of identity of location, embracing related 'age-groups' embedded in a historical-social process." Historian Susan Ware has listed elements that "locate" an individual within a generation, which include date of birth, socioeconomic class, gender, socialization process in childhood, and access to education. "The unity of a generation comes from the common experiences of its members within the society as a whole," she writes. In considering "the historical problem of generations," Alan Spitzer concluded: "Groups of coevals are stamped by some collective experience that permanently distinguishes them from other age groups as they move through time."[114] But if a definition of generations includes class, access to education, and consciousness of similar, shared experiences in time, this conceptual framework can still be used to differentiate and exclude certain groups.

Nevertheless, there are compelling reasons why a generational approach to the history of US feminism might still be more useful than the metaphorical "wave" approach. Bracketing of generations considers the age of a generational cohort as opposed to the wave model, which is linked to specific decades.[115] Born in the years between 1873 and 1896, the four women in this book were part of a cluster of women's rights advocates that at least one of their contemporaries described as "the generation after the great pioneers." Distinguished by their sense of mission and bonded through the experiences of their age cohort of middle-class women that included increasing access to higher education, progressivism, participation in the woman suffrage movement, World War I, the Depression, and widening public opportunities, this was a distinctive generation of women.[116]

A generational approach addresses the slippage of those who came to feminism between waves or who worked to keep feminist ideas and activism alive in the lull between the waves, like the four women in this book. As Nancy Hewitt has argued, while the chronology of feminist activism charted in the wave metaphor suggests discrete and separate waves, in reality such movements "overlapped and intertwined across U.S. history." "The decades excluded from the waves—before 1848 or from 1920 to 1960—are assumed to be feminist-free zones," she states.[117] Being left out of the wave metaphor of feminism can feel personal. As sociologist Nancy Naples remarked, "in terms of the political generational view of feminism, I am neither second nor third wave. Consequently, I find myself in the awkward position of being an outsider to my own historical generation and to the generational labels created in the context of efforts to historicize feminism and women's movement politics." She suggests differentiating between waves of protest and political generations, which, she writes, "interact, learn from each other, and in the process contribute to transformations in political analyses and strategies." Political generations, she notes, are not bounded by particular movements but are involved in diverse movements simultaneously: feminists active in these campaigns range in class, age, race and ethnicity, and in their understanding of feminism.[118] Nancy Whittier's idea of "micro-cohorts" addresses the clumsiness of fitting individual feminist activists into one wave or another. Her definition of feminist generations includes those who came into feminist consciousness at different historical moments and at various ages; those who entered via personal and community-based struggles and those who came in through women's organizations.[119]

Envisioning US feminism as a nonlinear continuum can help solve this problem. Even in its supposed nadir in the post-suffrage decade and the Depression era, the movement was alive. Many feminists continued to wage the battle for women's rights on a variety of fronts, in different organizations moving toward a multiplicity of goals. Although the continuum model does not differentiate periods of more active, mass involvement from quieter phases, it does demonstrate the continuity of ideas that have characterized the history of feminism in the United States. In addition, this model allows for circling back and borrowing from earlier ideas, and it guards against the arbitrary divisions that historians develop.[120]

How would the four women in this book have responded to these concerns? They lived in a time before the wave metaphor that currently charts the history of US feminism was created. Three of the four wrote women's history books, and one was a historian by profession. If they knew one thing it was that history can be interpreted in multiple ways, can be seized, shaped, and distorted for purposes of politics or race (they lived through Hitler's ascension and fall), and that to get it "right" is difficult, if not impossible. Stevens illustrated this understanding in a 1958 open letter to her Omaha High School classmates. She described being under "the stress and strain of trying to put down a final word about what really happened a long time ago," as she reviewed the papers and memories from a lifetime of feminist activism. "I am more than ever convinced," she confided, "of how difficult it is to arrive at historical accuracy, even when dealing with events in which I took part. The old clichés about truth being elusive take on a fresh meaning. Properly to evaluate how and why certain things happened, who of the vast personnel involved was angel or devil, who blocked or advanced various proposals and why; this is a tough job."[121]

All four women experienced the judging that occurs when history is being written and its meaning debated. The main feminist historiographical struggle of their era was over the way the history of the woman suffrage movement would be told. Irwin's history of the militant suffrage campaign, *The Story of the Woman's Party* (1921), infuriated some NAWSA members who criticized it as "a distortion of history." Twelve years later, Irwin was again caught up in an ugly feminist dispute about *Angels and Amazons*. The National Council of Women originally asked her to write a history of American women of the last century, to be published as part of the Century of Progress exposition at the July 1933 World's Fair in Chicago. Irwin found writing the book, her twenty-third, exceedingly difficult because of bitterness between feminists and the fine line she had to walk to please both factions. Her depiction of the NWP and the NAWSA so angered Carrie Chapman Catt that she accused Irwin of "tainting the memory of persons who are dead and gone." "To my mind," Catt wrote, "the most important thing in the history of women that happened in the last one hundred years was the winning of the vote and that story is, I fear, not at all correctly told. I regret it, but I shall not feel sad about it because some day, somebody will write a history of these past few years and merge the truth about everything and everybody in such a way that the story will be told without injustice to any group and that story will probably stand the test of acceptance by the nation at large as the truth about woman suffrage."[122] Irwin responded heatedly: "In a life which has been devoted to the cause of women ever since I was old enough to think about it, I have had but one disillusion. And that is the treatment by the National American Woman Suffrage Association of the National Woman's Party. It appalled and horrified me at the time; it appalls and horrifies me now." At the same time, Irwin wrote Park, mailing her the transcripts of her correspondence: "I want you to know all about it. If I hurt you, again I apologize."[123] When some NWP members were dissatisfied with Irwin's treatment of their organization, she resigned from the organization in dismay. Receiving her resignation, Anita Pollitzer urged her to reconsider: "we do not want to lose you. You are not only known to everyone as a very earnest believer in the capacity of women, and the truest of feminists, but your name, like Georgia O'Keeffe's, gives us distinction with a group in the world at large." Withdrawing her resignation, Irwin stated sincerely, "I yield to nobody in loyalty to its [the National Woman's Party's] tenets and to no one in admiration for Alice Paul."[124]

Beard exasperated both equal rights and social feminists in her insistence that the women's rights movement was not the centerpiece of women's history but a side note in the history of a gender that had been contributing to civilization in multiple ways through millennia. Like some contemporary scholars, Beard would have been dissatisfied with the use of the wave metaphor to chart the history of the US women's rights movement, since it is limited and excludes the richness of women's contributions on so many different fronts. But she would have been pleased that such an accessible metaphor allows the general public—rather than only the intellectual elite—to realize that feminism does have a history in the United States; so many believe that it does not. Beard, along with Irwin, Stevens, and Pruette cared deeply about women's history, and understood its importance and its connection to activism. This belief fueled their writing that was, for the most part, intended for general audiences. They appreciated the importance of "historicizing feminism" and understood this to be an essential factor in its survival.

The four women in this collective biography, separated in age by twenty-three years, came to the women's rights movement at different historical moments, for diverse reasons and at varying ages. Inez Irwin heard about the woman suffrage movement as a Boston schoolgirl and heard the term "feminism" as a Radcliffe student in the 1890s. Mary Beard first came to a concern about women's lives as a young wife in a working-class British town in the dawning years of the twentieth century. Doris Stevens became a suffrage activist as an Oberlin College student in the 1900s, while nine-year-old Lorine Pruette fretted about women's overwork on the porch of her rural Tennessee home and began to write her first feminist text as a girl in 1905. A myriad of factors inspired each of them to care about women, and their resolute persistence in fighting for women's rights over decades was inclusive in its intellectual range. Although they struggled with activists who held competing ideas about women's equality and its meaning, their approach to feminism was never narrow in scope. They linked their definitions to other political and social movements—pacifism, anti-poverty and labor, internationalism, progressivism—and they sought to reshape social institutions including marriage and the family. As Beard insisted, "We must do everything at once!" All four would have rejected a restricted definition of feminism that did not include reproductive rights, women's health concerns, work and family issues, and women's leadership. Their evolving feminist philosophies illustrate their quests for a synthetic model that would include gender equality with difference and expand the rigid ways we have thought about equal rights versus social feminism between 1910 and 1940.

Irwin, Beard, Stevens, and Pruette also cared a great deal about continuity in the women's rights movement, so it is possible that a generational approach to the history of the US movement would have appealed to them. They were not unique in their self-consciousness about their own generational placement and the obligation they owed to their forerunners. A sense of feminist continuity was a defining feature of this generation. A contemporary, Sue Shelton

White, commented to her peers in 1929, "We should be a bit ashamed to stand on ground won by women in the past without making some effort to honor them by winning a higher and wider field for the future. It is our business. It is a debt we owe."[125] Irwin, Beard, Stevens, and Pruette looked to the generation of women activists and thinkers who came before them—with reverence and gratitude at times, anger and frustration on other occasions—and they self-consciously saw themselves as part of a moving stream of women though time. They were part of that feminist stream, even in the 1920s, 1930s, 1940s, and 1950s, decades that have been left out of the wave metaphor. What has been called a dormant, stagnant feminist interlude between the 1920 winning of suffrage and the resurgence of a mass women's movement in the late 1960s was instead a rich, painful, varied, tumultuous period in the history of the feminist movement in the United States. If the seas appeared calm, that was an illusion—fluid energy was propagating, mixing under the surface. Feminism is a continuum, as these four women well knew, and it so captivated them that they devoted long, purposeful lives to ensuring its survival and success.

Notes

INTRODUCTION

1. Christine Stansell, *American Moderns: Bohemian New York and the Creation of a New Century* (New York: Henry Holt, 2000); Elaine Showalter, ed., *These Modern Women: Autobiographical Essays from the Twenties* (Old Westbury, NY: Feminist Press, 1978); Elizabeth Francis, *The Secret Treachery of Words: Feminism and Modernism in America* (Minneapolis: University of Minnesota Press, 2002).

2. My use of Inez Haynes Irwin's name will remain consistent, although it changed several times. She was Inez Haynes until her marriage to Rufus Gillmore, and Inez Haynes Gillmore during her first marriage (1897–1913) and until she married William Irwin in 1916. From 1916 to the end of her life she went by Inez Haynes Irwin.

3. Lorine Pruette, "I Don't Want to Play This Game Anymore!," Box 2, Folder 61, LPP.

4. Cited in Elaine Showalter, "In Search of Heroines," *Guardian*, June 13, 2011.

5. Susan Ware, *Beyond Suffrage: Women in the New Deal* (Cambridge, MA: Harvard University Press, 1981), 13–42.

6. Mari Jo Buhle, Teresa Murphy, and Jane Gerhard, *Women and the Making of America* (Upper Saddle River, NJ: Pearson Prentice Hall, 2009), 459.

7. Barbara Welter, "The Cult of True Womanhood, 1820–1860," *American Quarterly* 18 (Summer 1966): 151–175.

8. Francis, *Secret Treachery*, xxvii.

9. Dorothy Dunbar Bromley, "Feminist—New Style," *Harper's*, October 1927, 560.

10. Francis, *Secret Treachery*, xii.

11. Estelle Freedman, "Separatism as Strategy: Female Institution-Building and American Feminism," *Feminist Studies* (Fall 1979): 512–579, see 513.

12. Buhle et al., *Women and the Making of America*, 506; Francis, *Secret Treachery*, xiv.

13. Christina Simmons, *Making Marriage Modern: Women's Sexuality from the Progressive Era to World War II* (New York: Oxford University Press, 2009).

14. Showalter, *These Modern Women*, 3, 8.

15. Anne-Marie Slaughter, "Why Women Still Can't Have It All," *Atlantic*, July/August 2012; http://www.theatlantic.com/magazine/archive/2012/07/why-women-still-cant-have-it-all/309020/.

16. Lorine Pruette, "Why Women Fail," *Outlook* 158 (August 12, 1931): 460–462+. Reprinted in V. F. Calverton and Samuel Schmalhausen, eds., *Woman's Coming of Age* (New York: 1931), 257–258.

17. Irwin, Stevens, and Pruette donated their papers to the Schlesinger Library, now part of the Radcliffe Institute at Harvard University. This book is largely based on those three collections.

18. *The Other Women's Movement*, for example, analyzes labor feminists from the 1940s to the twenty-first century. Dorothy Sue Cobble, *The Other Women's Movement: Workplace Justice and Social Rights in Modern America* (Princeton, NJ: Princeton University Press, 2004).

19. Julie Des Jardins, *Women and the Historical Enterprise in America: Gender, Race, and the Politics of Memory, 1880–1945* (Chapel Hill: University of North Carolina Press, 2003), 80.

20. Nancy F. Cott, *The Grounding of Modern Feminism* (New Haven, CT: Yale University Press, 1987).

21. Francis, *Secret Treachery*, xiii.

22. Alys Eve Weinbaum, Lynn Thomas, Priti Ramamurthy, Uta Poiger, Madeleine Yue Dong, and Tani Barlow, eds., *The Modern Girl around the World: Consumption, Modernity, and Globalization* (Durham, NC: Duke University Press, 2008); Christine Stansell, *The Feminist Promise: 1792 to the Present* (New York: Random House, 2011), 180–181.

23. Lorine Pruette, "The Flapper," in *The New Generation: The Intimate Problems of Modern Parents and Children*, edited by V. F. Calverton and Samuel D. Schmalhausen (New York: Macaulay, 1930), 572–590.

24. Historians created the term "social feminist" to group together women who were civic reformers, club members, settlement house residents, and labor activists. See William O'Neill, "Feminism as a Radical Ideology," in *Dissent: Explorations in the History of American Radicalism*, edited by Alfred F. Young (DeKalb: Northern Illinois University Press, 1968), 275–277. Although historians have criticized the term as imprecise, it is still useful and has gained wide usage, so I employ it in this book. See Nancy F. Cott, "What's in a Name? The Limits of 'Social Feminism': or, Expanding the Vocabulary of Women's History," *Journal of American History* 76, 3 (December 1989): 809–829.

25. Glenda Elizabeth Gilmore, *Gender and Jim Crow: Women and the Politics of White Supremacy in North Carolina, 1896–1920* (Chapel Hill: University of North Carolina Press, 1996); Paula Giddings, *When and Where I Enter: The Impact of Black Women on Race and Sex in America* (New York: William Morrow, 1984).

26. Rosalyn Terborg-Penn, "Discontented Black Feminists: Prelude and Postscript to the Passage of the Nineteenth Amendment," in *Decades of Discontent: The Women's Movement, 1920–1940*, edited by Lois Scharf and Joan Jensen (Westport, CT: Greenwood, 1983), 263; Louise Newman, *White Women's Rights: The Racial Origins of Feminism in the United States* (New York: Oxford University Press, 1999).

27. Katherine H. Adams and Michael L. Keene, *Alice Paul and the American Suffrage Campaign* (Urbana: University of Illinois Press, 2008).

28. Jacquelyn Dowd Hall, *Revolt against Chivalry: Jessie Daniel Ames and the Women's Campaign against Lynching* (New York: Columbia University Press, 1993); Paula J. Giddings, *A Sword among Lions: Ida B. Wells and the Campaign against Lynching* (New York: HarperCollins, 2009).

29. Terborg-Penn, "Discontented Black Feminists," 267–268.

30. Beard to Alma Lutz, January 29, 1937, Series I, Reel 58, NWP Papers.

31. William Chafe, *The Paradox of Change: American Women in the 20th Century* (New York: Oxford University Press, 1992).

32. Seth Koven and Sonya Michel, "Introduction: 'Mother Worlds,'" in *Mothers of a New World: Maternalist Politics and the Origins of Welfare States*, edited by Seth Koven and Sonya Michel (New York: Routledge, 1993), 1–42, see 4.

33. Joan W. Scott, "Deconstructing Equality-versus-Difference: Or, the Uses of Poststructuralist Theory for Feminism," *Feminist Studies* 14, 1 (Spring 1988): 32–50.

34. Estelle B. Freedman, *No Turning Back: The History of Feminism and the Future of Women* (New York: Ballantine Books, 2003), 4.

35. Cott, *Grounding of Modern Feminism*.

36. Susan Kent, "Worlds of Feminism," in *Women's History in Global Perspective*, edited by Bonnie G. Smith (Urbana: University of Illinois Press, 2004), 275–312, see 275–277.

37. Cott, *Grounding of Modern Feminism*, 5.

38. Burnita Shelton Matthew to Doris Stevens, December 7, 1932, Box 4, DSP.

39. Amy Butler argues this in *Two Paths to Equality: Alice Paul and Ethel M. Smith in the ERA Debate, 1921–1929* (Albany: State University of New York Press, 2002), 5.

40. Cobble, *The Other Women's Movement*, 7.

41. See Wendy Sarvasy, "Beyond the Equality versus Difference Policy Debate: Postsuffrage Feminism, Citizenship, and the Quest for a Feminist State," *Signs* 7, 2 (Winter 1992): 329–362.

42. Rosemarie Tong, *Feminist Thought: A More Comprehensive Introduction* (Boulder, CO: Westview, 2009), 1.

43. Ibid., 3.

44. Cott, *Grounding of Modern Feminism*, 3.

45. Marie Jenney Howe, "Feminism," *New Review* 2, 8 (August 1914): 441. Irwin is quoted in Judith Schwartz, *Radical Feminists of Heterodoxy: Greenwich Village 1920–1940* (Norwich, VT: New Victoria Publishers, 1986), 18.

46. Freedman, *No Turning Back*, 4.

47. Kent, "Worlds of Feminism," 300–302.

48. Myra Marx Ferree, "Globalization and Feminism: Opportunities and Obstacles for Activism in the Global Arena," 3–23 (see 13); and Aili Mari Tripp, "The Evolution of Transnational Feminisms: Consensus, Conflict, and New Dynamics," 51–78, both in *Global Feminism: Transnational Women's Activism, Organizing, and Human Rights*, edited by Ferree and Tripp (New York: New York University Press, 2006).

49. Tong, *Feminist Thought*, 1–2, 11–47, 34.

50. Ibid., 43. See Chela Sandoval, *Methodology of the Oppressed* (Minneapolis: University of Minnesota Press, 2000).

51. Tong, *Feminist Thought*, 2–3, 48–50.

52. Denise Riley, "Am I That Name?" *Feminism and the Category of "Women" in History* (London: Macmillan, 1987).

53. Nancy A. Hewitt, ed., *No Permanent Waves: Recasting Histories of US Feminism* (New Brunswick, NJ: Rutgers University Press, 2010); Estelle B. Freedman, "Beyond the Waves: Rethinking the History of Feminism," in *Exploring Women's Studies: Looking Forward, Looking Back*, edited by Carol Barkin (New York: Prentice Hall, 2005), 11–24.

54. A number of historians have contested the claim that US feminism was dead between 1920 and 1960. See Cott, *Grounding of Modern Feminism*; Leila J. Rupp and Verta Taylor, *Survival in the Doldrums: The American Women's Rights Movement, 1945 to the 1960s* (New York: Oxford University Press, 1987); Cobble, *The Other Woman's Movement*; Barbara Ransby, *Ella Baker and the Black Freedom Movement: A Radical Democratic Vision* (Chapel Hill: University of North Carolina Press, 2002).

55. William O'Neill, *Everyone Was Brave: A History of Feminism in America* (Chicago: Quadrangle, 1969), viii; Pruette to Sherna Gluck, n.d. (1974); see also Pruette to Sherna Gluck, March 1, 1974; William O'Neill to Sherna Gluck, March 22, 1971, all in Feminist History Research Project Collection, Special Collections and Archive, Library, California State University Long Beach.

56. Stansell, *The Feminist Promise*, 154.1

CHAPTER 1 — PLANTING THE SEEDS

1. Laura Lovett, *Conceiving the Future: Pronatalism, Reproduction, and the Family in the United States, 1890–1938* (Chapel Hill: University of North Carolina Press, 2007), 7.

2. Mari Jo Buhle, Teresa Murphy, and Jane Gerhard, *Women and the Making of America* (Upper Saddle River, NJ: Pearson Prentice Hall, 2009), 243, 248.

3. Stephanie Coontz, *Marriage, a History: From Obedience to Intimacy or How Love Conquered Marriage* (New York: Viking, 2005), 181.

4. K. A. Clements, "The New Era and the New Woman," *Pacific Historical Review* 73, 3 (August 2004): 425–462, see 426.

5. Coontz, *Marriage*, 187.

6. Lovett, *Conceiving the Future*, 7.

7. Elaine Tyler May, "The Pressure to Provide: Class, Consumerism, and Divorce in Urban America, 1880–1920," *Journal of Social History* 12 (Winter 1978): 180–193, see 192.

8. Carl Degler, *At Odds: Women and the Family in America from the Revolution to the Present* (New York: Oxford University Press, 1980).

9. Lovett, *Conceiving the Future*, 7; Thomas Gossett, *Race: The History of an Idea* (New York: Oxford University Press, 1997).

10. Lovett, *Conceiving the Future*, 7.

11. Ibid., 7, 2–3.

12. Amy Richter, *Home on the Rails: Women, the Railroad, and the Rise of Public Domesticity* (Chapel Hill: University of North Carolina Press, 2005), 60–61.

13. Buhle et al., *Women and the Making of America*, 466–467.

14. Lovett, *Conceiving the Future*, 5.

15. Inez Irwin, "The Making of a Militant," in *These Modern Women: Autobiographical Essays from the Twenties*, edited by Elaine Showalter (Old Westbury, NY: Feminist Press, 1978), 33–40.

16. See ibid. and Irwin's unpublished autobiography, "Adventures of Yesterday," Microfilm M-59, Reels 974–975, no. 17 in IHGP.

17. Gideon Haynes, *Pictures from Prison Life: An Historical Sketch of the Massachusetts State Prison, with Narratives and Incidents, and Suggestions on Discipline* (Boston: Lee and Shepherd, 1871). The University of California Press digitized this in 2004, and it is available online.

18. Irwin, "The Making of a Militant," 36.

19. Ibid., 35; "Adventures of Yesterday," 92, 91.

20. Irwin, "The Making of a Militant," 36–37.

21. Inez Irwin, Diary #11, Volume 11, Box 1 (no page numbers or date), IHGP.

22. Inez Irwin to Maud Wood Park, July 29, 1938, Container 17, Reel 11, NAWSA Papers; Irwin, "The Making of a Militant," 35; Inez Haynes Gillmore, "Confessions of an Alien," *Harper's Bazaar* 46 (April 1912): 170–171, quote from 170.

23. Irwin, "The Making of a Militant," 38–39; "Adventures of Yesterday," 79; "Confessions of an Alien," 170.

24. Irwin, "Adventures of Yesterday," 134–137.

25. Buhle et al., *Women and the Making of America*, 385–387.

26. Ann Braude, *Radical Spirits: Spiritualism and Women's Rights in Nineteenth-Century America* (Boston: Beacon, 1989).

27. Irwin, "The Making of a Militant," 38; "Adventures of Yesterday," 188–189.

28. Irwin, "Adventures of Yesterday," 183.

29. Inez Haynes Diary, June 10–August 23, 1893, Box 1, Volume 2, IHGP.

30. Howard I. Kushner, "Women and Suicide in Historical Perspective," *Feminist Research Methods: Exemplary Readings in the Social Sciences*, edited by Joyce McCarl Nielsen (Boulder, CO: Westview, 1990), 193–206.

31. Inez Haynes Diary, June 10–August 23, 1893, Box 1, Volume 2, IHGP; "Adventures of Yesterday," 191.

32. On Park, see Barbara Sicherman and Carol Hurd Green, eds., *Notable American Women: The Modern Period* (Cambridge, MA: Belknap Press of Harvard University Press, 1980), 519–522; the Women's Rights Collection (WRC); and the papers of the League of Women Voters (LWV), Women's Joint Congressional Committee (WJCC), National American Woman Suffrage Association (NAWSA), and Carrie Chapmann Catt Papers, all in the Library of Congress.

33. Maud Wood Park, "Inez Haynes; Supplementary Notes," February 1943, Box 6, Folder 82, WRC.

34. Irwin, "Adventures of Yesterday," 210–211.

35. Ibid., 208–209; Irwin to Maud Wood Park, July 29, 1938, Container 17, Reel 11, NAWSA Papers.

36. Inez Gillmore Diary 12, 1898, "Sketches towards an Autobiography"; 1893 Diary, Box 1, Volume 2, IHGP.

37. Ibid.

38. Barbara K. Turoff, *Mary Beard as Force in History* (Dayton, OH: Wright State University Press, 1979), 7; Ann J. Lane, ed., *Mary Ritter Beard: A Sourcebook* (New York: Schocken Books, 1977), 7; Miriam Vagts to Barbara Turoff, July 16, 1975, quoted in Turoff, *Mary Beard as Force*, 7; Mary Ritter Beard, *The Making of Charles A. Beard* (New York: Exposition Press, 1955), 36.

39. Lane, *Mary Ritter Beard*, 11–14, and Turoff, *Mary Beard as Force*, 7–10. Their sources were primarily the Eli F. Ritter and Mary Beard Papers at DePauw University Archives.

40. Ibid.; MB Papers. Quote from Mary Beard to Mr. Knowlton, December 13, 1948, Macmillan Papers, Manuscript Division, New York Public Library Annex.

41. Lane, *Mary Ritter Beard*, 14, and Turoff, *Mary Beard as Force*, 8; Beard to Margaret Grierson, January 25, 1951, SSC.

42. Richter, *Home on the Rails*, 90.

43. Coontz, *Marriage*, 182; Jan Doolittle Wilson, *The Women's Joint Congressional Committee and the Politics of Maternalism, 1920–1930* (Urbana: University of Illinois Press, 2007), 3.

44. Coontz, *Marriage*, 188.

45. Mary Beard to Professor Longden, April 14, 1931, MB Papers.

46. 1897 Yearbook, MB Papers.

47. Mary Beard, "Memory and Human Relations," *Key of Kappa Kappa Gamma* (December 1, 1936): 308–311, quotation on 308.

48. Beard described this initial meeting in "Mary Beard's 15th Book Nears Publication," *Indianapolis Star*, July 29, 1955, clipping in Marjorie White Papers, SL.

49. Turoff, *Mary Beard as Force*, 14.

50. Eric F. Goldman, "Charles A. Beard: An Impression," in *Charles A. Beard: An Appraisal*, edited by Howard K. Beale (Lexington: University of Kentucky Press, 1954), 3.

51. Compiled from Carrie Koopan Stevens's obituary, Box 1, Folder 20; Doris Stevens, "Ebenezer Toby's Billiard Table," *Time and Tide*, June 17, 1927, 569–571, Box 7, Folder 214; "Doris Stevens, An Apostle of Action," *Time and Tide*, October 26, 1928 (reprinted in *Equal Rights*, November 7, 1928), 325; manuscript written by Stevens's father, H. H. Stevens (no title or date), Box 1, Folder 20; Alice Stevens Burns to Doris Stevens, April 10, 1935, Box 1, Folder 20, all in DSP.

52. Carrie Koopman Stevens Mortuary, n.d., Box 1, Folder 20; Stevens, "Dukie's Introduction to Politics," February 26, 1945, Box 7, Folder 216, both in DSP.

53. Elihu Root was Theodore Roosevelt's secretary of state and won the Nobel Peace Prize in 1912.

54. Doris Stevens, "Autobiographical Jottings," Box 8, Folder 251; "Dukie's Introduction to Politics," both in DSP.

55. Stevens, "Ebenezer Toby's Billiard Table," 569.

56. "Doris Stevens, An Apostle of Action," 325; Stevens, "Ebenezer Toby's Billiard Table," 569; Stevens to Dudley Field Malone, September 20, 1932, Box 2, Folder 41, all in DSP.

57. Stevens, "Ebenezer Toby's Billiard Table," 569; "Address by Miss Doris Stevens to the Eastern Regional Conference National Woman's Party," Atlantic City, N.J., June 16, 1946, Box 2, Folder 26; "Autobiographical Jottings," Box 8, Folder 251, all in DSP.

58. "Address by Miss Doris Stevens to the Eastern Regional Conference National Woman's Party"; "Autobiographical Jottings."

59. Stevens, "Ebenezer Toby's Billiard Table," 569; "Doris Stevens, in Tribute to Her Father, Lauds Independent Views," *Omaha Herald*, May 24, 1930, Box 8, Folder 231; Stevens to Jonathan Mitchell, May 21, 1930, Box 3, Folder 65; Stevens, "Letter to Mother," January 21, 1948, Box 1, Folder 23, all in DSP.

60. Information drawn from an article on the Class of 1905's 50th reunion (no title available), *Omaha World-Herald Magazine*, September 11, clipping, Box 5, Folder 149, DSP.

61. On Stevens's college years, see her 1908 Diary, Box 6, Folder 181, DSP; "Doris Stevens, An Apostle of Action," 325.

62. Doris Stevens, "Autobiographical Jottings"; Doris Stevens, "An Apostle of Action," 325.

63. Stevens described the loan incident in Box 8, Folder 251; *The Hi-O-Hi*, Volume 21, Class of 1911, Box 8, Folder 262, both in DSP.

64. Leila Rupp, "Sexuality and Politics in the Early Twentieth Century: The Case of the International Women's Movement," *Feminist Studies* 23, 3 (Autumn 1997): 577–605.

65. "Doris Stevens, An Apostle of Action," 325.

66. Lorine Pruette, "The Making of a Feminist," Box 3, Folder 66; "The End Is in the Beginning," Box 3, Folder 46; "Male Chauvinists I Have Known," Box 3, Folder 87, all in LPP.

67. Soule College was founded as the Female Academy in Murfreesboro, Tennessee, in 1825. It closed during the Civil War, reopened after, and closed permanently in 1916. "Tennessee Colleges that Have Closed, Merged, Changed Names," last modified February 14, 2013, http://www2.westminster-mo.edu/wc_users/homepages/staff/brownr/TennesseeCC.htm.

68. Lorine Pruette, "The Evolution of Disenchantment," in Showalter, *These Modern Women*, 69–73. Pruette, "The Making of a Feminist"; "Molly, Who Did Not Cry!" Box 3, Folder 96; "I Was the Odd Ball," Box 4, Folder 147; "In My Father's House," Box 2, Folder 64; "The End Is in the Beginning," all in LPP.

69. Pruette, "The End Is in the Beginning."

70. Ibid.; "In My Father's House," Box 2, Folder 64, LPP.

71. Buhle et al., *Women and the Making of America*, 376–378.

72. Pruette, "The Making of a Feminist."

73. Buhle et al., *Women and the Making of America*, 419–420, 449.

74. Pruette, "The Making of a Feminist"; "Trio for Strings," Box 4, Folder 150, LPP; "The Evolution of Disenchantment," 71.

75. Pruette, "Trio for Strings."

76. Pruette, "The Evolution of Disenchantment," 70.

77. Pruette, "The Making of a Feminist"; "Trio for Strings"; "I Was the Sick One," Box 4, Folder 145, LPP.

78. Pruette, "I Was the Sick One"; "I Was the Bright One," Box 4, Folder 146, LPP; "The Evolution of Disenchantment," 70–71.

79. Lorine Pruette, "Logos: The Shield," Box 3, Folder 78; "I Was the Odd Ball," Box 4, Folder 147, both in LPP; "I Was the Sick One."

80. Pruette, "The Evolution of Disenchantment," 71.

81. Pruette, "Male Chauvinists I Have Known"; "I Was the Bright One"; "Draft Pages, Notes," Box 4, Folder 159; "On The Trail of the Endocrines," Box 4, Folder 103, all in LPP.

82. Lorine Pruette, "And in the End" (1918 Lecture), Box 1, Folder 14, LPP; "The Making of a Feminist"; "I Was the Bright One"; "I Was the Sick One." Unfortunately Pruette's college speeches have been lost.

83. Pruette, "The Evolution of Disenchantment," 70–71.

84. Lorine Pruette, "Apologia," Box 4, Folder 146, LPP; "I Was the Bright One"; "I Was the Odd Ball."

CHAPTER 2 — SETTING THE STAGE

1. Jean Baker, ed., *Votes for Women: The Struggle for Suffrage Revisited* (New York: Oxford University Press, 2002); Christine A. Lunardini, *From Equal Suffrage to Equal Rights: Alice Paul and the National Woman's Party, 1910–1928* (San Jose, CA: Excel Press, 2000).

2. Ellen Carol DuBois, *Harriot Stanton Blatch and the Winning of Woman Suffrage* (New Haven, CT: Yale University Press, 1997); Margaret Finnegan, *Selling Suffrage: Consumer Culture and Votes for Women* (New York: Columbia University Press, 1999).

3. Christine Stansell, *American Moderns: Bohemian New York and the Creation of a New Century* (New York: Henry Holt, 2000), 228.

4. On the NWP's history see Inez Irwin, *The Story of the Woman's Party* (New York: Harcourt, 1921); Doris Stevens, *Jailed for Freedom* (New York: Boni and Liveright, 1920); Linda Ford, *Iron-Jawed Angels: The Suffrage Militance of the National Woman's Party, 1912–1920* (Lanham, MD: University Press of America, 1991); Katherine H. Adams and Michael L. Keene, *Alice Paul and the American Suffrage Campaign* (Urbana: University of Illinois Press, 2008); Nancy Cott, "Feminist Politics in the 1920s: The National Woman's Party," *Journal of American History* 71, 1 (June 1984): 43–68, and *The Grounding of Modern Feminism* (New Haven, CT: Yale University Press, 1987), 51–82.

5. Lunardini, *From Equal Suffrage*, xiv, xiii.

6. Ibid., xiv.

7. Stevens, *Jailed for Freedom*, 11.

8. Anne O'Hagan, "The Serious-Minded Young—If Any," *Woman's Journal* 13 (April 1928): 6; Julia Adams, "The 'Serious Young' Speak Up," *Woman's Journal* 13 (May 1928): 8–9.

9. Christine Stansell, *The Feminist Promise: 1792 to the Present* (New York: Random House, 2010), 149.

10. Beard described the incident in Genevieve P. Herrick, "Women in the News," *Country Gentlemen*, May 1936; Mrs. Vagts to Barbara Turoff, January 26, 1979; both cited in Barbara Turoff, *Mary Beard as Force in History* (Dayton, OH: Wright State University Press, 1979), 16.

11. Turoff, *Mary Beard as Force*, 16; second quote in Ann Lane, ed., *Mary Ritter Beard: A Sourcebook* (New York: Schocken Books, 1977), 21; Beard to Marjorie White, October 17, 1946, MBC.

12. Nancy Cott, ed., *A Woman Making History: Mary Ritter Beard through Her Letters* (New Haven, CT: Yale University Press, 1992), 6, 341.

13. See DuBois, *Harriot Stanton Blatch and the Winning of Woman Suffrage*.

14. Ellen Carol DuBois, "The Next Generation: Harriot Stanton Blatch and Grassroots Politics," in Baker, *Votes for Women*, 159–173, 161.

15. Ronald Schaffer, "The New York City Woman Suffrage Party, 1909–1919," *New York History* 43 (July 1962): 269–287.

16. Paula Giddings, *When and Where I Enter: The Impact of Black Women on Race and Sex in America* (New York: William Morrow, 1984), 119–131; Rosalyn Terborg-Penn, *African American Women in the Struggle for the Vote, 1850–1920* (Bloomington: Indiana University Press, 1998).

17. Terborg-Penn, *African American Women*, 1, 6; Giddings, *When and Where I Enter*, 124.

18. Stansell, *Feminist Promise*, 163.

19. Terborg-Penn, *African American Women*, 99–102.

20. Ibid., 100–102.

21. Stansell, *Feminist Promise*, 150.

22. Mary Beard to Elizabeth Schlesinger, September 19, 1944, MBC; Julie Des Jardins, *Women and the Historical Enterprise in America: Gender, Race, and the Politics of Memory, 1880–1945* (Chapel Hill: University of North Carolina Press, 2003), 82.

23. Mary Beard, "Votes for Workingwomen," *Woman Voter* 3 (September 1912): 3–5.

24. Ibid.; Beard to Alice Paul, 1913 (February?), Reel 2, NWP Papers.

25. Stansell, *Feminist Promise*, 151; Mari Jo Buhle, Teresa Murphy, and Jane Gerhard, *Women and the Making of America* (Upper Saddle River, NJ: Pearson Prentice Hall, 2009), 491.

26. Mary Beard, "Mothercraft," *The Woman Voter* 1–2 (January 1912): 12–13. Emphasis in original.

27. Alice Paul to Beard, June 2, 1913, Reel 3, NWP Papers; Beard to Alice Paul, July 26, 1916, NWP Papers, quoted in Lane, *Mary Ritter Beard*, 14.

28. Stansell, *Feminist Promise*, 163; Mary Beard, "The Legislative Influence of Unenfranchised Women," *Annals of the American Academy of Political and Social Science* 56 (November 1914): 54–61.

29. Mary Beard to Alice Paul, undated [February 1913], in Cott, *A Woman Making History*, 70–71.

30. Mary Beard to William Beard, August 18, 1951, Vagts private collection. In Cott, *A Woman Making History*, 69–70.

31. Turoff, *Mary Beard as Force*, 23.

32. Des Jardins, *Women and the Historical Enterprise*, 62–63.

33. Mary Beard, *Woman's Work in Municipalities* (New York: D. Appleton, 1915). Quotations from Arno Press 1972 edition, vi, 268.

34. Filene portrayed Beard as tied down by domestic obligations. Peter G. Filene, *Him/Her/Self: Sex Roles in Modern America* (New York: Harcourt Brace, 1975), 61.

35. Miriam Beard Vagts to Barbara Turoff, January 26, 1979. Turoff, *Mary Beard as Force*, 27.

36. Mary Beard to Alice Paul, July 5, 1913, Reel 3, NWP Papers; Beard to Mrs. Catt, June 8, 1915, Container 48, Reel 33, NAWSA Papers; Beard to Alice Paul, May 15, 1914, Reel 10, NWP Papers.

37. Mary Beard to Alice Paul, August 15, 1914, Box 1, Tray 29, NWP Papers.

38. Mary Beard to Miss Kalb, April 9, 1919, Box 5, Tray 13, NWP Papers; Miriam Vagts to Barbara Turoff, July 16, 1975, quoted in Turoff, *Mary Beard as Force*, 26.

39. "Prize for Essay on Equal Suffrage," *The Tech* 20, no. 109; http://www.tech.mit.edu/archives/Vol_020.

40. Stansell, *Feminist Practice*, 149.

41. "Address by Maud Wood Park, at the College Evening of the National American Woman Suffrage Association, 1908," Container 57, Reel 32, NAWSA Papers.

42. Inez Irwin, *The Lady of Kingdoms* (New York: George H. Doran, 1917), 360–363.

43. Inez Irwin, *The Story of the Woman's Party* (New York: Harcourt, Brace, 1921), frontispiece.

44. "College Women's Suffrage League," *College Women*, March 24, 1900, Container 77, Reel 32, NAWSA Papers.

45. "Excerpt from minutes of Massachusetts Woman Suffrage Association, March 2, 1900 and other dates," Container 57, Reel 32; Inez Irwin to Maud Wood Park, March 29, 1910, Container 57, Reel 32, both in NAWSA Papers.

46. Irwin, *Story of the Woman's Party*, 33–34.

47. Cott, *Grounding of American Feminism*, 33; Doris Stevens, "Women in Industry," chapter 2, 5, Box 8, Folder 245, DSP.

48. Inez Irwin, "Adventures of Yesterday," 281, IHGP.

49. Ibid.

50. Stansell, *Feminist Promise*, 159. On Younger, see also Lunardini, *From Equal Suffrage*, 10, 86–87.

51. Irwin, "Adventures of Yesterday," 305–306.

52. Stansell, *Feminist Promise*, 159–160.

53. Inez Irwin to Maud Park, n.d. (1913), Container 17, Reel 11, NAWSA Papers.

54. Stansell, *Feminist Promise*, 157.

55. Inez Irwin to Maud Park, n.d. (1913), , Container 17, Reel 11, NAWSA Papers.

56. See Irwin, "Adventures of Yesterday," Chapter 7 ("The Adventure of California").

57. Ibid.

58. Inez Irwin, "The Making of a Militant," in *These Modern Women*, edited by Elaine Showalter (Old Westbury, NY: Feminist Press, 1978), 33–39; quote from 36. "Adventures of Yesterday," 456.

59. Irwin, "Adventures of Yesterday," 456.

60. Will Irwin, *A Reporter in Armageddon: Letters from the Front and Behind the Lines of the Great War* (New York: D. Appleton and Company, 1918).

61. Inez Irwin, "1916 War Diary," Microfilm M-59, Reels 974–975, no. 17, IHGP.

62. "WWI Casualty and Death Tables"; http://www.pbs.org/greatwar/resources/casdeath _pop.html.

63. Irwin, "1916 War Diary."

64. Ibid., 18, 201, 248.

65. Buhle et al., *Women and the Making of America*, 489.

66. Irwin, "1916 War Diary," 9, 220, 385.

67. Stansell, *Feminist Promise*, 152.

68. Irwin, "1916 War Diary," 461.

69. Maud Younger, "Revelations of a Woman Lobbyist," *McCall's,* September, October, November 1919.

70. Inez Irwin, *The Story of the Woman's Party* (New York: Harcourt, Brace, 1921), 124–125.

71. Irwin, "Adventures of Yesterday," 468.

72. Stevens, "Women in Industry," chapter 2, 5.

73. Quoted in Cott, *Grounding of Modern Feminism*, 58.

74. Quoted in Irwin, *Story of the Woman's Party*, 314–315.

75. Edith Lobert, "Miss Doris Stevens, 'Political Agent' for Congressional Union, Knows Exactly Who's Who in the Halls of Legislation," *Washington Times*, March 22, 1914, Box 8, Folder 231, DSP.

76. "Woman Suffrage Is Live Political Issue, Says Doris Stevens," *Evening Express* (Portland, ME), December 29, 1915, clipping in Box 2, Folder 30; Beard to Stevens, November 14, 1935, Box 4, Folder 79, both in DSP.

77. Frank Walsh to Stevens, postmark January 24, 1916, Box 2, Folder 34; Frank Walsh to Stevens, postmark illegible, Box 2, Folder 35, DSP.

78. "An Apostle of Action: Doris Stevens" (no author given), *Time and Tide*, October 26, 1928, 1004–1006; reprinted in *Equal Rights*, 14 November 17, 1928, 325.

79. Stevens, *Jailed for Freedom*, 11; quotation on Stevens cited in "Recorded in The Suffragist; 1916," Box 8, Folder 266, DSP; Stevens to Alice Paul, October 24, 1914, Reel 13. NWP Papers. See also Stevens to Alice Paul, November 27, 1914, Reel 13, NWP Papers.

80. Amanda Mackenzie Stuart, *Consuelo and Alva Vanderbilt: The Story of a Daughter and a Mother in the Gilded Age* (New York: HarperCollins, 2005), 207.

81. Ibid., 25, 22, 327.

82. Doris Stevens, "Memorandum: General Statement," Box 5, Folder 132, DSP.

83. "Memorandum for Mr. Littleton," Box 5, File 132, DSP.

84. Stevens, "Memorandum—General Statement."

85. Frank Walsh to Stevens, Postmark October 17, no year (probably 1915), Box 2, Folder 31, DSP. Gertrude S. Hunff to Stevens, September (5?), 1916, Reel 33; Elizabeth W. Colt, postscript on letter, Stevens to Lucy Burns, May 6, 1915, Reel 16; Stevens to Alice Paul, September 27, 1917, Reel 48, all NWP Papers.

86. Mary Beard to Lucy Burns, June 8, 1915, Box 4, Tray 29, NWP Papers.

87. Inez Irwin to Maud Wood Park, July 29, 1938, Container 17, Reel 11, NAWSA Papers.

88. Inez Irwin to Maud Wood Park, March 14, 1921, Container 17, Reel 11, NAWSA Papers.

89. Irwin to Maud Wood Park, July 29, 1938.

90. Mary Beard to Lucy Burns, February 1914, Box 1, Tray 29, NWP Papers; Beard to Mrs. Catt, June 8, 1915, Container 48, Reel 33, NAWSA Papers.

91. Carol O'Hare ed., *Jailed for Freedom* (Troutdale, OR: New Sage Press, 1995), 21. Although she never joined the picket lines, Irwin claimed she gave Paul the idea of picketing the president, "labor-union fashion." Irwin, "Adventures of Yesterday," 460. See also Will Irwin, "Inez Haynes Irwin," Box 6, Folder 82, WRC, 3.

92. O'Hare, ed., *Jailed for Freedom*, 59, 62.

93. Linda Ford, "Alice Paul and the Politics of Nonviolent Protest," in Baker, *Votes for Women*, 174–188.

94. Amy Butler, *Two Paths to Equality: Alice Paul and Ethel M. Smith in the ERA Debate, 1921–1929* (Albany: State University of New York Press, 2002), 52.

95. O'Hare, ed., *Jailed for Freedom*, 219.

96. Butler, *Two Paths*, 52.

97. See Stevens, *Jailed for Freedom*, 99–121 for a description of her arrest and three-day imprisonment. Irwin described this in *Story of the Woman's Party*, 225–226.

98. Stevens to Alice Paul, April 1, 1917, Reel 41, NWP Papers.

99. Stevens, "Mrs. Belmont: 1914," Box 8, Folder 266, DSP.

100. O'Hare, ed., *Jailed for Freedom*, 134.

101. Despite resolutions from the Republicans and the New York Legislature, Senator Wadsworth voted against the federal woman suffrage amendment in 1918. His vote was sufficient to prevent the passage of the measure in New York. Vira B. Whitehouse to the Editor, "Senator Wadsworth: Mrs. Whitehouse Says Suffragists Want an Explanation from Him," *New York Times*, March 9, 1920.

102. O'Hare, ed., *Jailed for Freedom*, 141–146; the letter was Stevens to Elsie Hill, August 1918 (?), Reel 64, NWP Papers.

103. Lunardini, *From Equal Suffrage*, xii–iv.

104. Buhle et al., *Women and the Making of America*, 494.

105. O'Hare, ed., *Jailed for Freedom*, 158, 174.

106. Stevens, *Jailed for Freedom*, 219.

107. Buhle et al., *Women and the Making of America*, 494–495.

CHAPTER 3 — DETENTION BY THE MALE

1. Mari Jo Buhle, Teresa Murphy, and Jane Gerhard, *Women and the Making of America* (Upper Saddle River, NJ: Pearson Prentice Hall, 2009), 504–507.

2. John D'Emilio and Estelle Freedman, *Intimate Matters: A History of Sexuality in America* (New York: Harper & Row, 1988), 188–189.

3. Sandra Gilbert, "Soldier's Heart: Literary Men, Literary Women, and the Great War," in *Behind the Lines: Gender and the Two World Wars*, edited by Margaret Randolph Higonnet, Jane Jenson, Sonya Michel, and Margaret Collins Weitz (New Haven, CT: Yale University Press, 1987), 197–226.

4. Buhle et al., *Women and the Making of America*, 504–507.

5. Christine Stansell, *The Feminist Promise: 1792 to the Present* (New York: Random House, 2010), 154.

6. Mari Jo Buhle, *Feminism and Its Discontents: A Century of Struggle with Psychoanalysis* (Cambridge, MA: Harvard University Press, 1998), 28.

7. Jonathan Mitchell, "A Bend in the River," Side 2, DS Tapes. Stevens and Mitchell recorded these tapes in 1961, when Stevens was suffering from heart disease and organizing her papers to donate to Radcliffe.

8. Buhle, *Feminism and Its Discontents*, 42–44.

9. Havelock Ellis, *Studies in the Psychology of Sex* (Philadelphia: F. A. Davis, 1913); Edward Carpenter, *Love's Coming of Age* (New York: M. Kennerley, 1911); Buhle, *Feminism and Its Discontents*, 35–42.

10. Ellen Key, *Love and Marriage* (New York: Putnam, 1911).

11. Christine Stansell, *American Moderns: Bohemian New York and the Creation of a New Century* (New York: Henry Holt, 2000).

12. Christina Simmons, *Making Marriage Modern: Women's Sexuality from the Progressive Era to World War II* (New York: Oxford University Press, 2009), 79–94.

13. Mari Jo Buhle, *Women and American Socialism, 1870–1920* (Urbana: University of Illinois Press, 1981); June Sochen, *The New Woman: Feminism in Greenwich Village, 1910–1920* (New York: Quadrangle Books, 1971).

14. Nancy Cott, "Passionlessness: An Interpretation of Victorian Sexual Ideology, 1790–1850," in *A Heritage of Her Own*, edited by Nancy Cott and Elizabeth Pleck (New York: Simon and Schuster, 1979), 162–181.

15. Linda Gordon, *Woman's Body, Woman's Right: Birth Control in America* (New York: Grossman/Viking, 1990), 62–64, 94–115.

16. Simmons, *Making Marriage Modern*, 94.

17. Gordon, *Woman's Body, Woman's Right*.

18. In 1873, the US Congress passed the Comstock Law, which made it illegal to send any "obscene, lewd, and/or lascivious" materials through the mail, including contraceptive devices and information.

19. D'Emilio and Freedman, *Intimate Matters*, 222–223. In 1972, when abortion was illegal in the United States, several dozen women signed "We Have Had Abortions," a statement in *Ms.* magazine. It was a petition to the government and a way to raise awareness. See http://womenshistory.about.com/od/feministtexts/a/we_have_had_abortions.htm.

20. Doris Stevens, "False Social Barriers to Women's Psychic Release," speech to Sixth International Neo-Malthusian and Birth Control Conference, convened at the Hotel McAlpin, New York, from March 25 to March 31, 1925, Box 4, Folder 85, DSP.

21. Margaret Sanger to Stevens, April 10, 1925, Box 4, Folder 85, DSP. Excerpts were reprinted as Doris Stevens, "Birth Control and Women's General Advance," *Birth Control Review*, April 1926, 122–123.

22. Stansell, *The Feminist Promise*, 165.

23. Jessie Rodrique, "The Black Community and the Birth-Control Movement," in *Unequal Sisters: A Multi-cultural Reader in U.S. Women's History*, edited by Ellen Carol DuBois and Vicki Ruiz (New York: Routledge, 1990), 333–344.

24. Nancy Milford, *Savage Beauty: The Life of Edna St. Vincent Millay* (New York: Random House, 2001), 241–242; Jonathan Mitchell, interview with Nancy Milford, December 1975, cited ibid., 242.

25. Leila Rupp, "Feminism and the Sexual Revolution in the Early Twentieth Century: The Case of Doris Stevens," *Feminist Studies* 15, 2 (Summer 1989): 289–309; see 296; also Stevens, "False Social Barriers to Women's Psychic Release."

26. Simmons, *Making Marriage Modern*, 61; Hazel Carby, "'It Jus Be's dat Way Sometime': The Sexual Politics of Women's Blues," in *Unequal Sisters*, edited by DuBois and Ruiz, 238–249.

27. Simmons, *Making Marriage Modern*, 71–72; Paula Giddings, *When and Where I Enter: The Impact of Black Women on Race and Sex in America* (New York: William Morrow, 1984), 85–94.

28. D'Emilio and Freedman, *Intimate Matters*, 186–187.

29. Simmons, *Making Marriage Modern*, 72. See also Angela Davis, *Women, Race, and Class* (New York: Random House, 1981), 172–201.

30. D'Emilio and Freedman, *Intimate Matters*, 190–191; Nancy Sahli, "Smashing: Women's Relationships before the Fall," *Chrysalis* 8 (Summer 1979): 17–27.

31. D'Emilio and Freedman, *Intimate Matters*, 193.

32. Simmons, *Making Marriage Modern*, 67–68.

33. Floyd Dell, "Can Men and Women Be Friends?" in *Our Changing Morality: A Symposium*, edited by Freda Kirchwey (New York: Albert and Charles Boni, 1924), 184.

34. D'Emilio and Freedman, *Intimate Matters*, 193.

35. Ibid., 171–173; Katharine Bement Davis, *Factors in the Sex Life of Twenty-Two Hundred Women* (New York: Harper and Row, 1929), 263.

36. Inez Irwin Diary, June 13, 1891, quoted in Peter Filene, *Him/Her/Self: Sex Roles in Modern America* (New York: Harcourt Brace, 1975), 61.

37. Inez Irwin to Maud Wood Park, June 20, 1929, Container 17, Reel 11, NAWSA Papers.

38. Inez Irwin, "Adventures of Yesterday," IHGP, 179–180.

39. Mary Beard, "The Economic Background of the Sex Life of the Unmarried Adult," in *The Sex Life of the Unmarried Adult: An Inquiry into and an Interpretation of Current Sex Practices*, edited by Ira S. Wile (New York: Vanguard, 1934), 155–185. An abridged version is reprinted in Ann Lane, ed., *Mary Ritter Beard: A Sourcebook* (New York: Schocken Books, 1977); quotations from Lane, 229, 233.

40. Inez Irwin to Maud Wood Park, September 26, 1909, Container 17, Reel 11, NAWSA Papers; D'Emilio and Freedman, *Intimate Matters*, 181–183, 208–215.

41. Mary Beard, *Women's Work in Municipalities* (New York: D. Appleton, 1915), quotations from Lane, *Mary Ritter Beard*, 117–119.

42. Alice Stone Blackwell to Kitty Barry Blackwell, March 1, 1912; Carrie Chapman Catt to Margaret Sanger, November 24, 1920, both cited in Filene, *Him/Her/Self*, 62–63; Charlotte Perkins Gilman, "Toward Monogamy," in Kirchwey, *Our Changing Morality*, 50–66, quotation 63; Jane Addams, *Second Twenty Years at Hull House* (New York: Macmillan, 1930), 195–196.

43. Inez Irwin to Maud Wood Park, October 25, 1908, Container 17, Reel 11, NAWSA Papers.

44. Inez Irwin to Maud Wood Park, November 10, 1945; December 27, 1912; n.d. (1913); March 14, 1921; Irwin to Edna Stantial, February 27, 1958, all in Container 17, Reel 11, NAWSA Papers.

45. K. A. Clements, "The New Era and the New Woman," *Pacific Historical Review* 73, 3 (August 2004): 425–462, 426.

46. Genevieve Taggard, ed., *May Days: An Anthology of Verses from Masses-Liberator* (New York: Boni and Liveright, 1925), 7; Stevens is quoted in Mary Beard to Stevens, November 14, 1935, Box 4, Folder 79, DSP. Stevens discussed Duncan in "Address by Miss Doris Stevens to the Eastern Regional Conference National Woman's Party," Box 2, Folder 26, DSP.

47. Nancy Cott, *The Grounding of Modern Feminism* (New Haven, CT: Yale University Press, 1987), 150–151.

48. "Statement by Jonathan Mitchell," in DS Tapes, "A Bend in the River," Side 2.

49. Doris Stevens, "Women in Industry," Chapter 10, 26, Box 8, Folder 246, DSP.

50. Milford, *Savage Beauty*, 249.

51. Milford, *Savage Beauty*, xiii; Edna St. Vincent Millay, "First Fig," first published in *Poetry*, June 1918, 130.

52. Mitchell, interview with Nancy Milford, December 1975; cited in Milford, *Savage Beauty*, 250.

53. D'Emilio and Freedman, *Intimate Matters*, 230–231.

54. Cott, *Grounding of Modern Feminism*, 42. Frank Walsh to Stevens, n.d.: postmark December 27, 1915 (Box 2, Folder 32); postmark smudged except for year 1916 (Box 2, Folder 30); postmark May 7, 1916 (Box 2, Folder 30); postmark January 9, 1916 (Box 3, Folder 35), all in DSP.

55. Frank Walsh to Stevens, postmark May 4, 1916, Box 2, Folder 30; postmark September 12, no year, Box 2, Folder 32, both in DSP.

56. Dudley Field Malone to Stevens, January 6, 1919; December 9, 1920; December 4, 1920; April 1, 1921, all in Box 2, Folder 38, DSP.

57. Rupp, "Feminism and the Sexual Revolution," 294.

58. Frank Walsh to Stevens, postmark December 27, 1915, Box 2, Folder 32; Stevens, Undated memorandum, cover page reads in part: "The following memorandum refers to incidents which happened during the year 1931 which may be related to Mrs. Belmont's

revocation of the legacy," Box 5, Folder 132; Stevens to Jonathan Mitchell, June 26, 1931, Box 3, Folder 67; Jonathan Mitchell to Stevens, July 8, 1931, Box 3, Folder 66, all in DSP.

59. Frank Walsh to Stevens, postmark May 7, 1916, Box 2, Folder 35; Sara Bard Field to Stevens, April 1, 1916, Box 4, Folder 112, both in DSP.

60. See Amelia R. Fry's oral history of Field in "Suffragists Oral History Project," University of California at Berkeley, Regional Oral History Office, http://www.oac.cdlib.org.

61. Stansell, *American Moderns*, 299.

62. Simmons, *Making Marriage Modern*, 80, 75–77.

63. Caroline Ware, *Greenwich Village, 1920–1930* (Boston: Houghton Mifflin, 1935), 258.

64. Simmons, *Making Marriage Modern*, 83.

65. Ibid., 84–85.

66. Buhle, *Feminism and Its Discontents*, 37.

67. Max Eastman, *Enjoyment of Living* (New York: Harper and Row, 1948), 211.

68. Simmons, *Making Marriage Modern*, 86.

69. Stevens, "Episodes which cause trouble," Box 3, Folder 43; "Primus-A Satire on Marriage," Box 7, Folder 210; "Marriage," Box 3, Folder 43, all in DSP.

70. Stevens ("Julia") to Jonathan Mitchell, August 4, 1923, Box 3, Folder 47, DSP.

71. D'Emilio and Freedman, *Intimate Matters*, 237, 234.

72. Stansell, *The Feminist Promise*, 154.

73. "Statement by Jonathan Mitchell." The debate was with Raymond (Gram) Swing on Wages for Wives, Box 8, Folder 235, DSP.

74. Gail Bederman, *Manliness & Civilization: A Cultural History of Gender and Race in the United States, 1880–1917* (Chicago: University of Chicago Press, 1995), 84; Stansell, *Feminist Promise*, 154.

75. Jonathan Mitchell to Stevens, February 2, 1928; November 9, 1932, Box 3, Folders 66 and 67, DSP.

76. Rupp, "Feminism and the Sexual Revolution," 299–300, 302.

77. Stevens to Sara Bard Field, n.d. (1916 or 1917), Wood Papers; Sara Bard Field to Stevens, January 30 (1917), Box 4, Folder 112, DSP.

78. Bobbie O'Dare, "Auxiliaries Are Bores, Declares Doris Stevens; Feminist Says Women and Men Should Belong to Same C. of C.; Says Ego Must Be Fed," *Omaha Evening Bee*, September 28, 1927, Box 8, Folder 232, DSP.

79. Jonathan Mitchell to Stevens, September 14, 1928, Box 3, Folder 61, DSP.

80. Rupp, "Feminism and the Sexual Revolution," 293.

81. "Address by Miss Doris Stevens to the Eastern Regional Conference National Woman's Party."

82. Stevens to Jonathan Mitchell, postmark May 23, 1924, Box 3, Folder 50, DSP.

83. Buhle et al., *Women and the Making of America*, 454–456.

84. Lorine Pruette publicity card, February 1931, Clippings, LPP; Pruette, "The Flapper," in *The New Generation*, edited by F. Calverton and Samuel Schmalhausen (New York: Macaulay,1930), 572–590; quote on 582.

85. Cott, *Grounding of Modern Feminism*, 153.

86. Lorine Pruette, "A Study of the Mores and the Totemic Concepts," M.A. thesis, Clark University, 1920. Held in the Clark University Archives, Worcester, MA; quotations 28, 29.

87. Nathan Hale Jr., *Freud and the Americans: The Beginnings of Psychoanalysis in the United States, 1876–1917* (New York: Oxford University Press, 1971), 462.

88. See Lorine Pruette, "G. Stanley Hall, the Playboy of Western Scholarship," *Century* (October 1924): 766–772; Pruette, *G. Stanley Hall: A Biography of a Mind* (New York: D. Appleton, 1926); Dorothy Ross, *G. Stanley Hall: The Psychologist as Prophet* (Chicago: University of Chicago Press, 1972); Bederman, *Manliness and Civilization*, 77–120; Lesley Diehl, "G. Stanley Hall: Foe of Coeducation and Educator of Women," *American Psychologist* 41, 8 (1987): 867–878.

89. Pruette, "G. Stanley Hall, the Playboy," 769.

90. Ibid., 766; Pruette, *G. Stanley Hall*, 6.

91. Lorine Pruette, "The True Companion," Box 4, Folder 13, LPP.

92. Bederman, *Manliness and Civilization*, 95.

93. Michael Kimmel, *Manhood in America: A Cultural History* (New York: Oxford University Press, 2011), 131.

94. Lorine Pruette, "The Decline of the Male," Box 2, Folder 38, LPP.

95. Bernard Handlbauer, *The Freud-Adler Controversy* (London: One World Publications, 1998).

96. Edward Hoffman, *The Drive for Self: Alfred Adler and the Founding of Individual Psychology* (New York: Perseus Books, 1997).

97. Elaine Showalter, ed., *These Modern Women: Autobiographical Essays from the Twenties* (Old Westbury, NY: Feminist Press, 1978), 3.

98. Beatrice Hinkle, "Why Feminism?" in *These Modern Women*, edited by Elaine Showalter (Old Westbury, NY: Feminist Press, 1978), 137–141.

99. John B. Watson, "The Weakness of Women"; Joseph Collins, "Half-Confessions"; Lorine Pruette, "The Evolution of Disenchantment," all in *These Modern Women*, edited by Elaine Showalter (Old Westbury, NY: Feminist Press, 1978), 141–147; quotes 142, 145, 147. See also Cott, *The Grounding of Modern Feminism*, 152–156.

100. Pruette, "The Flapper," 579.

101. Lewis M. Terman, *Psychological Factors in Marital Happiness* (New York: McGraw-Hill, 1938), 321.

102. William Chafe, *The American Woman: Her Changing Social, Economic, and Political Roles, 1920–1970* (New York: Oxford University Press, 1972), 94–96.

103. Wile, *The Sex Life of the Unmarried Adult*, xi.

104. Pruette, "The Flapper," 577.

105. Ibid., 581, 580, 579.

106. Ibid., 580–581, 582, 578; Pruette, "Conditions Today; Some Modern Portraits and Their Interpretation," in Wile, *The Sex Life of the Unmarried Adult*, 278–303, quotation 301.

107. Lorine Pruette, "Draft Pages, Notes," Box 4, Folder 159, LPP; "The True Companion."

108. Pruette, "Draft Pages, Notes"; "Parthenope on the Mountain," Box 4, Folder 158, LPP.

109. Kimmel, *Manhood in America*, 127–132.

110. Little is known about John Woodbridge Herring. He published *Social Planning and Adult Education* in 1933, which focused on the Chester County Health and Welfare Council in West Chester, Pennsylvania.

111. John Herring, "Lines for a Lady," *Poetry Quarterly* 1, 3 (Spring 1931): 31; Lorine Pruette, "Courage," *New York Herald Tribune*, 1933, LPC.

112. Lorine Pruette, *School for Love* (Garden City, NY: Doubleday, Doran, 1936). *New York Times*, May 23, 1936; *Chattanooga News*, May 24, 1936, 22, both in LPC.

113. Pruette, "The Flapper," 581; "Conditions Today," 283, 285, 286–287; *Saint in Ivory: The Story of Genevieve of Paris and Nanterre* (New York: D. Appleton, 1927). Pruette is quoted in William O'Neill to Pruette, May 19, 1972, Box 1, Folder 7, LPP.

114. Stansell, *Feminist Promise*, 158.

115. Pruette, "The Flapper," 573.

116. Pruette, "The Evolution of Disenchantment," 71–72; "The Flapper," 583, 587.

117. Cott, *Grounding of Modern Feminism*, 151.

118. Doris Stevens to Dudley Field Malone, June 21, 1927, Box 2, Folder 4, DSP.

119. Doris Stevens, "Why Did She Do It?," Box 8, Folder 229, DSP.

120. Pruette, "Conditions Today."

121. Stevens to Sara Bard Field, 1917, Folder 22, Wood Papers; quoted in Cott, *Grounding of Modern Feminism*, 45.

CHAPTER 4 — OLD IDEAS VERSUS NEW

1. Seth Koven and Sonya Michel, "Introduction: 'Mother Worlds,'" in *Mothers of a New World: Maternalist Politics and the Origins of Welfare States*, edited by Koven and Michel (New York: Routledge, 1993), 1–42; see 2, 4.

2. Mary Beard, *Women's Work in Municipalities* (New York: D. Appleton, 1915).

3. Molly Ladd-Taylor, *Mother-Work: Women, Child Welfare, and the State, 1890–1940* (Urbana: University of Illinois Press, 1995).

4. Gwendolyn Mink, *The Wages of Motherhood: Inequality in the Welfare State, 1917–1942* (Ithaca, NY: Cornell University Press, 1995), 5–6.

5. Koven and Michel, "Introduction," 2–3.

6. Ibid., 4.

7. Seth Koven, "Borderlands: Women, Voluntary Action, and Child Welfare in Britain, 1840 to 1914," in *Mothers of a New World*, edited by Koven and Sonya Michel (New York: Routledge, 1993), 94–135.

8. Mink, *Wages of Motherhood*, 8; Alice Kessler-Harris, *In Pursuit of Equity: Women, Men, and the Quest for Economic Citizenship in 20th-Century America* (New York: Oxford University Press, 2001), 33–34.

9. William Chafe, *The Paradox of Change: American Women in the 20th Century* (New York: Oxford University Press, 1992), 22–44.

10. *Woman Citizen*, September 25, 1920, 445.

11. Jane Doolittle Wilson, *The Women's Joint Congressional Committee and the Politics of Maternalism, 1920–1930* (Urbana: University of Illinois Press, 2007).

12. Ibid., 31, 43, 27–49.

13. Ibid., 50–51.

14. Kessler-Harris, *In Pursuit of Equity*, 40–41, 31.

15. Quoted in Chafe, *Paradox of Change*, 49.

16. Ibid., 48.

17. Wilson, *Women's Joint Congressional Committee*, 21.

18. Alva Belmont, "Women as Dictators," *Ladies' Home Journal* 39 (September 1922): 7, 43.

19. Amanda Mackenzie Stuart, *Consuelo and Alva Vanderbilt: The Story of a Daughter and a Mother in the Gilded Age* (New York: HarperCollins, 2005), 406–411; quote 408.

20. Wilson, *Women's Joint Congressional Committee*, 148–149, 54, 129–132.

21. Ibid., 149–150; Stanley Lemons, *The Woman Citizen: Social Feminism in the 1920's* (Urbana: University of Illinois Press, 1973), 210–212; Mari Jo Buhle, *Women and American Socialism, 1870–1920* (Urbana: University of Illinois Press, 1981), 69–94.

22. Nancy Cott, ed., *A Woman Making History: Mary Ritter Beard through Her Letters* (New Haven, CT: Yale University Press, 1992), 36–37.

23. Beard to Elsie Hill, July 19, 1921, Series I, Reel 9, NWP Papers.

24. Ibid.

25. Miriam Beard Vagts to Ann Lane, undated, received January 2, 1977. Quoted in Ann Lane, ed., *Mary Ritter Beard: A Sourcebook* (New York: Schocken Books, 1977), 4–5.

26. The Beard home is described in June Allison, "Mary Beard's 15th Book Nears Publication," *Indianapolis Star*, July 29, 1955, and in a 1954 article in the *Waterbury Sunday Republican*. Clippings in Marjorie White correspondence, MB Papers.

27. Miriam Beard Vagts to Ann Lane, January 11, 1977, quoted in Lane, *Mary Ritter Beard*, 4–5.

28. Richard Hofstadter, *The Progressive Historians: Turner, Beard, Parrington* (New York: Vintage Books, 1970); Clyde W. Barrow, *More Than a Historian: The Political and Economic Thought of Charles Beard* (New Brunswick, NJ: Transaction, 2000).

29. Mary Beard, *A Short History of the American Labor Movement* (New York: Harcourt, Brace & Howe, 1920); quote from preface.

30. Orleck described the Workers Education Bureau as "the nerve center for labor education." Annelise Orleck, *Common Sense and a Little Fire: Women and Working-Class Politics in the United States, 1900–1965* (Chapel Hill: University of North Carolina Press, 1995), 184. The Beards created the bureau with Alexander Fichandler, journalist Arthur Gleason, and labor advocate Fannia Cohn.

31. Charles Beard, "Cooperation and the New Century," *Young Oxford* 2 (December 1900): 98; Mary Beard, "Struggling toward Civilization," address to the morning session of the International Congress of Women, July 17, 1933, both cited in Cott, *A Woman Making History*, 7–8, 341.

32. Hofstader, *The Progressive Historians*, 299.

33. Cott, *A Woman Making History*, 277.

34. See Charles Beard to the Macmillan Co., June 11, 1927, Macmillan Papers, Ms. Division, New York Public Library Annex; Mary Beard to Florence Kitchelt, May 18, no year, Florence Kitchelt Papers, SL.

35. Mary Beard to Rosika Schwimmer, October 14, 1935, WCWA Papers; Beard to Dorcas Campbell, August 31, 1946, MBC.

36. "Statement of Mrs. Mary Beard of New York City," in Committee on Woman Suffrage, Hearing before the Committee on Rules, U.S. House of Representatives, December 3, 4, & 5, 1913 (Washington, DC: Government Printing Office, 1914), 27.

37. See Mary Beard to President Jordan, June 10, 1944, MBC.

38. Julie Des Jardins, *Women and the Historical Enterprise in America: Gender, Race, and the Politics of Memory, 1880–1945* (Chapel Hill: University of North Carolina Press, 2003), 81.

39. Mary Beard, "The Twentieth-Century Woman Looking Around and Backward," *Young Oxford* 2, 15 (December 1900): 100–104; "The Nineteenth-Century Woman Looking Forward," *Young Oxford* 2, 16 (January 1901): 119–122, quoted in Nancy Cott, "Two Beards: Coauthorship and the Concept of Civilization," *American Quarterly* 42, 2 (June 1990): 277–300, 284.

40. Mary Beard, *On Understanding Women* (New York: Grosset and Dunlap, 1931), 122, 404–405.

41. Sue Shelton White, "This Feminism—A Review of Mary Beard's Book ON UNDERSTANDING WOMEN," *Equal Rights*, January 9, 1932, 391.

42. Mary Beard, ed., *America through Women's Eyes* (New York: Macmillan, 1933), 4–5, 7.

43. "Mary Beard Revalues Women," *Equal Rights*, November 25, 1933.

44. Quotations from Mary Beard to Margaret Grierson, December 10, 1950; Beard to Margaret Grierson, August 13, 1950, SSC; both quoted in Lane, *Mary Ritter Beard*, 53. Mary Beard, "In Pioneer Days," *Independent Woman*, September 1939, 290.

45. Interview with Mary Beard in the *Louisville Courier-Journal*, March 22, 1946, MBP, quoted in Lane, *Mary Ritter Beard*, 53; "Mary Beard's 15th Book Nears Publication."

46. Mary Beard to Anne Martin Grey, February 27, 1947, Bancroft Library, quoted in Lane, *Mary Ritter Beard*, 67; Beard to Eva Hansl, August 11, 1944, MBC.

47. John Higham, "Charles A. Beard: A Sketch," *International Encyclopedia of the Social Sciences* (New York, 1968), 2:33–37; cited in Cott, "Two Beards," 274.

48. Howard K. Beale, ed., *Charles A. Beard: An Appraisal* (Lexington, KY, 1954), 300 n 44; cited in Cott, "Two Beards," 275.

49. Mary Beard to Lena Madisen Phillips, April 28, 1935; Beard to Miriam Holden, June 13, 1940; both cited in Cott, *A Woman Making History*, 18.

50. Lorine Pruette described this book (the manuscript is missing) in an interview in the *Chattanooga Times*, March 3, 1946, LPC; Mary Beard to Elizabeth B. Schlesinger, May 30, 1944, MBC.

51. Mary Beard to Marjorie White, August 18, 1948, MBC.

52. Mary Beard to William Beard, n.d. [1951 or 1952] in personal collection of Detlev Vagts, Cambridge, MA; cited in Cott, "Two Beards," 275.

53. Mary Beard to Luella Key, October 21, 1951; Beard to Florence Kitchelt, March 30, 1951, both in MBC.

54. Mary Beard to Lena Madesin Phillips, October 10, 1948; quoted in Cott, "Two Beards," 295.

55. Koven and Michel, "Introduction," 3; Charlotte Perkins Gilman, "New Mothers of a New World," *Forerunner* 4 (1913): 149.

56. William Irwin published over thirty books. See Will Irwin, *The Making of a Reporter* (New York: G. P. Putnam's Sons, 1942); *The National Cyclopaedia of American Biography*, Vol. 35 (New York: James T. White, 1949): 271–272; *New York Times*, February 25, 1948 (obituary).

57. Inez Irwin, "Adventures of Yesterday," IHGP, 574–575.

58. Louise Bryant to John Reed, July 8, July 15, 1917; quoted in Christine Stansell, *American Moderns: Bohemian New York and the Creation of a New Century* (New York: Henry Holt, 2000), 256.

59. "Their Wives Are Literary, Too," *Time*, October 8, 1923.

60. Irwin, "Adventures of Yesterday," 574–575; Irwin to Carrie Chapman Catt, April 8, 1933, Container 17, Reel 11, NAWSA Papers; Irwin, *Angels and Amazons: A Hundred Years of American Women* (Garden City, NY: Doubleday, Doran, 1933).

61. Inez Irwin to Charlotte Perkins Gilman, July 30, 1921, Gilman Papers, Reel 143, SL.

62. Inez Irwin to Maud Wood Park, July 29, 1938, Container 17, Reel 11, NAWSA Papers; Irwin, "Adventures of Yesterday," 412–413.

63. Irwin, "Adventures of Yesterday," 418; "Adelaide Hawley (Radio) Interview with Inez and Will Irwin—Theme: Will Women Run the World?" Adelaide Fish Hawley Cumming Papers, Box 2, Folder 22, SL.

64. See Nancy Cott, *The Grounding of Modern Feminism* (New Haven, CT: Yale University Press, 1987), 12, 38; Will Irwin, "Inez Haynes Irwin," May 1943, Box 6, Folder 82, WRC; "Adelaide Hawley Radio Interview with Inez and Will Irwin."

65. Irwin, "Adventures of Yesterday," 548–549, 590.

66. Inez Irwin to Mrs. Stantial, April 20, 1952, Container 17, Reel 11, NAWSA Papers.

67. Cott, *A Woman Making History*, 18.

68. Irwin, "Adventures of Yesterday," 589, 518–519, 573.

69. Inez Irwin, "1893 Diary #2," Box 1, Volume 4, IHGP; "The Making of a Militant," in *These Modern Women*, edited by Elaine Showalter (Old Westbury, NY: Feminist Press, 1978), 33–39.

70. Inez Irwin, "Diary #14, 1904," Box 1, Volume 14, IHGP, 66; "Diary #17, 1908," 160 (January 27, 1908), Box 2, Volume 17, IHGP. Rufus Gillmore (1879–1935) published three mysteries between 1912 and 1914 and several more in the 1930s, including his most well known, *The Ebony Bed Murder* (1932).

71. Inez Haynes Gillmore, "The Life of an Average Woman," *Harper's Bazaar* 46 (June 1912): 281–282, quote on 282; "Confessions of an Alien," *Harper's Bazaar* 46 (April 1912): 170–171, 210, quotes on 170, 210.

72. Charlotte Rich, "From Near-Dystopia to Utopia: A Source for *Herland* in Inez Haynes Gillmore's *Angel Island*," in *Charlotte Perkins Gilman and Her Contemporaries*, edited by Cynthia J. Davis and Denise D. Knight (Tuscaloosa: University of Alabama Press, 2004). *Herland* was published in 1915.

73. Inez Haynes Gillmore, *Angel Island* (New York: Henry Holt, 1914), 80, 86–87. *Angel Island* was first published by the Phillips Publishing Company in 1913.

74. Ibid., 237, 238.

75. Inez Irwin to Maud Wood Park, February 2, 1916; November 3, 1945, Reel 17, File 11, NAWSA Papers.

76. Sonya Michel, *Children's Interests/Mother's Rights: The Shaping of America's Child Care Policy* (New Haven, CT: Yale University Press, 1999), 3.

77. Irwin, "1916 War Diary," Reel 975, II Papers, 279.

78. Michel, *Children's Interests/Mother's Rights*, 73–90; Mink, *Wages of Motherhood*, 32.

79. Eirinn Larsen, "Feminist Scholars Define Maternalism and Maternal Policy," http://www.ub.uib.no/elpub/1996/h/506002/eirinn/eirinn-Feminist-2.html.

80. Mink, *Wages of Motherhood*, 28.

81. Ibid., 31–33.

82. Ibid., 37–38, 44, 47.

83. Michel, *Children's Interests/Mothers' Rights*, 86–89.

84. Inez Irwin, *The Lady of Kingdoms* (New York: George H. Doran, 1917); Irwin, *Gertrude Haviland's Divorce* (New York: A. L. Burt, 1925).

85. Irwin, *The Lady of Kingdoms*, 38–39, 27.

86. Ibid., 43, 255, 82–83.

87. Ibid., 35–36.

88. Ibid., 245.

89. Ibid., 225, 478, 122.

90. Ibid., 178–179.

91. Ibid., 437.

92. "Briefer Mention," *The Dial*, March 14, 1918, 248.

93. Inez Haynes Irwin, "Discarded," *American Magazine*, May-November 1925.

94. Irwin, *Gertrude Haviland's Divorce*, 8, 15.

95. Ibid., 8, 15, 143–144.

96. Ibid., 365, 371, 375, 379, 381.

97. Irwin, "The Life of an Average Woman," 282; *Gertrude Haviland's Divorce*, 26.

CHAPTER 5 — THIS VAST LABORATORY

1. Christine Stansell, *The Feminist Promise: 1792 to the Present* (New York: Random House, 2010), 154–155.

2. Ben Lindsey and Wainwright Evans, *The Revolt of Modern Youth* (Garden City, NY: Garden City Publishing, 1925); *The Companionate Marriage* (New York: Boni & Liveright, 1927).

3. Peter Filene, *Him/Her/Self: Sex Roles in Modern America* (New York: Harcourt Brace, 1975), 146.

4. Ruth Hale, *Equal Rights*, 1924.

5. Floyd Dell, *Love in the Machine Age* (New York: Farrar, 1930), 6.

6. Christina Simmons, *Making Marriage Modern: Women's Sexuality from the Progressive Era to World War II* (New York: Oxford University Press, 2009), 114–118.

7. Nancy Cott, "Giving Character to Our Whole Civil Polity: Marriage and the Public Order in the Late Nineteenth Century," in *U.S. History as Women's History*, edited by Linda Kerber, Alice Kessler-Harris, and Kathryn Kish Sklar (Chapel Hill: University of North Carolina Press, 1995), 107–121; Simmons, *Making Marriage Modern*, 60.

8. Nancy Cott, *Public Vows: A History of Marriage and the Nation* (Cambridge, MA: Harvard University Press, 2000), 11–12.

9. Ibid., 150.

10. Robert Lynd and Helen Lynd, *Middletown* (New York: Harcourt Brace, 1929), 114–115.

11. Cott, *Public Vows*, 150–151.

12. Paula Fass, *The Damned and the Beautiful: American Youth in the 1920's* (New York: Oxford University Press, 1977).

13. Stephanie Coontz, *Marriage, A History: From Obedience to Intimacy or How Love Conquered Marriage* (New York: Viking Press, 2005), 202.

14. Both quotes cited in Mari Jo Buhle, Teresa Murphy, and Jane Gerhard, *Women and the Making of America* (Upper Saddle River, NJ: Pearson Prentice Hall, 2009), 511.

15. Cott, *Public Vows*, 195.

16. Coontz, *Marriage*, 204.

17. Doris Stevens, "How Many People Marry Mates?," Box 8, Folder 239, DSP.

18. Cited in Lillian Faderman, *Surpassing the Love of Men: Romantic Friendship and Love between Women from the Renaissance to the Present* (New York: Oxford University Press, 1977).

19. Phyllis Blanchard and Carolyn Masasses, *New Girls for Old* (New York: Macaulay, 1930), 179–180.

20. Lorine Pruette, "Married or UnMarried? Or to Be or Not to Be?" Box 3, Folder 91, LPP.

21. Helen Archdale to Stevens, November 2, 1936, Box 4, Folder 78, DSP.

22. See Arlie Russell Hochschild, *The Time Bind: When Work Becomes Home and Home Becomes Work* (New York: Metropolitan Books, 1997); Joan Williams, *Unbending Gender: Why Family and Work Conflict and What to Do about It* (New York: Oxford University Press, 2000); the Families and Work Institute at http://www.familiesandwork.org/.

23. Lorine Pruette, "Why Women Fail," *Outlook* 158, August 12, 1931, 460–462+.

24. The local Omaha newspaper interviewed Stevens's mother on December 5, 1921; the article was reprinted in the *New York Times*, December 6, 1921, clipping in Box 8, Folder 231, DSP.

25. John Reddy, "Dudley Field Malone: Magnificent Failure," *Esquire*, August 1951, 29+.

26. Ibid.

27. Doris Stevens, "Mental Cruelty," Box 3, Folder 43; Stevens to Dudley Malone, September 20, 1932, Box 2, Folder 41; Stevens, "Marriage," all in DSP.

28. Doris Stevens 1924 Diary, Box 6, Folder 182, DSP. The first is dated May 14, 1924, the second undated; Stevens, "Mental Cruelty"; "Marriage."

29. Jonathan Mitchell, *Goose Steps to Peace* (New York: Gordon Press, 1973). Mitchell's papers are held by the Schlesinger Library.

30. Jonathan Mitchell to Stevens ("Caroline"), postmark July 24, 1924 (letter undated), Box 3, Folder 50, DSP.

31. Stevens, "Marriage."

32. Jonathan Mitchell to Stevens, May 9, 1924, Box 3, Folder 51, DSP.

33. Hale is quoted in the *New York Herald Tribune*, September 19, 1934, clipping in Box 3, Folder 70, DSP.

34. Jonathan Mitchell to Stevens, March 28, 1926, Box 3, Folder 54, DSP.

35. Doris Stevens, Preface to "Women in Industry," Box 8, Folder 246, DSP.

36. Simmons, *Making Marriage Modern*, 127–132; Coontz, *Marriage*, 196–215.

37. Doris Stevens ("Julia") to Jonathan Mitchell, August 25, 1923, Box 3, Folder 47, DSP.

38. Jonathan Mitchell to Stevens, September 23, 1928, Box 3, Folder 5, DSP.

39. William Chafe, *The Paradox of Change: American Women in the 20th Century* (New York: Oxford University Press, 1992), 113.

40. Alice Kessler-Harris, *In Pursuit of Equity: Women, Men, and the Quest for Economic Citizenship in 20th-Century America* (New York: Oxford University Press, 2001), 21.

41. Doris Stevens quoted in "Woman's Party Delegates Sail for Conference," *New York Tribune*, May 1, 1926, clipping in Box 8, Folder 231, DSP.

42. The Pact of Paris, also known as the Kellogg-Briand Pact, was a treaty that attempted to outlaw war. Drafted by France and the United States, fifteen nations signed it on August 27, 1928, and by 1933 sixty-five had pledged to observe its provisions. Considered a milestone for international peace, three of its signatories—Japan, Germany, and Italy—all committed aggressions that helped precipitate World War II.

43. "Doris Stevens Urges Nuptial Contract on Visit to Miami," *Miami Daily News*, March 26, 1926, clipping in Box 8, Folder 231, DSP.

44. "Malone's Wife Clings to Miss," *New York Evening Sun*, April 21, 1922, clipping in Box 2, Folder 44, DSP.

45. "Doris Stevens Urges Nuptial Contract."

46. "World Tending toward Matriarchy, Declares Doris Stevens" (New York newspaper, title missing), April 22, 1922, Box 8, Folder 231, DSP.

47. Buhle et al., *Women and the Making of America*, 513; Lynn Weiner, *From Working Girl to Working Mother* (Chapel Hill: University of North Carolina Press, 1983), 89; Nancy Cott, *The Grounding of Modern Feminism* (New Haven, CT: Yale University Press, 1987), 182–183.

48. Chafe, *The Paradox of Change*, 69.

49. Buhle et al., *Women and the Making of America*, 513; Beverly Guy-Sheftall, ed., *Words of Fire: An Anthology of African American Feminist Thought* (New York: New Press, 1995), 9.

50. Chafe, *The Paradox of Change*, 73–75.

51. Ibid., 76; Kessler-Harris, *In Pursuit of Equity*, 50–56.

52. Research Materials, "Women in Industry," Box 8, Folder 247, DSP.

53. Stevens, "World Tending toward Matriarchy."

54. Kessler-Harris, *In Pursuit of Equity*, 9.

55. Arlie Russell Hochschild, *The Second Shift: Working Parents and the Revolution at Home* (New York: Viking, 1989).

56. Doris Stevens, "Things That Could be Done at Once," n.d. [ca. 1926], Research Materials, "Women in Industry."

57. John Bowman and Alyson Cole, "Do Working Mothers Oppress Other Women? The Swedish 'Maid Debate' and the Welfare State Politics of Gender Equality," *Signs* 35, 1 (Fall 2009): 157–184.

58. Ann Crittenden, *The Price of Motherhood: Why the Most Important Job in the World is Still the Least Valued* (New York: Macmillan, 2001), 58–61.

59. "Debate—Hays vs. Stevens," Box 8, Folder 240, DSP. The debate was published as Doris Stevens, "Wages for Wives: The Home as a Joint-Stock Company," *Nation*, January 27, 1926, 81–83.

60. Wendy Sarvasy, "Beyond the Difference versus Equality Policy Debate: Post-Suffrage Feminism, Citizenship, and the Quest for a Feminist Welfare State," *Signs* 17 (Winter 1992): 329–362; Molly Ladd-Taylor, *Mother-Work: Women, Child Welfare, and the State, 1890–1930* (Urbana: University of Illinois Press, 1994), 135–166.

61. "The 'Blanket' Amendment—A Debate," *The Forum* 72, 2 (August 1924): 145–160, quote 148; 149.

62. Ladd-Taylor, *Mother-Work*, 115–116.

63. Stevens, "Wages for Wives"; "Debate—Hays vs. Stevens"; "Doris Stevens Urges Nuptial Contract."

64. "Doris Stevens Urges Nuptial Contract."

65. Bobbie O'Dare, "Auxiliaries Are Bores, Declares Doris Stevens; Feminist Says Women and Men Should Belong to Same C. of C.; Says Ego Must Be Fed," *Omaha Evening Bee*, September 28, 1927, Box 8, Folder 232, DSP.

66. Stevens-Hays debate on "Wages for Wives." See Cott, *Grounding of Modern Feminism*, 185–188.

67. Doris Stevens, "Women in Industry."

68. Doris Stevens to Mr. Conner, June 23, 1927, Box 3, Folder 43; Stevens to Dudley Malone, no date or title, begins with "1. Is it right to go from one another while we still suffer at the going?," Box 2, Folder 41; Dudley Field Malone to Stevens, June 11, 1927, Box 2, Folder 43; Stevens Diary, June 27, 1927, July 1, 1927, Box 6, Folder 183, all in DSP.

69. "Shall Dudley Pay the Piper? No Alimony for His Wife Say Persons Who Discuss Her Petition for Divorce," *Omaha Evening Bee*, July 17, 1927, Box 2, Folder 40; "Feminist Divorces Dudley Field Malone," *New York Times*, July 21, 1927, Box 2, Folder 41, both in DSP. Stevens discusses alimony in a letter to her attorney, Mr. Conner, June 23, 1927, Box 3, Folder 43; Folder 183; Jonathan Mitchell, "The Bend in the River," Side two, all in DSP.

70. Doris Stevens to Jonathan Mitchell, November 12, 1923, Box 3, Folder 47; Stevens to Jonathan Mitchell, postmark September 1925, Box 3, Folder 52; Stevens to Dudley Malone, December 1925, Box 2, Folder 39, all in DSP.

71. Mitchell, "The Bend in the River," side two; Stevens to Jonathan Mitchell, n.d. [February or March 1927], Box 3, Folder 56; Jonathan Mitchell Journal, October 12, 1931, Box 3, Folder 66, all in DSP.

72. Mitchell, "The Bend in the River," side two. Stevens and Mitchell were married in Portland, Maine, on August 31, 1935. "Doris Stevens Wed in Maine Ceremony: Former Wife of Dudley

Field Malone is Married to Jonathan Mitchell," *New York Times*, September 1, 1935; http://select.nytimes.com/gst/abstract.html?res=FB0C12FF3D5A107A93C3A91782D85F418385F9.

73. Jonathan Mitchell to Stevens, March 8, 1926, Box 3, Folder 54; Stevens, "Marriage"; Stevens to Dudley, September 20, 1932, Box 2, Folder 41, all in DSP.

74. Doris Stevens to Jonathan Mitchell, n.d. [1927], Box 3, Folder 55, DSP.

75. Doris Stevens, Preface to "Women in Industry."

76. Cott, *Grounding of Modern Feminism*, 127.

77. Doris Stevens, "Chapter 5: Attacking What Proponents say on Protection," 4–5, "Women in Industry."

78. Ibid., 5–8.

79. Ibid., 10–11.

80. Doris Stevens, "Will Men Become Housekeepers?," n.d., Box 8, Folder 239, DSP.

81. Stevens-Hays debate on "Wages for Wives."

82. Lorine Pruette, *Women and Leisure: A Study of Social Waste* (New York: E. P. Dutton, 1924). Pruette dedicated the book to her mother, and to the novelist Dorothy Canfield (Fisher) "for writing *The Homemaker*."

83. Lorine Pruette, "The End Is in the Beginning," Box 3, Folder 46, LSP; "The Evolution of Disenchantment," *These Modern Women: Autobiographical Essays from the Twenties*, edited by Elaine Showalter (Old Westbury, NY: Feminist Press, 1978), 68–73; quote 72.

84. Pruette, "The Evolution of Disenchantment," 72; Pruette, "Memento Mori," Box 4, Folder 157, LPP.

85. Pruette, "The Evolution of Disenchantment."

86. Pruette, "Married or Unmarried? To Be or Not to Be?"

87. Pruette, "Male Chauvanists [*sic*] I Have Known," Box 3, Folder 87, LPP.

88. Lorine Pruette, "G. Stanley Hall, the Playboy of Western Scholarship," *Century* 108 (October 1924): 766–772; see 771.

89. Pruette, "Male Chauvanists [*sic*] I Have Known." See also "The Making of a Feminist," Box 3, Folder 86 and "On the Trail of the Endocrines," Box 3, Folder 103, all in LSP.

90. Lorine Pruette, "A Woman Who Was Not Intelligent," Box 3, Folder 103, LPP.

91. Lorine Pruette, "The Elders Cast Long Shadows," Box 4, Folder 157, LPP.

92. Lorine Pruette, "The Decline of the Male," Box 2, Folder 38; "The Sorceror & the Young Prophet," Box 3, Folder 104; "Addendum to Dr. Freud," Box 2, Folder 23; and "To Sigmund, with Love," Box 4, Folder 126, all in LPP.

93. Pruette, "Why Women Fail."

94. Lorine Pruette, "According to Taste," Box 2, Folder 22; "Don't Look Homeward, Angel!," Box 2, Folder 43, both in LPP.

95. Lorine Pruette, "Second Wife," Box 4, Folder 30; "Not Magic in Mountains," Box 3, Folder 113, both in LPP.

96. Pruette, "On the Trail of the Endocrines"; Pruette to Mary Lee, September 18, 1958, Box 1, Folder 6, LPP.

97. Charlotte Perkins, *Women and Economics* (Boston: Small, Maynard, 1900); Olive Schreiner, *Woman and Labor* (New York: Frederick A. Stokes, 1911).

98. Pruette, *Women and Leisure*, 116–190; quote 186–187.

99. Ibid., 187.

100. "Auxiliaries Are Bores, Declares Doris Stevens."

101. Lorine Pruette, "The Business Professions for Women," in *Vocational Self-Guidance: Planning Your Life Work*, edited by Douglas Fryer (Philadelphia: J. P. Lippincott, 1925), 337.

102. Lorine Pruette, "The Part-Time Job," *Woman's Journal* 15, 22 (March 1930); "The Married Woman and the Part-time Job," *Annals of the American Academy of Political and Social Science* 143 (May 1929): 301–306.

103. Pruette, "The Business Professions for Women," 323, 329.

104. Ibid., 58. *The Effects of Labor Legislation on the Employment of Women*, Women's Bureau Bulletin no. 68 (Washington, DC: Government Printing Office, 1928), 27.

105. Lorine Pruette, "Equal Rights or Easier Work? Are Working Women Handicapped by Protective Labor Laws? The Women's Bureau Answers," *Woman's Journal* 14 (January 1929): 14–15, 44.

106. Ibid., 44, 15.

107. Ibid., 44.

108. Alice Kessler-Harris has written that economic citizenship includes access to social benefits, wage work, and credit (without regard to gender, marital status, or race). Kessler-Harris, *In Pursuit of Equity*, 4–5, 66, 56.

109. Cott, *Public Vows*, 158.

110. Coontz, *Marriage*, 218.

111. Cott, *Public Vows*, 173; Kessler-Harris, *In Pursuit of Equity*, 59.

112. Kessler-Harris, *In Pursuit of Equity*, 60, 309–310.

113. Lorine Pruette, *Women Workers through the Depression: A Study of White Collar Employment Made by the American Woman's Association* (New York: Macmillan, 1934), 1, 20, 21.

114. Ibid., 35–37.

115. Ibid., 55, 86, 90, 110–111, 119.

116. Pruette, "The End Is in the Beginning."

117. Pruette, "The Business Professions for Women," 337, 340.

118. Doris Stevens to Betty Gram Swing, January 8, 1946, Box 5, Folder 164, DSP.

CHAPTER 6 — TO WORK TOGETHER FOR ENDS LARGER THAN SELF

1. Carlos Davila, "The Montevideo Conference: Antecedents and Accomplishments," May 1934, Box 2, Folder 31; "The IACW: Documents Concerning Its Creation and Organization," Box 3, Folder 32; IACW Bulletins and Press Releases; DS Notes toward a book on IACW, Box 8, Folder 251; L. E. Elliot, "Woman's Progress towards Equal Rights; Feminist and World Treaties; Work of the Inter American Commission of Women," *Pan-American Magazine* (December 1928): 205–214, Box 2, Folder 28; "Outline of the History of the Inter American Commission of Women," Box 3, Folder 33; "Address of Miss Doris Stevens Made Before a Special Plenary Session of the Sixth Pan American Conference February 7, 1928, Habana, Cuba," *Congressional Record*, Box 2, Folder 18, all in DSP.

2. Leila Rupp, "Challenging Imperialism in International Women's Organizations, 1888–1945," *National Women's Studies Association Journal* 8 (Spring 1996): 8–27.

3. Ibid., 8.

4. Leila Rupp, *Worlds of Women: The Making of an International Women's Movement* (Princeton, NJ: Princeton University Press, 1997), 147.

5. Rupp, "Challenging Imperialism," 10.

6. Ibid., 18; Rupp, *Worlds of Women*, 78–80.

7. "Doris Stevens Speaks at Headquarters," *Equal Rights*, March 3, 1928, 27.

8. Doris Stevens, "In Behalf of the Equal Rights Treaty," reprinted in *Equal Rights*, March 10, 1928, 37–39.

9. "Mrs. Belmont Urges a Woman's Government," *New York Times*, September 24, 1923, clipping in Box 5, Folder 2, DSP.

10. In an 1891 speech before the inaugural meeting of the National Council of Women, Women's Christian Temperance Union Leader Frances Willard argued for women to organize "a miniature council in every town and city," made up only of women. "We should thus have within the National Government, as carried on by men, a republic of women." Cited in Mari Jo Buhle, Teresa Murphy, and Jane Gerhard, *Women and the Making of America* (Upper Saddle River, NJ: Pearson Prentice Hall, 2009), 399–400.

11. Paula Giddings, *When and Where I Enter: The Impact of Black Women on Race and Sex in America* (New York: W. Morrow, 1984), 164–166.

12. Amy Butler, *Two Paths to Equality: Alice Paul and Ethel M. Smith in the ERA Debate, 1921–1929* (Albany: State University of New York Press, 2002), 58.

13. Giddings, *When and Where I Enter*, 167.

14. Cited ibid.

15. Butler, *Two Paths*, 58.

16. Freda Kirchwey, "Alice Paul Pulls the Strings," *Nation* 112 (March 2, 1921): 333.

17. Giddings, *When and Where I Enter*, 169.

18. Cited in Butler, *Two Paths*, 58.

19. Ibid., 57, 59.

20. K. Lynn Stoner, *From the House to the Streets: The Cuban Woman's Movement for Legal Reform, 1898–1940* (Durham, NC: Duke University Press, 1991), 187.

21. On the IACW's creation, see *Equal Rights* articles "Why We Are in Havana," January 28, 1928, 402, and "Showing the Way," February 25, 1928, both in DSP; Stevens, "International Feminism is Born," *Time and Tide*, April 13, 1928; quote from "International Action," *Equal Rights*, December 21, 1929, 364.

22. "Equal Rights Treaty," Box 4, Folder 78, DSP.

23. Doris Stevens to Jonathan Mitchell, January 16, 1928, Box 3, Folder 57, DSP.

24. Stoner, *From the House*, 187.

25. The League of Nations was an intergovernmental organization created after World War I with the objective of maintaining world peace. At its 1935 height it had fifty-eight members. The United States never joined, largely because of Senate objections to interference in foreign wars. The United Nations replaced it after the end of World War II.

26. "Doris Stevens Addresses International Club," *Equal Rights*, October 20, 1928, 293–294; Stevens, "International Feminism Is Born."

27. Stoner, *From the House*, 193–195, 108–126.

28. Ibid., 112, 113.

29. "Wants International Party," *Equal Rights*, September 14, 1929, 254; "Doris Stevens Heads Pan-American Women's Commission," *Equal Rights*, April 14, 1928, 77.

30. Doris Stevens to Dr. Freund, August 1, 1928, Box 4, Folder 103, DSP.

31. Doris Stevens, "The Rights of Women in Inter-American Relations," July 5, 1934, speech at the University of Virginia Institute of Public Affairs, Box 2, Folder 24, DSP.

32. Doris Stevens to Alice Paul, September 1, 1928, Box 2, DSP.

33. "Feminists Try to Crash Peace Pact Ceremony," *Los Angeles Examiner*, August 29, 1928; Rupp, *Worlds of Women*, 138–139.

34. Alva Belmont to Alice Paul, August 29, 1928, Box 9; Elizabeth Rogers to Alice Paul, September 30, 1928, Box 2, both in DSP.

35. Jonathan Mitchell to Stevens, August 29, 1928, Box 3, Folder 61, DSP.

36. "Who Is Doris Stevens?" *Equal Rights*, November 3, 1928, 311; "An Apostle of Action," *Time and Tide* (October 26, 1928): 1004–1006, in Box 8, Folder 238, DSP.

37. Lady Margaret Rhondda to Stevens, n.d. [probably 1928], Box 5, Folder 154, DSP.

38. Margaret Rhondda to Stevens, August 27, 1928, Box 5, Folder 154, DSP.

39. Simone Tery, "Doris Stevens at The Hague," *Equal Rights*, May 31, 1930, 131–133.

40. Jonathan Mitchell to Stevens, October 2, 1928, Box 3, Folder 61, DSP.

41. Susan Becker, "International Feminism between the Wars: The National Woman's Party versus the League of Women Voters," in *Decades of Discontent: The Women's Movement, 1920–1940*, edited by Lois Scharf and Joan M. Jensen (Westport, CT: Greenwood, 1983), 223–242.

42. Muna Lee de Munoz Marin, "Equal Rights Approved by the American Institute of International Law," November 28, 1931, 339–340; "Congratulations to Doris Stevens," December 19, 1931; "Slowly but Surely," February 6, 1932; "A Good Intelligence Test," February 27, 1932, 32; "Havana Delegation Receives Warm Welcome," March 22, 1930, all in *Equal Rights*.

43. "Doris Stevens Returns," *Equal Rights*, July 13, 1929, 181. On her fatigue, see Stevens to Mrs. John Milholland, January 28, 1933, Box 5, Folder 136, DSP.

44. Doris Stevens, "Memorandum: General Statement" (p. 15), Box 5, Folder 132, DSP.

45. Doris Stevens Diary, July 18, 1927, Box 6, Folder 183, DSP; see also "Memorandum for Mr. Littleton," Box 5, Folder 132, DSP; "Memorandum: General Statement."

46. Stevens, "Memorandum: General Statement."

47. Alva Belmont to Stevens, April 5, 1929. Stevens retyped this letter and included it in the chronology of her relationship with Belmont, described in "Memorandum: General Statement."

48. Leila Rupp, "Feminism and the Sexual Revolution in the Early Twentieth Century: The Case of Doris Stevens," *Feminist Studies* 15, 2 (Summer 1989): 289–309; see 300.

49. Stevens, "Memorandum: General Statement," 24.

50. Ibid., 28. Stuart described this final meeting in Amanda Mackenzie Stuart, *Consuelo and Alva Vanderbilt: The Story of a Daughter and a Mother in the Gilded Age* (New York: HarperCollins, 2005), 444.

51. Harry Stevens to Doris Stevens, December 2, 1932, Box 1, Folder 20, DSP.

52. Vivian (Pierce?) to Doris Stevens, n.d., Box 1, Folder 20, DSP.

53. Jonathan Mitchell to Stevens, Wednesday night (n.d.) in 1929, Box 3, Folder 65, DSP.

54. Stuart, *Consuelo and Alva Vanderbilt*, 441–446.

55. "Press release for Alva's funeral on Sunday February 12, 1933," Jane Norman Smith Papers, SL; "Eulogy Gven by Doris Stevens at Alva's Funeral," February 12, 1933, DSP.

56. Doris Stevens, *Jailed for Freedom* (New York: Boni & Liveright, 1920), dedication page. On her evolving feelings toward Paul, see "Memorandum on year 1931, on incidents related to Mrs. Belmont's revoction [*sic*] of the legacy," Box 5, Folder 132, DSP.

57. Doris Stevens to Gaeta Boyer, August 1, 1940, Box 4, Folder 87, DSP.

58. Stuart, *Consuelo and Alva Vanderbilt*, 448.

59. Alice Burns to Stevens, March 1933, Box 1, Folder 20, DSP.

60. Stuart, *Consuelo and Alva Vanderbilt*, 448.

61. Martin Littleton to Stevens, "Memo on Alva Belmont's will, 1934," n.d., Box 5, Folder 132, DSP.

62. Doris Stevens to Sara Bard Field, September 1, 1933, Box 4, Folder 112, DSP.

63. Stuart, *Consuelo and Alva Vanderbilt*, 448; see Rupp, "Feminism and the Sexual Revolution," 300–301.

64. Rupp, "Feminism and the Sexual Revolution," 301; Alva Belmont to Stevens, n.d. (February 1927), Box 9, Folder 1, DSP; Stevens, "Memorandum," n.d., Box 5, Folder 32.

65. Rupp, *Worlds of Women*, 140. The Treaty of Versailles, signed in June 1919, was one of the peace treaties at the end of World War I.

66. Becker, "International Feminism," 224–228. Catt had been president of the International Woman Suffrage Alliance from 1904 until 1923.

67. Ibid., 227; Alice Paul to Stevens, cable, May 30, 1926, Jane Norman Smith papers, Box 5, SL.

68. Lady Margaret Rhondda to Doris Stevens, January 6, 1928, Box 5, Folder 154, DSP.

69. Rupp, *Worlds of Women*, 146–150.

70. Quote from "Commission Studies Nationality Laws," *Equal Rights*, August 4, 1928, 205; see also "Nationality? In a Nutshell," *Equal Rights*, January 25, 1930, 403.

71. Becker, "International Feminism between the Wars," 230.

72. Stevens quoted in Ruby A. Black, "United States Refuses to Accept Unequal Code," *Equal Rights*, April 19, 1930, 83; and "Doris Stevens Tells the Story of The Hague," *Equal Rights*, May 24, 1930, 126–127.

73. Rupp, *Worlds of Women*, 147–148.

74. Becker, "International Feminism between the Wars," 235–236; Doris Stevens to James Brown Scott, cable, December 14, 1933, Box 5, Folder 160, DSP.

75. Becker, "International Feminism between the Wars," 235–236.

76. Stevens, "Memorandum on year 1931."

77. Quotation from Stevens's 1934 speech at the New York Herald Tribune Conference on Current Problems, Box 2, Folder 18a, DSP.

78. Ibid.; see "The First Treaty Giving Complete Equality to Women in the History of the World Signed at Montevideo," *Equal Rights*, July 7, 1934, 179–183; "Brilliant Throng Fetes Doris Stevens in New York," *Equal Rights*, February 17, 1934, 20.

79. Stoner, *From the House*, 190–192.

80. Dudley Malone to Stevens, December 22, 1933 telegram, Box 2, Folder 41, DSP.

81. "The Victory Conference," *Equal Rights*, December 30, 1933; "We Cross the Rubicon," *Equal Rights*, May 19, 1934.

82. "Praise for Two Ladies," *Baltimore Evening Sun*, December 21, 1933; quoted in *Equal Rights*, February 3, 1934, 7; William Kimberly Palmer, "Alice Paul and Doris Sevens," *Equal Rights*, February 10, 1934, 16; Scott is quoted on the cover of *Equal Rights*, February 17, 1934, under a drawing of Stevens.

83. Leila Rupp, "Sexuality and Politics in the Early Twentieth Century: The Case of the International Women's Movement," 23, 3 *Feminist Studies* (Autumn, 1997): 577–605, see 594.

84. Ibid., 590.

85. Rupp, *Worlds of Women*, 149.

86. Becker, "International Feminism," 230–233.

87. Susan Ware, *Beyond Suffrage: Women in the New Deal* (Cambridge, MA: Harvard University Press, 1981), 16.

88. Ibid., 78–79.

89. Becker, "International Feminism," 232.

90. Jonathan Mitchell to Stevens, December 12, 1938, Box 3, DSP; Becker, "International Feminism," 236–238.

91. Mary A. Murray, "Muchas Gracias, Senator Burke," *Equal Rights*, September 1939, 111.

92. "Letter to Governing Board of Pan American Union," *Equal Rights*, March 1, 1939, 40.

93. Becker, "International Feminism," 237.

94. Rupp, *Worlds of Women*, 148.

95. Doris Stevens to Frank (?), n.d. (probably 1941), in Box 5, Folder 151, DSP.

96. "A Changed Commission," *Equal Rights*, November 1940, 32; Mrs. Fanny Chipman to Doris [Stevens] and Jonathan [Mitchell], February 24, 1939, Box 4, Folder 97, DSP.

97. Doris Stevens to Eleanor Roosevelt, February 22, 1942, Box 5, Folder 152, DSP.

98. Beard, "A Test for the Modern Woman," *Current History* (November 1932): 179–193; quotes 179, 183.

99. Jane Norman Smith to Stevens, August 3, 1932; December 29, 1932, Box 5, Folder 163, DSP.

100. Beard to Harriot Stanton Blatch, July 16, 1934, in *A Woman Making History: Mary Ritter Beard through Her Letters*, edited by Nancy Cott (New Haven, CT: Yale University Press, 1992), 115–116.

101. Julie Des Jardins, *Women and the Historical Enterprise in America: Gender, Race, and the Politics of Memory, 1880–1945* (Chapel Hill: University of North Carolina Press, 2003), 237.

102. Cott, *A Woman Making History*, 42–43, 154.

103. Mary Beard, "Women and Social Crises," *Independent Woman*, January 1935, 31; Beard, *A Changing Political Economy as It Affects Women* (Washington, DC: American Association of University Women, 1934).

104. Carrie Foster, *The Women and the Warriors: The U.S. Section of the Women's International League for Peace and Freedom, 1915–1946* (Syracuse, NY: Syracuse University Press, 1995), 153–154.

105. See Mary Beard to Florence B. Hilles, January 31, 1937; Beard to Mrs. Hilles, January 5, 1937; both Series I, Reel 58, NWP Papers.

106. Mary Beard to Alma Lutz, January 29, 1937, Series I, Reel 58, NWP Papers.

107. Cott, *A Woman Making History*, 43–44.

108. Nancy Cott, *The Grounding of Modern Feminism* (New Haven, CT: Yale University Press, 1987), 117–142; Leila Rupp and Verta Taylor, *Survival in the Doldrums: The American Women's Rights Movement, 1945 to the 1960s* (New York: Oxford University Press, 1987), 59–64.

109. Mary Beard to Alma Lutz, January 29, 1937, Series I, Reel 58, NWP Papers.

110. Jane Norman Smith to Stevens, December 29, 1932, Box 5, Folder 163, DSP.

111. On the WCWA, see WCWA File, MBPSL; WCWA Papers; Des Jardins, *Women and the Historical Enterprise in America*, 225–240; Cott, *A Woman Making History*, 46–49, 128–220; *Mary Ritter Beard: A Sourcebook*, edited by Ann Lane (New York: Schocken Books, 1977), 31–42, 210–214; Barbara Turoff, *Mary Beard as Force in History* (Dayton, OH: Wright State University Press, 1979), 51–69.

112. Des Jardins, *Women and the Historical Enterprise in America*, 227.

113. Rosika Schwimmer to Beard, August 4, 1935, in Cott, *A Woman Making History*, 129.

114. Mary Beard to Mrs. Boeckel, August 10, 1935, reprinted in Cott, *A Woman Making History*, 131; Beard to Florence Kitchelt, April 7, 1939, MBPSL.

115. Mary Beard to Lena Madisen Phillips, November 17, 1935; Beard to Stevens, November 14, 1935, both in Cott, *A Woman Making History*, 139–141, 138.

116. Mary Beard to Mrs. Dorothy Porter, March 31, 1940, in Cott, *A Woman Making History*, 48; "WCWA Desirable Materials," Box 1, Folder 1, MBPSL.

117. Mary Beard to Florence Kitchelt, April 4, 1939; "Mary Beard on Trail of Famous Women Lore, Seeks PWA Aid," [Bridgeport, CT] *Post*, March 6, 1936, both in MBPSL.

118. Mary Beard to Rose Arnold Powell, September 14, 1935, MBC; Beard to Rosika Schwimmer, August 16, 1935, quoted in Turoff, *Mary Beard as Force in History*, 45.

119. Cott, *A Woman Making History*, 144–145; Beard to Rosika Schwimmer, February 14, 1936, in Cott, *A Woman Making History*, 145–149.

120. Mary Beard to Rosika Schwimmer, April 11, 1935 (copy), and typescript, "Confidential discussion for the reasons of Madam Schwimmer's resignation from A World Center for Women's Archives between Madam Rosika Schwimmer, Mrs. Mary R. Beard, and Mrs. Inez Haynes Irwin, at Madam Schwimmer's apartment on May 1, 1936," quoted in Cott, *A Woman Making History*, 150.

121. Mary Beard to Rosika Schwimmer, May 12, 1936, in Cott, *A Woman Making History*, 150–152; Beard to Margaret Grierson, May 18, 1951, Box I, Beard Papers, SSC.

122. Des Jardins, *Women and the Historical Enterprise*, 232–236.

123. Mary Beard to Florence Brewer Boeckel, November 21, 1936, in Cott, *A Woman Making History*, 153; on the *New York Sun* list, see Cott, 157.

124. Mary Beard to Miriam Holden, March 12, 1938, in Cott, *A Woman Making History*, 169–171.

125. [Unknown] to Mrs. Catt, n.d., Container 2, Reel 2 (WCWA File), NAWSA Papers; Carrie Chapman Catt to Inez Irwin, May 5, 1937, Carrie Chapman Catt Papers, SSC, Container 6, Reel 4; Mary Beard to Miss Blackwell, July 29, 1938, Container 2, Reel 2, NAWSA Papers.

126. Des Jardins, *Women and the Historical Enterprise*, 235.

127. Mary Beard to Miriam Holden, March 9, 1939, in Cott, *A Woman Making History*, 183–185.

128. Mary Beard to Lena Madesin Phillips, May 11, 1939, in Cott, *A Woman Making History*, 187–188.

129. Cott, *A Woman Making History*, 195–207.

130. Mary Beard to Miriam Holden, March 25, 1940; Miriam Holden to Beard, April 5, 1940; Beard to Miriam Holden, April 2, 1940, all in Cott, *A Woman Making History*, 199–201; 202–205.

131. Des Jardins, *Women and the Historical Enterprise*, 36–38; Beard to Margaret Grierson, July 15, 1945, Box 1, Beard Papers, SSC.

132. Des Jardins, *Women and the Historical Enterprise*, 237; see Beard to W. K. Jordan, July 2, 1944, Box 2, Folder 30, MBPSL.

133. Mary Beard to Mrs. Saunders, May 22, 1940, Carton 2, WCWA File, NAWSA Papers; Beard to Florence Kitchelt, October 28, no year [1940], MB Papers; "1940—Corporation of the WORLD CENTER FOR WOMEN'S ARCHIVES Dissolved," Marjorie White Papers, SL.

134. Miriam Holden to Eva Hansl, June 13, 1940, in Cott, *A Woman Making History*, 210; see Beard to Members of the Board of the WCWA, June 26, 1940, in Cott, *A Woman Making History*, 210–213.

135. Rosika Schwimmer quoted in Cott, *A Woman Making History*, 212–213; Beard to Rosika Schwimmer, July 10, 1940, in Cott, *A Woman Making History*, 213–214.

CHAPTER 7 — FEMINISM AS LIFE'S WORK

1. Lorine Pruette, "I Don't Want to Play This Game Any More!," Box 2, Folder 61, LPP.

2. Lorine Pruette, "I Don't Want to Play!"

3. Anne-Marie Slaughter, "Why Women Still Can't Have It All," *Atlantic*, July/August 2012; http://www.theatlantic.com/magazine/archive/2012/07/why-women-still-cant-have-it-all/309020/.

4. Leila Rupp and Verta Taylor, *Survival in the Doldrums; The American Women's Rights Movement, 1945 to the 1960s* (New York: Oxford University Press, 1987), 7.

5. Inez Irwin to Maud Wood Park, August 1, 1940, December 16, 1940, Container 17, Reel 11, NAWSA Papers.

6. Mari Jo Buhle, Teresa Murphy, and Jane Gerhard, *Women and the Making of America* (Upper Saddle River, NJ: Pearson Prentice Hall, 2009), 580, 602–610.

7. "Adelaide Hawley (Radio) Interview with Inez and Will Irwin," March 22, 1944, Box 2, Folder 22, Adelaide Fish Hawley Cumming Papers, SL.

8. Inez Irwin to Maud Wood Park, November 10, 1945, Container 17, Reel 11, NAWSA Papers; Lorine Pruette, "The True Companion," Box 4, Folder 163, LPP.

9. Sonya Michel, "American Women and the Discourse of the Democratic Family in World War II," in *Behind the Lines: Gender and the Two World Wars*, edited by Margaret Randolph Higonnet, Jane Jenson, Sonya Michel, and Margaret Collins Weitz (New Haven, CT: Yale University Press, 1987), 154–167; quote from 167.

10. Edna Capewell to Alice Paul, November 24, 1945, Reel 88, NWP Papers; Doris Stevens to Betty Gram Swing, January 8, 1946, Box 4, DSP.

11. Dorothy Sue Cobble, *The Other Women's Movement: Workplace Justice and Social Rights in Modern America* (Princeton, NJ: Princeton University Press, 2004), 3–4.

12. Jane Mansbridge, *Why We Lost the ERA* (Chicago: University of Chicago Press, 1986), 9.

13. Rupp and Taylor, *Survival*, 25. For her 1940 role, see Doris Stevens to James Scott, July 31, 1940, Box 5, Folder 161, DSP.

14. Rupp and Taylor, *Survival*, 25, 38–43; Leila Rupp, "The Women's Community in the National Woman's Party, 1945 to the 1960s," *Signs* 10 (1985): 715–740.

15. Rupp and Taylor, *Survival*, 27–32.

16. Lucy Burns to Stevens, November 18, 1942, Box 4, File 79, DSP.

17. Doris Stevens to Katherine Callery, October 7, 1944, Box 4, Folder 92; Jeannette Marks to Stevens, April 12, 1946, Box 5, Folder 139, both in DSP.

18. Doris Stevens to Katherine Callery, June 23, 1946, Box 4, Folder 93, DSP.

19. Located at 144 Constitution Ave NE in Washington, DC, the building is known today as the Sewall-Belmont House and Museum.

20. Anna Kelton Wiley, Laura Berrien, and Doris Stevens to Alice Paul, April 29, 1947, Reel 91, NWP Papers.

21. Laura Berrien and Doris Stevens, "An Open Letter to Miss Alice Paul," July 30, 1947, in Rupp and Taylor, *Survival*, 30.

22. Doris Stevens to Westbrook Pegler, May 3, 1946, cited in Rupp and Taylor, *Survival*, 36.

23. Rupp and Taylor, *Survival*, 30–31.

24. Stevens noted her departure in "Fiftieth Reunion Omaha High School Class of 1905," Box 5, Folder 149, DSP.

25. Rupp and Taylor, *Survival*, 31–36, 26.

26. Mary Walton, *A Woman's Crusade: Alice Paul and the Battle for the Ballot* (New York: Palgrave Macmillan, 2010); Linda Ford, *Iron-Jawed Angels: The Suffrage Militancy of the National Woman's Party, 1912–1920* (Lanham, MD: University Press of America, 1991); Christine Lunardini, *From Equal Suffrage to Equal Rights: Alice Paul and the National Woman's Party, 1910–1928* (San Jose, CA: Excel Press, 2000).

27. Katherine Adams and Michael Keene, *Alice Paul and the American Suffrage Campaign* (Urbana: University of Illinois Press, 2008), xvi–xviii.

28. Amy Butler, *Two Paths to Equality: Alice Paul and Ethel M. Smith in the ERA Debate, 1921–1929* (Albany: State University of New York Press, 2002), 1–11.

29. Ella Winter, "Eve's Numerous Daughters," *Saturday Review*, n.d. 1946, Box 26, Volume 150a; James H. Hexter, "The Ladies Were There All the Time," *New York Book Review*, March 17, 1946, Box 26, Volume 150e; Stephen Peabody, "Fools Gold for Women," publication unknown, April 14, 1946, Box 26, Volume 150e; all in Sue Shelton White Papers, SL.

30. Julie Des Jardins, *Women and the Historical Enterprise in America: Gender, Race, and the Politics of Memory, 1880–1945* (Chapel Hill: University of North Carolina Press, 2003), 254–255.

31. Pruette, "The True Companion"; Mary Beard to Marjorie White, January 16, 1950, December 10, 1950, MBC.

32. Des Jardins, *Women and the Historical Enterprise*, 255–257.

33. Mary Beard to Marjorie White, January 16, 1951; Beard to Florence Kitchelt, March 30, 1951; Beard to Luella Key, July 24, 1953; Beard to the Keys, Easter 1954, all in MBC.

34. Mary Beard to Luella Key, June 25, 1953; Beard to Dorcas Campbell, July 16, 1955, both in MBC.

35. Mary Beard to V. O. and Lulebelle Key, April 5, 1955; Beard to the Keys, July 20, 1955, both in MBC. Mary Beard, *The Force of Women in Japanese History* (Washington, DC: Public Affairs Press, 1953); Beard, *The Making of Charles A. Beard* (New York: Exposition Press, 1955).

36. See Mary Beard and Martha Bensley Bruère, eds., *Laughing Their Way: Women's Humor in America* (New York: Macmillan, 1934).

37. William Beard to Dorcas Campbell, January 15, 1957; February 4, 1957; August 5, 1958; William Beard to the Keys, August 9, 1958, all in MBC.

38. Donald Lowe to Stevens, December 18, 1959, Box 5, Folder 148, DSP.

39. Doris Stevens to Arthur Pell, October 26, 1961, Box 5, Folder 133, DSP.

40. Ralph [Stevens] to Jon [Mitchell], June 25, 1961, Box 2, Folder 26; June 25, 1963, Box 2, Folder 29, both in DSP.

41. Inez Irwin, *Many Murders* (New York: Random House, 1941); Irwin, *The Women Swore Revenge* (New York: Random House, 1946).

42. Inez Irwin, *Maida's Little Shop* (New York: Grosset & Dunlap, 1909), *Maida's Little Treasure Hunt* (New York: Grosset & Dunlap, 1955).

43. Inez Irwin to Maud Wood Park, November 10, 1945; Irwin to Mrs. Stantial, July 8, 1959, both in Container 17, Reel 11, NAWSA Papers.

44. Inez Irwin to Mrs. Stantial, September 29, 1959, II Correspondence. Maud Wood Park, *Front Door Lobby*, edited by Edna Lamprey Stantial (Boston: Beacon, 1960).

45. Inez Irwin to Mrs. Stantial, September 29, 1950, II Correspondence.

46. Irwin to Mrs. Stantial, June 7, 1958, January 11, 1959, Container 17, Reel 11, NAWSA Papers; "Inez Haynes Irwin, Author, Feminist, 97," *New York Times*, October 1, 1970.

47. Buhle et al., *Women and the Making of America*, 665–685.

48. Sara Evans, *Tidal Wave: How Women Changed America at Century's End* (New York: Free Press, 2003).

49. Ibid, p. 1.

50. Buhle et al., *Women and the Making of America*, 689–700.

51. Becky Thompson, "Multiracial Feminism: Recasting the Chronology of Second Wave Feminism," in *No Permanent Waves: Recasting Histories of U.S. Feminism*, edited by Nancy A. Hewitt (New Brunswick, NJ: Rutgers University Press, 2010), 39–60.

52. Benita Roth, *Separate Roads to Feminism: Black, Chicana, and White Feminist Movements in America's Second Wave* (New York: Cambridge University Press, 2004).

53. Kimberly Springer, *Living for the Revolution: Black Feminist Organizations, 1968–1980* (Durham, NC: Duke University Press, 2005).

54. Buhle et al., *Women and the Making of America*, 700–705.

55. Interview with Lorine Pruette, *Chattanooga Times*, February 12, 1964, LPC; Pruette, "Mental Health for Oldsters," Box 3, Folder 95, LPP.

56. Una Stannard, who corresponded with Pruette in the last several years of her life, stated, "we did develop friendly feelings for each other, in part because we both felt that we were feminists ahead of our time." Una Stannard to Mary Trigg, February 9, 1985, in the author's possession. Dr. Stannard is the author of *Mrs. Man* (San Francisco: Germaine Books, 1977), a study of women taking their husbands' names. She met Pruette through her research.

57. Kate Millet, *Sexual Politics: The Classic Analysis of the Interplay between Men, Women, and Culture* [1970] (Urbana: University of Illinois Press, 2000); Buhle et al., *Women and the Making of America*, 708–709.

58. Lorine Pruette to Sherna Gluck, December 12, 1973; Lorine Pruette Oral History (January 1974), Feminist History Research Project Collection, Special Collections and Archive, Library, California State University Long Beach. Gluck described Pruette's interview as "titillating and frustrating. . . . what happened was that a friend of hers taped. I then sent an outline for further interviewing, and she flatly refused to do any more"; Sherna Gluck to Mary Trigg, June 11, 1984, in the author's possession. Sherna Gluck, ed., *From Parlor to Prison: Five American Suffragists Talk about Their Lives* (New York: Vintage Books, 1976).

59. "What Is Success? Seven Women Answer . . . ," *Chattanooga News-Free Press*, August 4, 1974, LPC.

60. William O'Neill, *Everyone Was Brave: A History of Feminism in America* (Chicago: Quadrangle, 1969), viii; Pruette to Sherna Gluck, n.d. (1974); see also Pruette to Sherna Gluck, March 1, 1974; William O'Neill to Mrs. Gluck, March 22, 1971, all in Feminist History Research Project Papers.

61. Alice Rossi to Pruette, April 9, 1974, Box 1, Folder 7, LPP.

62. Lorine Pruette to Norman Cousins, June 24, 1962, Box 1, Folder 6, LPP.

63. Lorine Pruette, "How to Choose and Change Your Doctors," Box 3, Folder 109, LPP.

64. Moya Lloyd, *Beyond Identity Politics: Feminism, Power, and Politics* (London: Sage, 2005), 4.

65. Pruette, "The Making of a Feminist," Box 3, Folder 86; "Male Chauvanists [*sic*] I Have Known," Box 3, Folder 87, both in LPP; Pruette Oral History.

66. Shulamith Firestone, *The Dialectic of Sex: The Case for Feminist Revolution* (New York: Morrow, 1970).

67. Pruette, "Male Chauvinists I Have Known."

68. Mansbridge, *Why We Lost the ERA*, 90–91, 3, 1.

69. Lorine Pruette to Scott Meredith, May 19, 1967; Pruette to Joe King, January 5, 1964, both in Box 1, Folder 10, LPP. Pruette to Mary Sue Bethea, June 26, 1970, Box 1, Folder 7, LPP; Pruette to Sherna Gluck, December 12, 1973, Feminist History Research Project Papers; Pruette to AAPP Insurance Plan, August 9, 1967, Box 1, Folder 10, LPP.

70. Pruette, "The True Companion"; Account of dreams [1967?], Box 1, Folder 11, LPP.

71. Inez Irwin, "1916 War Diary," 385, Microfilm M-59, Reels 974–975, no. 17, IHGP.

72. Inez Irwin, *Angels and Amazons: A Hundred Years of American Women* (Garden City, NY: Doubleday, Doran, 1933), 438.

73. "WCWA Desirable Materials," Box 1, Folder 1, MBPSL.

74. Des Jardins, *Women and the Historical Enterprise*, 241.

75. Simone Tery, "Doris Stevens at The Hague," *Equal Rights*, August 27, 1928; "Doris Stevens Returns," *Equal Rights*, July 13, 1929.

76. Rupp and Taylor, *Survival*, 30.

77. *Iron Jawed Angels* was released in 2004. Hilary Swank portrays Alice Paul in the movie.

78. Doris Stevens's songs, copyrighted in 1952, are part of her collection at the SL and are also available at the Nebraska State Historical Society.

79. "Doris Stevens Chair in Women's Studies, Princeton University," http://fmrsi .wordpress.com/2008/12/08/doris-stevens-chair-in-womens-studies-princeton-university/.

80. Center for American Women and Politics, Rutgers University: http://www.cawp .rutgers.edu.

81. Dorothy Dinnerstein, *The Mermaid and the Minotaur: Sexual Arrangements and Human Malaise* (New York: Harper & Row, 1976); Nancy Chodorow, *The Reproduction of Mothering* (Berkeley: University of California Press, 1978); Carol Gilligan, *In a Different Voice: Psychological Theory and Women's Development* (Cambridge, MA: Harvard University Press, 1982).

82. Cobble, *The Other Women's Movement*, 7.

83. Butler, *Two Paths*, 2–3.

84. Mansbridge, *Why We Lost the ERA*, 195–99; Lenore Weitzman, *The Divorce Revolution* (New York: Free Press, 1988).

85. Cobble, *The Other Women's Movement*, 7.

86. Lorine Pruette, "My Life among the Doctors," Box 3, Folder 108; Pruette, "On weekending in heaven, the living in Hell," Box 3, Folder 118, both in LPP. Mary Beard to Margaret Gettys Hall, 1946, MBC; Irwin, "Adventures of Yesterday," Microfilm M-59, Reels 974–975, no. 17, IHGP 49; Inez Irwin to Maud Wood Park, September 26, 1909, Container 17, Reel 11, NAWSA Papers.

87. July 3, 1929, IACW press release, A-104, v. 28, SL; Doris Stevens "1920 Diary," December 13, 1920, Box 6, Folder 182, DSP.

88. First quotation December 12, 1938 *New York Times* article (title missing); second, "Lorine Pruette Nominates 'Real New Deal' Cabinet, All-Feminine, for Roosevelt," *World Telegram*, December 16, 1932, 3, both in LPC. The American Woman's Patriotic Association opposed Einstein's 1932 visit because of his socialist views. After cross-examination, Einstein was granted a visa, and eventually renounced his German citizenship and became an American citizen.

89. Lorine Pruette, "LOGOS: The Shield," Box 3, Folder 78, LPP.

90. Lorine Pruette, "The Long Shadows," Box 4, Folder 148, LPP.

91. Leila Rupp, "Feminism and the Sexual Revolution in the Early Twentieth Century: The Case of Doris Stevens," *Feminist Studies* 15, 2 (Summer 1989): 289–309.

92. "Statement by Jonathan Mitchell," in DS tapes, "A Bend in the River," Side 2.

93. Lucy Burns to Doris Stevens, November 18, 1942, Box 4, Folder 79, DSP.

94. Karen Offen, "Defining Feminism: A Comparative Historical Approach," *Signs* 14, 1 (Autumn 1988): 119–157; quotes from 120, 121, 135–136.

95. Ibid.

96. Ibid., 138.

97. Mary Beard to Stevens, May Day [1937], in Nancy Cott, ed., *A Woman Making History: Mary Ritter Beard through Her Letters* (New Haven, CT: Yale University Press, 1992), 165–167.

98. Offen, "Defining Feminism," 139.

99. Ibid., 140.

100. Ibid., 143; see Rosalind Rosenberg, *Beyond Separate Spheres: Intellectual Roots of Modern Feminism* (New Haven, CT: Yale University Press, 1982).

101. Offen, "Defining Feminism," 147, 149.

102. Wendy Sarvasy, "Beyond the Difference versus Equality Policy Debate: Post-Suffrage Feminism, Citizenship, and the Quest for a Feminist Welfare State," *Signs* 17 (Winter 1992): 329–362; see 330.

103. Ibid., 329–331.

104. Cobble, *The Other Women's Movement*, 7.

105. Estelle Freedman, *No Turning Back: The History of Feminism and the Future of Women* (New York: Ballantine Books, 2003), 10.

106. See Ginia Bellafante, "It's All about Me!," *Time*, June 29, 1998; Sam Bennet, "Sarah Palin's Brand of 'Feminism' Hurts Women," *Huffington Post*, May 25, 2010; http://www .huffingtonpost.com.

107. Freedman, *No Turning Back*, 11.

108. Nancy Hewitt, "Introduction," in *No Permanent Waves: Recasting Histories of U.S. Feminism*, edited by Nancy A. Hewitt (New Brunswick, NJ: Rutgers University Press, 2010), 1.

109. Nancy Hewitt, "No Permanent Waves," paper presented at May 13, 2005 symposium, Institute for Research on Women, Rutgers University.

110. Hewitt, *No Permanent Waves*, 5, 4.

111. Melody Berger, "Introduction," in *We Don't Need Another Wave: Dispatches from the Next Generation of Feminists*, edited by Melody Berger (Emeryville, CA: Seal Press, 2006), 19–22; quote 20.

112. Kimberly Springer, "Third Wave Black Feminism?" *Signs* 27, 4 (2002): 1059–1082; quote 1061, 1063–1064.

113. Kimberly Springer, "Strongblackwomen and Black Feminism," in *Different Wavelengths: Studies of the Contemporary Women's Movement*, edited by Jo Reger (New York: Routledge, 2005), 3–21; quote 3.

114. Karl Mannheim, *Essays on the Sociology of Knowledge* (London: Routledge and Kegan Paul, 1959), 292; Susan Ware, *Beyond Suffrage: Women in the New Deal* (Cambridge, MA: Harvard University Press, 1981), 19; Alan Spitzer, "The Historical Problem of Generations," *American Historical Review* 75 (December 1973): 1385.

115. Ware, *Beyond Suffrage*, 19.

116. Quote from Molly Dewson, cited in Ware, *Beyond Suffrage*, 19.

117. Hewitt, "Introduction," 5.

118. Nancy Naples, "Confronting the Future, Learning from the Past: Feminist Praxis in the Twenty-First Century," in *Different Wavelengths: Studies of the Contemporary Women's Movement*, edited by Jo Reger (New York: Routledge, 2005), 215–235; see 217, 220.

119. Nancy Whittier, *Feminist Generations: The Persistence of the Radical Women's Movement* (Philadelphia: Temple University Press, 1999), 15.

120. Lynne Phillips and Sally Cole, "Feminist Flows, Feminist Fault Lines: Women's Machineries and Women's Movements in Latin America," *Signs* 35, 1 (2009): 185–211.

121. Doris Stevens to Omaha High School Classmates, June 10, 1958, Box 5, Folder 149, DSP.

122. Inez Irwin, *The Story of the Woman's Party* (New York: Harcourt, Brace, 1921); *Angels and Amazons*. Catt is quoted in Irwin to Carrie Chapman Catt, March 22, 1933, Container 17, Reel 11, NAWSA Papers.

123. Inez Irwin to Maud Wood Park, April 15, 1933, Container 17, Reel 11, NAWSA Papers.

124. Anita Pollitzer to Irwin, October 6, 1933; Irwin to Anita Pollitzer, October 1933, both in Series I, Reel 52, NWP Papers.

125. Ware, *Beyond Suffrage*, 19.

Index

Business and Professional Women's Foundation, 142
Butler Act, 123

California: Central Trades and Labor Council, 54; and CESL, 52; eight-hour work law for women in, 53; and Ford-Suhr case, 54; Industrial Commission, 54; and Irwin, 52–54; and IWW (Industrial Workers of the World), 54; and labor movement, 53–54; and Stevens, 59, 123
The Call (socialist newspaper), 69
capitalism, 5, 13; and Beard, 5, 46, 104–105, 167, 182; and Irwin, 116
careers, 1, 3–6, 14, 22, 119–144; and Beard, 26–27, 104–105, 182–183, 193; and "careerism," 183; and career-marriage dilemma, 135–144, 176; and companionate marriage, 3, 6, 119–144; home-based, 135; and Irwin, 22, 107, 113; and Pruette, 6, 38–39, 83–84, 92, 135–144, 176, 195; and sexual revolution, 83–84, 92–93; and Stevens, 30–31, 119–128, 184. *See also* professional women; work, productive; *types of careers*
care-focused feminism, 11, 13, 18–19, 95, 176, 196–197, 200; and Beard, 49, 100, 104; and child care, 27; and Pruette, 13. *See also* maternalism
Carpenter, Edward, 68, 74–75, 78
Catholic Church, 72, 77, 117
Catt, Carrie Chapman, 205; and Beard, 49, 62–63, 172; and birth control campaign, 73; and international feminism, 150, 157, 161; and NAWSA, 49, 61; and WCWA, 172
Census (US), 130
CESL (College Equal Suffrage League), 6, 14, 50–52; and "equal suffrage theory" essay contest, 51; and Irwin, 6, 14, 32, 50–52, 192; and merger of state leagues, 52; and Park, Maud Wood, 32, 50–52; and Stevens, 6, 32; and suffrage movement, 50–52. *See also* Park, Maud Wood
A Changing Political Economy as It Affects Women (Beard), 166
Chaplin, Charlie, 123
Chattanooga (TN), 37, 91–92; Alexian Brothers nursing home, 191; High School, 39
chauvinism, male, 33, 189; and Pruette, 33, 39, 137
Chicago, 28, 45
Chicanas, 186–187
Child, Lydia Maria, 22

childbirth, 17; difficult, 33–34, 36; dying in, 20; and Firestone, 189; and Pruette's family, 33–34, 36, 38, 143
childrearing, 17, 49, 189
children, 18; and Addams, Jane, 114; and Beard, 18, 25, 43–44, 46, 48–50, 101, 104, 106, 182–184; and Belmont, Alva, 60, 154, 156; and child care, 27, 113–114, 129, 135, 176, 178, 196; and child labor laws, 18, 99–100; and companionate marriage, 119, 122, 125, 127–129, 133; and Equal Nationality Treaty, 158; and Gilman, Charlotte Perkins, 107; health/welfare of, 18, 95–97, 99–100, 113; and IACW, 158; and infant mortality, 96; and Irwin, 108, 110–111, 113, 115–118; and Pruette, 33–34, 139, 141, 143–144, 187, 191; and Pruette's family, 36–38; and Stevens, 133, 135, 158; and "These Modern Women" (*The Nation*), 3; and working women, 128–129; and World War I, 113. *See also* maternalism; motherhood
Children's Bureau (US), 113, 163
Chile, 146, 148, 194
Chodorow, Nancy, 194
Christman, Elizabeth, 134, 163
churches: and Irwin, 196; and suffrage movement, 42, 45; women as church members, 22; and women clergy, 22, 65. *See also* religion
cigarettes, 8, 92, 114
citizenship: economic citizenship, 142, 178, 230n108; and Equal Nationality Treaty, 158; and gendered citizenship, 95; and maternalism, 95, 97–98; and protective legislation, 97–98; and Schwimmer, Rosika, 168–169
civil disobedience, 23; in France, 150–151; and Irwin, 23, 41, 54–55, 62, 192, 197; and Stevens, 61, 127, 150–151, 193; suicide as tactic of, 23, 41, 54–55, 62, 192, 197
civilizing agents, women as: and Beard, 6, 26–27, 29, 46, 48–49, 72–73, 105, 165, 197; and fascism, 72; and sexual revolution, 68, 72–73
civil rights movement, 186, 193, 203; Civil Rights Act (1964), 181
Civil War, 20; and Beard's father, 26–27; Confederate States of America, 34; and New South, 35–36, 214n67; and Pruette's family, 34–35, 38; and Reconstruction, 35–36
Clark University, 84, 136; Clark Lectures, 84
class, 6, 9; and Beard, 43–44, 46, 49, 100, 169, 192–193; and birth control campaign, 69; and classism, 64; and companionate

About the Author

MARY K. TRIGG is associate professor of women's and gender studies at Rutgers University. She is also the director of leadership programs and research at the Institute for Women's Leadership. A graduate of the University of Michigan, Carnegie-Mellon University, and Brown University, she edited *Leading the Way: Young Women's Activism for Social Change*, which was published in 2010. She lives in Bernardsville, New Jersey, with her husband, Ronald Rapp, and has two grown daughters.